EARLY KINGDOMS IN MADAGASCAR
1500-1700

EARLY KINGDOMS IN MADAGASCAR 1500-1700

Raymond K. Kent

University of California, Berkeley

Iddio vi salvi, benigni uditori,
quando e' per che dependa
questa benignità da lo esser grato.
Se voi seguite di non far romori,
Noi vogliàn che s'intenda
un nuovo caso in questa terra nato.

Niccolò Machiavelli, *La Mandragola*
Clizia-Belfagor, "Prologo."

HOLT, RINEHART AND WINSTON

New York · Chicago · San Francisco · Atlanta
Dallas · Montreal · Toronto · London · Sydney

Photo credits: All photographs in the book with one exception are from the Bibliothèque Grandidier at Tsimbazaza-Tananarive, courtesy of the Institut de la Recherche Scientifique de Madagascar. The photograph of Sakaombé tombs, 1965, original in color, was taken by the author.

To Gabriel Ferrand
and Emil Birkeli

PREFACE

The present work questions the findings of previous scholarship in respect to the Malagasy past between about 1500 and 1700, the period when the Great Island developed its early kingdoms. The results run counter to what is still widely held, believed, and perpetuated both within and outside of Madagascar.

Difficulties regarding the past of Madagascar cannot be attributed to any lack of interest in it. Since 1902, the Académie Malgache has been the collecting and clearing house for historically oriented research and publication. Individuals working outside the Académie, long before it was established by General Gallieni as well as since, have contributed perhaps an even greater share. Bibliographical entries concerning Madagascar exceed 30,000 and are by no means inclusive of everything extant, either in print or in manuscripts. Indeed, in comparison with other "preliterate" societies, Madagascar ranks very high in terms of what is available for the study of its past. Rather, the hard truth is that there has been a paucity of trained historians, that research has been extremely uneven, and that too many writers could neither use the materials actually available nor yet apply to those used the very basic criteria and methods of history as a discipline. To this must be added an intellectual orientation which developed in the nineteenth century and which still retains strong roots in Madagascar, in part because the Great Island is more isolated than, for example, nearby Africa from the crosscurrents of the post-colonial period.

In one sense then, the present work is one of "revisionism," representing simply a return to the *métier d'historien*, with his special concern for pre-existing sources and the critical use thereof, for change and the contexts in which data are found, for chronology and time perspective, causality and repercussion, for the particular and the general, the unique and the common. The very nature of the subject has also required many departures from the written source and into the oral tradition, ethnography, linguistics, and anthropology. In so departing, the author does not claim or wish to convey more than partial training in these "auxiliary" fields along with having made an effort as a historian to seek their aid to the best of his ability. No method is foolproof and no discipline is immune from criticism by others. But both linguistics and anthropology have shared considerable benefits by turning to history, and there is no reason to doubt that reverse borrowing can produce analogous results. Many contemporary historians who study "preliterate" societies have alluded to the great need for such borrowing while remaining wedded to written documents, unreconstructed narrative, neglect of local cultures and languages, and to fairly recent periods. The present work is, therefore, also an attempt to practice what one preaches.

Paris, France   R. K. K.
December 1969

ACKNOWLEDGMENTS

The following institutions have allowed me to consult unpublished materials: the French National Archives, Overseas Section, and the Bibliothèque Nationale, Department of Manuscripts; the Académie Malgache, the Scientific Research Institute of Madagascar (I.R.S.M.) which houses the Bibliothèque Grandidier at Tsimbazaza-Tananarive, the National Archives of the Malagasy Republic, the University of Madagascar and particularly its Humanities Department and Law Faculty which acquired in 1965 the hitherto private library of Charles Poirier, former Inspector of Colonies. Substantial parts of Chapters 3, 4, and 5 have been published in the *Journal of African History,* under the general heading of "Madagascar and Africa," and I am grateful to the Editors for allowing them to be incorporated into the present volume.

Madame B. Dandouau and Madame and Maitre Gabriel Pain of Tananarive, Professor Hubert Deschamps of Paris, and Doctor Michel Jospin of Majunga have generously permitted me to consult their private libraries. Madame Monique Adam, Mlle Juliette Ratsimandrava, M. Jean Valette, Madame Jean Poirier, Madame Annie Rouhette, and Professor Edouard Ralaimihoatra have helped me with book and manuscript loans, translations, suggestions, and kind advice.

Professor Jan M. Vansina of the University of Wisconsin has given me more than priceless criticism of an earlier draft. It is largely to him that I owe an awakening to the many possible ways in which one can approach and think about the past of preliterate societies. He has been an inspiring teacher and is perhaps the last of genuine Renaissance men in our own moment in time.

No success in fieldwork and in the collection of oral Malagasy texts would have been possible without the unselfish and elegantly given help of Madame and M. Frank Amiot of Morondava, of the late Madame

Maurice Upton, and of Mlle Luciani, both of Majunga. My principal Malagasy informants in 1965 were Raphael Mahonjobé, oral historian of Menabé; Naketrana, village elder of Marovoay (area of Morondava), Menabé; Abderrahmane Said Ben Ali of Majunga Chief Nintsy, Mamory-bé, and Tsimanohitra Tombo, oral historians and guardians of the Iboina-Sakalava royal relics and tombs at Mirinarivo-Majunga. I am also indebted to direct-line descendants of Andriantsoli, last Sakalava king of Iboina, and of Ramena, ruler of eighteenth-century Menabé. A collective gratitude is herewith expressed to a number of informants who, for one reason or another, have asked me not to mention their names in print.

The financial support for research and travel connected with this work came from the Foreign Area Fellowship Program of the Ford Foundation and in conjunction with the Social Science Research Council and the American Council of Learned Societies.

None of the institutions and individuals cited here are in any way contributors to errors of judgment or fact, for which I am alone to blame.

R. K. K.

CONTENTS

MAPS

MAJOR SUBDIVISIONS OF MALAGASY (1964)

EASTERN MADAGASCAR	POPULATION	PRONUNCIATION
Betsimisaraka	915,000	*Betsimšārák'*
Anteimoro	212,000	*Těmūrú*
Anteifasy	40,000	*Těfaš'*
Antambahoaka	22,000	*Tămbahouák'*
Antaisaka	325,000	*Têšak'*
Tanala	237,000	*Tânaľ*

SOUTHERN MADAGASCAR		
Antanosy	149,000	*Tânuš'*
Antandroy	326,000	*Tândrui*
Bara	228,000	*Bār'*
Mahafaly	91,000	*Maafaľ*

WESTERN MADAGASCAR		
Sakalava	360,000	*Šákkállăvâ*
Makoa	65,000	*Makua*

NORTHERN MADAGASCAR		
Antankarana	42,000	*Tankaran'*
Tsimihety	429,000	*Tsimiét'*

CENTRAL MADAGASCAR		
Betsileo	736,000	*Betsileu*
Bezanozano	44,000	*Bezanuzan'*
Merina	1,570,000	*Meern'*
Sihanaka	135,000	*Siánák'*

ABBREVIATIONS

AA	Antananarivo Annual
AAM	Archives de l'Académie Malgache
AASC	Annales de l'Académie des Sciences Coloniales
ADE	Annales d'Ethiopie
AFL	Africa (London)
AM	Académie Malgache (library)
AMGRHR	Annales du Musée Guimet, Revue de l'Histoire des Religions
ANTHV	Anthropos (Vienna)
ANSOMCM	Archives Nationales, Section Outre-Mer, Correspondence Madagascar
ARM	Archives de la République Malgache
ASBS	African Studies (ex-Bantu Studies)
AUM	Annales de l'Université de Madagascar
AV	Annales des Voyages
AVG	Annuaire des Voyages et de la Géographie
AZ	Azania
BAM	Bulletin de l'Académie Malgache
BCM	Bulletin du Comité de Madagascar
BDP	Bibliothèque Dandouau-Pain (Tananarive, private)
BEM	Bulletin Economique de Madagascar
BGT	Bibliothèque Grandidier (Tsimbazaza-Tananarive)
BM	Bulletin de Madagascar
BMF	Bulletin of the Madras Fisheries
BMSAP	Bulletin et Mémoires de la Société d'Anthropologie (Paris)
BODE	Bulletin Officiel de la Direction de l'Eneignement (Madagascar)
BP	Bibliothèque Charles Poirier (now public)
BS	Bantu Studies
BSG/BSGP	Bulletin de la Société de Géographie de Paris
BSGL	Boletim da Sociedade da Geographia de Lisboa
BSGT	Bulletin de la Société de Géographie de Toulouse
BSSAIR	Bulletin de la Société des Sciences & Arts de l'Ile de la Réunion
CDCMPV	Collection des Ouvrages Anciens Concernant Madagascar et Pays Voisins
CLMS	Chronicle of the London Missionary Society

CM	Civilisations Malgaches
COACM	Collection des Ouvrages Anciens Concernant Madagascar
ESA	Ethnographic Survey of Africa
IRSM	Institut de la Recherche Scientifique de Madagascar
JA	Journal Asiatique
JAH	Journal of African History
JAI/JRAI	Journal of the (Royal) Anthropological Institute (London)
JAS	Journal of the African Society
JEAUNHS	Journal of the East African (Universities) Natural History Society
JOM	Journal Officiel de Madagascar
JSA	Journal de la Société des Africanistes
JTG	Journal of Tropical Geography
MAM	Mémoires de l'Académie Malgache
MM	Mariner's Mirror
MOZ	Moçambique
MSP	Mémoires de la Société Philomatique
NADA	Native Affairs Department Annual (Southern Rhodesia)
NEMBN	Notices et Extraits des Mss. de la Bibliothèque Nationale (Paris)
NGM	Ny Gazety Malagasy
NJ	Nyasaland Journal
NRE	Notes, Reconnaissances et Explorations
NRJ	Northern Rhodesian Journal
NTS	Norsk Tidsskrift for Sprogvidenskap
OEMB	Oslo Etnografske Museum, *Bulletin*
OTT	Oral Traditions Taped (1965)
RA	Revue Anthropologique
RBAAT	Revue de Botanique Appliquée et d'Agriculture Tropicale
RE	Revue d'Ethnographie (Paris)
REES	Revue des Etudes Ethnographiques et Sociologiques (Paris)
RETP	Revue d'Ethnographie et des Traditions Populaires
RFHOM	Revue Française d'Histoire d'Outre-Mer
RJ	Rhodesian Journal
RLC	Rhodes-Livingstone Communications
RLJ	Rhodes-Livingstone Journal
RLOP	Rhodes-Livingstone Occasional Papers
RM	Revue de Madagascar
RS	Revue Scientifique
RSE	Rassegna di Studi Etiopici
RTC	Revue des Troupes Coloniales
SGCBB	Société de Géographie Commerciale de Bordeaux, *Bulletin*
TNR	Tanganyika Notes and Records
UJ	Uganda Journal
UN	Uganda Notes
ZA	Zaire
ZGE	Zeitschrift des Gesellschaft für Erdkunde (Berlin)

GLOSSARY OF
REOCCURRING TERMS

Andevo: slave
Andriana: lord, ruler, sovereign, king, chief, noble
Arivo: thousand, thousands, great number
Bilo: spirit possession, possessing spirit itself
Buki: old African name for Malagasy, sometimes prefixed by *wa-*
Dady: grandparent, ancestor, relic
Fanany/fanane: serpent, snake
Fatidra/fatitra: blood-drawing incision, blood covenant
Foko: family, class, clan, tribe, community
Hova: commoners, freemen in Imerina
Kibory: tomb in southeastern Madagascar
Kitabo/katibo: scribe, writer
Lakam-piara: outrigger canoe
Lamba: traditional cloth worn in toga-like manner
Lovan'tsofina: heritage of the ears, oral tradition
Masikoro: nontribal name given to peoples of the southern interior
Mpanjaka: lord, ruler, king, chief, sovereign
Ody: protective amulets usually worn by individuals
Ombiasy: priest, diviner, doctor, sacerdotal person
Raza: family
Sampy: amulets usually protecting a group; called "idols" by missionaries
Sikidy: divination, oracles
Sombily: legal right to exclusive slaughter of domestic animals
Sora-bé: Arabico-Malagasy manuscripts
Tantara: oral tradition, history
Tomboka: tattoo, tattooing
Tompontany: masters of the soil, original inhabitants
Tromba: possession by spirit, spirit that possesses
Tsangambato: megalith
Vazimba: now extinct early inhabitants of Imerina with surviving pockets on the western coast of Madagascar
Vezo: seagoing fishermen of southwestern Madagascar
Volamena: gold; literal, red silver
Ziwa: joking relationship, palship

chapter 1 THE MYTH OF THE WHITE KING

> The Negro speakers of the early Bantu languages were
> brought under the influence of a semi-Caucasian race. . . .
> Descendants of such ancient civilizers of Central Africa
> are . . . to be seen at the present day in the . . . aristoc-
> racies . . . , "royal" families . . . and the many handsome-
> featured pale-skinned castes and ruling clans in so many
> of the Bantu peoples.
>
> Sir Harry H. Johnston (1919)

A visitor to Madagascar will usually land at Arivonimamo, the international airport of the Malagasy Republic. In less than an hour, he will
reach its capital, Tananarive, situated on the high plateau almost in the
very heart of the Great Island, the fourth largest in the world. If he has
any geographical and historical background, the visitor might expect to
find Tananarive inhabited by an African-speaking and essentially black
population. The island is, after all, separated from Africa by a mere 250
miles of water known as the Mozambique Channel.

This expectation will be negated at once by what the visitor sees and
hears. The central-plateau inhabitants, known by their group name of
Merina (or less frequently Hova), are deficient in melanin and are
predominantly Asian-looking. The polysyllabic local language, Malagasy,
sounds nothing like the idioms spoken on the African mainland. It belongs, in fact, to the Indonesian branch of Malayo-Polynesian languages.
Our hypothetical visitor will probably join the ranks of a very long and
old line of amateurs and scholars who have wondered about this African
island inhabited by a people whose ancestral language is spoken thousands of miles away across the Indian and Pacific oceans. Sooner or later,

he will turn to the numerous books about Madagascar to satisfy his curiosity about their origins.

He will then learn that the island was either uninhabited before the arrival of Indonesian settlers or else that these migrants found and absorbed completely some very primitive human antecedents from Africa. These Indonesian proto-Malagasy crossed the vast oceans in their outriggers anywhere between 2000 B.C. and A.D. 400, according to the sources our visitor consults. They came in several migratory movements, not a single one. But, they were not the sole ancestors of present-day Malagasy. In more recent times, men of other origins came to Madagascar. The greater the number of books referred to, the larger becomes the variety of early settlers: Malay, Maori, Indians, Arabs, Persians, Jews, Phoenicians, Chinese, Japanese. Thus, the population of Madagascar, taken as a whole, is of multiple origins. It also includes Europeans and the more recent Negroid element, introduced from Africa through slave trade. Unless the newcomer develops a sustained interest in the earlier periods of Malagasy past, he too will eventually repeat what others have written about the ancestors of Malagasy.[1]

A somewhat longer excursion into the literature will, however, lead to increasing doubts and dissatisfaction with the testimony of the experts. The authors simply quote one another, and while the "Problem of Malagasy Origins" is universally discussed, most of the claims are presented as established fact. A chronological span of about 3500 years that encompasses ten or twelve distinct migrations soon becomes meaningless, if not vapid. Even the very able and hardy Indonesian seafarers would have had some trouble crossing the huge Pacific in their outriggers several times to come directly to Madagascar. A number of reported overseas migrations turn out to have been sheer fantasies of one or two writers.[2] And, the few items acceptable as archaeological evidence—lack

[1] Cf. R. K. Kent, *From Madagascar to the Malagasy Republic* (1962), pp. 5–6; and V. Thompson and R. Adloff, *The Malagasy Republic* (1966), pp. 3–4.

[2] Ancient accounts attest to the trading or migratory movements of the Chinese, Indians, Malays, Jews, Persians, Arabs, and even the Japanese along the coastal belts of southern Arabia, eastern Africa, and the Indian subcontinent. In an absolute sense, thus, any of the enumerated peoples *could* have reached Madagascar as well in outriggers, dhows, junks, or any other type of old but seafaring craft, with the help of winds and currents. The mere possibility of maritime contact allows, however, no automatic inference for any significant contributions to the peopling of Madagascar and to the Malagasy cultures unless these can be ascertained within the island itself. Against this basic criterion, one can safely attribute the "reality" of many postulated migrations into Madagascar only to unsubstantiated statements in the following texts: (Phoenicians) Court de Gebelin, *Le Monde primitif*, Vol. I (1781), pp. 52, 538, 553, and M. I. Guet, *Les Origines de l'Ile Bourbon et de la colonisation française à Madagascar* (1886), p. 34, *passim* thereafter; (Chinese, Japanese, and Persians)

of human presence in the prehistory of Madagascar or attested ruins of old Arab settlements—stand out in marked contrast to the total literary output. The Indonesian archipelago itself contains a great variety of linguistic, ethnic, and cultural units. To see thus the proto-Malagasy as Indonesians on the basis of broad linguistic classification is not quite the same as to know which of the Indonesian peoples might be involved and what their own past cultures might have been at the time of overseas migrations.

To "crack" the Malagasy origins has been the stated or secret dream of

---

A. Grandidier, *Ethnographie de Madagascar*, Vol. I, Tome 1 (1908), pp. 116, n. 7, 135, n. 2, 139, n. 2, 169–170; (Maori) F. Vernier, "Hovas et Maoris," *BAM*, I (1902), 80–82. For the Arab and Indian migrations see the text of this chapter, below. As the foremost practitioner of inferential technique, Grandidier often relied on single-sentence statements in old accounts. Thus, the Chinese were mentioned in southwestern Madagascar by Payrard de Laval, *Voyages des français aux Indes Orientales*, Vol. I (1611), Ch. III, p. 24. In a 1650 letter from Fort-Dauphin, the Lazarist missionary Abbé Nacquart reported to Vincent de Paul in France that a local ruling lineage derived from Persian migrants who came to Madagascar 500 years earlier; cf. Nacquart to Vincent de Paul, February 5, 1650, in *Mémoires de la congrégation de la mission des Lazaristes*, Vol. IX (1866), p. 60. De Laval, who visited Madagascar in 1602, based his statement about the Chinese on the somatological characteristics of Mongoloid-looking *individuals* among the southwestern Mahafaly people. Grandidier himself noted this type as being *prevalent* among the Mahafaly aristocracy, an argument rejected by the more detailed studies of Robert David, "Observations anthropométriques et sérologiques chez les mahafaly du sud-ouest de Madagascar," *BAM*, XXIII (1940), 12–29, particularly 24–27. In respect to one or more Jewish colonies in ancient Madagascar, there is no real evidence for them. Some missionaries of the London Missionary Society believed that all of the Malagasy religious antecedents derive from Hebrew religion itself and even that "all Malagasy" are supposed to be the descendants of "Jews who came to Madagascar in Phoenician ships." Cf. Rev. J. Cameron, "On the Early Inhabitants of Madagascar," *AA*, I (1877), 1–10; A. Jully, "Ethnographie de Madagascar," *RM*, VIII/12 (1906), 1025–1054; for the listing of thirty-five traits common to all Malagasy and to the ancient Jews, see A. Grandidier, *Ethnographie*, pp. 100–103 and notes. The evidential value of these claims is discussed adequately by Gabriel Ferrand, "Les Migrations musulmans et juives à Madagascar," *AMGRHR*, LII (1905), 381–417; Lars Dahle, "The Race Elements of the Malagasy: A Truth in Regard to Their Origin," *AA*, II (1883), 216–228; and Arnold Van Gennep, *Tabou et totémisme à Madagascar* (1904), pp. 3–11, *passim*. It is probable that the whole subject would never have been discussed if Etienne de Flacourt, French governor of Fort-Dauphin, had not visited the northeastern islet of Sainte-Marie between October and November 1652. At the islet, Flacourt reported the discovery of what he believed to be the remnants of an ancient Jewish colony; cf. *Histoire de la grande ile Madagascar* (1661), reprinted as Vol. VIII, in *COACM* (1913), pp. 12–13, 46–50, 55–57. Since the work of Flacourt is on the whole of undisputable historical value, it has been widely quoted, if little studied. On Flacourt, see Arthur Malotet, *Etienne de Flacourt ou les origines de la colonisation française à Madagascar, 1648–1661* (1898), pp. 59–261, and *COACM*, Vol. VIII (1913), pp. xxii–lix.

most *Malgachisants.* Many went back in time to search, in the ancient and medieval accounts, for some concrete fact that relates to the Great Island. Others engaged in anthropometry to determine ethnic substrata among the Malagasy, an endeavor that still finds a response in spite of its questionable value.[3] Not infrequently, Malayo-Polynesian and Malagasy customs were compared in such a way that the feedback confirmed the input without the slightest regard for chronological possibilities and geographical and ethnographic contexts.[4] To this day, hardly a few years pass without a report of some major find, be it a mysterious inscription carved on a rock or part of an ancient shipwreck imbedded in the sands of the endless Malagasy seashore.[5] In short, the dream has been frustrated, and the continuous proliferation of hypotheses is best accounted for by the conclusion of a recent symposium in Tananarive that Malagasy origins remain obscure and urgently require new methods and new research.[6]

Against this background, the formation of early kingdoms in Madagascar, the subject of the present study and one hardly unrelated to the problem of Malagasy origins, arouses no controversy or demand for new methods and research. This is quite strange, at least on first glance. Around 1550, a striking change began to take shape in Madagascar. In three geographically distant areas of this huge island, royal lineages came into being more or less concurrently and gradually imposed a larger political organization on the pre-existing petty chiefdoms, which were centered mainly on the village. However, this more or less synchronic advent of new and durable dynasties did not produce analogous historical results.

[3] M.-C. Chamla, *Recherches anthropologiques sur l'origine des Malgaches* (1958). The use of anthropometric methods to establish the Malagasy origins has been increasingly questioned in recent times. Somatological comparisons tend to rest on a limited number of samples, and within a research context they often are far from being satisfactory. Moreover, anthropometry itself is ill-suited to the problem of Malagasy origins after centuries of a melting-pot situation.

[4] For example, R. S. Codrington, "Resemblances Between Malagasy Words and Customs and Those of Western Polynesia," *AA*, II (1882), 122–127; A. Grandidier, *Ethnographie*, pp. 16–71; J. Faubleé (ed.), *Ethnographie de Madagascar* (1946), pp. 129–140. Despite over seventy pages of text and more than 150 footnotes, the authors cite no primary or secondary sources for Asia. The Malayo-Polynesian world covers nearly 2 million square kilometers and thousands of islands and islets. It thus becomes impossible to treat the whole area as a single culture or to assume any ethnographic affinities without strictest scholarly controls.

[5] Ch. Poirier, "Réflexions sur les ruines de Mailaka situées au fond de la Baie de Passandava, côte nord-ouest de Madagascar," *BAM*, XXVIII (1947–1948), 97–98 (the inscription is reproduced in n. 3, p. 97); and G. Pain, "Découverte d'une étrave de navire," *BAM*, XL (1964), 81–82.

[6] L. Molet, "L'Origine des Malgaches," *CM*, I/1 (1964), 43–52. The "new" methods enumerated by Molet were proposed by Dahle over eighty years ago. An outline of Dahle's proposal will be found in the Appendix.

ISLE DE
MADAGASCAR
autrement
ISLE DE S. LAURENT
Par N. B. Ing.ᵉ de la Marine
1747.
Echelles
Lieues Marines de France et d'Angleterre

Cap Natal
ou
Cap d'Ambr.
Cap S. Sebaiïen

Baye de Vohemare

Baye d'Antongil
NOSSI HIBRAHIM
ou
Isle d'Abraham
aujourdhui
ISLE DE S.ᵗ MARIE
Isle de S.ᵗ Marie

S.ᵗ Jean de Nove
ou
Christeava

HAZON

Ringhets

Voluts

Angombe

La He Fonu
Conchaa

Erin
Dranou

La Basse d'Inde

B. S. Augustin

Sivych   Machicores

Carenbole   Ampatres

Cap S.ᵗ Marie

Fort Dauphin

S.ᵗ Luce

TROPIQUE DU   CAPRICORNE

Remarque
La Partie du Sud Est de cette Isle
comprise entre la Riviere de Mandrerey
et celle d'Antavare demande un détail
particulier qu'on n'a pu inscrire ici, on
le trouve dans la Carte du S.ʳ de Flacourt
publiée en 1656.

Longitude du Meridien de l'Isle de Fer.

Tom I. N.º

In one case, the imposition of the dynasty was followed by a radical social transformation within a limited territorial domain and was implemented by an internally strong monarchy. In another, it gave birth to a vast territorial empire, held together by branches of the same royal family. This empire caused enormous human displacement while incorporating many different local populations. In still another, a theocracy without significant military and political power, torn by lasting internal strife, not only changed the nature of the local economy and society but also came to influence indirectly most of the other Malagasy as well. The dynasties alluded to are those of *Andriana, Maroserana,* and *Anteony,* respective rulers of the Merina, west-coast Sakalava, and the southeastern Anteimoro.

Historically minded students of Madagascar have indeed recognized that these royal families mark a very real political transition from fragmented chiefdoms to genuine states, centered around the monarchy and attested both by their own historical traditions and external sources, some of which are of considerable antiquity. Yet, this capital dynastic transformation within Madagascar, second in historical importance only to the actual peopling of the Great Island, has produced thus far just two general theories of explanation. Both of them were conceived in the concluding decades of the nineteenth century. The less complicated one has been that of Antony Jully, amplified some years later by J. V. Mellis—namely, that *all* of the Malagasy royal dynasties derive from an Arab family.[7] Since it is not easy to account for a political phenomenon that betrays no apparent single origin and that manifests itself in three separate and distant locations and, yet, accords closely in timing, Jully and Mellis provide an attractive explanation. However, it encounters insoluble difficulties from the outset.

Muslim and Arabic-speaking colonies existed in the northern part of Madagascar, both on its western and eastern littoral, since at least the twelfth century. Recent archaeological excavations at the northeastern site of Vohémar, known by its ancient name of Iharana, have yielded an entire culture complex based on external commerce and dominated by traders who wrote Arabic.[8] The combined evidence of archaeology, oral traditions, and written sixteenth-century accounts shows that early Mus-

---

[7] A. Jully, "Origine des 'Andriana' ou nobles," *NRE*, IV (1898), 890–898; "L'Habitation à Madagascar," *NRE*, IV (1898), 909–920; "Ethnographie de Madagascar," *RM*, VIII/12 (1906), 1025–1054; and J. V. Mellis, *Volamena et Volafotsy* (1938).

[8] Mouren and Rouaix, "Industrie ancienne des objets en pierre de Vohémar," *BAM*, XII/2 (1913), 3–13 of reprint edition; and P. Gaudebout and E. Vernier, "Notes sur une campagne de fouilles à Vohémar," *BAM*, XXIV (1941), 91–114. The principal Arabic inscription reads: "Year 515 Chaik Salim ben Radjab."

lim traders had two important settlements on the northwestern coast of Madagascar, not far from present-day Majunga.[9]

The ancient presence of Arab colonies, on the one hand, and the absence of any real Malagasy kingdoms until centuries later, on the other, make Jully's theory ill-suited to the historical problem it sought to resolve. It has been established that the old Arab colonies of northwestern Madagascar had nothing to do either with the advent of the Maroserana kings or with the creation of the Sakalava empire in the seventeenth century. Although, following Jully, Iharana is still sometimes considered a possible center of political influence, there is nothing to support such a view.[10] On the contrary, the early inhabitants of the Vohémar area, known as Onjatsy, are noted for their acephalous past and lack of any tradition that reveals the slightest trace of ancient kingship.[11] Moreover, the method of Jully and Mellis consisted of extracting certain traditions and customs of political elites in Madagascar, making them interchangeable in order to conclude that such similarities must presuppose a common source. Since personal names of royalty in Madagascar were widely prefaced with *Andria/Andriana* (Malagasy, lord), this provided a linguistic proof for their theory.[12] If *Andria* were indeed an Arabic loan-word, Jully's theory would have some merit, pending more solid research for other types of evidence. It belongs, however, to common Malagasy, the etymon being completely unrelated to Arabic. In reality, any single-origin theory

[9] Ch. Poirier, "Terre d'Islam en Mer Malgache," *BAM*, special issue (1954), 71–116; L. Jacquier, "Les Royaumes Sakalava Bemihisatra de la côte nord-ouest de Madagascar," unpublished typescript, *BP* (now housed at the University of Madagascar), not dated but prepared *ca.* 1914 (reproduced in the Appendix to this work); *COACM*, Vol. I (1903), pp. 14–31 *passim* for Portuguese reports on northwestern Madagascar in 1506–1510 as given mainly by Portuguese chroniclers. See also text below.

[10] Faublée, *Ethnographie*, p. 127; H. Deschamps, *Histoire de Madagascar*, 2nd ed. (1961), p. 55, n. 2; and R. Cornevin, *Histoire de l'Afrique*, Vol. I (1962), pp. 386–389.

[11] R. T. Batchelor, "Notes on the Antankarana and Their Country," *AA*, I (1877), 31; J. M. Hildebrandt, "Ausflug zum Ambergebirge in Nord Madagaskar," *ZGE*, XV (1880), 275; Ch. Bernier, *Rapport sur une mission sur la cote nord-est de Madagascar*, manuscript, pp. 1–136, December 27, 1834 (based on a mission of 1831), *ANSOMCM*, Carton XVII, Dossier 8; and Th. Fleury, "Quelques Notes sur le nord de Madagascar," *SGCBB* (1886), 194–209, 226–245, 257–282, 290–312. The Antankarana, who encompass the Onjatsy, obtained kings from the Sakalava.

[12] Jully, "Origine des 'Andriana,'" 890, 896–897; Mellis, *Volamena et Volafotsy*, pp. 56–58, 10–14; see also in the Appendix to this work extracts from J. V. Mellis' unpublished typescript, *Autour du Tombeau du prince qui fait peur: legendes, coutumes et moeurs sakalava* (not dated), pp. 1–123, Document 0752, Library of Institut de Recherche Scientifique de Madagascar (IRSM), Tsimbazaza-Tananarive. See also Chapters 2 and 7 below for an explanation of how the term Andriana diffused.

for the three oldest royal dynasties in Madagascar is confronted by an entire chain of written sources, oral traditions, and linguistic and ethnographic documents that make it completely untenable.

The plainly impossible task of finding evidence to support such a monolithic theory points to one reason why it has failed to gain acceptance. Yet, the fundamental belief of Jully that the political transition itself must have been induced by Asian outsiders has been shared by all of the several hundred *Malgachisants*, yesterday as well as today. The psychological and historical roots of this belief can be traced to a local Malagasy phenomenon, the Merinization of Europeans in Madagascar.

Following the Napoleonic Wars in Europe, the Anglo-French rivalry in the western Indian Ocean gave a British governor of Mauritius an opportunity to extend Britain's influence into Madagascar. Having played a similar role earlier in Asia, the governor looked for the most "promising" group in Madagascar. He found the Merina to fit his plans and concluded a politicomilitary alliance with them. His agents trained the Merina army along the European model in the second decade of the nineteenth century while Mauritius supplied modern British weapons. In turn, the Merina proceeded to build rapidly their own subempire. The Anglo-Merina alliance also introduced the London Missionary Society into Tananarive. Not without some setbacks, its missionaries gradually identified with the Merina and came to serve openly the political and economic ends of their monarchy. The cordial relations between the Merina and the London Missionary Society were attested by the fact that Protestantism became the official religion of the Merina state in the late 1860s.[13]

Individual missionaries of the society when writing about the island concentrated mainly on the Merina, giving a false impression of their cultural and political omnipresence there. This tradition was never to be reversed. It began with the 1838 *History of Madagascar*, in two volumes, by Reverend William Ellis. Although there were references to other Malagasy, the volumes were confined in effect to the Merina. Later, in periodicals like the *Antananarivo Annual* (1875–1900), *Chronicle of the London Missionary Society* (in London after 1867), and countless pamphlets, the society's numerous spokesmen contrasted the Merina in unjustly sharp terms with other Malagasy, who often were reported as comparative savages, and held that extension of Merina control over other provinces was synonymous with the spread of civilization. Tananarive, the center of a local Merina subempire, was more densely inhabited,

[13] On this chapter of Malagasy history, see R. K. Kent, "How France Acquired Madagascar, 1642–1896," *Tarikh*, University of Ibadan, Nigeria, special number (January 1969), 20 pp.; and S. E. Howe, *The Drama of Madagascar* (1938), pp. 115–248.

imposing, and advanced in its arts and crafts than any other Malagasy town of the period. The court of the Merina monarchs had no peers elsewhere in the island. Visually—then as now—the Merina were the "whitest" of Malagasy, other groups appeared to be invariably "darker." A number of them were already under Merina control by mid-nineteenth century.

It was only a matter of time before race, culture, politics, and history became hopelessly intermixed. The relatively recent Merina political supremacy was constantly attributed to superior culture, itself a product of a superior race of Asians, or Malays, as the Merina were often called in those days. The pre-existing fascination of many contemporary Europeans with old civilizations of Asia, the strong influence of missionary writers, the perennial testimony of the "naked eye," the Merina success story itself, and the important fact that educated Europeans resided mainly in Tananarive, led the French *Malgachisants* to much the same premise that the first kingdoms in Madagascar were founded by overseas Asians.[14] Voiced inadequately by Jully, this hypothesis awaited only a weightier scholar to provide a more serious framework along with evidence that would not be taxed by inner contradiction.

This need was filled by Alfred Grandidier, the most important and influential *Malgachisant* of all time. Aided by his son Guillaume, Alfred Grandidier began in 1865 an encyclopedic effort which was to have culminated in the fifty-two-volume *Histoire Physique, Naturelle et Politique de Madagascar*.[15] For almost a century (1865–1955), the Grandidiers worked tirelessly to amass information about every aspect of the Great Island. They collected oral traditions along with specimens of flora and fauna, purchased Arabico-Malagasy manuscripts and mapped the island, compiled old travel accounts and local vocabularies, and studied the traditional Malagasy customs, economies, and religious and political institutions. If measured only by joint publications, some 250 articles and 15 in-quarto volumes devoted exclusively to Madagascar, their contribution is already unique. But it is vastly more encompassing. The Grandidiers inspired numerous collaborators, created many disciples, induced several agencies to print bibliographical and substantive data about Madagascar, and researched and catalogued materials relative to the

---

[14] R. K. Kent, "Alfred Grandidier et le 'Mythe des Fondateurs d'États Malgaches d'Origines Asiatiques,'" *BM*, nos. 277–278 (June–July 1969), pp. 603–620. While a number of authors have been willing to grant that Africans, too, contributed to the peopling of Madagascar, no one has ever connected this aspect with the political and cultural history of the Malagasy.

[15] By 1958, thirty-two volumes had been published—twenty-five devoted to the flora, fauna, geography and meteorology, three to political history, and four to ethnography. A number of the volumes appear in more than one tome or fascicule.

island in nearly fifty public and private archives and libraries of Europe. They devoted not only their physical and intellectual energies to the Grand Island, but their personal fortune as well. If Madagascar happens to be better documented than most preliterate areas, the credit belongs largely to Alfred and Guillaume Grandidier.[16]

Because Alfred Grandidier came to confirm a widespread belief that only new migrants coming from Asia could have fathered the early kingdoms in Madagascar, there was no predisposition to doubt him. The Great Island is an extremely isolated place even in the era of air travel, and *Malgachisant* scholarship has reflected this factor by being oriented mainly inward. The present had to be explained by a past that would fit the observable phenomena, and since the most Asian of Malagasy had also attained the highest degree of technological and political supremacy in the island, the historical task was clearly predefined. Over the years, some minor points were modified or a few dates were made more plausible. But, there were no trained historians who advocated a course of research contrary to this possibly useless conception of historical craft. No one considered questioning Grandidier's conclusion or examining its supporting pillars. The stature and massive scholarship of the man became the shield for disciples who continued to quote him as the penultimate authority.

Grandidier began his study of Madagascar with several strong advantages over any previous student of the island. He collected, first, a vast number of early sources written by Portuguese, Dutch, English, and French travelers who had visited Madagascar before 1800. On the basis of these, he was able to establish a valid point of departure—namely, that no large or powerful state was reported on the island before the 1660s. Up to at least 1614, this was confirmed by an astute observer, who circumnavigated nearly half of the Madagascar coast, from present-day Majunga in the northwest to Fort-Dauphin in the southeast. In Madagascar, he reported, "the government is [in principle] monarchical [but] the kinglets, who are extremely numerous and for this very reason command slight power . . . are absolute masters [only] in their own districts. . . . Moreover, because [the island] is partitioned among countless chiefs who are not in accord with one another, warfare is frequent, one could even say continuous, yet [politically] unimportant since it aims [only] at pillage."[17] Although most Europeans used "chief" and "king" indiscriminately, their accounts leave no doubt that the entire coast of Madagascar was fragmented into small and usually riverain sovereignties,

---

[16] See Kent, "Alfred Grandidier." *BM,* 277–278 (1969), pp. 603–620.
[17] L. Mariano, *Relation du voyage de découverte fait à l'Ile Saint-Laurent, 1613–1614,* in *COACM,* Vol. II (1904), p. 9.

that the principal concern of their politics was redistribution of wealth by force and not territorial expansion. In addition, none of the Europeans before 1650 heard of any important state in the interior.

Grandidier had another important advantage over other students of Madagascar in that, as a professional explorer, he managed to visit many parts of the island before the French annexation of 1896. Traditional institutions, although affected to some extent by Merina conquests here and there, were still very much alive, and Alfred Grandidier was no casual observer. In the 1860s, there were other kingdoms besides the Merina one, and not a few preserved their own *lovan'tsofina*, or heritage of the ears, about the past. The Merina and Anteimoro possessed in addition some written history. Grandidier purchased the "Hova Manuscripts" and the Anteimoro *Sora-bé* (Arabic, "Great Writings"), both in Malagasy but written in Latin and Arabic scripts. Where there were no written documents, he set down the oral texts and described local institutions on some 2500 manuscript pages, entitled *Cahiers de Notes sur l'Histoire et les Moeurs des diverses Peuplades de Madagascar.*[18] From these local sources, Grandidier was able to calculate that although the

[18] These notes were compiled between 1868 and 1870. They include accounts of: *Iavibola*, southeastern coast of Madagascar, pp. 1–41; the *Antifiherenana*, people of the southwestern coast, pp. 42–197; the *Andrevola kings of Fiherenana*, pp. 198–202; the *Antanosy migrants* in southwestern Madagascar, pp. 398–488; the *Mahafaly people*, pp. 489–528; coastal *Sakalava* between Tuléar and Morondava, pp. 569–629; the *Sakalava of Menabé* (Antimenabé) between Morondava and Mahabo, pp. 630–720; the *Sakalava and Vazimba of Menabé*, pp. 721–912, 920–923; the *Sakalava and Arabs of Maintirano*, pp. 913–920, 923–924; coastal *Sakalava north of Maintirano*, pp. 925–928; the *Sakalava and Antankarana of the islet of Nosy-bé*, pp. 929–952; the *Sakalava of the northwestern coast between the Bays of Ampasindava and Anorontsangana* (with notes on the Antalaotra and Hova settlers among them), pp. 952–1046; notes on the *Hova* found on the route from Majunga to Tananarive, pp. 1046–1138; *land of the Merina* (Imerina) with various notes, pp. 1159–1454, 1516–1847; *from Tananarive to Morondava*, pp. 1454–1516; *the (west-coast) Vazimba*, pp. 1848–1856; the *Sakalava of Menabé*, notes taken at Manja, pp. 1856–1876; the *Hova, Bezanozano, and Sihanaka*, pp. 1877–1944; the *Sakalava between Morondava and Manja and at Midongy*, pp. 1945–2012; *from Midongy to Mananjary* (east coast), with notes on the Betsileo, Tanala, Zafindraminia, and Anteisaka, pp. 2013–2197; *from Mananjary to Matitana*, with notes on the Antaimoro and Zafindraminia, pp. 2198–2265; the *Vorimo and Betsimisaraka*, pp. 2266–2337; the *Hova and Bezanozano*, pp. 2337–2409; the *Betsimisaraka*, pp. 2409–2438 (and Hova), pp. 2439–2487. Although these manuscript notes are in the possession of a private party who will show them to no one, much of the primary data has found its way into print for the Merina (Hova), Vazimba, Bezanozano, Antaimoro, Zafindraminia, Antanosy, Betsileo, Sihanaka, and Mahafaly. The material that remains unpublished pertains mainly to the Sakalava. However, Hubert Deschamps has kindly allowed me to consult the unpublished typescript of Guillaume Grandidier, "Essai d'histoire des Malgaches de la région occidentale: les Sakalava" (not dated), pp. 1–78, with extensive notes based primarily on his father's original manuscript notes.

early kingdoms did not exist in the 1500s, their founders were present in Madagascar by the middle of the sixteenth century. He could also reject safely some of the Merina genealogical trees, through which attempts were made to push their kingdom back in time to periods long antedating the 1500s.[19]

During his early travels, Grandidier formed some personal impressions that would never leave him, impressions that are fundamental to an understanding of how he arrived at the accepted version of dynastic origins and the foundation of the first kingdoms in Madagascar.

Throughout Madagascar, he observed, "nearly all of the chiefs and rulers" were of an "origin different from the mass of people," as attested by special or royal vocabularies, for example, vocabularies with "words from their mother tongues."[20] But, even more striking was the observable fact that the rulers were physically different from their subjects. Others, too, noticed this in the Merina province, for "just about everyone agrees that [its] inhabitants belong to the Malay race" and while this need not apply to all of them, "it is . . . among certain *Andriana* . . . , descendants of the conquerors, that one discovers the most characteristic traits of [the] Malayan race which came and mastered the Indonesian one at a comparatively recent period."[21] While on a ship, Grandidier "saw together a Javanese . . . and an Andriana of Imerina and they did not appear to belong just to the same people but to the same family."[22]

The Andriana then, as seen in the late 1800s, were descendants of Malays from Java. The Merina texts, moreover, suggested to Grandidier that the arrival of the Andriana into the central highlands was substantiated by conquests of pre-existing Vazimba chiefdoms and by the ensuing sudden and radical change in society and religion.[23] Since written accounts of Madagascar went back to the 1500s, he felt, they should reveal one or more Javanese landings in Madagascar, leading eventually to the ancestors of the Andriana. To narrow down the documentary search, it was necessary to determine which section of the vast Malagasy coast would be most likely to reveal the suspected landings. Following this approach, Grandidier decided to trace internal migrations from oral sources in order to discover the points of overseas landings.

[19] A. Grandidier, *Ethnographie*, pp. 75–87; and G. Grandidier, *Histoire politique et coloniale*, Vol. I (1942), pp. 37–47; compare with the mythical genealogy going back to 1300, as given by Father Malzac in his *Histoire du Royaume Hova* (1912), pp. 30–31.

[20] A. Grandidier, *Ethnographie*, pp. 6–7, and n. 2.

[21] A. Grandidier, "The Vazimba: The Earlier Inhabitants of Imerina," *AA*, V (1894), 134; original in French as "Note sur les Vazimba de Madagascar," *MSP*, commemorative issue (1888), 155–161.

[22] A. Grandidier, *Ethnographie*, pp. 73, n. 1.

[23] See Chapter 6 below for discussion of this change.

From traditions recorded by others and by himself, he found that the Indonesian Vazimba had participated in an early migration from the western coast into the central highlands.[24] But, the Andriana came from the eastern littoral, as much to escape a malarial environment as to avoid being subjugated by the Arabs who had been there for some time.[25] In addition to the evidence derived from oral traditions, one could claim an Andriana landing in eastern Madagascar in other ways. The "very position of their earliest dwelling sites on the plateau, southeast of Tananarive . . . shows well enough that they came from the east." And, "quite naturally, the currents and prevailing winds in the Indian Ocean would have brought them to the eastern littoral."[26] Good evidence of this was furnished by the Krakatoa volcanic eruption. Its debris reached Tamatave in 1884. Five months later, following a major cyclone, the Krakatoa debris scattered along the entire eastern seaboard of Madagascar as well.[27] To this could be added that at the turn of the nineteenth century several Javanese vessels were pushed by winds and current into the Tamatave area,[28] a fact hardly lost on Grandidier.[29]

Considering the currents and winds as well as the fact that western

[24] A. Grandidier, *Ethnographie*, pp. 73–74 and n. 2. The Vazimba are discussed both in the Merina and Sakalava chapters below.

[25] *Ibid.*, p. 74, n. 1. It is well-known that the inhabitants of the central highlands do not resist malaria as well as some of the coastal populations. The latter appear to have built some immunity through the sickle-cell anemia. There is, however, no evidence in the Malagasy past of malaria-induced migrations. On malaria in Madagascar, see: R. Blanchard, "Le Paludisme à Madagascar," *Archives de Parasitologie*, XI (1907), 185–214; R. Lhuerre, *Le Paludisme et la peste à Madagascar* (1937), pp. 1–134; M. M. Monier, *Charactères de l'anophélisme sur les plateaux de l'Emyrne* (1937), pp. 1–56; and J. Doucet, *Les Anophélines de la région malgache* (1951), pp. 24–195.

[26] A. Grandidier, *Ethnographie*, pp. 74–75, n. 1. The currents, seasonal winds, and weather disturbances in the Indian Ocean and around Madagascar are far too complicated and unstable for any a priori arguments concerning overseas migrations. Cf. R. P. Poisson, "Sur l'Etude des cyclones de l'Océan Indien," *BAM*, XVII (1934), 1–6; M. Jehenne, *Renseignements nautiques* .(1850), pp. 5–7 (northwestern Malagasy waters and Mozambique Channel); J. Emon, *L'Inversion de l'Alizé dans l'Océan Indien sud-ouest* (1949), pp. 1–269; M. Menaché, "Etude systématique de l'hydrographie du Canal de Moçambique," *Le Naturaliste malgache*, V/2 (1953), 129–136; Ch. Ph. De Kerhallet, *Considérations générales sur l'Océan Indien* (1859), pp. 6–7, 87, 104–109, 120–121; and M. Destombes, *Cartographie de la compagnie des Indes Orientales, 1593–1743* (1941), pp. 1–99 and maps.

[27] A. Grandidier, *Ethnographie*, p. 9 and note.

[28] See B. Hugon, "Lois, police et coutumes de Madagascar," manuscript, pp. 1–45, *ANSOMCM*, Carton XI, Dossier 2, Item 3, dated February 1818. Barthélemy Hugon reported to have seen them in 1808 and that some of the stranded sailors were incorporated into the local militia at Tamatave by the French agent Sylvain Roux (p. 30 verso).

[29] A. Grandidier, *Ethnographie*, p. 9, n. 2(b).

Madagascar faces nonmaritime Africa and eastern Madagascar faces maritime Asia, a scholar could conclude that *all* of the dynastic founders in Madagascar must have landed on the eastern-southeastern littoral. The entire spread of kingship in Madagascar, thus, proceeded from east to west. It remained simply to turn now to the Portuguese chroniclers of the sixteenth century to pinpoint the Andriana or, for that matter, any other dynastic group. Two Portuguese accounts, contained in Diogo do Couto's *Da Asia*, namely those of Balthazar Lobo de Souza, who visited Madagascar in 1557, and Luis Fernandez de Vasconcellos, whose vessel sank off the Malagasy coast in 1559, gave Grandidier the evidence sought. Claiming that both had actually been on the eastern littoral of the island, Grandidier stated that finds were made there of Javanese shipwrecks between Matitana and Mahanoro. There is, he added, "a remarkable overlap of the time of this shipwreck and the advent [in Imerina] of the first king belonging to the Malay dynasty."[30] He turned next to the Maroserana.

This dynastic family, unlike the Andriana of Imerina, gave rulers to more than one Malagasy group—to the Sakalava, Bara, Mahafaly, Antandroy, and Anteisaka—and it thus extended its influence across the southern plateau, from the eastern coast (Antaisaka) to the opposite one (Sakalava). But, as in the Andriana-Merina case, it was not difficult to visualize the true Maroserana antecedents. All of the Maroserana were white in comparison to their subjects, yet certainly not Mongoloid. Rather, the Bara princes resembled greatly the Malabari of India and the Sinhalese of Ceylon. The Sakalava royal women were Tamil-looking. There was no doubt, as others had noted also at the time, that all of the politically prominent families in western Madagascar were direct descendants of Indians from India.[31] The Maroserana, "who rule among the Mahafaly, the Sakalava [of Menabé and Boina], as well as the *Zafy Manely* dynastic Bara chiefs, and the *Zafy Manara*, chiefly dynasty of the

---

[30] *Ibid.*, p. 82 and n. 1. Grandidier placed the first king of the Malay dynasty on the Merina throne in 1590, calculating a thirty-year generation from about 1560.

[31] Cf. M. E. F. Knight, "From Fort-Dauphin to Fianarantsoa," *AA*, V (1895), 367, and his *Madagascar in War Time* (1896), p. 50; A. Jully, "Mission en Extrême-Orient," *BAM*, II (1903), 73, 78; and E. O. McMahon, "First Visit of a European to the Betsiriry Tribe," *AA*, IV (1891), 278–279. In citing the Tamil-looking Sakalava women as taken from McMahon, A. Grandidier (*Ethnographie*, 169, n. 1) should have given the full quote, which reads: "From all I saw I should say that most of [the Betsiriry-Sakalava] religious beliefs and customs are African, such as their splitting the ears [of cattle], painting their faces and chests, tattooing, and ornamentation of their hair with rows of crocodiles' teeth, wire, beads, etc., as well as their lazy habits, yet the Sakalava women are much more like the Tamil women than the African type" (pp. 278–279). See the photographs of Sakalava women in this work.

Antandroy . . . are all descendants of the Anteisaka rulers who [them-
selves] descend from Indians of Gudjerat or Malabar."[32] These Indians
would have then landed on the southeastern littoral, moving north to
found the Anteisaka kingdom. Thereafter, part of the Maroserana proceeded on their way toward the west coast. In their passage from east to
west, they gave rulers to the southern-plateau Bara, founded the Mahafaly
kingdom in the southwest, and branched out again in two directions.
North of Mahafaly, they created the Sakalava kingdom of Menabé and
east of the Mahafaly they became the *Zafimanara* kings of the Antandroy,
who occupy the southernmost part of Madagascar. From Menabé, the
Sakalava-Maroserana expanded north, along the western littoral, founding
the Boina kingdom in the northwest. The very name *Sakalava* came from
the site of *Isaka*, the etymon thus affirming the Anteisaka origin of the
Sakalava.[33] Grandidier held that while the whiteness of Sakalava-Maroserana had led some to assume an Arab origin, this was inadmissible
because of historical proof that the Maroserana king who founded the
first Sakalava kingdom of Menabé, *Andriandahifotsy* (white king), ate
pork.[34]

According to Grandidier, the "direct arrival of Indians" to Madagascar
was no simple "hypothesis but a historically proven fact."[35] "Toward
1300, ships sent from Cambay [Western Gudjerat] to East Africa and
the Cape of Good Hope by the Muslim ruler of Gudjerat, were wrecked
on the southern coast of Madagascar as a result of a tempest."[36] This
information was found in the *Commentários do Grande Afonso de Albuquerque*, written in 1557 and reproduced since in several editions and
translations. And, it was certain that the *Zara Behavana*, or Anteisaka
chiefs, derive from this particular group of Indian shipwrecks.[37] In
addition to the Portuguese sources, Grandidier reported that he had
found equally convincing evidence "in local traditions and customs of
certain families."[38]

[32] A. Grandidier, *Ethnographie*, pp. 128 n., 168, 212, 214, 278, 279–280 n. 4.

[33] Isaka is noted on Flacourt's 1661 map as an eastern littoral site. From this,
Grandidier proposed that the west-coast Sakalava were *Antaisakalava* (ant-a+I+
saka+lava), or people who crossed long distances, in his "Un Voyage scientifique à
Madagascar," *RS*, 2nd series, I/46 (May 1872), 1086. Grandidier's etymon is as
unreal as a number of others proposed, *inter alia*: long cats (lava+saka); the defiant
ones (*Sakaray*); people of the long plains, (*Sakany*). *Isaka* and *Sakalava* are *not*
derivatives and neither is a Malagasy term as will be shown. The first to suggest
that Sakalava may be a non-Malagasy name was an early linguist, Rev. S. E.
Jorgensen, *Notes on the Tribes of Madagascar*, *AA*, III (1885), 33.

[34] A. Grandidier, *Ethnographie*, pp. 168; I/2 (1908), 648, notule 2.

[35] *Ibid.*, p. 11, notule 6.

[36] *Ibid.*, p. 118, n. 2.

[37] *Ibid.*, pp. 168, 206, n. 5.

[38] *Ibid.*, p. 166, n. 1.

Finally, the Arabs too contributed royal dynasties, but only to the southeastern Anteimoro of Matitana and the Antanosy of the area that was to be the French settlement Fort-Dauphin. Together with the Malays from Java and Indians from India, they conclude the list of king-makers in old Madagascar. Their migrations did not take place in the same time period and some of the arrivals were Arabs only in a nominal sense.

The first migration, around 1100, produced the so-called descendants of Raminia (*Zafindraminia*). They landed first at Iharana (Vohémar), in the northeast. Some two centuries later, between 1300 and 1350, a group of Sunni Arabs from Malindi came to Iharana to establish a trading center and expelled the Zafindraminia.[39] They dispersed, moving gradually down the eastern littoral into the valley of Mananjara River. Here, they acquired the ethnic name of Antambahoaka, but some of the Zafi Raminia went into Antanosy and became local kings (*roandrian*). But, the first Portuguese navigators to visit the Fort-Dauphin area in 1508 did not find them there as yet.[40] Who then were Raminia and his companions? They were, argued Grandidier, Karamatians (Bātinī) who had fled to the Malabar coast of India in the tenth century. At the turn of the twelfth century, these Indianized Arabs left the port of Mangalore, probably to go back to Arabia, but the currents pushed them instead into the waters of northeastern Madagascar.[41]

That the Zafi Raminia sailed from an Indian port mentioned in an Arabico-Malagasy manuscript and their own oral traditions as related to two Europeans at Fort-Dauphin in the first half of the seventeenth century did not constitute the only evidence of Raminia's Indian origin. When European residents at Fort-Dauphin began to write about the Antanosy, they noticed that incest was an accepted custom among the Zafi Raminia.[42] They also noticed that the Antanosy society below the Zafi Raminia ruling class consisted of indigenous chiefly families (called *voajiry*), commoners and freemen (*lohavohits* and *ontsoa*), and slaves (*ondeves*).[43] "Only" the Batini Muslims allowed incest. And since there was "in the valley of Indus, north of Gudjerat, a half-Afghan and half-Indian tribe" named Voajiry, Grandidier also found plausible proof for

[39] *Ibid.*, pp. 139–141.

[40] *Ibid.*, p. 141.

[41] *Ibid.*, pp. 109, 128, 130, 137, 139–140.

[42] This aspect of local society seems to have been noticed particularly by Christian missionaries, like Father Manoel d'Almeida in 1616–1617 and Father Domingo Fernandez Navarrete in 1671. Cf. *COACM*, Vol. II (1904), pp. 197; and *COACM*, Vol. III (1905), pp. 350. In effect, what they observed was, on the whole, levirate, which appears to have been fairly wide-spread at one time in the island.

[43] Flacourt, *Histoire*, *COACM*, Vol. VIII (1913), pp. 25–27.

the earlier Indian shipwrecks whom the Zafi Raminia "designated as Voajiry."[44]

The ancestors of present-day Anteimoro did not reach either Madagascar or the Matitana area before the turn of the sixteenth century. They, too, did not come directly from Arabia. It is difficult to determine just where they might have paused in the meantime. Grandidier would not exclude eastern Africa or the Comoro Islands as probable points of departure. Unlike the Zafi Raminia, the Anteimoro were pure Arabs in the ethnic and cultural sense. Their king-making or noble clans were composed of Sunni Arabs and of 'Alides.[45] Grandidier's deductions in respect to the Anteimoro rested mainly on linguistics. The script of their *Sora-bé* is Arabic, and many of their texts reveal a relatively high percentage of Arabic loan-words. At least one of them mentioned some mountains of Arabia, pointing to fairly "recent" toponymic associations.[46]

These are essentially the findings of Grandidier relative to the most important political transition in Madagascar before the nineteenth century. They are far more sophisticated than the feeble excursions of Jully or the myriad guesses of others who did not have Alfred Grandidier's knowledge of Madagascar and its historical sources, written as well as oral and ethnographic. It is safe to say that, in more than half a century since he published his major work, no one else has advanced an overview of Malagasy precolonial past without repeating in one way or another what Grandidier has written. In the past few years, with the growth of general interest in the "Third World," several authors have started to disseminate his findings outside of Madagascar.[47] There is, however, every reason to doubt them.

[44] A. Grandidier, *Ethnographie*, pp. 143, 167 and n. 2.

[45] *Ibid.*, p. 156. The 'Alid dynasties ruled at Mecca, Yemen, Maghreb, western Sudan, and southern Spain; see H. A. R. Gibb and J. H. Kramers, *Shorter Encyclopedia of Islam* (1953), pp. 32–33.

[46] A. Grandidier, *Ethnographie*, p. 639, n. 139; and Flacourt, *Histoire, COACM*, Vol. VIII (1913), p. 94, and n. 1–3 by Grandidier. In this instance, Grandidier was juxtaposing two totally disparate sources, an Antanosy tradition reported by Flacourt in the 1650s and an Anteimoro tradition recorded by the French administrator Marchand around 1900; cf. Marchand, "Les Habitants de la province de Farafangana," *RM*, III (1901), 484. In both, the term *zabally/zobaly* recurs as a prefix that Grandidier translated as mountain (from arabic, *djebel*). This could well apply to the text of Flacourt but not to that of Marchand. The problem is discussed below in the Anteimoro chapter (Chapter 3).

[47] In Madagascar: "Before the arrival of the Zafindraminia in Antanosy, there was already a colony of Indians from Goudjerat"; "It can be presumed, in accordance with the name Voajiry, that they originated from the valley of the Indus, where a half-Indian, half-Afghan tribe by that name is to be found" (both in Guillaume Grandidier and Raymond Decary, *Histoire politique et coloniale*, Vol. V, Tome III [1958], pp. 71–72); "Alfred and Guillaume Grandidier have advanced the hypoth-

Let us begin with the Andriana of Imerina. The Portuguese sources cited and used by Grandidier tell a completely different story. Balthazar Lobo de Souza never went beyond the northwestern littoral of Madagascar, which he and his men explored on orders of the viceroy at Goa, Barreto, in 1557.[48] De Souza provided some important detail about the part of Madagascar actually explored, but he had nothing to say about the opposite or eastern coast of the island. Rather, it was Do Couto himself who, in relating de Souza's account, inserted the sentence "it is *presumed* that this Island was once conquered by the Javanese and that the inhabitants of eastern [Madagascar] are composed of the Javanese and indigenous *métis*."[49] De Vasconcellos, also, never landed at any point on the Malagasy shore. The only Malagasy seen by his crew were those who came with outriggers to the Portuguese sloop to trade.[50] Where Grandidier, moreover, gave the two accounts an individuality of primary sources, Do Couto placed them together into the seventh decade of Portuguese overseas expansion, taken as a "unit" of history, paraphrased them half a century after the events (1602–1616) and, in doing so, transformed them into a secondary source.

In paraphrasing the information extracted from de Vasconcellos, the

---

esis that the dynasties which, since the 16th century, ruled over most of the southern and western tribes in Madagascar, descend from Indian immigrants. . . . We will [now] try to show that this hypothesis accords perfectly with oral tradition" (cf. M. E. Fagering, "Contribution à l'histoire de Madagascar: etude sur les immigrations anciennes à Madagascar et sur l'origine des principales dynasties du sud et de l'ouest de l'ile," BAM, XXV [1942–1943], 168–169 (his twenty-page article, 165–174, merely cites the Grandidiers in respect to Indians and adds *nothing* by way of oral tradition]); "The names of the descendants of Zafiramini . . . are found in tribal names of the Zarabehavana, Mahafaly, Masikoro—all kinsmen—and whose chiefs were Indian *métis* who did not have an aversion to pork-eating" (cf. H. Rusillon, "Notes explicatives à propos de la généalogie maroserana zafimbolamena," BAM, VI [1922–1923], 179); "The Zafi-Raminia of Antanosy superimposed themselves on the *Voajiry* caste, probably of Indian origin . . . but the Zafi-Raminia themselves were apparently Indian immigrants"; "The term *andriana* became a chiefly prefix . . . among peoples who obtained chiefs from the new arrivals of the Medieval period, the Iharanians, Indians and Indonesians" (cf. Deschamps, *Madagascar*, pp. 50–51 and 55, n. 2.

Outside Madagascar: R. Cornevin, *Histoire de l'Afrique*, Vol. I (1962), pp. 386–388; G. P. Murdock, *Africa: Its Peoples and Their Cultural History* (1959), p. 216 ("the original culture was exclusively Indonesian, and all immigrants prior to the middle of the first millennium were overwhelmingly Mongoloid"); and the chapter on Madagascar in Ivan Hrbek (ed.), *Dejny Afriky* (History of Africa), Vol. I (1966), with a table of would-be migrations.

[48] Do Couto, *Da Asia* (Decade VII) (1555–1564) (1616), in *COACM*, Vol. I (1903), p. 98.

[49] *Ibid.*, p. 99. Italics added.

[50] *Ibid.*, pp. 109–110.

Portuguese chronicler stated again that he "would not deny that the eastern coast of the Island was once conquered by the Javanese."[51] This is the only link between the two accounts. Here, Do Couto went on to elaborate on what grounds he had made the same statement twice. "Our compatriots have found, in some of the bays, *individuals* who *seemed Javanese to them,* from which *they* concluded that the east coast was inhabited [actually] by the Javanese, whose language the local people speak." But, Do Couto could not accept such a conclusion. "As for us [personally], we believe . . . that these individuals must have been [recent] *shipwrecks* [for] it seems inadmissible to us that they could [otherwise] have *retained* the language of their ancestors."[52]

In contrast to the data found for northwestern Madagascar in 1557, which consist of linguistic items attesting to a faithful reproduction by Do Couto, nothing comparable exists in the context of his summary of the 1559 account. It would have been indeed surprising if the Portuguese sailors failed to notice that some individuals who came to their sloop looked Javanese since, to this day, many individual Malagasy could easily pass for Indonesians from Java. In the absence of any real contact with the mass of east-coast inhabitants, it would have been equally normal for them to conclude that the entire eastern littoral was inhabited by the Javanese. For that matter, another Portuguese chronicler, a contemporary of Do Couto and using the same 1559 account, held that the Javanese superimposed themselves on the pre-existing population of "Blacks from the coast of Southeastern Africa."[53] It is also most unlikely that the crew of de Vasconcellos knew at the same time a variety of Malagasy east-coast dialects and the idioms of Java or that they could make any valid comparisons. And even Do Couto could accept the linguistic argument only by manufacturing contemporary shipwrecks from Java. The *real* evidence, thus, contradicts Grandidier completely.

We are thus dealing with a hypothesis that has no foundation in historical facts. The Andriana appear in Merina texts even earlier than the one generation Grandidier estimated it would take to get them from an invented mid-sixteenth-century shipwreck, hundreds of miles away, to the local throne in 1590.[54] Only *one* tradition, itself a mere statement

---

[51] *Ibid.,* p. 111.

[52] *Ibid.,* pp. 110–111. Italics added.

[53] Francisco d'Andrada, *Cronica del Rey Dom João III,* Vol. IV (1613), Ch. CXX, p. 145 verso.

[54] Cf. F. Callet, *Tantaran'ny Andriana (Histoire des rois),* Vol. I (1953), trans. into French by G. S. Chapus and E. Ratsimba, pp. 27–29, 123–135. On the basis of Callet's *Tantara* and the Merina manuscripts, Guillaume Grandidier revised the chronology of his father in respect to the Malay kings, pushing the 1590 date back to the 1530s, which is somewhat too early; see his *Histoire politique,* Vol. I (1942), p. 45, and the Merina chapter in this work.

elicited from local informants recently by pointed questioning and accompanied by no detail, claims that the Andriana came to Imerina from the southeastern coast "after" a previous Arab settlement.[55] The early sites in Imerina, southeast of Tananarive, attributed to the Andriana, involve microdistances of 5–10 kilometers from the capital, hardly enough for postulating migratory directions. The would-be Andriana migration into the central plateau applies in reality to the Hova, a name that in time came to designate all freemen in Merina society. These Hova constitute the only true Mongoloid element in Imerina, and while, by Grandidier's time, many Andriana looked white, other Europeans observed the very opposite—namely, that some Andriana were much darker than their Hova subjects.[56]

In dealing with the Anteimoro overseas migrations, Grandidier was by no means wrong about the approximate dates of arrival in Madagascar. His suggestion of 'Alid connections, opens some intriguing possibilities for the role of religion in history. Conversely, the use of *written* language as proof that the Anteimoro were pure Arabs, uncontaminated by physical contact and cultural borrowing from one or more societies that were neither Arab nor Malagasy, merely augments the discrepancies that begin with the Andriana.

As the language of the Quran, classical Arabic, survives in written texts throughout Muslim communities, from Bosnia to Java, even where

[55] Callet, *Tantara*, pp. 118–119. The pointed and leading informant questioning is clear from the text. On the almost normal distortions of this technique, see J. M. Vansina, "History in the Field," in D. G. Jongmans and P. C. W. Gutkind (eds.), *Anthropologists in the Field* (1967), and his *Oral Tradition* (1965), pp. 1–186. See also W. J. Samarin, *Field Linguistics* (1967), pp. 140–150. It is not very surprising that the translators of Callet add also the speculations of Grandidier immediately after the reported "native tradition" (pp. 119–121).

[56] Some of the early London Missionary Society missionaries saw the Merina king Radama I (1810–1828) as an African and stated so in a now extremely rare pamphlet, *Radama: The Enlightened African*. Even the nineteenth-century sketch reproductions and paintings by Reverend Wm. Ellis and A. Coppalle depict Radama I in sharp contrasts, one as a very white English nobleman with a Roman toga over his shoulder and the other as a dark and Malay-looking sovereign dressed in European military uniform. The sketches given by William Ellis of Merina officers and nobility are equally revealing; cf. his *History of Madagascar*, Vol. I (1838), pp. 116–117, and his *Three Visits to Madagascar* (1858), pp. 129, 413, 417. Obviously, as a criterion of origin, the whole question of pigment is useless and has loomed large only in the hypotheses. There is no doubt that this "pigmental" preoccupation of Europeans has poisoned intra-Malagasy relations since the early nineteenth century, polarizing the lighter-skinned Merina from other and darker islanders beyond the purely political and economic differences. The problem, conceived in historical terms, is essentially one of Merina formation, noble and commoner classes and their evolution, involving the Vazimba, Hova, and Andriana, none of whom can be confused with any other. See Chapter 6 on the Merina.

direct contacts with Arabs from Arabia are not known. That the Anteimoro scribes and priests wrote in Arabic script is just as certain as the
fact that the language of their *Sora-bé,* even the oldest available, has been
Malagasy. The Arabico-Malagasy manuscript in which Grandidier found
Arabian toponymic names is paralleled by another document of similar
nature that allows a totally different linguistic interpretation.[57] In short,
the *Sora-bé,* as linguistic documents, are of slight evidential help to the
argument of cultural purity and can only shed light on the question of
origins within the context of local ethnography and history, both of which
Grandidier dealt with in a fragmentary fashion. The notion that the
Anteimoro were likewise "pure" or "white" Arabs is contradicted by the
author of the first history of Madagascar, Etienne de Flacourt, who
reported in 1661 that members of the then ruling royal Anteimoro clan
"are darker than the other Whites but are nonetheless their masters."[58]

The would-be Indian origin of Raminia was rejected almost immediately by Gabriel Ferrand, an important Arabist and student of Muslim
communities in Asia, Africa, and Madagascar.[59] It was also Ferrand who
alone questioned many other views of Grandidier about the Malagasy
past. Yet, because he focused mainly on Islam, because his commitment
to Madagascar was less extensive and continuous, and because Grandidier
contested bitterly almost everything Ferrand wrote about the island,[60]
many of his ideas never found a place in the accepted body of historical
knowledge. According to Ferrand, the place-names of Mangalore and
Mangadsini, which crop up in connection with Raminia's origin, did not
necessarily reflect sites on the Indian subcontinent.[61] The tolerance of
incest in Antanosy could not be used to determine the Zafi Raminia
origin either. And, although he never elaborated on the reasons for so
stating, Ferrand wrote that the presupposed Indian migration belonged

[57] In Marchand, "Les Habitants . . . Farafangana," 484.

[58] Flacourt, *Histoire, COACM,* Vol. VIII (1913), p. 40.

[59] See, among others, G. Ferrand, *Les Musulmans à Madagascar et eux Iles
Comores,* 3 vols. (1891–1902); *Les Çomaḷis* (1903); *Voyages et textes géographiques
arabes, persanes et turks relatifs a l'extrême-orient du VIIIe au XVIIIe siècles,* 2 vols.
(1913–1914); and *Instructions nautiques et routieres arabes et portugais des XVe et
XVIe siècles,* 4 vols. (1923–1928).

[60] A. Grandidier, *Ethnographie,* Vol. I, Tome 1, pp. 3, 10, 75–76, 104, 117–119,
126, 129, 133, 145–150, 153–158, 166, 170, 199, 207, 300; Vol. I, Tome 2, pp. 619,
627–639, 654, and on all these appropriate notes and notules.

[61] G. Ferrand, "Le Pays de Mangalor et de Mangatsini," *T'oung-pao* (Leiden),
Series 2, X/1 (1909), 1–16; and his *Musulmans,* Vol. III (1902), pp. 129–130.
Ferrand saw two alternatives, namely, that Mangatsini stood for Mogadisho in
Somalia or else that both sites applied in effect to Madagascar itself and were located
between the present-day Tamatave and Fenerive area (note the *manga-* in both
Mangalore and Mangatsini).

to the type of conjecture which "deserves no further notice."[62] Instead, Ferrand held that Raminia and his companions were partly Islamized Indonesians from Java and Sumatra who had sailed along the coast of India, southern Arabia, and eastern Africa before coming to Madagascar. They were the enigmatic Wak-Wak of ancient sources, the term being synonymous with Indonesians and finding its phonetic equivalent in the Malagasy *Antambahoaka*, or people of Wak-Wak (Malagasy, *Ant* = people; *mb/v* and *h/k* conversions being common in Malagasy = *Anta* + *vak/o/ak*). Ramini, moreover, was the old name of Sumatra.[63] Actually, the strongest argument in favor of Ferrand is that neither the ancient nor modern Malagasy vocabularies reveal much in the way of an Indian linguistic influence, including the term *voajiry*.[64] Again, in none of his voluminous writings did Grandidier present the Indian evidence presumably discovered in local traditions and customs of certain families.

Indeed, the least tolerable use of sources by Grandidier occurs precisely in relation to the Maroserana, the "Indians from India" who had founded so many royal lineages in southern and western Madagascar. The *Commentários* of F. Albuquerque refer specifically to Moors from the islet of Bete, shipbuilders and traders who took their fleet successfully to

[62] G. Ferrand, "Le Peuplement de Madagascar," *RM*, IX/2 (1907), 87.

[63] G. Ferrand, "Les Voyages des Javanais à Madagascar," *JA*, 10th series, XV/2 (1910), 281–330, esp. 327–330; "Les Iles Râmny, Lâmery, Wâkwâk, Komer des géographes arabes et Madagascar," *JA*, 10th series, X/3 (1907), 433–566.

[64] E. Renan had once observed that "etymology is the science of fools" and modern linguists appear to feel the same way by shunning etymology altogether. With the return, however, of historical linguistics in recent years (cf. W. P. Lehmann, *Historical Linguistics: An Introduction* [1962]), it is clear that etymology is invaluable under proper safeguards (see Chapter II for a discussion of loan-words). In respect to Grandidier's *voajiry* as being Indian, such safeguards are entirely lacking. For example, at least two alternative etymologies are much more probable. The Anteimoro also called traditional chiefs in the Matitana area *vuaziri* (phon. of *voajiry*), a title which may derive from Arabic *vizir*. The Anteimoro manuscripts mention *vuaziri* at least fifteen times; cf. G. Mondain, *L'Histoire des Tribus de l'Imoro au XVIIe Siècle* (1910), pp. 85, 89, 91, 93, 97, 99, 115, 123. In a number of southeast and east African idioms, the root *zira* means, among other things, to abstain oneself from the forbidden (Ch. Sacleux, *Dictionnaire swahili-français*, Vol. II [1941], p. 1039). With *wa-* as a plural prefix, *-zira* becomes in effect *ziri* (*waziri*). One of the principal characteristics of rulers in Madagascar, as in most of Africa indeed, was that they had to observe rigorously the group *fady* (taboos) because when a ruler violated them the whole group was endangered in a religious sense. That the *voijiry* were not confined to Antanosy area is also confirmed by an unpublished manuscript, cf. Duhamel, Count of Precourt, *Mémoire* (April 1784), *ANSOMCM*, Carton VIII, Dossiers a-c, which mentions a chief in the valley of Amboule whose title was *voadziri*, or prince, who was "rich in cattle and iron but feeble in war" (this document bears the new docket number C5A8bis/195 since the archives are being reclassified).

Malindi, not to any Indians. On their way to the Cape of Good Hope, strong winds forced them to take shelter on the Island of São Lourenço (Madagascar), and it was there that they *"povoárem alguns portos, e dizem que destas náos naiceo haver* povoação de mouros *na Ilha São Lourenço."*[65] There is no mention of southern Madagascar or, again, of any Indians. The earliest conceivable date for the formation of the Maroserana family would be ± 1550, which means that it took some 250 years to derive this dynasty from the migration of 1300.

Grandidier also found in the chronicle of João de Barros, *Da Asia*, written between 1552 and 1563, a secondary account relating the journey of Diogo Lopes de Sequeira around Madagascar in 1508. In the French translation provided by Grandidier, one learns that Diogo Lopes came to a Malagasy port that *"les naturels appellent* Turubaya *(le Fort-Dauphin actuel) du nom du capitaine d'un navire du Goudjerat qui s'y est perdu jadis. Tous les habitants de cette région, suivant le récit qu'ils en firent à Diogo Lopes, descendent des matelots de ce navire."*[66] In the Original Portuguese text, de Barros states:[67]

> *começou Diogo Lopes correr a costa da ilha té chegar a um reino, a que es da terra chamam* Turubaia, *do nome de um capitão de ũa nau de gouzarates, que ali se perdeu. Da gente da qual nau (segundo estava na memória daqueles homens que Diogo Lopes ali achou), êles vinham todos; e aqui estava outre moço per nome António . . . per meio da qual, por já saber a lingua da terra, o Rei, que se chamava Diamom.*

The problem, again, is one of using secondary sources as if these were firsthand reports. *Diamom*, the title name of a local kinglet (*Andria* + *mamy*), is Malagasy and not Indian. Turubaya, as Grandidier himself argued in an obscure footnote, could be a Malagasy term as well.[68] As a matter of record, an Italian chronicler wrote in 1576 that this name,

[65] Albuquerque, F. *Commentários*, 4th ed. (1922), Part III, Ch. XXIII, p. 300.
[66] *COACM*, Vol. I (1903), p. 47.
[67] J. de Barros, *Asia*, 6th ed. (1945), Second Decade, Book 4, Ch. III, p. 171. The Portuguese text (certified as conforming to the original) clearly indicates that this information was obtained from some of the men Diogo Lopes could meet, not from the "entire population of the area" as would appear in the French translation. Equally, António, a young Portuguese, learned to speak the *lingua da terra*, or local Malagasy dialect, through which communication with *diamom* (Malagasy, *andria* prefix being apparent) was possible. There was no Indian language even in 1508.
[68] A. Grandidier, *Ethnographie*, Vol. I, Tome 1, p. 118, notule a; and Vol. I, Tome 2, p. 629, n. 103, where it derives from Malagasy, *Androbaia*; and his *Histoire de la géographie de Madagascar*, rev. ed. (1892), p. 108 and n. 2, where it derives from Malagasy, *Taolankara+baya*, or Portuguese for bay. The last etymology is very likely accurate and should be retained as having nothing to do with *any* overseas immigrants.

spelled by him *Torombaja*, belonged originally to a Javanese captain.[69] There is also on hand a French translation by Grandidier of a secondary account concerning the 1508 visit, by Fernando Lopes de Castañeda, in his 1552 *Historia de los Descobrimentos de los Portugueses*. It states that Diogo Lopes came to a "grand village" named Tourouaya, *"que gouvernait un roi maure avec lequel vivait un autre Portugais, nommé Antoine."*[70] There is no reference to Goudjerati descendants in this village (not region). Instead, as was the Portuguese custom of the time, Diogo Lopes placed two of his ship's *degradados* on the Malagasy littoral and ordered them to scout it for some 50 leagues before contacting the vessel at a prearranged point. They told Diogo Lopes that nothing of commercial value could be found except some *"gingembre marron."* They did, however, encounter *"deux Indiens de Cambaye, les* seuls survivants *de l'equipage d'un navire qui, se rendant à Sofala, s'était perdu dans ces parages* trente ans auparavant."[71]

De Castañeda is thus the only secondary source to actually mention any Indians in a concrete manner, but the context in which they were found can no more be used to formulate an important theory of dynastic origin than the conflicting statements of an Italian and a Portuguese chronicler. If a paramount Indian impact existed, it would have had to manifest itself in language, traditions, culture, and institutions, and of these there is no trace whatsoever. The claim that the Maroserana founder of the Sakalava kingdom of Menabé must have been an Indian because he was white as the name suggests (-*dahefotsy*, from Malagasy *lahe fotsy*, or white male) and because he did not observe the Islamic interdiction of eating pork, is yet another instance of Grandidier's proclivity to manufacture "evidence" where none is to be found. The personal and nonwhite slave of Etienne de Flacourt bore exactly the same name of *Lahefouty* by which the Sakalava monarch was known to mid-seventeenth-century Frenchmen at Fort-Dauphin.[72] For the third time, in respect to the main dynastic families, one finds whiteness to be an obsession and all the more so since the Europeans who saw the two sons of Lahefouty (Andriandahifotsy), who ruled respectively over the Sakalava kingdoms of Menabé and Boina, held them to be anything *but* white.[73]

[69] Quoted by Jerome Megiser, *Description . . . de l'Ile . . . Saint-Laurent* (1609), from J.-L. Anania's *Cosmographia* (1576), in *COACM*, Vol. I (1903), p. 434 and n. 2.

[70] A. Grandidier, *COACM*, Vol. I (1903), p. 49.

[71] *Ibid.*, p. 50. This gives the date of ±1480.

[72] E. de Flacourt, *Relation de la Grande Ile Madagascar, 1642–1657* (1661), in *COACM*, Vol. IX (1920), p. 139.

[73] Cf. Robert Drury, *Madagascar or Robert Drury's Journal during Fifteen Years on That Island*, 7th ed. (1890), p. 262—originally published in 1729; and Captain De la Merveille, "Récit," (August 7, 1708), in *COACM*, Vol. III (1905), p. 620, in small print.

The information about pork-eating was extracted by Grandidier from a single, and again paraphrased, source—Du Bois' 1674 account of southeastern Madagascar.[74] It should be noted that Du Bois never went beyond Fort-Dauphin, and that in his own text no actual mention is made of Lahefouty (or l'Hayfouchy to conform phonetically to French) eating pork. Rather, Du Bois himself reports secondhand on a voyage made by Sieur Desbrosses, a cattle trader for Fort-Dauphin, in 1671, to southwestern Madagascar and the Sakalava ruler. Desbrosses simply observed that many pigs were to be seen in the land of this king. In the margin next to the pertinent text, Du Bois added himself that *"ce l'Hayfouchy fait nourir des Porcs & en mange contre le coûtume des gens de ce pais."*[75] The reason for this inference is an obvious one. Familiar with the Fort-Dauphin Zafi Raminia who did not consume impure meat, Du Bois assumed that this was also observed on the opposite coast of the island. In reality, even the term *cochon* is inaccurate since the reference is to wild boar and not to domesticated pig, an animal not yet introduced from Europe. Even if there was some proof that the Sakalava monarch did consume pork, this would not be a solid argument for his Indian origin, certainly no more so than the inverse custom in Antanosy would be enough to negate that the Zafi Raminia did not come from India. The different attitudes toward the wild boar in two parts of Madagascar are easily explained by economic factors. The Antanosy, an agricultural people, could not tolerate wild boars and exterminated them to save their crops. The Menabé Sakalava, on the other hand, were pastoralists. Having no plantations to speak of, they allowed the wild boar to multiply. It is this difference between the Antanosy and the Sakalava that struck Desbrosses, and nothing else.

Grandidier was the first European to suggest that kinship ties linked the ruling families of Sakalava, Mahafaly, Bara, Antandroy, and Antaisaka, and that all of them were Maroserana-derived. This is more accurate than even he could have known at the time. Unfortunately, the effort to transform the Maroserana into Indians from India forced him to invent the Antaisaka long before this group formed on the eastern coast, to postulate the spread of Maroserana rulers from east to west, and to argue that the Sakalava were nothing else but Anteisaka migrants. No Sakalava tradition, published or not,[76] has advanced such an internal origin. All

---

[74] Du Bois, *Les Voyages faits par le Sieur D. B. aux Isles Dauphine ou Madagascar, & Bourbon, ou Mascarenne, és années 1669–1672* (1674); cf. A. Grandidier, *Ethnographie*, Vol. I, Tome 1, p. 216, n. 1, and Vol. I, Tome 2, pp. 647–648, n. 168 and notule 2.

[75] Dubois, *Voyages*, p. 107, printed margin.

[76] This includes Sakalava Oral Traditions taped by myself in 1965 in both Menabé and Boina, as well as G. Grandidier's unpublished typescript "Les Sakalava," pp. 1–78, based on manuscript notes of his father.

of the Antaisaka traditions state that they were originally west-coast
Sakalava who migrated east and were led by the royal kin of the Maroserana, the *Zarabehavana*. This is amply attested by Anteisaka oral traditions collected by Marchand and Deschamps as well as by others
belonging to contiguous groups.[77] Thus, the Anteisaka moved in reality
from *west to east*. There are genealogical problems concerning the birth
of the Maroserana family, but—as will be seen—the overwhelming
verdict of local tradition is that it formed in the southwest, roughly
in the present-day land of the Mahafaly people.

Western Madagascar faces Africa, and eastern Madagascar faces Asia.
When the huge importance attached to the points of landing as an indication of overseas origins is taken into consideration, it is not surprising
to find that no royal dynasty of Madagascar has ever been allowed to
form on the western side of the island. Undoubtedly, internal migrations
play an important role in Malagasy history. They can lead to the discovery of cultural and political influences flowing from one local group
into another. The matter of overseas migrations is different. Whether an
ancient vessel docked at Majunga or Fort-Dauphin, it is not possible to
determine from such a fact alone the ethnic origin of its crew or to
attribute to it a historical importance that cannot be demonstrated on
other grounds. Given the hazards of ancient navigation, one has only the
right to infer that, irrespective of a vessel's flag, point of departure, or the
nationality of the crew, winds and currents could be expected to push a
particular ship toward these two particular points along the coast of
Madagascar.

It is abundantly clear by now that while some of the data collected
by Grandidier retain their value, his hypotheses are worthless and no
longer merit the uncritical acceptance of yesterday. They fail to explain
the advent of early kingdoms in Madagascar, and they decidedly impede
the reconstruction of Malagasy past through the fabrication of origins
that can nowhere be substantiated. The primacy accorded to India
comes from something entirely unconnected with Madagascar, namely
Grandidier's pre-Malagasy experience. Years before turning his attention
to the Great Island, Grandidier had been a devotee of India's civilization.
He studied Buddhism and Indian architecture, wrote about the Sinhalese
of Ceylon, and wanted to live on the plateau of Tibet.[78] Circumstances
prevented him from becoming an Indianist, but Grandidier could not

---

[77] Cf. Marchand, "Les Habitants . . . de Farafangana," 485–486; and H. Deschamps,
Les Antaisaka (1936), pp. 162–164, *passim*; and J. Boto, "Tradition relative à
l'origine des Betsimisaraka-Betanimena," *BODE*, XXV (1923), 252–253. See also
Chapter 5 on the Sakalava.

[78] A. Grandidier, *Notice sur les travaux scientifiques* (1884), pp. 4–5, 47–48.

part with his early association and hence tended to see Indians in Madagascar as well. It is also obvious that his hypotheses about Malagasy dynastic origins, taken together, spell out what might be called the "Myth of the White King." Crudely stated, it holds that all major advances in material culture and political organization within Madagascar were the doings of men with skins lighter than those of the populations they came to influence, dominate, and rule.

A trained historian might have approached the problem in other ways. The sixteenth century, it is worth noting, was a harbinger of new times in Madagascar. Coastal populations came into contact with Europe, represented mainly by the Portuguese. Certain domesticated plants were introduced, while the uses of iron underwent both expansion and refinement. A limited number of firearms passed into Malagasy hands, and slave trade began to increase considerably. It would thus be tempting to link iron weapons and firearms with the export of slaves and state building. A trained historian has suggested as much recently.[79] The destruction of several Muslim trade centers along the Malagasy littoral could also be seen as stimulating local political initiative, and some shipwrecked Portuguese sailors and mercenaries could have given this impulse additional impetus.

Again, supporting evidence offers slight encouragement in these directions, tidy as they appear to be. Firearms, like the export of slaves, began to loom large toward the end of the 1600s but *not* in the preceding century. Even around 1650, there were few places along the coast of Madagascar where firearms could be found in important quantities. For example, in the area of Fort-Dauphin in 1650, among some 10,000 men the Antanosy could put into the field, there were only nine flintlocks, half of them secured from shipwrecks and the other half from individual Europeans.[80] A sharp contrast may be noted a century later, when about 10,000 flintlocks were imported from Mauritius into the Fort-Dauphin area within a single year.[81] The Portuguese involvement in the export of Malagasy slaves was minimal. This was, on the whole, an "Arab" enterprise, the term in quotes being necessary since it incorporated men of very different origins who claimed Arab ancestry. The slave trade was, moreover, confined in the 1500s to the northwestern coast of Madagascar, and this is, indeed, where it can be shown that it did have a stimulating political role. Elsewhere in Madagascar, this type of early trade could

[79] R. Oliver, "The Great Island," *JAH*, I/2 (1960), 319–321; and R. Oliver and A. Atmore, *Africa Since 1800* (1967), p. 28.

[80] Flacourt, *Relation*, *COACM*, Vol. IX (1920), pp. 121–122.

[81] Together with 100,000 pounds of powder, 120,000 lead bullets, and some 300,000 *pierres a fusil*, all in the year 1768, according to Count de Maudave, *Journal*, manuscript *ANSOMCM*, Carton II, Dossier I, Item D.

not have amounted to much in terms of volume or impact. If the discovery of a few black Portuguese in southeastern Madagascar is an indication of some politicomilitary activity, the circumstances in which they were found are not very favorable to the idea that their involvement was in any way significant.[82]

The sole area where iron weapons and dynastic change come into fairly close chronological contact is the mid-sixteenth-century Imerina. This can be explained by the general absence of the iron-headed spear among the local Vazimba. It constitutes, in no way, proof of any overseas migration into the central highlands. The Vazimba, as will be shown, may not have known how to work iron, but iron weapons were not entirely unknown to them. Other groups in Madagascar used them long before the 1550s, as a number of European accounts attest.[83] A site near Fort-Dauphin, explored in 1957, has revealed a maritime culture familiar with both iron and iron-headed spears with a given Carbon-14 date of A.D. 1100.[84] Two gold coins and two dinars found in Iharanian tombs, of Fattimid and Abbassid mints, span the tenth- to thirteenth-century period and point to an equally ancient and iron-using culture.[85] As late as the nineteenth century, there were still some isolated groups in Madagascar unfamiliar with the iron spear, most of them being the west-coast Vazimba. On the other hand, as early as the twelfth century, this particular type of weapon was known to inhabitants of two opposite tips of Madagascar, nearly a thousand miles apart.

The only alternative still open to obtain historical answers is to do the hard work and investigate in detail the *Merina, Anteimoro,* and *Sakalava*

---

[82] Several Portuguese shipwrecks are attested in the old sources, both in southwestern and southeastern Madagascar, the crews being absorbed by the Malagasy or else simply disappearing in the island. Among the Antanosy, however, where the Portuguese had a fort early in the sixteenth century, intermarriage with the Zifindraminia kinglets appears to have taken place leading to reports of Black Portuguese; cf. *COACM*, Vol. II (1904), pp. 26, 30, 33–34, 36, 37–38, 40–47, 50–54, 58–59, 69, 75–79, 175–179, 180, 184–185 and notes; Vol. III (1905), pp. 285, 295–300, 305, 329; Vol. VIII (1913), pp. 42, 58–60.

[83] For specific mention of the iron-headed spear, see *COACM*, Vol. I (1903), pp. 54 (year 1516), 82 (year 1529), 89 (year 1539), 118 (year 1572), 139 (year 1575), and 174–174bis (year 1595) for reproduction of spears. Most accounts mention spears; many mention arrows without saying what the heads consist of. To the best of my knowledge, there is only one mention (in 1506, northwest coast of Madagascar) of a group along the coast that did *not* have iron-headed spears but rather bone-headed spears.

[84] P. Vérin, "Première Datation d'un site par le radio carbone à Madagascar," *BAM*, XXIV (1941), 106, 113–117.

[85] The dinars are reproduced in A. Grandidier, *Ethnographie*, Vol. I, Tome 1, 140bis. For the Iharanian weapons, see P. Gaudebaut and E. Vernier, "Fouilles à Vohémar," *BAM*, XXIV (1941), 106, 113–117.

roughly between 1500 and 1700. To these must also be added the *Bara*, the fourth principal case study. This choice is dictated by a special circumstance in that the Bara occupy a geographically and historically strategic position in south-central Madagascar and their past, although unstudied, cannot be left out as a result. A number of Malagasy peoples— the Antaisaka, Mahafaly, Antaifasy, and Antandroy—are peripheral to the problem at hand and will be alluded to as the discussion requires.

The spread of early kingship does not necessarily accord with the numerical importance of each Malagasy group. The *Betsimisaraka*, for example, the third largest ethnicity of Madagascar, began to form kingdoms only in the eighteenth century through the royal lineage of the *Zanamalata* or *métis* of European pirates and local women.[86] Two of the earliest kingdoms of the *Betsileo*, second largest Malagasy group, do not antedate the seventeenth century, although the origin of their rulers is of considerable interest to this study.[87] A number of intermediary populations, like the *Tanala, Tsimihety,* and *Antankarana*, also obtained rulers from other king-making Malagasy. The Antanosy Zafi Raminia will be discussed mainly in the Anteimoro chapter. The concern of this study is, thus, mainly with those units that gave rulers to others without receiving any in return.

If this study of early kingdoms in the island is meant to be primarily a contribution to the local Malagasy history, and it could not be conceived in any other way irrespective of the culture to which the author belongs, the historian in him is also faced with an unavoidable question that no one has really asked: Is there anything significant that Africa might have contributed to the past which is being investigated? It is inconceivable that the proximity of the Great Island to its mainland has really been of no importance whatsoever to the Malagasy past. Indeed, this is precisely the missing factor that invalidates all previous hypotheses. However, first it must be given a proper perspective.

[86] The only worthwhile monograph on the Betsimisaraka past is the unpublished *Histoire de Ratsimilahoe roi de Foulepointe et des Bétsimiçaracs*, by Nicolas Mayeur (written in 1806 and based on a long residence in Madagascar since 1774) in the British Museum, Department of Manuscripts, Farquhar Collection, No. IV. My own typescript copy totals 136 pages. Guillaume Grandidier has given a brief outline of this manuscript in "Histoire de la fondation du royaume des Betsimisaraka," *BCM*, IV (1898), 275–286.

[87] See H. M. Dubois, *Monographie des Betsileo* (1938), pp. 102–226; and Chapter 6 on the Merina below.

chapter 2 MADAGASCAR AND AFRICA

There is a world of difference between the Malagasy islander and the black African . . . separated only by the Mozambique Channel. These differences do not come from more advanced education but from the diversity of origins and organization. The African gets attached to soil, is obedient, works without introspection; his sole thought is to satisfy the physical needs; and his imagination, confined to a small brain, hardly taxes the function of his stomach: he thrives and improves in slavery, and the sentiment of liberty develops in him only when the treatment is excessively harsh—this black *par excellence*, one that replaces so well the horse and the mule! But, give something to a Malagasy to carry, no matter how light he will find it heavy, too heavy. . . . Yes, indeed, the superiority of Malagasy over the African is certain.

Augustine Billiard (1829)

The great and only real hope for the future prosperity of the Malagasy lies in the Hova dominion. . . . The Hova is evidently born to rule: he has the air and gait by nature of a king of men; and better still, he has great sagacity, indomitable perseverance, great powers of endurance, much patience, strong self-restraint, and a natural adaptability to trade and intercourse with the foreigner; in all these respects he stands out in marked contrast to the neighbouring and subject tribes.

Reverend Henry W. Little (1884)

Northwestern Madagascar has some thousands of lately-freed Africans, mostly belonging to the Makoa tribe, black, tattooed, shiningly moist, and good-naturedly lazy beyond description. For several years after their emancipation these had contrived to support themselves by jobbing in the town, the women making mats, drawing water, carrying stones for building, and acting as nurses, charwomen, and cooks to any person able to afford them food and clothing; the men collecting palm leaves for roofing, digging stones, salting, storing, and shipping hides, and working as sailors on board the dhows.

Reverend W. Clayton Pickersgill (1893)

Where shall I throw this *faditra* (bad object)? To the East? That is where the Sun comes out. To the North? That is the road travelled by the Sovereign on way to Ambohimanga (Merina Necropolis). I shall throw it to the West for this is where the Mozambiques live and they can stand the garbage.

A Merina traditional priest (before 1896)

The ease with which foreign elements abandoned their national distinctiveness while taking roots in the Great Island is one of the main causes of the impenetrable obscurity encountered by ethnographic research concerned with the question of . . . origins.

Eugene de Froberville (1839)

Despite the factor of geographical proximity, no detailed or sustained examination has ever been made to determine the nature and scope of Africa's possible impact upon Madagascar. It is not only the formation of early kingdoms but also the older problem of Malagasy origins that remains encapsulated in the framework and ideas provided over half a century ago by Alfred Grandidier. Until late in the last century, countless European travelers assumed that, at least in part, Africa had contributed to the peopling of Madagascar if not to its government, religion, and society.[1] It was Grandidier who eliminated Africa completely as a prob-

---

[1] At the very least, five dozen sources can be cited in this connection, from Tristan da Cunha in 1506 to the anthropologist Zaborowski in 1897. As items of evidence, they can be restricted to only a few firsthand accounts that will be reported in the body of this work. Most of the others have no greater evidential value than those of the Indonesian school. Some are, nonetheless, worth being noted as rather interesting suggestions. In an unpublished *Mémoire sur Madagascar* (1813), sent as a

able cultural contributor to the Malagasy. His own perception of Africa as a cultural wasteland is amply demonstrated in a quarto volume of 711 pages dealing with the Malagasy ethnography and history. It discusses Africans of Madagascar in less than three full pages or roughly in the same amount of space as allotted to extremely hypothetical Chinese and

letter to Charles Telfair, Rondeaux advanced the idea that there was a considerable influx of migrants from Africa between the twelfth and sixteenth centuries as a result of "revolutions" that had taken place on the mainland's eastern littoral. Cf. Barthélemy Huet, Chevallier de Froberville, *Dictionnaire madécasse et français*, manuscript (1816), compiled at Mauritius in five volumes), Vol. V, Appendices, Rondeaux *to* Telfair, pp. 1–24, the British Museum, Department of Manuscripts, No. 2 of the Farquhar Collection. Under the popular heading of *Le Grand Dictionnaire de Froberville*, the five volumes are being gradually published by the *Bulletin de Madagascar*. Carpeau du Saussay, in his *Voyage de Madagascar*, published in 1722 but actually written in 1663, saw the blacks of Madagascar as an original population on whose origins he did not speculate. But, he was certain that all of the "Whites came some time ago from Mazambique (to Madagascar) having been expelled by the Tyrant of Quiloe" (p. 246). Lesson, who along with many others perceived the duality of Malagasy peoples, held that they should be called Cafro-Madécasses or Afro-Malagasy. Cf. *Voyage autour du monde de la 'Coquille*, Vol. I (1826), pp. 87 and 101. According to V. A. Barbié du Bocage, the only distinguishable Africans in Madagascar of the 1850s were to be found among the west-coast populations, *"chez lesquelles des migrations plus récentes ont entretenu le type originel, tandis qu'un climat différent, des révolutions qui nous sont inconnues et des croisements successifs avec d'autres races, venues de pays plus lointains, ont modifié la nature première des autres habitants,"* in his *Madagascar, possession française depuis 1642* (1859), p. 63. A number of authors have referred specifically to the African origins of one or more Malagasy ethnic groups. Thus, D. W. Cowan believed that there were four Malagasy groups of African origin or Sakalava, Bara, Betsileo, and Tanala, cf. "Geographical Excursions in the Betsileo, Tanala and Bara Countries," *Proceedings of the Geographical Society*, London (June 1882), 521–537. Robert Drury, in 1729, and anthropologist Th. Waitz, in 1860, had opened the door to the hypothesis that the Malagasy Vazimba came from Africa, a view repeated by many others since. Cf. Robert Drury, *Journal*, 8th ed. (1890), p. 34, or the 1729 original, *The Adventures of Robert Drury during Fifteen Years of Captivity in the Island of Madagascar*, p. 14; and Th. Waitz, "Die Malgaschen," in *Anthropologie der Naturvölker*, II (1860), 426–446. An African origin for the Sakalava has, also, been advanced with some consistency, on the basis of not only physical traits but also custom and usages. The most important early statement on the Sakalava came from the German explorer and scholar J. M. Hildebrandt, who had spent one year in Madagascar and seven years in east Africa. In his view, the Sakalava were identical with east African pastoralists whom he had observed at close hand. Moreover, Hildebrandt maintained that the "Negroid element is predominant among the Malagasy, and if there is a linguistic unity in the island, this is because the warriors coming from Africa intermarried with (non-African) women, the children taking over the language of their mothers," in his "West-Madagaskar," *ZGE*, XV (1880), 81–131. Hildebrandt died prematurely in Madagascar, and it is almost a foregone conclusion that under more fortunate circumstances he would have given a solid alternaitve to the hypotheses of Grandidier.

Japanese migrations into the island.[2] Actually, he managed to explain *away* the Negroid Malagasy first through slave trade with Africa and, second, by postulating an Indo-Melanesian origin for most of them. He saw Africans as nonmaritime peoples incapable of taking to the high seas and without previous record of voluntary overseas migration.[3] Therefore, such Africans, that did come to Madagascar could *only* have been brought over as *slaves*, first by the Arab and later by European traders. In a condition of bondage, thus, the African could make no impact in any Malagasy society.

"On what grounds did I link the Malagasy," wrote Grandidier, "apart only from the Andriana of Imerina and the chiefs of principal tribes, to the Far Eastern Negroes rather than to those on the African continent as all of the [earlier] authors and even anthropologists used to do?"[4] His answer was threefold, namely the unity of language, the uniformity of customs, and the widely shared physical traits in the "mass of the people." In some sixty-five pages and more than two hundred notes, he then proceeded to outline these three aspects while comparing them to "identical" ones in the Malayo-Polynesian world.[5]

It is safe to say that this legacy of Grandidier is the major reason why the Great Island has been disconnected from its mainland. Even the most recent monographs on Malagasy art or the institution of joking relationship between individuals and groups, important as an agent for reduction of conflict and tension, reject a priori any African antecedents.[6] The fact,

---

[2] A. Grandidier, *Ethnographie de Madagascar*, Vol. I, Tome 1 (1908), pp 170–171 (Africans), 169–170 (Japanese and Chinese); Vol. I, Tome 2 (1908), pp. 414–415 (Africans), 518 (Chinese).

[3] *Ibid.*, Vol. I, Tome 1, p. 170 and n. 3; Vol. I, Tome 2, p. 414.

[4] *Ibid.*, Vol. I, Tome 1, p. 5.

[5] *Ibid.*, pp. 5–71. One cannot neglect to point out that Grandidier cites *no sources* from which the would-be comparative materials have been extracted. This section is at complete variance with his consistent concern to cite the sources elsewhere. In effect, the nonreferential footnotes have been substituted themselves as evidence. The method is to mention a trait in the text as Malagasy and then state in footnotes that it is "found in" Timor Borneo, Tonga, Thai of Tonkin, Melanesia, Marshall Islands, Hawaii, New Zealand, or the Caroline Islands, to name only a few. Since there are some 500 Caroline Islands alone, such geographical referents are worthless. The total "comparative" area includes southeast Asia and exceeds many millions of square miles. The context in which a trait is found and the time periods are revealed nowhere. Of the six or seven sources cited in all of the footnotes, not a single one deals directly with the Malayo-Polynesian world. A close reading of the text clearly shows that the enumerated traits are to be found in Madagascar and that the vast majority were *assumed* to exist in Asia without any proof.

[6] J.-C. Hébert, "La Parente a plaisanterie à Madagascar," *BM*, VIII/142 (1958), 182–216; VIII/143 (1958), 268–335; and M. Urbain-Faublée, *L'Art malgache* (1963), particularly pp. 5 and 10. Madame Urbain-Faublée states without the slightest reservation that Malagasy art is that of a region "belonging to the world of

nonetheless, remains that the island-wide term for joking relationship is the Bantu *ziva* (*isiwa*), and numerous Malagasy art objects and musical instruments could have come from no other place than Africa.

An English historian has suggested:[7]

> It has long been notorious that the island [of Madagascar] had actually been excluded from most of the general works on African history and ethnography . . . and yet Madagascar with its peculiar mixture of Malayo-Polynesian language and material culture with African social organization and religious beliefs, presents some problems of the greatest importance for the history of Africa as a whole.

This perception of a long-time student of Africa's past derives from no idle speculation. The question of human contact between Indonesia and Africa, at least since the first century of our era, constitutes the most interesting historical problem left in this part of the world. Some hypotheses have been certainly advanced, but all of them rest on a small variety of items found in Africa so far—outriggers, equipentatonic xylophones, and Malaysian yams and bananas.[8] To these, one could add a passage or two in the accounts of ancient mariners and travelers.[9]

Oceania and Indonesia" and it forms together "a coherent whole," (p. 5). There is no single Malagasy art style and some of the group and regional styles in Madagascar are strikingly different from one another. Since the same author disputes the linguistic fact that Malagasy *omby* (*ombe, ngmobe*) for cattle is the common Bantu *ngombe* (p. 10), one cannot take seriously the sweeping categorization of Malagasy art, and all the more so since some of this art is unique to the island itself and owes nothing to external borrowing.

[7] R. Oliver, "The Great Island," *JAH*, I/2 (1960), 319–320, being a review of Hubert Deschamps *Histoire de Madagascar* (1960)—the second edition, 1961, is used in the present work.

[8] Cf. A. M. Jones, *Africa and Indonesia: The Evidence of the Xylophone and Other Musical and Cultural Factors* (1964); J. Hornell, "The Affinities of East African Outrigger Canoes," *Man*, No. 55 (July 1919), 97–100; "The Common Origin of the Outrigger Canoes of Madagascar and East Africa," *Man*, Nos. 66–67 (September 1920), 134–139; "The Outrigger Canoes of Indonesia," *BMF*, No. 12 (1920), 43–114; "Indonesian Influence on East African Culture," *JRAI*, 64 (1934), 305–333; "The Outrigger Canoes of Madagascar, East Africa and the Comoro Islands," *MM* (January 1944), 3–18, and (October 1944), 170–185; D. N. McMaster, "Speculations on the Coming of the Banana to Uganda," *JTG*, XVI (1962), 57–69; J. H. Hutton, "West Africa and Indonesia: A Problem in Distribution," *JRAI*, 76 (1946); and G. P. Murdock, *Africa* (1959), pp. 22–23; A. T. and G. M. Culwick, "Indonesian Echoes in Central Tanganyika," *TNR*, 2 (1936), 60–66.

[9] The most significant one is to be found in the itinerary of Ibn al-Mujāwir, *Tārīh al-mustabṣir*. Its author died in 1291 and the original manuscript appears to have been composed in the mid-1230s. Gabriel Ferrand gives a translation of its copy, manuscript 6021 of the Bibliothèque Nationale's *Fonds Arabe*: "The Al-Ḳomr peoples used to leave Al-Komr to reach Aden in fleets and using a single monsoon [but] these people have now disappeared since their power came to end and since the route

While their ultimate origin is beyond dispute, the watercraft and musical instruments retain no Indonesian linguistic survivals in Africa.[10] A study of terminology associated with the Malaysian food plants in Africa has hardly begun.[11] The diffusion of material objects and plants in question may or may not imply a substantial Indonesian presence in Africa. In short, a great deal has been postulated already on the evidence that suffers both in quality and quantity of written sources and in linguistic and ethnographic data. Yet, the probability of an early Indonesian colonization of Africa or at least its eastern littoral remains high *because* of Madagascar.

Its proximity to Africa, its language, the physical aspects of some Malagasy, its outriggers (both single and double), its taro, cocoyam, and banana varieties, and certain of its musical instruments stand out as

---

of their travel has been closed . . . From Aden to Mogadišo there is one monsoon . . . from Mogadišo to Kilwa there is a second monsoon and from Kilwa to Al-Ḳomr there is a third one. These people managed to unite the three monsoons into one. A single vessel from Al-Komr thus went (once) directly to Aden . . . in the year 626 [A.D. 1228–1229]. It was to have gone to Kilwa but it docked at Aden instead. The vessels [of the peoples of Al-Ḳomr] have outriggers because the seas [around Al-Komr] are . . . dangerous. . . . [But following the conquest of Aden] these people lost power and the Barābar [people of Berbera, port on the African side of the Red Sea] came to them . . . attacked them and chased them out of Aden." Cf. G. Ferrand, *"Le K'ouen-Louen et les anciennes navigations interocéaniques dans les mers du sud,"* *JA*, 11th series, XIII/3, (1919), 476–477. A contemporary of this traveler, Ibn Sa'id (d. 1286) held that the people of Al-Ḳomr gave their name to the mountain (of the moon, *djabal al-ḳamar*), which was in the African interior but that these people were not Africans but rather the "brothers of the Chinese," in Ferrand, just cited, p. 445. Although other passages (reproduced in the Appendices to this work) can be brought to bear on this topic, there can be slight doubt that Indonesians had contacts with Africa and that these came to end early in the thirteenth century.

[10] Cf. J. Hornell, "The Sea-going *Mtepe* and *Dau* of the Lamu Archipelago," (*MM*, January 1941, for original printing) reproduced in *TNR*, XIV (1942), 27–37; and J. D. Fage's review article of A. M. Jones' *Africa and Indonesia*, in "Xylophones and Colonists," *JAH*, VI/3 (1965), 413–415. See also, V. L. Grottanelli, *Pescatori dell' Oceano Indiano* (1955), pp. 48–83, 321–344, and vocabulary (Bàjuni) 350–364; and Murdock, *Africa*, pp. 206–209. A. H. J. Prins has attempted to question the Indonesian origin of the East African outrigger in his article "Uncertainties in Coastal Cultural History. . . ," *TNR*, No. 53 (1959), 205–213. No doubt, the Indonesian provenance of the xylophone in Africa will eventually be questioned as well. Such efforts derive in part from a new trend that, in seeking to end the old bias against an imagined lack of originality in Africa, could go too far in the direction of disallowing or discouraging research into cultural borrowings from outside.

[11] A useful beginning has been made at the Hartford Seminary Foundation by Charles P. Blakney's Master of Arts thesis in Linguistics, *On "Banana" and "Iron," Linguistic Footprints in African History* (1963), typescript, pp. 1–125. I am indebted to Jan M. Vansina for lending me his copy. See also footnote 63 below for the problem of the banana term *akondro*.

living testimony of old Indonesian migrations into the western Indian Ocean, migrations that could not have easily by-passed the eastern littoral of Africa.[12] Hence, once shown that Madagascar does indeed possess the peculiar mixture of Africa and Indonesia, the problem assumes an altogether different dimension and demands a new system of priorities. It is, for example, no longer necessary to dwell on probability but rather to search for the types of evidence available within Madagascar from which to infer what is at the moment lacking in Africa. Of particular interest here would be the degree of Indonesian penetration of Africa—into the lake regions, the Zambezi valley, possibly the Congo basin, and even (as some have suspected) west Africa. On the mainland, thus, human and cultural contact and influence could involve the Cushitic-speaking inhabitants of northeastern Africa as well as the more widespread speakers of Swahili and other Bantu languages. There are reasons to envisage that Bantu-Malagasy ties in particular may even have been considerable.

To make the case of Madagascar even stronger, one need only point out that Madagascar can claim not only the rare possession of written precolonial archives,[13] but also one of the most extensive bibliographies known to exist for a preliterate society.[14] Without any claims for statistical precision, it can be said that the Negroid element dominates the human composition of Madagascar.[15] The sheer promise of contribution from the Malagasy side to Africa and from the African side to Madagascar has so far been thwarted by an anti-African orientation of *Malgachisant* scholarship since Grandidier. There are also some subsidiary causes.

[12] One can note here the negative but important evidence of the Mascarene Islands, facing the eastern littoral of Madagascar, which the Portuguese and the Dutch found uninhabited as late as the sixteenth century. Subsequent research in Mauritius and Réunion has failed to reveal any traces (skeletal remains, artifacts) of earlier non-European settlement. On this subject, see De Constantin, *Recueil des voyages*, Vol. II (1725), pp. 155–164; G. Azéma, *Histoire de l'Ile Bourbon* (1862); and in general the *Revue historique et littéraire de l'Ile Maurice*.

[13] These include letters, memoranda, and reports of the Merina officers and governors stationed outside Imerina from about 1830 until 1896. The manuscripts run into several thousand but remain to be inventoried and classified before the contents can be published. I have been able to examine only a small fraction of one carton while in Tananarive. See also J. Valette, "L'Historiographie malgache, son passé, son devenir," *BM*, IX/157 (1959), 467–469; and his *Inventaire de la série mi des archives de la République Malgache* (1963), pamphlet, pp. 3–16. See also footnote 5 of Chapter 6 below.

[14] G. Grandidier, *Bibliographie de Madagascar* (1905–1957) four tomes in three volumes containing 23,000 entries.

[15] About the only attempt to determine this composition will be found in A. Rakoto-Ratsimamanga, "Tache pigmentaire héréditaire et origine des Malgaches," *RA* (January–March 1940), 5–130. According to the author about 54 percent of the Malagasy are Negroid and 32 percent Indonesian-Mongoloid. The sampling methods are, however, inadequate. Many of the conclusions are also highly questionable.

Since the 1890s, only five trained historians and anthropologists, two of whom have had some familiarity with Africa as well, bothered to study Madagascar. The Merina alone have been presented in considerable detail. Some Malagasy groups remain almost unknown, while a dozen others can claim nothing comparable to what is available for the Merina. Among them are the Sakalava, Bara, and Anteimoro, peoples as important in the precolonial history of the island as the Merina themselves. In turn, because equal knowledge for the other Malagasy needs to be brought together with some idea of purpose in mind, much of what is usually presumed to apply to all Malagasy is limited in essence to the Merina. Thus, a part of the total wealth of bibliography and of the historical, linguistic, and ethnographic materials attributed to Madagascar as a whole must be subtracted from the encompassing category. Next comes the abnormally high bibliographical contribution of naturalists and of amateur historians and ethnographers who compile the raw data without perceiving in most cases their value, meaning, and the importance of contextual accuracy. Finally, most of the non-Merina materials are fragmentary in nature, scattered in hundreds of unrelated, multilingual and often very obscure sources. Circumstances of this type are not conducive to the asking of meaningful historical questions that must provide the raw data and the generalities one wishes to advance. This becomes apparent when the search begins for some tangible evidence from which to argue for an Afro-Indonesian cultural mixture in Madagascar, as the English historian has done. It is confined to a few pages of two recent books by George P. Murdock and Hubert Deschamps.

Murdock begins by warning scholars not to engage in what he calls "trait-chasing," undoubtedly a reaction to an older and much criticized culture historical school of ethnology.[16] This can, of course, not be taken seriously since a good part of his own work rests on the chasing of traits and since it would at once preclude any comparative study of Africa and Indonesia in Madagascar. Here, according to Murdock, the economy and social organization of the Malagasy as a whole reflect most clearly the Indonesian antecedents in their culture.[17] African influences, on the other hand obtrude in animal husbandry and in government of the Malagasy. But, he finds that African political institutions are especially prominent

[16] Murdock, *Africa*, pp. 40–43. This school has been attacked most vehemently by certain social anthropologists often by taking some of its statements out of context. Moreover, most of the antagonists never refer to the major statement on the school by Father Wilhelm Schmidt, *The Culture Historical Method of Ethnology* (1939), pp. 1–389, translated from German by S. A. Sieber. This is equally absent from Murdock's own bibliography (p. 47). A detailed examination of Schmidt's work will show, to any detached student, that it contains, along with some questionable segments, a very large amount of seminal materials.

[17] Murdock, *Africa*, p. 220.

among the Merina and postulates that these must have been brought over by them from the section of east African littoral known by its ancient name of Azania.[18] This is surprising in several respects. The Merina speak the purest form of Malagasy and provide to this day the largest numbers of Mongoloid individuals in Madagascar. As an ethnicity, they do not even begin to form before the late 1500s, in contrast to two pre-existing populations of the central plateau—the ancient Vazimba and more recent Hova. The Merina state, in Murdock's terms, would then have influenced decisively the government of all other Malagasy. The Merina became paramount in Madagascar politically during the first half of the nineteenth century and a backward projection cannot work since their state begins to assume historical importance toward the 1770s or far too late to make the Azanian hypothesis even relevant to the problem.

The basic settlement of an uninhabited Madagascar by migrants from Indonesia must have taken place before the advent of great empires in Borneo, Java, and Sumatra, with a probable date of no later than the fifth century. Their elaborate sculpture and architecture are not even remotely reproduced in Madagascar. The Malagasy language is somewhat archaic in nature, with a paucity of Sanskrit words.[19] The technically crude megaliths and the retention in Madagascar of early Indonesian watercraft, without evolution toward the Borobudur outrigger ship of greater size and more complex construction, show that the proto-Malagasy represent the old Indonesian society. The often-claimed argument that the proto-Malagasy must have been Deutero-Malays, or bearers of iron tools and weapons, is based on no solid evidence. The earliest Carbon-14 date for an iron implement in Madagascar—the iron-headed spear—is A.D. ± 1100. Moreover, this find occurs with a pottery style that has no parallels in Indonesia. Merina oral traditions, which are detailed and of high quality, reveal that the use of iron-headed spears was not known either to the Vazimba or the Hova. There is no earlier date for an iron implement in Madagascar than A.D. ± 1100. The associated pottery find, on the southern littoral of Madagascar, belongs to the style known as combed (peignée) and the nearest center of which was in southern Rhodesia.[20] The words in Malagasy vocabulary for iron, pot, and spear show that the first has an Indonesian etymon (curiously, these have been encountered in small segments of Africa as well), that the second allows for both Indonesian and African etymons, while the

[18] Ibid., pp. 220–221.

[19] Cf. Solange Bernard-Thierry, "A propos des emprunts sanskrits en Malgache," JA (1959), 311–348, which may be taken as the most up-to-date monograph.

[20] Desmond Clark informed me of this.

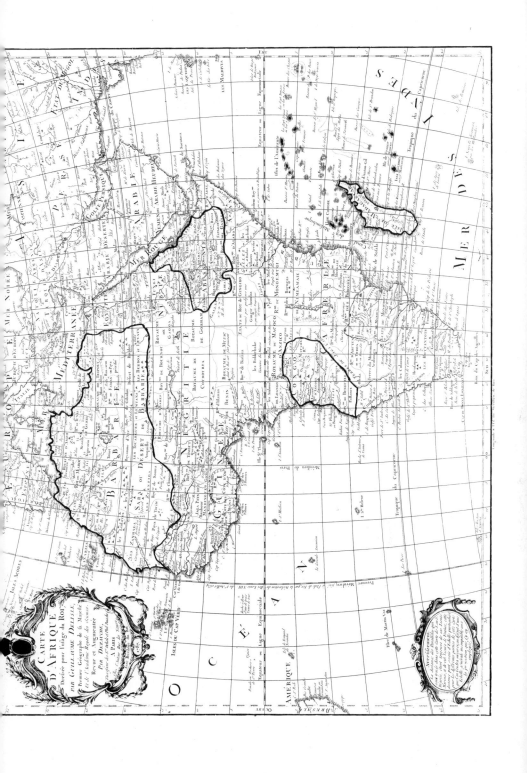

CARTE
D'AFRIQUE
Dreſſée pour l'uſage du ROI,
PAR GUILLAUME DELISLE,
Premier Geographe de ſa Majeſté
& de l'Academie Royale des Sciences.
Revue et Augmentée
PAR DEZAUCHE,

À PARIS
Succeſſeur des S.rs Delisle & Phil. Buache.
1.er Geographe du Roi, rue des Noyers,
près celle des Anglois.

third has no parallels in Indonesia.[21] Thus, it is not unlikely that a group
of Afro-Indonesians with an unknown degree of linguistic and cultural
admixture introduced iron smelting into Madagascar long after the arrival
of proto-Malagasy but before the second millennium began.

Assuming (as will be seen, correctly) the presence of more clearly
defined human and cultural antecedents from Africa, one could allow
for Murdock's contention that African influences in the government of
Malagasy societies have been substantial. Ultimately, these would affect
the central-highlands Merina and even become more apparent as their
state gained local supremacy and earned the major attention of European
scholars. Murdock, however, hardly begins to tell us what makes the
Merina institutions African or indeed what the material culture and
social organization—let alone government—of other Malagasy happen
to be. Actually, his startling claim for the Merina is not rooted in any
solid study of this paramount state. It comes from his own model of an
abstracted African despotic state, defined through eighteen general
traits.[22] Much of this model would force anyone familiar with the past
of Madagascar to conclude that Indonesia contributed virtually nothing
in the realm of government.

As Father Luis Mariano, a Jesuit missionary, reported early in the
seventeenth century, Murdock's feature of "monarchical absolutism" appeared to have been widespread in Madagascar when it was still atomized
into myriad chiefdoms. Later, it extended to Malagasy kings as well,

[21] In Malagasy, iron is *vy*. The words for pot are *vilany* and *nongo*, while the
island-wide general term for the spear is *lefona*. *Nongo* is a Bantu loan (see notes
58 and 59 below) as well as *lefona* (see notes 34 and 35 below). *Vy* and *Vilany*
belong to the Indonesian vocabulary. The term *vy* for iron has been noted as *vi*
among two very small ethnicities, Hina and Tera, in the vicinity of Lake Chad
(Blakney, *Linguistic Footprints*, p. 97). This may not mean anything in connection
with Indonesia since in the ancient Egyptian the word for iron is the compound
bi-nu-pet, the prefix *bi/vi* being present. This would confirm the findings of Paul
Huard, outlined in the "Introduction et diffusion du fer au Tchad," *JAH*, VII/3
(1966), 377–404, and arrived at on nonlinguistic grounds. However, the Gisu and
Rimi (east-central Africa, near Mount Elgon and south of Lake Victoria) terms for
iron *bia/via* contain the cognate *vi/vy* as well, and here the Indonesian link may be
well worth investigating.

[22] Murdock, *Africa*, pp. 37–39: (1) monarchical absolutism; (2) eminent domain;
(3) divine kingship; (4) ritual isolation; (5) insignia of office; (6) capital towns;
(7) royal courts; (8) protocol; (9) harems; (10) queens (commonly endowed with
independent estates); (11) territorial bureaucracy; (12) ministers; (13) duality of
ministerial roles (double function of minister at court and governor of province);
(14) titles; (15) security provisions (in one way or another, removal of potential
"palace revolutionaries"); (16) electoral succession (by designation, by election
through ministers, generally from correct royal lineages); (17) anarchic interregnums
(due to absence of central authority or through organized violence by rivals); and
(18) human sacrifice as part of royal funerary rites.

along with one or more attributes belonging to the "complex of divine kingship." Irrespective of the known time periods, all political entities in Madagascar had some perception of what their "eminent domain" was, although the Malagasy idea of political boundaries was by no means rigid. Malagasy chiefdoms and kingdoms had single seats of government—or Murdock's "capital towns," "courts," some form of "protocol," a "territorial bureaucracy" with "dual role" for the high-ranking officials. The high-ranking officials served at the court but retained in the home village or region their positions as headmen in chiefdoms and chiefs in kingdoms. As a rule, chiefs and kings had many concubines and less often more than one official wife as well, a feature called "harem" by Murdock. The principle of "electoral succession" and some "security provisions" were also widespread in Madagascar. A chief or king normally designated his own successor who, by custom, had to be from the proper lineage, chiefly or royal. To avoid palace revolts, Malagasy rulers often exiled from their capitals royal sons who were not favored, a practice that has had much to do with proliferation of rulers from a single dynastic family in different Malagasy states. Court officials were rarely anything else but men from nonroyal lineages or religious specialists without local kin ties. The "Queen Mother" and "Queen Sister," whom Murdock stresses, generally occupied positions of privilege as would be normal for immediate female kin of a ruler in any society. "Independent Queens" occurred in two Malagasy empires, Sakalava and Merina, along with such contemporaries as Maria Theresa, Queen of Hungary and Bohemia, and Queen Victoria, Empress of India. Indeed, the thirteen features of Murdock have slight comparative value since they can be found in a model of older despotisms throughout the globe.

A case can be made for African "interregnums" and a stronger one for African "royal funerary rites," involving entire clusters of features and not just one or two. But, Malagasy interregnums have not been studied, while funerary rites for Malagasy monarchs have been described without any search for African antecedents.[23] The "ritual isolation" of African Monarchs is also well-grounded. It connects religion and government in ways typical of African sovereignties. The remaining two features, "titles" and "insignia of office," are valuable. Nomenclature similarities through

[23] No specific piece of writing has ever been devoted to Malagasy interregnums. On the funerary rites, see: A. Dandouau, "Coutumes funéraires dans le nord-ouest de Madagascar," *BAM*, IX (1911), 157–172; "Rites funeraires (Sakalava)," manuscript, 1–33 (in-folio), on kind loan from Mme and Maitre Gabriel Pain and Mme B. Dandouau; L. Aujas, "Les Rites du sacrifice à Madagascar," *MAM*, II (1927), 65–75; J. Sibree, "Remarkable Ceremonial at the Decease and Burial of a Betsileo Prince," *AA*, VI (1898), 195–208, translated from Malagasy (see Appendix below for reproduction); and R. Decary, *La Mort et les coutumes funéraires à Madagascar* (1962), pp. 21–301.

loan-words or loan-translations are capable of providing in many instances good evidence of borrowing by one society from another. But, since the ritual isolation of Malagasy monarchs has not been brought out, and because Malagasy titles and symbols of office have never been linked with any counterparts in Africa, the value of Murdock's entire model was nil at the time of presentation. The three cultural features should, nonetheless, be kept in mind.

Hubert Deschamps, a *Malgachisant* since the 1930s, hardly suffers from the difficulty of being unfamiliar with the island. One of the few modern students of Madagascar who has had the courage to go at least in part against the traditional bias, Deschamps provides his own list of traits, both Indonesian and African, found in the Great Island. It is not only conceived in a way different from Murdock's, but the list is vastly more extensive. Many of the items were obviously compiled from sources only a historically trained *Malgachisant* could know about. Still, what is known personally to Deschamps is not conveyed to the reader, and his list turns out to be far less valuable than might have been expected. The criteria and methods used to prepare the list reveal a lack of familiarity with anthropology and add up to at least five major and fatal flaws. It is only after the flaws are perceived that there remains a residue of items that are worth considering and that can lead to some interesting possibilities.

In the realm of nonmaterial culture, Deschamps cites sixty-one traits as being common to Indonesia and Madagascar and seventeen to Africa and Madagascar.[24] Fifteen of the African-designated ones are duplicated

---

[24] Deschamps, *Madagascar*, pp. 22–23.

Indonesia and Madagascar: (1) patrilineal clans with matrilineal traits; (2) endogamic taboo more pronounced for descendants of two sisters; (3) sexual liberty of young girls and prenuptial relations; (4) wives offered to the host (notably among ancient Sakalava); (5) juridical liberty of female spouse and her moral authority; (6) limited polygamy; (7) classificatory kinship; (8) age classes; (9) father takes the name of his child; (10) twin infanticide (among the Antambahoaka); (11) infanticide to exorcise evil; (12) no restrictions on child behavior; (13) frequency of child adoption; (14) blood brotherhood (blood covenant); (15) land owned by the clan or extended family; (16) social stratification into three classes (nobility, commoners, slaves); (17) use of spears in warfare; (18) ambush; (19) use of marine shells to announce attacks; (20) tabooing of royal name after death; (21) cult of royal relics; (22) chief's council; (23) rear section of slaughtered cattle given to chiefs; (24) nonspilling of royal blood; (25) king travels in palanquin; (26) slaves generally secured as war prisoners and treated humanely; (27) ephemeral god; (28) water and high-place (site) spirits; (29) ancestral cult; (30) offerings at funerals; (31) sacrifices at funerals; (32) slaughter of cattle at funerals; (33) two-stage funerals; (34) phalli or other stones near the tomb decorated with pieces of cloth; (35) graves in the forest or near family dwellings; (36) tomb enclosures decorated with sculptures of humans, animals, and birds; (37) bodies enveloped in mats; (38) placing of bodies in canoelike coffins; (39) caves used for burials;

by those attributed to Indonesia without a single hint how to determine
when a trait should be considered African or Indonesian.[25] Two of the
seventeen, the joking relationship and age groups, can be accepted as
African for reasons that Deschamps does not mention.[26] And, although
this is nowhere stated, the majority of would-be Indonesian traits are also
found in Africa.[27] Some of them appear in African contexts far stronger

---

(40) megaliths; (41) a second *fête des morts*; (42) spirit possession; (43) death-
causing spells; (44) trial by ordeal employing red-hot stones, (45) by boiling water,
(46) by swimming across a river full of crocodiles, (47) by internally taken poison;
(48) funerary dances; (49) hand dancing; (50) short-gesture dancing; (51) hand
clapping; (52) professional dancers; (53) effeminate posture of dancers (male);
(54) young people dances under moonlight accompanied by chants; (55) satirical
chants; (56) amorous poetry; (57) metaphoric and symbolic poetry; (58) metaphorical eloquence; (59) knowledge of decimal enumeration; (60) knowledge of
points cardinaux; (61) knowledge of the stars.

Africa and Madagascar (Rhodesia, Zambezi, Mozambique, Swahili): (1) patriarchal
clan with special rights of maternal uncle; (2) sexual freedom for the unmarried of
both sexes; (3) respect for the female spouse; (4) absence of dowry as important
feature; (5) *images d'accouplements*; (6) incest considered as reinforcing power
(according to Grandidier and Ferrand, among the Zafi-Raminia); (7) atmospheric
god; (8) ancestral cult; (9) royal body placed in a river after death; (10) serpent
ancestors; (11) joking relationship; (12) mass trial by ordeal through liquid poison;
(northeastern and eastern African Hamites); (13) castes; (14) age groups; (15) freemen assemblies curtailing chiefly powers in government; (16) "divinized" princes;
and (17) social importance of cattle.

[25] Compare in footnote 24 above the African items with the Indonesian ones in
the order that follows: (1)–(1); (2)–(3); (3)–(5); (4) with no mention of dowry
in Indonesia; (5)–(36); (6)–(2); (7)–(27); (8)–(29); (9)–(38); (12)–(47);
(13)–(2); (14)–(8); (15)–(22); (16)–(24)+(25); and (17)–(23)+(32).
Deschamps states disarmingly (*Madagascar*, p. 23) that "some traits are common to
Africa and Asia" and that "no scientific work has been devoted to such comparisons."
This is a truism that is detrimental in its effect because of the context in which it is
presented. The Indonesian traits listed by Deschamps have been taken entirely from
Alfred Grandidier (*Ethnographie*, Vol. I, Tome 1, 13–71, subchapter entitled "Etude
comparative des Malgaches et des Indo-Océaniens,"). This subchapter *presupposed*,
on linguistic grounds, that Malagasy features are *also* Indonesian ones or even more
broadly Indo-Oceanian. To repeat, in such an easily accessible outline form, an
extremely superficial list of half a century ago is to infuse it with new life to which
it is by no means entitled.

[26] Age groups in Madagascar are restricted to a single ethnicity, the Anteimoro.
There is no doubt that they alone imported this institution into Madagascar and that,
as such, its study constitutes an important, even major, hint as to the Anteimoro
origins (see Chapter 3). As noted earlier, joking relationship in Madagascar is designated by the Bantu loan *isiwa* or Bisa term for the same institution, cf. E. Birkeli,
Les Vazimba de la côte ouest de Madagascar (1936), p. 63.

[27] Cf. H. Baumann and D. Westermann, *Les peuples et les civilisations d'Afrique*
(1962); J. G. Frazer and R. A. Downie, *The Native Races of Africa and Madagascar*
(1938); and Murdock, *Africa*. The indices of Baumann and Westermann and Frazer
and Downie will easily lead to most of the same traits mentioned by Murdock, whose
index is restricted to tribal names only.

and more suggestive of relatively recent borrowing from the mainland than of more remote introduction from Indonesia. This is the case, for instance, of one major cultural feature—the cult of royal relics.

Malagasy *kingdoms*, as distinct from less imposing political entities ruled by elders or chiefs, do not appear in local history much before the seventeenth century. For some of them, the date of dynastic formation can be pushed back half a century in time. This is still far too late to allow for the admission into Madagascar of both the royal relics and the cult that goes with them from Indonesia, home of earlier ancestors. The cult of royal relics existed in traditional societies of Africa and Indonesia, but it was far more developed and sophisticated in Africa. It existed within Madagascar in only three local societies and survives only in two at the present time. Taken in the context of a whole cluster of cultural features, the most imposing Malagasy cult of royal relics (*dady*), among the Sakalava of western Madagascar, points immediately to a rather well-defined African counterpart. This is confirmed beyond any doubt, as will be seen, from written contemporary accounts.[28]

Some of Deschamps' Indonesian features are also too widely diffused in preliterate societies to be taken at face value and without highly controlled conditions. Strictly speaking, therefore, of the entire set of would-be Indonesian traits, one alone cannot be denied such an origin.[29] The major flaws thus emerge with great clarity. Even if we do not consider the dogmatic adumbration of certain anthropologists, too easily horrified by any comparison of traits, Deschamps has not taken into account some of the valid reservations that have emerged from the rebellion against the culture historical school. There is no allowance in his list for cultural features that can have an *independent* origin in almost any primitive society—the hunting with spear, for example. The problem of a feature *common* at the same time to Madagascar, Indonesia, and Africa, is not dealt with at all. For instance, the division of society into nobility, commoners, and slaves obtains in all three areas. Because this division presupposes some political organization, it does become important to discover if it evolved first in a Malagasy society and then diffused locally, if it were carried over initially from Indonesia, borrowed later from Africa, or if all three processes occurred independently within different Malagasy societies. Deschamps' method offers no succor here. It addresses itself neither to external borrowing nor to local diffusion, both of which are crucial to the problem at hand.

[28] See the *Letters* (1616–1617) of Father Luis Mariano, in Chapter 5 on the Sakalava.

[29] This is the association of marine shell with royalty, common to Indonesia but rare in Africa where it occurs only in the Rhodesian culture area, according to Baumann and Westermann, *Les Peuples*, p. 80.

The *isolation* of cultural features from their ethnographic, chronological, and linguistic contexts is another major flaw. In one place, Deschamps lists the filing of teeth, very likely a feature borrowed from Africa, as being contemporary to Madagascar. It could hence be assumed that the Malagasy of today generally file their teeth and that such a widespread and surviving African antecedent indicates an aesthetic influence of no small proportions. For a historian who sets out to pioneer a work on one or more aspects of Africa's impact in Madagascar, this would be a very valuable datum if he were to depend on the synchronic listing of Deschamps alone. In reality, the factor of isolation from context does not permit this dependence. The filing of teeth was reported in another time period, within a restricted geographical area.[30] It has never been an island-wide custom, and it no longer obtains in Madagascar. This trait within its proper context of ethnicity, time, and place can only serve to confirm something quite different, namely, that the old ways become harder and harder to find in the contemporary setting. And, it is not difficult to find a predecessor of some thirteen decades ago who anticipated this trend through alarm that Merina political supremacy over "hitherto independent provinces will effect the erasure of . . . distinctions between the tribes which could have guided us in research as to their origin."[31] It is also easy to understand why one must turn on the whole to history (its concern for chronology, change in time perspective) for the unique *and* the general rather than to present-day anthropological descriptions of Malagasy as a single ethnicity.

The flaw of linguistic isolation is even more dangerous because linguistics can often provide vital help either to confirm the otherwise probable borrowing or even to reveal with a measure of certainty a borrowing that has not been suspected. The shield, for example, is not used in Madagascar any more, but it did exist as a weapon of defense and was employed in many sections of the vast island. Early European ac-

[30] In the 1650s, an old man told Flacourt of a group in the interior called Ontayasatrouha and whose members had "les dents aigues." The account of this group in Flacourt is extremely similar to that of the famous Wazimba in East Africa as described by Dos Santos. Flacourt, however, refused to believe the old man while reporting the story itself. Cf. E. de Flacourt, *Histoire de la Grande Ile Madagascar* (1661), in *COACM*, Vol. VIII (1913), pp. 17–18; and the English translation of the Wazimba passage from Dos Santos in G. S. P. Freeman-Grenville (ed.), *The East African Coast—Select Documents from the First to the Earlier Nineteenth Century* (1962), or else G. M. Theal (ed.), *Records of South-Eastern Africa*, 9 vols. (1898–1903), Vol. VII, pp. 1–370. For the original, see Fr. João dos Santos, *Ethiopia Oriental* (1609). See also Chapters III and IV for Malagasy Vazimba and Ontayasatrouha.

[31] E. de Froberville, "Aperçu sur la langue malgache et recherches sur la race qui habitait l'ile de Madagascar avant l'arrivée des Malais," *BSG*, XI (1839), 261.

counts contain innumerable references to it.[32] In the nineteenth century, several photographs were made of it, and the shield survives as an archaism of the Malagasy vocabulary. As it is not very likely that such an object of material culture was invented in Madagascar, one way to ascertain its origin would be to study the shield construction and try to find an overseas replica or prototype. The Malagasy shield varieties would make this a cumbersome task at best. A much faster and no less promising way is to look in Madagascar at the word that designates it—ampinga, Bantu for shield.[33]

An Indonesian origin for the Malagasy shield widely called by its Bantu name becomes less tenable, but one can go a step beyond. A spear is the offensive and intimate counterpart of the shield, and it is most likely that the spear was diffused simultaneously with the shield. The suspicion must then be that the spear, too, should have an African name and that it survives along with the spear, used now mainly for hunting. If the two linguistic terms diverge radically, a hypothesis of dual origin needs to be introduced. Conversely, the case for a single borrowing of both items from Africa is greatly reinforced if they do not. The Malagasy term for spear, island-wide, is lefona (phonetics, lēfúna).[34] Its phonetic relatives, and with the same meaning, occur in many parts of central Africa, east-central as well as south-central, involving a number of empire builders as well.[35]

---

[32] For the sixteenth century alone. see COACM, Vol. I (1903), pp. 22, 101, 202bis, 206–234 passim. These eye-witness accounts applied to northwestern and north-eastern Madagascar, reported in 1506, 1557, and 1595 both by the Portuguese and the Dutch. They distinguished two types of Malagasy shield, or grands boucliers en bois, with a see-through hole near the top, and the much smaller and completely round shield, or the rondache. For a reproduction of the first type see the drawing in COACM, Vol. I (1903), p. 202bis; for the second type, see the Sakalava rondache in the photographic appendix to this work. Flacourt notes the different shields in Madagascar also, Histoire, COACM, Vol. VIII (1913), pp. 140–141.

[33] Cf. J. Webber, Dictionnaire malgache-français (1853), p. 32; J. Richardson, A New Malagasy-English Dictionary (1885), p. 36; A. Abinal and V. Malzac, Dictionnaire malgache-français (1888), p. 30; and Ch. Sacleux, Dictionnaire swahili-français, Vol. II (1941), p. 751, under pinga (meaning to block, shield, arrest); also mpinga, both applicable to east and southeast African littoral. Webber, whose dictionary is the only one to include most dialects, gives ampinga as the general Malagasy term for shield. Abinal and Malzac note that, in addition to being a term for shield in Imerina (the sole dialect in their dictionary), ampinga means figuratively protection.

[34] Webber, Dictionnaire, p. 425; Richardson, Dictionary, p. 386; and Abinal and Malzac, Dictionnaire, p. 360. The Malagasy, lefona appears sometimes with the prefix reni (renilefona), which makes it the "mother spear," normally one to be thrown last or seldom. In old warfare many Malagasy carried from five to twelve spears. For other weapon nomenclatures, see the Appendix.

[35] In Tonga and Botatwe, lisumo (sing., first; pl., second); in Seshukulombwe (Ila), isumo; in Bisa, ifumo; in Bemba, the closest Malagasy equivalent, or lifumo

The effort of Deschamps is devoid of what may be called simply a sense of *control*. Many of the features stated to be Indonesian are Malagasy ones assumed to be Indonesian. Not a few were extracted uncritically from Grandidier's much earlier speculations about Oceanian features in Madagascar.[36] Others are unsupported by any bibliographical reference to sources for Indonesia. The traits themselves are lumped together indiscriminately, and they do not always have the same historical and social quality. They can be present in numbers or in isolation within a given context. This requires a controlling mechanism of quantity and even more of quality, basic to any study of culture contact.

According to Deschamps, there is roughly a four-to-one (61:17) ratio of Indonesian as against African features found in Madagascar. Unlike his predecessors, he thus gives Africa at least some credit in Malagasy nonmaterial culture while stating, in effect, that Indonesian traits are paramount. This could be inferred from the Malagasy language alone. Otto Dahl's study has shown that Malagasy belongs to the Indonesian language family, having its closest relative in the Maanjan of Borneo.[37] The frequent assertion that Malagasy is a Malayo-Polynesian language stands as a substitute for knowing that it does have a more precise

---

(sing.) and *lifuma* (pl.); in Swahili, Karanga, Ganda, Ndau, Manyika, *fumo, pfumo, pfomo, ipfumo*. Cf. E. Hoch, *Bemba Pocket Dictionary* (1960), p. 196; C. M. Doke, *A Comparative Study in Shona Phonetics* (1931), "Appendix 'f'"; J. T. Brown, *Secwana Dictionary* (1954), p. 158; E. W. Smith, *A Handbook of the Ila Language* (1907), pp. 341 and 405; J. Torrend, *Bantu-Botatwe Dialects of Northern Rhodesia* (1967 reprint of 1931 edition), p. 525, and *A Comparative Grammar of the South-African Bantu Languages* (1891), p. 89 (index, paragraph 411, and comparative word list for spear). An onomatopoeic possibility cannot be seriously accepted. Further research will most likely reveal a much greater spread of the cognate for spear in central Africa. *Fumo* is also a chiefly title in Africa.

[36] Compare the sixty-one traits from Deschamps listed above in note 24 with A. Grandidier, *Ethnographie*, Vol. I, Tome 1, pp. 5–71. There is a false implication in the two lists that the Bantu-speaking Africans had no knowledge of the decimal system, cardinal points, and celestial phenomena. It is instructive to read in this connection, for example, Louis Massignon's *Les Nuages de Magellan et leur découverte par les Arabes* (1962), p. 3, where he makes a comparison of Sakalava perception of Magellanic Clouds and compares it to those of the Chagga of Kilimanjaro, of the Bawenda (northeast Transvaal) and Ndala. The Bawenda-Sakalava analogy is clear, and what may be said of the Sakalava applies equally to the Bara, cf. Jean-Claude Hébert, "La Cosmographie malgache," *AUM*, special issue (1965), 111 and note; and Gottschling's note on this subject in *JAI*, XXXV (1905), 382, cited by Massignon on page 3. Equally false is the implication that elaborate forms of poetry or "metaphorical eloquence" have been absent from traditional Africa. To take only the example of Rwanda, one can easily consult the following works of Alexis Kagame: "Le Poésie pastorale au Rwanda" and "Avec un Troubadour du Rwanda" in *Zaire*, I/7 (1947), 791–800, and III/7 (1949), 765–769; *La Poésie dynastique au Rwanda* (1951), pp. 1–240; *La Divine Pastorale* (1952), pp. 1–109; and *La Philosophie bantu-rwandaise de l'etre* (1956), pp. 1–448.

[37] Otto Chr. Dahl, *Malgache et Maanjan* (1951), pp. 5–372.

affinity. Since most *Malgachisants* know that Dahl has refined the problem of affinity in favor of more immediate Indonesian descent, it becomes safe to transfer linguistic supremacy into the realm of culture. Such a transfer list may not even be vital to the argument, but there is no harm in confirming the fact of language. In essence, Deschamps' list is a statement of Malagasy cultural unity, quantified in terms of common traits. Very few, however, are common to *all* Malagasy; many are restricted to one or two local ethnicities at best. In short, until a cluster of features is presented in its ethnographic, chronological, and linguistic contexts, the factor of *quantity* has no value either.

This is immediately related to *quality*, of which two types must be noted: historical and social. When properly detailed ethnographic and linguistic data ascertain a borrowed feature, this feature acquires thereby a historical quality. In itself, the particular feature may not be terribly important. An adequately described form of wrestling, for example, is known in southwestern Madagascar as *ringa*, a Bantu term descriptive of the same style.[38] Both the area and context are therefore conveyed. This is valuable as yet another indication of cultural influence from Africa, but it cannot imply anything of great social consequence or of antiquity. A few Makoa slaves, imported into Madagascar in the first half of the nineteenth century,[39] might simply have started the *ringa*, and the sport took hold by imitation and purely as an amusement. Although its historical quality is reasonably high (known origin but uncertain time of introduction), its social quality is decidedly low since the *ringa* made no major imprint on local government, religion, or economy.

Mainly in connection with lexicostatistics, linguists like Rea and Gudschinsky have worked out a "core" vocabulary of 100 to 200 words that embodies the principles of quantity and quality. The lower numerals one to five, seventeen terms for parts of the body, many pronouns and items dealing with "natural" objects provide the bulk of this core vocabulary. In it, "quality" applies strictly to what is apt to be most stable in any language, and what informs the word selection is the "historical" desire to determine how long two *related* languages have been separated. The core is seen as having the same rate of retention and loss, and the relative percentages of its cognates thus "determine" the approximate date of separation. Quite apart from what can be said against lexico-

[38] In E. Mamelomana, *Les Mahafaly*, unpublished typescript (not dated), pp. 1–78 (unnumbered), No. 141 of *BP*, under *ringa*. Cf. Sacleux, *Swahili: français*, Vol. I (1939), p. 475, and Vol. II (1941), p. 777, where he places *ringa/linga* in Vanga-Rufiji, Gazi-Kilifi, Rasini Island, and the opposite coast.

[39] Some 40,000 Makua live today in western Madagascar in more or less distinct communities. Makua applies in Madagascar to a variety of Zambezi people, and it is also a synonym for Africans. A Makua vocabulary is given in the linguistic Appendix below.

statistical methods and assumptions, the core vocabulary has nothing to do with borrowing or with the purpose of the social quality to be assigned to Bantu loans in Malagasy. The two languages are *unrelated* and only three of the two hundred terms (snake = *pilo, fanane*; eye = *maso*; and *ana-ka* = children) are to be found both in Malagasy and Bantu vocabularies. Two of these, moreover (*maso* and *anaka*) may or may not be simply a matter of linguistic coincidence. To have thus an undisputed importance in the context of Bantu loans in Malagasy, a cultural feature must be sociohistorically of high quality. This can be illustrated with the feature of spirit possession that Deschamps attributes to Indonesia.[40]

Spirit possession appears in five basic linguistic forms within Madagascar—*ramanenjana* and *ambo* (Merina), *bilo* (Bara), *tromba* (Sakalava), and *salamanga* (Betsimisaraka). It is possible, even probable, that spirit possession of private individuals came into Madagascar both from Indonesia and Africa. Possession by a spirit, ancestral or otherwise, affects the realm of guilt—real or imagined—and may be seen as a form of psychological relief from mental anguish. Such features are notoriously difficult to trace. Yet, in one case, among the Sakalava of western Madagascar, there is a type of public *tromba* associated with defunct monarchs and regarded as a local institution. Special priest mediums go into the royal *tromba* (spirit possession) and "speak the will" of a particular king, usually to urge the Sakalava into some activity.[41] In practice, the mediums are the men serving a living monarch, attached to his court, and it is *his* will that is conveyed to the subjects who are not likely to disobey a would-be royal voice from the grave. The *tromba* here is an agent of royal government, used for political and social control through religion. This represents a cluster of features merging within the royal *tromba*, and of very high social quality among the Sakalava. There are no parallels elsewhere in Madagascar or in Indonesia. The royal *tromba*, surrounded by a cluster of very particular features, could not have been invented independently in Madagascar either. On the other hand, the same pivotal institution, having the same basic function and much the same but somewhat richer cluster of related features, occurs in the old, gold-bearing empire of Mwene Mutapa in southern Rhodesia, home of the Bantu-speaking Shona peoples.[42] Here, ethnographic data *alone* are strong enough to add the historical aspect of quality. The precise etymon

[40] Deschamps, *Madagascar*, p. 23.

[41] H. Rusillon, *Un Culte dynastique avec evocation des morts chez les sakalaves de Madagascar: le "Tromba"* (1912), pp. 117–135; this should be supplemented with A. Dandouau's manuscript *Le Trumba—Razana ou Angabé* (not dated), pp. 1–16, reproduced in the Appendix below.

[42] D. P. Abraham, "The Early Political History of the Kingdom of Mwene Mutapa, 850–1589," in *Historians in Tropical Africa*, mimeographed Proceedings of the Leverhulme Inter-Collegiate History Conference, University College of Rhodesia and

of *tromba* has never been explored.[43] It must, nonetheless, exist in the same general area of the mainland because it would be unusual for a feature of the highest quality to be disconnected from its original linguistic context. To find it, however, one must determine the Sakalava *meaning* of *tromba* and render the written term into its phonetic counterpart. The *tr* in Malagasy is a *t* obtained by pressing the tip of the tongue firmly behind the upper incisors. The Malagasy *o*, unless followed by the vowel *a* (aa), is equal to the English *oo* (u), as in the adverb *too*. Thus, *tromba* comes out phonetically *tumba* (*toomba* with terminal *a* barely audible). A Sakalava possessed by *tromba* is said to be "like dead," or a "living corpse," an accurate impression of pitch phase in the trance and a statement of representing the dead. This very meaning applies to *mTumba/kiTumba* in the Ki-Ngwana dialect of Swahili, used as commercial language in central Africa, from the Congo to Tanganyika.[44] We still do not know the precise linguistic birthplace of *tromba*, but the general area of Africa in which it is used cannot be disputed.

Deschamps does not limit himself to nonmaterial culture. For the material cultures of Madagascar, he reports thirty-six Indonesian and fourteen African items and techniques.[45] Certain of the components are most

---

Nyasaland, September 1960 (1962), pp. 62, 67, 77. Consult also F. W. T. Posselt, *Fact and Fiction* (1935), pp. 1–210, and M. Gelfand, *Medicine and Magic of the Mashona* (1956), pp. 1–266.

[43] Birkeli, *Vazimba*, p. 63, sees in it the Bisa *ntembo*, or prayer to the spirits. This is not too good phonetically or in terms of what is meant by *trumba* among the Sakalava.

[44] Sacleux, *Swahili-français*, Vol. I (1939), p. 415, and Vol. II (1941), p. 617.

[45] Deschamps, *Madagascar*, pp. 21–22.

Indonesian: (1) slash-and-burn farming; (2) long-handle spade; (3) inundated rice fields (wet rice cultivation); (4) cultivation of taro, (5) yams, (6) bananas, and (7) *cocotier*; (8) dog rearing; (9) fowl rearing; (10) "black" hog rearing; (11) importance of fishing, and the associated use of (12) harpoons, (13) poison, and (14) nets; (15) turtle catching; (16) whale catching; (17) hunting with spear and sling; (18) use of gourds and bamboos as utensils; (19) use of wooden plates and bowls; (20) pottery-making; (21) use of vegetable fibers for the manufacture of clothing; (22) mat and basket weaving; (23) sculpting in wood; (24) tattooing; (25) circumcision; (26) coloring of teeth; (27) body depilation; (28) underground kilns; (29) double-valve pump bellows; (30) making of fire through the rubbing of barks; (31) hill villages surrounded by (protective) ditches; (32) rectangular huts; (33) stone phalli; (34) quadrangular tombs; (35) small dolmens; and (36) internal tiering of tombs with flagstones.

African: (1) cultivation of millet; (2) social importance of cattle; (3) cattle markings; (4) wearing of togas; (5) pottery-making; (6) cotton weaving; (7) construction of silos (for grain storage); (8) indented sickles; (9) sculpting in wood; (10) filing down of teeth; (11) lancers; (12) round shields; (13) circumcision; and (14) custom of wearing a small disk on the forehead.

Note again, by Deschamp's own juxtaposition, the African items 5, 9, and 13 are identical with Indonesian items 20, 23, and 25.

reasonably defined in respect to their ultimate homes. The catching of tortoise and small whales,[46] the cultivation of certain plants and the plants themselves, the outrigger, and the double-valve pump bellows (often called piston bellows) can be taken to be just as Indonesian as the cultivation of millet, millet itself, the social importance of cattle and cattle-markings can be taken to be African, as the linguistic evidence confirms. Malagasy terms for cattle, *omby/ombe* (older *ngomby*, the *y* standing for any vowel in Malagasy) derive from Bantu *ngombe* (cattle), while those for millet, *ampemba* and *morama*, retain their Bantu form in Madagascar.[47]

The African origin of Malagasy cattle markings could be presupposed, as it would appear from Deschamps, on the basis of the argument that cattle came from Africa. The *bos* or zebu cattle and the cattle-milking complex are duplicated in eastern and southern Africa.[48] Western and southern pastoralists of Madagascar are exclusively ear markers, like most southern African Bantu and some groups in east Africa. Western Madagascar must have been the initial center of cattle diffusion into other parts of the island. But, there is a fair amount of oral evidence for this area to show that cattle raising is considerably older than the marking. The markings are, as Emil Birkeli has observed, ethnographic

---

[46] It should be noted that tortoise catching *in* Africa (east and southeast) is mentioned by early Arab geographers. On this aspect, see L.-M. Devic, *Le Pays des Zendjs ou la côte orientale d'Afrique au Moyen-Age* (1883). As for the whales, there is an extremely interesting passage in the Chinese "Records of Foreign Nations," (*Chu-fan-chi,*) authored by Chau Ju-kua, Inspector of Foreign Trade at Fukien, in the mid-thirteenth Century. It applies to the area of Africa known to the Chinese as Chung-li and identified as the Somali coast. It reads: "Every year there are driven on the coast a great many dead fish measuring two hundred feet in length and twenty feet through the body. The people do not eat the flesh of these fish, but they cut out their brains, marrow and eyes, from which they get oil, . . . and . . . mix this oil with lime to caulk their boats, and use it also in lamps. The poor people use the ribs . . . to make rafters, the backbones for door leaves, and they cut off vertebrae to make mortars with," F. Hirth, and W. W. Rockhill, *Chau Ju-kua* (1966—1st ed. 1911), p. 131. Also J. J. L. Duyvendak, *China's Discovery of Africa* (1949), p. 21.

[47] Cf., for Malagasy cattle, cow, and ox, Webber, *Dictionnaire*, pp. 496–497; Richardson, *Dictionary*, p. 460; Abinal and Malzac, *Dictionnaire*, p. 424. For millet, in the same order of authors, pp. 190 and 482; 35 and 444; 30 and 408. Compare with: word list for cattle in J. Torrend, *Grammar of the . . . Bantu Languages* (1891), p. 82 (index, paragraph 385 and list below); and Chr. Ehret, "Cattle-Keeping . . . in Eastern and Southern African History: The Linguistic Evidence," *JAH*, VIII/1 (1967), 1–17. For millet terms in Africa, see: Sacleux, *Swahili-français*, Vol. II (1941), pp. 606, 763, and 847 for *mtama* (millet) on Swahili littoral, *mrama* on Comoro Islands (*morama*, Malagasy) and for the millet variety *pumba* (*mtama wa-pumba=varieté de sorgho à panicule condensée et à grain blanc*).

[48] See L. Joleaud, "Le Bœuf de Madagascar, son origine, son rôle dans les coutumes sakalaves," *Anthropologie*, XXXIV (1924), 103–107.

documents of great value to the history of preliterate societies.[49] In western Madagascar they do indeed reveal more or less when cattle ears began to be marked and under what circumstances. Thus, it cannot be held that the ear-marking custom came to Madagascar with African cattle. Only the circumstances alluded to point to an African origin, and these need to be discussed in some detail before even this much can be claimed.[50]

It is apparent even from the limited examples of cattle, millet, and especially cattle markings that Deschamps' second list reproduces the flaws encountered in the earlier one. Whale catching is unknown today and was reported over three centuries ago in one specific coastal region of Madagascar.[51] From this very area, the outrigger has disappeared as well although it used to serve the unusual purpose of slave raiding as far as the Comoro Islands and the coast of east Africa in the late eighteenth and early nineteenth centuries.[52] Land clearing by fire (slash-and-burn method of farming) is hardly limited to Indonesia. No one can regard the making of fire by rubbing wooden barks as a technique confined to Asia, or the importance of fishing as something alien to Africa, along with the use of harpoons, fish poisoning, and nets.[53] The Malagasy stone phalli

---

[49] E. Birkeli, *Marques de boeufs et traditions de race: documents sur l'ethnographie de la côte occidentale de Madagascar* (1926), pp. 1–7.

[50] *Ibid.*, pp. 9–55; and Chapter 5 (Sakalava).

[51] In 1598, the Dutch fleet under Van Neck came across whale-catching Malagasy of the islet of Sainte-Marie, not far from the mouth of Antongil Bay. Cf. *COACM*, Vol. I (1903), pp. 246–254 and drawing on 246$_{bis}$. These Malagasy were the Betsimisaraka who lived on the islet, and all subsequent reports of whaling concern this single area. In 1786, two American vessels collected a full whale cargo at Sainte-Marie. The French commander of Sainte-Marie, De Valgny, imposed a tribute tax on local inhabitants of "one whale out of three" in 1767 (the French took possession of the islet on July 30, 1750). For these and other unpublished reports, see *ANSOMCM*, Piece 31, Carton I, De la Merveille to Pontchartrain (1712), and Piece 41, *Voyage de Raby* (1754); Carton II, Dossier 1(b), Valgny *to* Dumas (1767); Carton XI, Dossier 4(a), Mackau, *Report* (1818). There is one exception: Le Gentil, *Voyage dans les mers de l'Inde*, Vol. II.(1761), pp. 399, claimed that in addition to Sainte-Marie (pp. 561–567) whale catching took place on the southern littoral of Madagascar.

[52] For this aspect see in the Appendices E. de Froberville's "Historique des invasions madécasses aux Iles Comores à la côte d'Afrique," *AVG*, II (1845), 194–208.

[53] Cf. Lagercrantz, "The Harpoon . . . and Its Distribution in Africa," *ANTHV* (1934). Bone harpoons, of course, existed at Khartoum, Asselar, as well as eastern Africa since prehistoric times. On fishing with poison, see C. S. Alexander's "Fish Poisoning Along the Northeastern Coast of Tanganyika," *TNR*, 62 (1964). On the general importance of fishing in Africa a few references should be sufficient: C. M. N. White, "The Role of Hunting and Fishing in Luvake Society," *African Studies*, XV/2 (1956), 75–86; Th. Scudder, "Fishermen on the Zambezi," *Human Problems*, 27 (June 1960), 41–49; W. V. Brelsford, *Fishermen of the Bangwelu Swamps* (1946), on the Unga, pp. 1–169; M. C. Hoole, "Notes on Fishing and Allied Industries . . .

may well be a product of Indonesian megalithic culture. But, in the 1930s, Deschamps did not find any similarities. There is a good chance that northeastern Africa, with its own and well-developed megalithic complex, could have contributed its share in Madagascar.[54] The use of gourds and bamboos as utensils, mat and basket weaving, or the manufacture of clothing from vegetable fibers can in no way be ascertained as exclusively Indonesian. Wooden plates and bowls, too, are hardly absent from Africa. Moreover, the Malagasy term for bowl is the Bantu loan *finga*. Tattooing, also classified with certainty as a feature of Indonesian culture, is far too widespread in Africa to disregard the mainland completely. Of the two monographs on patterns and techniques in Malagasy tattooing, one claims borrowing from Africa, while the other admits some African influence but is largely an independent evolution within Madagascar.[55] Although it contained no reference to linguistic items, the earlier of the two monographs was in print before Deschamps published his own work.

One does not equally perceive at all why the Malagasy robes or togas (Malagasy, *lamba*), grain silos, and circumcision are given specifically as African. Sculpturing in wood is designated as Indonesian *and* African without making this duality meaningful in any way. It would take, of course, a great deal of knowledge of wood sculpture done in Madagascar, Indonesia and Africa to determine particular borrowings or a knowledge of the local inventiveness in Madagascar since it is impossible to see the Malagasy always as passive recipients of foreign loans. Again, students of Malagasy art, even when concerned with external borrowing, made their conclusions mainly through visual impression and not as a result of solid grounding in Indonesian or African art styles. The case for musical

---

among the Tonga of . . . West Nyasa," *NJ*, VIII/1 (1955), 25–36; C. M. Dobbs, "Fishing in the Kavirondo Gulf, Lake Victoria," *JEAUNHS*, XXX (1927), 97–109; H. A. Fosbrooke, "Some aspects of the Kimwani fishing culture," *JRAI*, 64 (1934), 1–22; O. Mors, "Notes on Hunting and Fishing in Buhaya," *Anthropological Quarterly*, XXVI/3 (1953), 89–93.

[54] The Indonesian *menhirs*, wrote Deschamps after a visit to the archipelago (July–October 1935) as representative of Madagascar to the exposition at Batavia, "*sont des pierres basses, carrées, au bout vaguement arrondi. Elles forment des alignements ou des cromlechs. L'analogie avec nos* tsangambato (Malagasy stone phalli, particularly Anteimoro) *est toutefois assez faible. Ce ne sont pas des dalles, mais des pierres massives.*" H. Deschamps, "Indonésiens et Malgaches," *BAM*, XVIII (1935), 61. For Africa, see the chapter on "Megalithic Cushites" in Murdock, *Africa*, pp. 196–203. For the *tsangambato*, see Chapter IV (Anteimoro) below.

[55] R. Decary, "Les Tatouages chez les indigènes de Madagascar," *JSA*, V/1 (1935), 1–39 (with 241 patterns for the Sakalava, Makoa, Mahafaly, Tandroy, Antanosy, Tanala, Betsimisaraka, and Betsileo); and J.–C. Hébert, "Les Tatouages sakalava dans l'ethnie culturelle malgache," *CM*, I/1 (1964), 115–165, and iconographic annex of 28 pages at the end of the volume.

instruments is different because a trained ethnomusicologist, Curt Sachs, did the initial ground clearing.[56] This has enabled Deschamps to list with accuracy, rarely present elsewhere, the Indonesian- and African-derived instruments in Madagascar.[57] Here, a point of unusual interest must be noted. The sole scientific study, making definite technical comparisons within a restricted field, reveals *equal* borrowing from Indonesia and Africa, six basic instruments being given for each of the two areas. Sachs confined this conclusion to the most primitive and therefore most ancient types of instruments. Thus, a case for any recent borrowings can not be made. On the strength of solid evidence for items that crosscut material and nonmaterial cultures, the Sachs' conclusion clearly contradicts those of Murdock and Deschamps. It is, however, limited to musical instruments alone.

Fowl rearing in Madagascar, according to Deschamps, came from Indonesia and yet he notes elsewhere in passing that the general Malagasy term for domesticated fowl is *akoho* (phon. *a'kūhú*), undoubtedly from Bantu *kuku*.[58] After listing the use of gourd as Indonesian, Deschamps allows Malagasy gourds and pots to come both from Indonesia and Africa. This is more reasonable. The old Merina idiom, however, preserved Bantu terms for them, *nongo* and *zinga*,[59] and both are found

---

[56] C. Sachs, *Les Instruments de musique à Madagascar* (1938), pp. 1–96.

[57] Deschamps, *Madagascar*, p. 22.

[58] *Ibid.*, compare pp. 36 and 21. See also Sacleux, *Swahili-français*, Vol. I (1939), p. 446, for Swahili *kuku*; the same term for fowl, structured at times as *in-kuku*, *n-kuku*, *n-khukhu*, *n-guku*, *n-goko*, *n-koko* appears in Tonga, Bisa, Gogo, Sagara, Shambala, Boondei, Taita, Nyanyembe, Sukuma, Kamba, Nyika, Senna, Ganda, Rotse as well as others, cf. word list for fowl in Torrend, *Grammar*, p. 83.

[59] F. Callet, *Tantara*, Vol. I (1953), p. 129, note that the *marmites de terre a rebord* of all types were called *nongo* and (p. 127) that "no one recalls the origin of pottery." This term is still in Abinal and Malzac, *Dictionnaire*, p. 417. There is no doubt of a Bantu loan, from the root *ongo* for clay, earth, soil, cf. Sacleux, *Swahili-français*, Vol. II (1941), p. 713. According to Sacleux, it appears with the same (Malagasy) generic meaning as *uwongo* in Ki-Amu (Lamu), being a Ki-Ngozi archaism there (p. 987); *uwongo* in Ki-Gunya and Ki-Ti-kuu (spoken on the Rasim islet and the opposite coast to the Equator), (p. 985); *vuongo* (p. 1006, same as p. 985 equivalent); and *udongo* among the southern African languages, spoken from Gasi to Mozambique or Ki-Mirima (Vanga to Rufiji), Ki-Mgao (Rufiji to Mozambique with Kilwa being the main center), Ki-Hadimu and Ki-Ungudya (Zanzibar), Ki-Pemba and Ki-Tumbatu (Pemba and Tumbatu), (p. 932). Its multiple meanings in the last group of languages include: soil, anything pertaining to soil, earth, clay mortar, clay for pottery (p. 932). For *zinga*, see entry by Richardson, *Dictionary*, p. 801, "A ladle or horn with a handle, used for lading water from a pitcher or water-pot. Swahili *mzinga*, a hollow cylinder"; by Abinal and Malzac, p. 808, "*Calebasse ou grande tasse en fer-blanc servant a puiser l'eau, dans la cruche, à la source, au puits, à la rivière.*" There are several more specific compounds: *zinga fotsy* (literally, white jug), or *zinga* (*en fer-blanc*); *zinga harona*, or gourd without handle; *zinga tandroka*, or *corne emmanachée*. It should be noted also that in Swahili *mzinga*

in the modern vocabulary.[60] When such linguistic context is reported, one can turn, for example, to at least one European resident in Madagascar who observed early in the 1700s that pottery-manufacturing centers were rare in the island and that the west-coast Vazimba, kin of the central-highlands Vazimba, were the most capable pottery-makers he knew.[61]

If the Malagasy quadrangular hut and stone tomb with single and narrow but round opening, the double-valve pump, or piston bellows, and double outrigger are eminently acceptable as being of Indonesian origin, Deschamps does not explore the African angle at all. The stone tomb described and the double outrigger are found *together* among the Bajun of Africa's eastern littoral.[62] In *west* Africa one finds Malaysian food crops, among which the banana duplicates the Malagasy term *akondro* (prefix *a + kūndrú* phon.).[63] It would have also been of some value to note that the piston bellows (both idea and artifact) have been reported in the seventeenth-century Gambia by Captain Barbot.[64] The Chopi (variously called Bi-Tonga, Batoka, Valenge and seen as deriving from the old Shona), who face southern Madagascar on the opposite side of the Mozambique Channel, merge at least three most interesting features: the highly developed xylophone culture, the quadrangular hut, and the piston bellows.[65] Quadrangular huts, common to all Madagascar,

---

applies to the cannon as well in the sense of hollow cylinder or even to a ship's anchor. It is, therefore, like the root *ongo* a basic term for any cylindrical and hollow vessel.

[60] *Zinga*, for example, appears as *ka-singy* in the current Sakalava dialect in the sense of calabash, while *nongo* is limited to Merina in contemporary use. Cf. B. H. Hoffmann, *Vocabulaire français-hova-sakalava-tsimihety*, unpublished typescript (not dated but compiled between 1940 and 1948), pp. 29 and 167, in *BP* without docket number.

[61] Drury, *Journal*, p. 280.

[62] Grottanelli, *Pescatori*, pp. 27–83, 321–344.

[63] This poses some interesting problems. The term *akondro* is prevalent in Imerina while elsewhere in Madagascar the term for banana is *ontsy* (Sakalava land) and *otsy* (east-coast Betsimisaraka). In Africa, the root word *konde* for banana is found from western Africa and the Cameroons to the Congo, among the Lunda and Lunda-influenced central Africans, in southeast and east-central Africa, as shown by Blakney's *Linguistic Footprints*, pp. 62–70. The *otsy* (phonetics, *utsi*) and *ontsy* (phonetics, *untsi*), both with barely audible terminal *i*, have been located as *huti* only among the Shambaa and Bondei (pp. 58–59). It is thus possible that the Imerina term represents and is an African loan, while the *utsi/huti* sequence would suggest the reverse or an Indonesian loan survival in Africa.

[64] Noted in A. M. Jones, *Africa and Indonesia* (1964), pp. 202–203.

[65] Cf. H. Tracey, *Chopi Musicians* (1948); J. Walton, *African Village* (1956); E. D. Earthy, *Valenge Women: An Ethnographic Study* (1933). It is Livingstone who noted first among the Batoka (village of Simariango, approximately 100 miles east of Victoria Falls) that "the bellows of the blacksmith here were somewhat different from the common goatskin bags and more like those of Madagascar"—

had started to displace at some points of the eastern African coast the older conical ones, an architectural change no one has as yet been able to attribute to independent invention.[66] It is true that the conical hut, common to the Bantu-speaking Africans, cannot be found today in Madagascar. Nonetheless, this type of hut was seen exactly a century ago, in June 1869, at one particular spot, a sand bar at the Manambolo River of western Madagascar.[67] If the piston bellows are indeed dominant in Madagascar, the African bag bellows have not been entirely absent from the Great Island either. The very observant French traveler Henry Douliot, after describing the Malagasy piston bellows, observed in 1892 that both in northwestern and southwestern Madagascar "on fait usage d'un autre systeme: c'est un soufflet en peau de chèvre, formé de deux outres qu'on presse avec la main."[68] A few isolated items of material culture do not, of course, permit the formulation of any major theory. But, when these begin to accumulate within properly defined contexts, one can be allowed to transform what is merely suspected into a plausible hypothesis of contact.

Thus, despite Deschamps' solid grounding in the sources for Malagasy history and ethnography as well as recent work with the traditional African past,[69] rare combination among students of Madagascar both past and present, his cultural items tend to be sterile and his lists potentially misleading because anthropology and linguistics have not been worked into them. Intellectually stimulating as they often are, cultural models turn out to be too congested, static, and seldom historically oriented. Murdock's model is no exception in terms of African societies,

---

Narrative of an Expedition to the Zambezi (1865), pp. 314–315 (or pp. 332–333 in the edition of 1866). Barrie Reynolds, in noting the Livingstone reference, uses the term cup bellows and states also that the valley Tonga smiths, "especially those in the western escarpment country," also are using the cup or drum bellows—The Material Culture of the Peoples of the Gwembe Valley (1968), p. 96. It is known from old Portuguese accounts that the old Barue Kingdom, populated by the Tonga, produced little gold but much iron.

[66] According to Baumann and Westermann, Les Peuples, p. 236: "On ne connaît point le pays d'origine de la case côtiere; c'est une maison quadrangulaire avec toit à pignon en palmes de cocoyer . . . elle porrait être d'origine malaise ou ouest-africaine. Cette case a pénétré loin à l'interieur, remplaçant la case à toit conique." Cf. A. Rita-Ferreira, Agrupamentos e Caracterização Etnica dos Indígenas de Moçambique (1958), p. 39.

[67] A. and G. Grandidier, Ethnographie de Madagascar, Vol. III (1917), p. 522. It was Alfred Grandidier himself who saw the conic huts that belonged to the Vazimba. They had a base diameter of about 2 meters and their height varied from 1.50 to 1.80 centimeters.

[68] H. Douliot, Journal du voyage fait sur la côte ouest de Madagascar, 1891–1892 (1895), p. 34.

[69] Cf. H. Deschamps, Traditions orales et archives au Gabon (1962).

many of which are noted in a few passing lines and not a few of which have been described in more meaningful ways by Baumann and Westermann. Insofar as the African despotism relates to Madagascar, there is no discernible evidence for detailed study of any or all Malagasy societies, while the absence of attempts at some time perspective is clear. His kinship algebra reveals the trained anthropologist, but it is far too dogmatic to be accepted as a valuable analytical and historical tool.[70] To the extent that Murdock uses linguistics in respect to Madagascar, this is done clearly to prove that the Maanjan of Borneo provided in effect the proto-Malagasy because the two languages are more or less closely related.[71] Murdock, hence, gives linguistics the highest evidential value. While this idea is by no means unwarranted, linguistics *alone* cannot be made to do *all* the work. There is no mechanistic overlap between the history of a language and that of its speakers, a matter on which many anthropologists and linguists have a common-sense agreement. Moreover, as W. G. Solheim shows, no one has as yet been able to reconstruct the old Maanjan culture as distinct from other and equally unknown cultures of Southeast Asia or actually prove through the comparative endeavor that the Maanjan are also the sole or undisputed ancestors of the Indonesian element among the Malagasy.[72] It is significant in this connection that Otto Dahl, who made the comparative linguistic study of Maanjan and Malagasy, refrained on the whole from migratory inferences.

It would, however, be unjust to say that Murdock and Deschamps give us nothing of value. If the real evidence is still to be presented, both have at long last alluded to a subject of incredible neglect. From Murdock, moreover, come the stress on government, hitherto advanced by no one, and five features promising for comparison. Deschamps makes us aware of broader possibilities in material and nonmaterial cultures of Madagascar. It thus becomes necessary to return first to the promise of

---

[70] "The social organization of the Malagasy, like their economy, clearly reflects the Indonesian antecedents of their culture . . . the whole social structure, indeed, corresponds almost exactly to what one would expect in a Bornean bilateral society that was subjected to patrilocal influences through Arab and Cushitic contacts. . . . Matrilineal exogamy, which constitutes the sole discrepancy, possibly reflects the mass impact of Bantu slaves . . . ," Murdock, *Africa*, p. 220. This is nothing short of an amazing set of postulates to make for the Malagasy.

[71] Murdock, *Africa*, pp. 214–215. He goes even further than that: Malagasy and Maanjan closest relatives=Malagasy dialects so similar that this suggests immigration by a relatively unified linguistic and cultural group=this contradicts various theories that the Island was peopled by diverse Indonesian elements=hence the Maanjan must also have been the ancient Azanians! Murdock does not know that dialectical divergence has been considerable in Madagascar, to mention only one factor, which, of itself, renders the rest of the equation without a connecting link.

[72] W. G. Solheim, "Indonesian Culture and Malagasy Origins," *AUM*, Hors Série (1965), 34–35.

linguistics and relate it to the problem at hand. Paying attention to some of Murdock's features, we shall then be able to insert in a general way some African antecedents in Madagascar that Deschamps did not look for.

A number of writers, most of them missionaries who lived in Madagascar for some time, have noted that Malagasy language contains a fair number of Swahili and Bantu loan-words in its vocabulary.[73] Recording mainly the vocabulary items which retain an original form, most of them presented longer or shorter loan-word lists, and they deduced, from these, three basic but widely divergent theories. The most popular one causes no surprise. It holds that mainland loans are relatively insignificant, having been obtained through recent commerce in the case of Swahili and/or through recently imported "agricultural slaves" from Africa in that of Bantu loans. As such, it is a linguistic counterpart to the traditional view of Africa's role in Madagascar. Its polar opposite, namely that Malagasy is in effect and in substance (vocabulary + syntax) an African language, has been accepted justly by no one except the sole proponent of this claim.[74] Somewhere in the middle, there is also a theory of Bantu substratum. Based on the antiquity of certain loans, it is in essence a hypothesis for a pre-Indonesian presence of Bantu-speakers in Madagascar.[75]

Old Bantu loans in Malagasy tax the prevalent view that Swahili traders and Bantu slaves who tilled the soil and hauled the water add up to all that can be said about Africa and Madagascar. But, the substratum cannot *prove* the broader claim. Old Bantu loans can be accounted for in other ways. The proto-Malagasy, as some recent scholars believe, must have resided on the mainland before settling in Madagascar.[76] By intermixing with the Bantu prior to their arrival in the Great

[73] Reverend Richardson's 1885 *Dictionary* has the unique feature of an *attempt* to give word etymologies, including Swahili, although this is restricted to cases where loans from Africa generally stand out in more or less *pure* forms. Cf. L. Dahle, "The Swaheli Element in the New Malagasy-English Dictionary," *AA* (1885), 99–115. It can safely be said, however, that Richardson and Lars Dahle (himself a linguist and writer of unusual interest) were the first to open the door to this subject.

[74] C. Tastevin, "Zimbabue, preuve de l'origine africaine des noirs de Madagascar et de la langue malgache," *Ethnographie*, XLI (1943), 379–391, and XLIII (1945), 51–70; "De l'Africanité de quelques phonèmes auxiliaries considérés à tort comme préfixes en malgache," *Ethnographie*, XLV (1947–1950), 178–202; and "L'Africanité des préfixes nominaux et verbaux du malgache," *Ethnographie*, XLVIII (1953), 63–68. The main thesis of Tastevin is untenable, but some of his research is valuable.

[75] Otto Chr. Dahl, "Le Substrat bantou en Malgache," *NTS*, Bind XVII (1953), 325–362.

[76] This is often called the Linton Hypothesis, after Ralph Linton—cf. "Culture Areas of Madagascar," *American Anthropologist*, XXX (1928), 363–390, and his *The Tanala*, Anthropological Series, Field Museum of Natural History (Chicago),

Island, the proto-Malagasy would thus have carried the old loans over. This must be modified. No dates are known for the earliest arrival of the Bantu in the immediate hinterland and coast of eastern and southeastern Africa. Next, Afro-Indonesian contacts can simply not be explained in terms of a single human migration from Indonesia toward Africa and Madagascar. Finally, to be sound, a hypothesis *must* explain at the same time why Indonesians disappeared from Africa, why the Malagasy language has an essential unity, and why it contains old Bantu loans, especially for certain domesticated animals and plants.

The unmodified hypothesis is far too simple to "solve" such a problem. Rather, the "true" proto-Malagasy would appear to have fled into Madagascar to avoid the oncoming Bantu, and their idiom should not have been contaminated with Bantu loans. Such a "pure" linguistic matrix would not easily yield to subsequent arrivals in Madagascar, a challenge that should not have been too great since *other* seafaring Indonesians followed them. They should, however, have been already Africanized in part. Reaching Africa's coastal belt facing the Indian Ocean only *after* the Bantu, they left eventually and by different routes for Madagascar. This was not done to avoid physical and cultural contact with the Bantu, but to prevent complete loss of linguistic and cultural identity within the dominant population groups. It is then this second important migratory movement into Madagascar, consisting of several separate crossings all of which ended by the thirteenth century (as can be deduced from one old account),[77] that introduced the loans, along with cattle, millet, and domesticated fowl. Finally, given the Malagasy maritime capabilities and some hints in written sources,[78] one must not exclude the possibility

---

XXI (1933), 1–334. Linton was by no means the first one to think of this possibility, but where the earlier writers made no effort to go beyond simple statements of this belief, Linton attempted at least a formulation of a hypothesis. The Tanala are discussed in this work in the chapters on the Anteimoro and the Bara, Chapter 3 and 4.

[77] See Ibn al-Mujāwir above in footnote 9 as well as Buzurg Ibn Shariyar in the Appendix below. Indeed, it is virtually certain that Indonesian contacts with Eastern Africa were arrested in the thirteenth century; cf. Gervase Mathew, "The East African Coast until the coming of the Portuguese, 100–1498," in R. Oliver and G. Mathew (eds.), *History of East Africa* (1963), pp. 94–127.

[78] Cf. E. de Froberville, "Invasions madécasses," reproduced in the Appendix below; the *Journal* of Captain Thomlison in Henry Salt's *Voyage to Abyssinia* (1814), pp. 97–101, reproduced in the Appendix below; and T. Frappaz, *Voyages* (1939). The French of Mauritius and Bourbon created a myth that the outrigger-fleet raids of the Betsimisaraka and the Sakalava on the Comoros and east Africa were initiated by Count Benyowsky at Antongil. This myth seems to have originated with the governor of Ile de France (Mauritius), Viscount de Souillac—cf. De Souillac *to* Minister of Colonies, letter of January 3, 1786, *ANSOMCM*, Carton VIII, Dossier 4. It has been possible to locate a Dutch account of 1719 that clearly reveals the

that a few old Bantu loans can be attributed to contacts maintained with
Africa by the Malagasy.

Actually, all of these hypotheses are inadequate to cope with the subject of contacts between Madagascar and Africa. The missionary linguists
in Madagascar made useful compilations of more or less pure African
loans with slight reference to their ethnographic context or the quality
of each loan-word. What is even more serious, there is a uniform un-
familiarity with ways in which the borrowing range can be evaluated and
with what the mechanics of borrowing might reveal about past contacts
with Africa. For this reason alone, if no other, a most valuable tool with
which to probe the extent and nature of African influences in the Great
Island has hardly been used. The science of linguistics does tell us how
to use this tool in Madagascar. Without necessarily attempting to master
the more technical aspects of linguistics, no historian worthy of his craft
can afford to remain ignorant of some very basic notions about borrowing. To find them, one can do no better than turn to L. Bloomfield and
W. P. Lehmann and extract a simplified outline in respect to the subject
of borrowing.[79]

The most common type of borrowing, and one with which the present
work is mainly concerned, consists of vocabulary items. Syntactic patterns
are borrowed much less frequently and even when borrowed are difficult
to maintain. Morphological and phonological patterns, on the other hand,
are rarely if ever borrowed. Since word-loans normally tend to violate
the phonetic pattern of the recipient language, borrowed words must be
fairly numerous to preserve their original form. The older the loan, however, the more likely that the borrowing language will develop a new
phoneme and modify the original form. In time, one is thus apt to find
a set of pure loans followed by a set of semiforeign forms that retain
the "look" of original imports but are altered to fit better into the local
"sound." A third set would be composed of loan-translations. These can
be seen as ideographic renditions into the recipient language of objects
and ideas borrowed, a process facilitated whenever the loaning and
receiving languages represent technologically similar cultures. A loan-
translation thus uses the same or analogous description conveyed by the
pure loan form while doing away with it.[80] Moreover, the recipient lan-

---

presence of long-distance war outriggers on the western coast of Madagascar that
could not have been used locally; cf. R. K. Kent, "Madagascar and Africa: The
Sakalava . . . before 1700," *JAH*, IX/4 (1968), pp. 517–546.

[79] L. Bloomfield, *Language* (1966), pp. 444–475; and W. P. Lehmann, *Historical
Linguistics* (1962), pp. 211–231.

[80] Lehmann, *Historical Linguistics*, p. 213. This process is to be distinguished
from *loan-shifts* and *extensions*. Actually, according to Lehmann, what is called in
this work a loan-translation would be in effect a loan-shift. He gives as an example

guage will develop a large amount of local compounds, hyphenated or not, if vocabulary borrowing is considerable.

Bloomfield and Lehmann stress the important distinction between *ordinary* cultural borrowing (diffusion) and *intimate* borrowing (acculturation), one often spontaneous and the other induced. The former does not presuppose direct human migrations along with the objects and ideas borrowed. Apart from a kin category of dialectical borrowing, intimate borrowing occurs only when two different speech groups cohabit the same geographical area. If the two do not form a single political community and one is isolated from its linguistic matrix, it will tend to be flooded sooner or later by loans from the other. Depending upon specific cultural and political situations, its response may be to resist and prolong the linguistic struggle, move toward bilingualism, or lose the idiom while retaining a substratum. If the two do, however, form one political community, its rulers will normally loan out items from their own vocabulary to subjects. Hence, the general rule is that intimate borrowing proceeds from the "higher" to the "lower" language. This rule is subject to some major exceptions and modifications.

Whenever subjects remain in contact with speech-fellows in other contiguous areas and the alien political elite is numerically weak, the loan pace will be quite slow. This obtains also when rulers are drawn entirely from one of the two groups that is isolated from speech-fellows. Political change in such a situation, usually in favor of rulers from the nonisolated speech group, becomes linguistically fatal. Loans now travel fast through the double filter of rulers and subjects, both of whom represent the flooding group. A language may be lost at times through a radical ethnographic change, ensuing in the wake of conquest the exodus of original inhabitants and their replacement by settlers of a completely different origin. Linguistic *assimilation* will occur when rulers without further contact with the original home intermarry with local women. If a scribal tradition exists, some of their idiom will survive within written survivals themselves without affecting the pattern of living-speech change. This pattern will move from one-way borrowing to bilingualism and toward disuse and ultimate extinction of old "elite" language. This introduces the last major exception in intimate borrowing, called by the perversion

---

the English borrowing of Greek *oxygen* as contrasted with the German loan-shift *sauerstoff*. His loan-translation would reproduce "the morphemes" of loaning language. In reversing the role of loan-shift and loan-translation I place the stress on *meaning* rather than phonetics and hence the qualifier "translation" seems much better suited than "shift," itself more appropriate to sound than meaning. Thus, in Slavic languages *samolot/samolet* for airplane would represent to this writer a clear-cut case of loan-translation descriptive of the object borrowed whereas, for example, the Serbo-Croat use of *avion* for airplane would be a loan-shift (Latin, *avis, aviarium*).

of linguists "aberrant." Here, a change in political and/or cultural conditions will lead first to a deliberate arrest of one-way borrowing. We can add to Bloomfield and Lehmann by saying that politically or religiously induced linguistic taboos lend themselves admirably to this arrest, followed by reverse (aberrant) borrowing from "lower" to "upper" language, either by reversing its position (political change) or by leveling it (religious-cultural change).

If these general notions and major exceptions are constantly kept in mind, it is not difficult to perceive a number of possibilities for Madagascar. Because of the sustained anti-African bias, semiforeign loans like *lefona* and *tromba* (*laifuna, mTumba*) were not apt to be explored too much. When on a rare occasion they were examined, as done by E. Birkeli and G. Ferrand,[81] African etymons were questioned and denied on the grounds of bad linguistics. The loan-translations, as far as it has been possible to ascertain, were never even considered.[82] Circumstances in Malagasy are most favorable to loan-translations. It is a language with a huge amount of compounds, suggested by unusually long nouns, adjectives, adverbs, and toponymic, ethnic, clan, lineage, family, and personal names.[83] But, this favorable linguistic environment is offset by the elusive nature of loan-translations, especially when preliterate societies of Africa and Madagascar are compared.

We do not have sound reports of every major and intermediary African culture and even less of each ethnicity within them. Written accounts for Bantu-speaking and Swahili-speaking Africa since about 1500 are infinitely more numerous than any one specialist can humanly handle.[84]

[81] Birkeli, *Les Vazimba*, pp. 57–67; and G. Ferrand, "L'Origine africaine des Malgaches," *JA*, 10th series, XI/3 (1908), 353–500.

[82] Allusions to it, however, can be detected here and there; cf. W. E. Cousins, "Characteristics of the Malagasy Language," *AA*, V (1894), 233–240; S. E. Jorgensen, "The Introduction of Foreign Words into Malagasy," *AA*, II (1881), 25–39; and Jorgensen's "The Use of the Hyphen in Malagasy, and Other Cognate Questions," *AA*, II (1882), 156–163.

[83] J. Sibree, "Malagasy Place-names," *AA*, V (1896), 401–413; "Malagasy Place-names, Part II," *AA*, VI (1898), 152–160, with 3 appendices, 160–166; O. Chr. Dahl, "Quelques etymologies du domaine religieux," *BAM*, XXII (1939), 55–64; G. Mondain, "De l'Origine de certains mots malgaches," *BAM*, XV (1932), 15–26; R. Decary, "Les noms français dans la toponymie de Madagascar," *BAM*, XXVI (1944–1945), 27–42; Solange Bernard-Thierry, "Les Onomatopées en Malgache," *BAM*, XXXVIII (1960), 245–271; G. Ramamonjy, "Essai sur la toponymie malgache," *BAM*, XXXII (1954), 17–28. In noting this elasticity of Malagasy, Reverend Jorgensen even attempted to formulate some rules for introduction of modern technology into the island via deliberately induced loans; cf., "The Want of New Words in the Malagasy Language, and the Way of Supplying Them," *AA*, II (1884), 396–402.

[84] Cf. J. Gay, *Bibliographie des ouvrages relatifs à l'Afrique et à l'Arabie*, 1875; O. Boone, *Bibliographie ethnographique de l'Afrique subsaharienne*, 33 volumes (1925–1960); R. Jones (ed.), *Africa Bibliography Series* (International African Institute), 5 volumes to 1968; A. M. L. Robinson, *A Bibliography of African Bibli-*

The researcher will rarely be able to track down every scrap of existing information for an African culture and society. In addition, the kind of cultural and linguistic data needed to identify loan-translations in Madagascar will not be found very often. The item sought in a recent account of an African society, say between 1860 and 1960, may well have died out by the time this society obtained its ethnographer. More often than not, the ethnographer is likely to miss survivals that do not appear as readily on the surface.[85] Because few traditional African states outlasted the colonial rule (some fell because of precolonial political cataclysms), a loss of data is most probable in the fields of government and religion, which are of special interest to this work. Now and then, a loan-translation becomes apparent, if the comparative data alone are ethnographically strong. Much more frequently, a suspected loan-translation will be of no value since no real evidence can be found to support the suspicion. In the present state of knowledge, therefore, loan-translations can be used in relatively few instances.

It is still possible to illustrate rather well that the triple layer of pure, semiforeign, and translated loans does operate in Madagascar according to linguistic rules derived from the study of more fortunate Indo-European languages. And, the illustrations will show not only the obstacles facing a researcher, but also will reveal what he otherwise might never have suspected. The field of botany and botanical linguistics offers some advantages for the illustrations.

Although the Mozambique Channel is a natural barrier to diffusion of African plants into Madagascar by land route, botanists have had no trouble in determining that a substantial number of yams, esculent herbs, and edible fruits found in Madagascar are native to Africa. A dozen such plants, picked at random, show that they have only Malagasy names.[86] Because their origin is known, if not how and when these were introduced

---

ographies (1955), to mention a few. A number of professional journals (*JSA, Africa, Bulletin—Institut Français de l'Afrique Noire*) contain bibliographical sections in each issue or annual volume. It is almost a frustrating experience to cope with sources for Africa.

[85] On this, see J. M. Vansina, "History in the Field," in O. G. Jongmans and P. C. W. Gutkind (eds.) *Anthropologists in the Field* (1967), and "The Use of Ethnographic Data as Sources of History," unpublished typescript.

[86] Extracted from H. Perrier de la Bathie, "Les Plantes introduites à Madagascar," *RBAAT*, XI (1931), No. 121, 719–729; No. 122, 833–837; No. 123, 920–923; No. 124, 991–999; XII (1932), No. 125, 48–52; No. 126, 128–133; No. 127, 213–220; No. 128, 296–301; and No. 129, 372–383. For example, many of the hibiscus species from Africa (*Shirensis, Ternatus, Physaloides*) are incorporated into *voa*-compounds; *Alectra Senegalensis* is *volombato* or *holakazo*; *Coleus Rotundifolla* is *voamitso*; *Coniza Aegyptaica* is *volohina*; *Lablad Vulgaris* is *voamahy*; *Triumfetta Annua* is *besofina*; *Desmodium Mauritanium* is *tsilanondrivotra*; *Adansonia Digitata* is *vonoa, bontony* or *sefo*; *Eragrostis Abyssinica* is *tefy*; and *Zizyphus Spina Christi* is *lamotifotsy*.

into the island, loan-translations are immediately suggested by a process not difficult to explain. All species of yams, esculent herbs, and edible fruits, no matter of what origin, would be easily absorbed through the Malagasy genera prefixes *ovy/ovi* (yams and potatoes), *anana* (herbs), and *voa* (fruits), followed by descriptive local suffixes or infixes and suffixes. Lack of botanical precision in Malagasy and pre-existing local species within the same plant family thus create an acute propensity for absorption. It would be normal to expect that the only plant loans to retain pure or semiforeign forms are those introduced recently or else under special circumstances.

The general pattern is confirmed by its exceptions. The Malagasy term for cucumber is *voantangombazaha*.[87] *Voa* gives the idea of fruit. *Tango* is Swahili for cucumber. *Mbazaha/bazaha*, more commonly *vazaha*, is a term for foreigner by which the Malagasy designate all Europeans. The compound reveals that the *tango* infix is retained because the cucumber came over recently from east Africa, that it is a *voa* (fruit) but one consumed mainly by resident Europeans. *Tango* is thus a foreigner's fruit. Similarly, the green pea brought a short time ago from France is called in Malagasy *pitipoa*, clearly a phonetic rendition of *petit pois*. Several types of beans are known by their Malagasy name of *tsaramaso* (literally, good eye).[88] The term is very descriptive. It shows that the bean is shaped like an eye and that the plant product is excellent for consumption. Since it is not a fruit, herb, or yam, the bean type could be a loan-translation or an independent Malagasy description of a plant borrowed without any contact with the original loan-word.

Against a rather long list of African plants with Malagasy names, pure and semiforeign loan counterparts are quite rare. At times, simple lack of linguistic information is at fault. Plants were often identified "professionally," by their Latin names alone.[89] The cultural referent for plant names and geography was, after all, European and not Malagasy. A few more or less pure loans survive in association with some form of specialized knowledge, like pharmacopoeia, or with an item of material culture. Certain medicinal herbs of western Madagascar are known under a gen-

---

[87] Richardson, *Dictionary*, p. 767. See also Dahle, "Swaheli Element," 110; and W. E. Cousins, "Words Resembling Malagasy in the Swahili language," *AA*, I (1876), 2nd printing, 149–151. On the isolation of roots in Malagasy, see Cousins "Malagasy Roots: Their Classification and Mutual Relations," *AA*, III (1886), 157–166. Reverend Cousins has also written the best short introduction in any foreign language to Malagasy, *A Concise Introduction to the Study of the Malagasy Language as spoken in Imerina*, 3rd ed. (1894), pp. 1–118.

[88] Richardson, *Dictionary*, p. 685. For Malagasy plant names this dictionary is basic.

[89] R. Baron, "Compendium des plantes malgaches," *NRE*, VI (1900), 349–393, 533–574; "Genera of Madagascar Plants," *AA*, II (1881), 94–97, and II (1883), 96–102; "On the Flora of Madagascar," *AA*, IV (1891), 322–357.

eral name *babonga*. This is a Bantu ideograph for medical powder or paste (*bunga, unga*) obtained from herbs.[90] In *mokoty*, the loan *mukuti* is applied to leaves of an imported fan palm used widely in roofing.[91] The clearest case of pure loan survivals, that of *ampemba* and *morama* (millet), has been mentioned. With millet as a cultigen, it is also the most striking one, to be explained by special circumstances.

Infrequently, a plant indigenous to Africa will have in one or more local dialects two equivalents, Malagasy and African. The descriptive *tsaramaso* for the African *phaseolus vulgaris* appears only in the Merina dialect. Here there is a curious coincidence in the root *maso* (eye, eyes), which is found in a number of Bantu languages and with the same meaning.[92] Elsewhere in Madagascar, the kin African *phaseolus calcaratus* is not described through the eye-bean analogy but bears the name *anatsamba*.[93] This may or may not be a semiforeign loan. *Ana* (extended *anaka*) is Malagasy for children of or issue of, while *ts/s* is merely a bridge between prefix and place-name *Amba*. As a plant "from Amba," the place-name is of no help. One can only say that the *calcaratus* is from Africa but, again, there is a curious linguistic coincidence. In many Bantu languages *ana* (with various extensions) duplicates exactly the Malagasy meaning.[94] Finally, another bean variety is the *voanemba*, combining Malagasy *voa* with the Bantu *émba* or bean.[95]

The last and most interesting category concerns plants that are not indigenous to Africa but carry African loans in Malagasy. *Mabiba/abiba* is a Swahili loan for cashew apple, native to tropical America and used mainly for nonpermanent tattooing in Madagascar.[96] The southeast Asian *zizyphus jujuba*, prickly shrub with edible fruit, is called in Malagasy

---

[90] Sacleux, *Swahili-français*, Vol. I (1939), p. 119, and Vol. II (1941), p. 955.

[91] Richardson, *Dictionary*, p. 441; Sacleux, *Swahili-français*, Vol. I (1939), p. 456, under *kuti, ma-kuti*, "*palme, feuille de palmier . . . palme tressée . . . pour couverture . . . ou pour entourage.*"

[92] Torrend, *Bantu Languages*, p. 88 (list under paragraph 411), as *meso* (always in plural) among fifteen groups and as *maso* (always in plural) among the Swahili, Pokomo, Nika, Senna, and Kilimane.

[93] Perrier de la Bathie, "Plantes," XI/121 (1931), 722.

[94] Torrend, *Bantu Languages*, p. 67 (list under para. 322), with *mu/ba* (sing.+ pl.) prefixes, as *ana* alone in Angola, lower Congo, Nywema, and Mozambique. In the Bantu language *ana* is also used to make diminutives with (little, small). The cases of both *maso* and *ana* are extremely interesting linguistically. If coincidence is ruled out, and if additional words of such basic quality crop up as well, it would not be too far fetched to claim that there must once have been an Afro-Malagasy or Afro-Indonesian language.

[95] Richardson, *Dictionary*, p. 766; and Dahle, "Swaheli Element," 113, *nyemba* at Sofala, Tette, and Sena; *niemba* in Maravi.

[96] Richardson, *Dictionary*, pp. 1, 405, from Swahili *bibo, mabibo*; also the cashew nut itself in Madagascar, *koroso*, corresponds to Swahili *korosho*. Cf. Sacleux, *Swahili-français*, Vol. I (1939), pp. 106, 348, 441.

moconazo, from Swahili *kunazi*.[97] The garlic, of Mediterranean origin, carries in Malagasy the loan *tongolo* (*túngúlú*).[98] Manioc, from Brazil, is found in Madagascar in three loan forms—*mahogo/muhogo, manga,* and *bala*, the last two often followed by Malagasy *hazo*, or tree. *Mahogo* is a Swahili loan, strictly limited to northwestern Madagascar.[99] *Manga* is a common term for manioc in a number of southeast-central Bantu languages.[100] It is prevalent as a loan in western and central Madagascar. *Bala* is found in central Africa, most obviously in the Kongo language for manioc.[101] In Madagascar, *bala* (or *balahazo*) prevails in the south-central part of the island.

All of these illustrations lead to several conclusions. Despite the natural sea barrier, a fairly large quantity of plants native to Africa crossed over to Madagascar. Some were introduced by Swahili traders on the northwestern coast and/or by resident Europeans seeking to "improve" their new colony. The *tango*, the *mabiba*, and the *mahogo* remain restricted to a small area in northwestern Madagascar, or else—as in the case of *tango*—the demand for a plant is mainly European. The diffusion of some plants is thus either recent or independent of human migrations. Other plants are of greater antiquity. Although botany does not give us the chronology, all of the African plants, and particularly certain cultigens, cannot be attributed to nonintimate borrowing. Also, the fact that loan-translations outnumber all other loans indicates, by linguistic rules, rather heavy borrowing.

As a cultigen, millet provides supporting evidence for nondiffusion. Its antiquity in Madagascar is not great. It came long after the goats, sheep, cattle, and domesticated fowl, all of them having Bantu loans in Malagasy.[102] But, millet was not introduced recently either. European

[97] Perrier de la Bathie, "Plantes," XII/128 (1932), 298–299; and Sacleux, *Swahili-français*, Vol. I (1939), 450.

[98] Perrier de la Bathie, "Plantes," VI/122 (1931), 836, gives *tongolo* for *Allium Satiuum* (garlic) while Richardson gives the same term for *Allium Cepa* (onion)— cf. his *Dictionary*, p. 662 for Swahili equivalent of *kitunguu*. Sacleux, *Swahili-français*, Vol. I (1939), p. 416, gives onion for *ki-Túnguu*.

[99] Richardson, *Dictionary*, pp. 274, 441, 406; Webber, *Dictionnaire*, p. 447. Hoffmann, *Vocabulaire*, p. 139, lists it for both Sakalava and Tsimihety (northwest) and Sacleux, *Swahili-français*, Vol. II (1941), p. 623, places it under *muHogo*.

[100] Sacleux, *Swahili-français*, Vol. II (1941), p. 501; *manga* being the exact equivalent for manioc in *ki-Bonde, ki-Nyika, ki-Sambara* and *ki-Ziga* idioms.

[101] W. H. Bentley, *Dictionary and Grammar of the Kongo Language* (1887), p. 32, field manioc=*bale*.

[102] Sheep in Malagasy is *ondry* and goat *osy*; Richardson, *Dictionary*, p. 468, gives the Swahili equivalent of goat as *mbuzi* and of sheep as *kondoo* (p. 463). In Deschamps, *Madagascar*, the two are reversed incorrectly (p. 36, chèvre=*osi*; mouton=*ondri*). Phonetically, Malagasy *osy* is *uzi* and *ondry* is *undrou*. See also Ch. Ehert, "Sheep and Central Sudanic Peoples in Southern Africa," *JAH*, IX/2 (1968), 213–221. The spread of form *-(k)ondri* from central Sudanic *ndri* is much

sources report millet in Madagascar already in the sixteenth century.[103] By the 1650s, they also reveal that millet with pure loan *ampemba* had reached eastern Madagascar from the western side.[104] Since the dialectical divergence in Malagasy, in some cases very considerable, must antedate the advent of millet in Madagascar, the local spread of pure loan *ampemba* along with the cultigen cannot be disconnected from internal human carriers familiar with the loan, the cultigen, and the cultivation techniques.

Another important cultigen—manioc—strengthens the millet evidence with a fairly precise chronology. *Manhiot utilissima* did not reach the Old World until the Portuguese took it out of Brazil sometime in the first half of the sixteenth century. Insofar as Africa is concerned, the Portuguese diffused it very unevenly. Manioc was not brought to the Kongo Kingdom much before 1600.[105] In this state the Portuguese did not need to augment the tropical food crops in order to survive. Their outposts along the Mozambique and east African littoral, on the other hand, had to be more or less self-dependent. No precise dates have been established, but some of the Portuguese enclaves in southeast Africa must have gotten manioc before 1550.

The earliest date for manioc in Madagascar is 1557, reported as *mungo* on its western littoral.[106] Half a century later, a firsthand account confirmed that manioc was cultivated in the same general area.[107] The retention in Malagasy of *manga* and *bala* loans as well as the spread of the cultigen repeat the millet pattern, already in progress at the time when manioc reached Madagascar. Like millet, manioc had to come from Africa with sufficient numbers of Africans capable of introducing the cultigen and sustaining it through the cultivation technique as well as the cooking one since unprepared bitter manioc is a poison. The *manga* and *bala* sequence in Madagascar attest that Bantu-speaking Africans were still arriving in Madagascar after 1550 but not after the 1620s when we enter into the "historical" period through written accounts that show that no important human migration has taken place since. It is certain that by the turn of the seventeenth century the Malagasy were

---

greater in Africa (western Tanzania, eastern shore of Lake Victoria, southeastern Kenya). The Malagasy *ondri* is very close to the pure cognate and the * *(k)ondri* form, which would show that the Malagasy might have gotten the sheep very shortly after they spread to eastern Africa.

[103] In 1595, the Dutch under de Houtman noted millet on the northeastern coast but in small quantities; see *COACM*, Vol. I (1903), p. 235 (small print).

[104] Flacourt, *Histoire*, *COACM*, Vol. VIII (1913), p. 170, under *ampembe*. He also reported *voanemba* as *voanghenbe*.

[105] J. M. Vansina, *Kingdoms of the Savanna* (1966), p. 21.

[106] *COACM*, Vol. I (1903), p. 101.

[107] L. Mariano, *Relation . . . 1613–1614*, in *COACM*, Vol. II (1904), p. 12, along with millet and beans.

formed as a people. By 1714, as an unpublished manuscript reveals, the *tongolo* (garlic) had reached the central highlands of Madagascar.[108] That *manga* (manioc) came to central highlands long before the 1700s as well has been shown in an article written in 1969.[109]

The insignificant cashew apple also leads to a whole chain of possibilities and overlaps that become rather striking when put together. First, the "apple" alerts one to look for some linguistic confirmation that tattooing itself might bear a stronger African imprint than suggested by the limited literature. Indeed, the general Malagasy term for tattooing by scarification is *tomboka* (*tumbuka*), from Swahili *tumbua* (root *tumbo*), to pierce.[110] Like many old customs, tattooing is receding in Madagascar, the oldest, or core, areas being those where it is still intact as a going practice. If one looks for these core areas on a distribution map, they occur in Menabé, the central Sakalava land of western Madagascar, and among the south-central Bara people.[111] The two core areas for tattooing correspond to those for manioc, one with *manga* loan (Sakalava) and the other with the *bala* one (Bara). At the same time, the Sakalava and Bara *alone* in Madagascar retain a very specific form of headdress noticed by a number of European travelers.[112] In origin, this headdress both for men and women is beyond doubt African.[113]

---

[108] Parat *to* Pontchartrain, *Letter*, September 19, 1714, ms., pp. 1–5, copy in *BGT*. Compare with Swahili *kitunguu* (onion in general). As garlic, Malagasy *tongolo* (phonetics, *tungulu*) is sometimes followed by qualifier *gasy* (*tongolo gasy*).

[109] R. K. Kent, "Note sur l'introduction et propagation du manioc à Madagascar," *Terre Malgache-Tany Malagasy* (January 1969), 177–183.

[110] Sacleux, *Swahili-Français*, Vol. II (1941), p. 911.

[111] See the distribution map in the annex to J.-C. Hébert, "Tatouages sakalava," *CM*, I/1 (1964). The annex was printed at the end of the volume, *viz.*, "l-Regression des zones de tatouages."

[112] See Chapter 4 (the Bara) for the *billes-de-billiard* style of hair dress (equidistant clumps of hair rolled in with mixture of lard and ochre). It was also worn by some Tanala, Mahafaly, and southern Sakalava clans and was noted among the Antanosy (see footnotes 153–156, Chapter 4).

[113] "A Chinese traveler who had apparently visited Mogadishu in 1417–1419 writes of the townspeople there that 'the men wear their hair in rolls which hang down all round' . . . and that the women 'apply a yellow varnish to their shaven crowns and hang several strings of disks from their ears,'" quoted by Mathew, "East African Coast," in Oliver and Mathew, *History*, p. 117. The source is Fei-Hsin, an officer of Cheng Ho, an admiral of Chinese commercial fleets that went to east Africa in 1417–1419 and 1421–1422. There is no doubt that this coiffure began to disappear in Madagascar in the precolonial period. An instance is given by H. Douliot, *Journal*, (1895), p. 27: "*Je reconnais divers hommes et femmes masikoro, dont l'élégance consiste à bourrer de suif leur chevelure qu'elles arrangent en une vingtaine de grosses boucles blanches. Rasoatra, la reine de Mahabo, a cependant interdit cette coiffure dans sa province, mais la coquetterie fait enfreindre la loi et j'ai vu encore quelques têtes ensuifées . . . mais elles sont rares.*"

Without any help from written history, the linguistic rules for cultural borrowing, botanical linguistics, and overlaps in socioethnographic contexts argue most powerfully that Madagascar *must* have had considerable human colonies from Africa on its soil. Some of them should still have been present as such when Europe began to have contacts with Madagascar. Therefore, it is logical to expect to find some written document of sufficient quality to reveal something about one or more African colonies in the island adduced from other types of data.

Admittedly, there is an abnormal paucity of written sources for Madagascar in the sixteenth century, when Portugal was the dominant maritime power in the western Indian Ocean.[114] But, "paucity" is a relative term, and a number of firsthand accounts of Madagascar have been incorporated into the publications of major Portuguese chroniclers. From unknown scribes belonging to the first Portuguese fleet to visit the waters of northwestern Madagascar, in 1506–1507, two distinct foreign colonies enter into the subsequent chronicles.

The Portuguese found important Arab trading towns at the mouth of the Mahajamba River and at Boina Bay, called Lulungane and Mazelagem. As in eastern and southeastern Africa, these Arab towns were located on islets while their "plantations" stood on the mainland. Lulungane, on the islet of Nosi Manja, reminded the Portuguese of Mozambique. The Arabs, or Moors, as the Portuguese called them, were chiefly from Mombasa and Malindi. In Lulungane, there were huge quantities of cloth, silver, and gold "for it was mainly from this port that dhows from Melindi and Mombas brought merchandise from Africa and Arabia to exchange for rice, of which there was so much that even twenty ships could not have taken all of it away." Slaves, beeswax, and cattle were also exported. Lulungane's Muslim population was seen as "more civilized and richer" than any other on this coast, the two aspects being obviously interrelated in the Portuguese mind. "Their mosque and most of the houses were of hard stone and limestone, with terraces like those of Kiloa and Mombas." The Moors, having no army, were promptly massacred and dispersed.[115]

The other type of colony was reported in a large bay, "named Cada or Sada" (Anorontsanga Bay at 13° 54′ 55″). Here, the Portuguese found an extremely dense population, "composed mainly of Cafres." Admiral Tristan da Cunha and his men were, however, in no position to deal with

---

[114] This is due in part to the need to re-examine the Goan archives, secular as well as of the Order of Jesus (now returned to Rome), and the state archives of Torre do Tombo in Portugal.

[115] See the accounts of Portuguese chroniclers Correa, Albuquerque, Barros, and Castanheda in *COACM*, Vol. I (1903), pp. 15, 20–22, 26–31, 36–37. They give much the same report for 1506–1507.

Sada as they did with Lulungane since "about 2000 Cafres armed with shields, spears, bows, and arrows" grouped on the beach. Who were these Africans, or Cafres? They were, according to the Portuguese, *former* "slaves of the towns of Melindi, Mombaz, and Mogdicho" who had taken refuge in Madagascar.[116]

This is the first mention in print of Africans living as a group in Madagascar. The Portuguese chronicles reveal that the slave traffic was going *from* Madagascar *to* Africa through Swahili intermediaries. Being on the rim of an Arab commercial empire, shortly to disintegrate because of European overseas expansion, Madagascar did not import slaves from Africa. There was no local demand for them in the sixteenth century either for economic or political reasons. Instead, the island was a sanctuary for men fleeing from bondage in Swahili urban centers of Africa. By about 1500, and probably much earlier, cattle was abundant in Madagascar to the extent that it constituted a fairly important export. Moreover, the highly developed Malagasy rice production had turned Madagascar into a rice granary for commercial towns of eastern Africa. The demand for slave labor from Madagascar was most probably connected with Swahili attempts to grow rice at home rather than depend on a distant outpost. Somewhat later, several rice wars on the Swahili coast attest that these attempts were partly successful.[117]

Thus, the earliest of written sources, which could easily have been examined for their *actual* content, provide a total negation of the subsequent and rather elaborate myth that no African colony existed in Madagascar as such, that Africans were always brought as individual slaves into the island, and that as slaves *from* Africa they remained slaves *in* Madagascar. It was not difficult to graft on to this related "fact of history" the idea that slaves cannot influence the master culture or create political entities of their own. It did not matter, of course, that such nonsense is refuted by the historical record in other lands and most notably in Brazil, where slaves from Africa altered significantly both the language and culture of European masters[118] and even created at least one important state as early as the seventeenth century.[119]

Almost eleven decades lapse before another written account mentions

[116] Fernan d'Albuquerque, *Commentários do Grande Alfonso d'Albuquerque* (1557), in *COACM*, Vol. I (1903), p. 22.

[117] Mainly in the first half of the eighteenth century between Pate and Mombasa over rice from the Pemba Island.

[118] R. Mendonça, *A Influencia Africana no Portugues do Brasil* (1935); J. H. Rodrigues, "The Influence of Africa on Brasil and of Brasil on Africa," *JAH*, III/1 (1962), 49–67; and G. Freyre, *The Masters and the Slaves: A Study in the Development of Brazilian Civilization* (1956).

[119] R. K. Kent, "Palmares: An African State in Brazil," *JAH*, VI/2 (1965), 161–175.

Africans in western Madagascar. The new information is, however, far more conclusive and the spread of African colonies more extensive. It comes down as a series of reports and letters from two men with firsthand experience on both sides of the Mozambique Channel. Father Luis Mariano, a Jesuit priest attached to Goa and transferred to Mozambique, visited western Madagascar in 1614 for several weeks and returned to spend a full year there, 1616–1617, along with his companion, Father Antonio d'Azevedo.[120]

During his first visit, Mariano reported that the western littoral of Madagascar:[121]

> . . . between Mazelagem and Sadia, some 130 leagues in length . . . spoke a language analogous to those of the Cafres . . . of Mozambique and of Melindi, while the inhabitants resemble in pigment and in culture the Negroes of Africa from whom they apparently derive. But, in the immediate hinterland of this coast as well as in the interior and other coastal sections, only the Buki language is spoken, one quite special to local inhabitants, completely different from the African tongues and very similar to Malay.

This coastal belt between the town of Sadia in the Manambolo delta (18° 55′–19° 1′) and Boina Bay, where the old Mazelagem stood, spans a distance of about three hundred miles. According to Mariano, the belt itself was called Bambala Coast.[122] The linguistic situation is clearly stated, *Buki* being the synonym of Malagasy, from Swahili *Wa-Bukue* for Madagascar, unknown by that name until Europe adopted it.[123]

After two years in Mozambique (1614–1616), Mariano and d'Azevedo could report at some length about their life and progress in western Madagascar and particularly in Sadia, during 1616–1617. Mariano himself knew the Buki language, while d'Azevedo learned the Bambala idiom and is known to have worked on a local vocabulary that has never been found.[124] D'Azevedo sent an occasional report to Goa, but it was Mariano who was the principal correspondent. Confirming his earlier statement, Mariano could now observe at firsthand that the idiom of Bambala Coast,

[120] For the exact itinerary and lengths of stay, see Sakalava Chapter 5 below, text and footnote 82.

[121] Mariano, *Relation, COACM*, Vol. II (1904), pp. 21–22.

[122] Mariano, *Letter*, August 24, 1619, in *COACM*, Vol. II (1904), p. 315.

[123] The etymon of Madagascar has never been convincingly explained. Deschamps, *Madagascar*, p. 59, attributes this to a would-be confusion of Mogadishu, Somalia, with the Great Island. This idea was first advanced by Thevet in 1575 but under very different circumstances that have little to do with Marco Polo, see Chapter 5 below, text and notes 115–116. There is also a Malagarasy River in east-central Africa.

[124] Mariano, *Letter*, May 24, 1617, in *COACM*, Vol. II (1904), p. 241; and *Letter*, October 22, 1616, in *COACM*, Vol. II (1904), p. 225.

"although it belongs to the family of Melindi-coast Cafres, is noticeably distinct and much richer [in vocabulary]."[125] But, having left the task to d'Azevedo, Mariano had nothing to say about the Bambala Coast vocabulary itself. A few words, nonetheless, are found in his texts.

Most of the toponymic names, dealing mainly with rivers, bear no resemblance to anything found in Malagasy.[126] Four of them are prefixed by *muto-*, the term for river in a number of Bantu languages, most obviously in Shambala.[127] Being concerned mainly with the domain of religion, Mariano transcribed two local terms for priest that also do not resemble the island-wide *ombiasa* (*ūmbiaš*). They are *maganga* from common Bantu *ma-ganga* and *cacis* (*kasis*) from Swahili *ukasisi*.[128] The "vital force" (in person or in act) appears as *kalakani* or *ukali* in Swahili.[129] The name of the person designated to be successor to the chief in Sadia is given as *Luquexa*, an exact phonetic equivalent of *Lukwesa*, the royal name of the Kazembe or the rulers of the ubiquitous central-African Lunda.[130] In Bambala itself, *ba-* is a Bantu locative prefix while *mbala* (Ambala, Bambala) reflects the ethnic name of peoples inhabiting the valleys of Kwango, Kasai, and middle Zambezi. Mariano also lists three ethnic names of groups found in the vicinity of Sadia— Ajungones, Quisaju, and Suculambas—stating that they are non-Buki, as is indeed apparent.[131]

With Mariano, historical evidence no longer shows an isolated and relatively small enclave of former slaves from Africa in Madagascar. Rather, some three hundred miles of its western coast are inhabited by Africans forming their own chiefdoms and having no slave role among

[125] Mariano, *Letter*, August 20, 1617, in *COACM*, Vol. II (1904), p. 256, in small print.

[126] They are: *Muto-Moculo, Muto-Moqunto, Muto-Ambuzi, Muto-Açambe, Iqualane, Quarecle, Camalila, Quivinjane, Satengoa, Sarangazo, Balue, Mani, Saume, Manaputa, Masimanga, Isango, Kasane.*

[127] Torrend, *Bantu Languages*, p. 78, word list for river under para. 370. Also *mto* (Swahili, *Bondei*).

[128] Mariano, *Letters*, October 21, and October 22, 1616, in *COACM*, Vol. II (1904), pp. 219, 230 and 254 (*Letter* of August 20, 1617). Cf. Sacleux, *Swahili-Français*, Vol. I (1939), p. 332 (ultimately from Arabic *quasis*), and Vol. II (1941), pp. 549, 678, and 942; Torrend, *Bantu Languages*, found the term *cacices* in Karanga oral traditions, pp. 286–288. *Nganga* is widespread in Bantu-speaking Africa.

[129] Mariano, *Letter*, August 20, 1617, *COACM*, Vol. II (1904), p. 258; and Sacleux, *Swahili-français*, Vol. II, pp. 941–942 (*ardeur, force, énergie*).

[130] Mariano, *Letter*, October 21, 1616, *COACM*, Vol. II (1904), p. 217 (cited many times elsewhere in his letters); A. C. P. Gamitto, *King Kazembe* (1831–1832), trans. by I. Cunnison, Vol. II (1960), pp. 13, 31, 48, 83, 86, 95, 103, 109, 115, 117, and 130 (Kazembe Lukwesa); and Vansina, *Kingdoms*, pp. 170–172, 228–232.

[131] Mariano, *Letter*, October 21, 1616, *COACM*, Vol. II (1904), pp. 218–221; and *Letter*, August 20, 1617, *COACM*, Vol. II (1904), p. 258 (Quisaju).

the Malagasy. The population of Sadia at its peak is given at about 10,000 and Mariano estimates that the total population of Bambala coast is substantial.[132] Mariano also reveals at first hand that just north of the Bambala Coast, at Boina and farther on, the old and independent Swahili outposts have been replaced. There are now Buki rulers served by Swahili traders and scribes. Many of the Buki subjects and most of the Buki rulers appear to have espoused Islam. A number of small but relatively powerful river chiefdoms have developed mainly through increased slave trade, and the African colony reported by the Portuguese in 1506 has completely disappeared.[133] There are contacts between Bambala groups and Boina Bay, and their "paganism" is beginning to be modified by "Muslim" influences.[134] At the same time, Mariano held that the peoples of Bambala Coast must have influenced some of the Buki as well.[135] There is no doubt that the Buki-Bambala contact existed as can be deduced from the richer vocabulary in Bambala plus the fact that Mariano cites the term *afo* as one which designated the ancestral spirit in Sadia.[136] *Afo* is Malagasy for fire, but the association of eternal fire with an ancestral spirit, especially for rulers, is distinctly Bantu and not Malagasy.[137]

[132] Mariano, *Relation, COACM*, Vol. II (1904), p. 20.

[133] Mariano, *Relation, COACM*, Vol. II (1904), p. 74; Father João Gomes, *Letter* (1620), in *COACM*, Vol. II (1904), p. 329; and R. K. Kent, "Sakalava," *JAH*, IX/4 (1968), 526.

[134] Mariano, *Relation, COACM*, Vol. II (1904), p. 65; and his *Letter*, October 22, 1616, *COACM*, Vol. II (1904), pp. 226 and 228.

[135] Mariano, *Letter*, May 24, 1617, *COACM*, Vol. II (1904), p. 235.

[136] Mariano, *Letter*, October 22, 1616, *COACM*, Vol. II (1904), pp. 228–229. This translation of *afo* is given by Grandidier in brackets. In terms of contextual meaning in original sentence ("assumes the role of *afo* and, taking his name . . ."), the translation appears to be correct. Nonetheless, Grandidier developed a standard habit of altering all terms as given in primary texts to conform to some accepted Malagasy ones. And, as in hundreds of other such transliterations by Grandidier, both obvious and suspected word loans were simply eliminated.

[137] Cf. Baumann and Westermann, *Les Peuples*, p. 143 and *passim*. *Afo* as word for fire in Malagasy does not displace yet another in Malagasy coastal dialects, namely *moto* for tinder and *motro* for fire, cf. Richardson, *Dictionary*, 445, from Swahili *moto*; cf. Sacleux, *Swahili-français*, Vol. II, pp. 581–582. Dahle, in his analysis of the "Swaheli Element," 107, explained *moto* as "a genuine African word occurring in many east African languages of the Bantu family . . . [but] here [in Madagascar] it occurs only on the coast; in the interior the Malayan *afo* . . . is the only word in use. When the Malayan invaders came, they probably took possession of *omby* (cattle), *amboa* (dog), and *akoho* (fowl) . . . of the African aborigines, and the *names* with *things*; but the fire was not to be taken captive in this way, and therefore it kept its Malayan name, leaving the African name to the African aborigines, whom they drove toward the coasts, where the word is still in use." Interesting as this explanation might be, in reality, the word *afo* has two principal meanings, fire and calamity. In this second meaning, it parallels the Swahili *afa* (danger, peril,

The limited linguistic evidence reveals that the Bambala Coast contained Bantu-speaking Africans with both east-African and Swahili connections as well as with some central African ties. A single-origin argument advanced by Mariano cannot, therefore, be accepted. Equally, the hypothesis of the peopling of Madagascar by "pure" Indonesians first and partly "Africanized" Indonesians next is incomplete without the "pure" African contingents. Just how and why these went into the Great Island or when remains obscure. Neither the Lunda nor Swahili-influenced terms would support the claim that Bambala was inhabited by any ancient migrants. The Lunda expansion into central and southeast-central Africa does not seem to antedate the sixteenth century by the best estimates.[138] The Swahili language and culture could not have been well developed much before the 1300s.[139] On the other hand, the Bambala colonies must have taken shape at least a generation before Mariano's visit, with a terminal date of ±1575. Perhaps a part of the explanation can be traced to A. Thévet and J. Megiser, who relate the following rather curious story. Sometime at ±1300, several merchants from Sofala landed by chance on the west coast of Madagascar and found it depopulated after a huge flood. At their urging, the "kings of Çefala and Mozambique ordered their ships to transport to the island three or four thousand persons so that it could be repeopled. The captain of this fleet was a pagan, born at Çefala and named Albergra."[140]

It is historically fortunate that Father Mariano came to live at Sadia in 1617 instead of 1717. Within a relatively short time after his stay at Sadia, the Maroserana would penetrate the area of Menabé, moving

---

calamity); cf. Sacleux, *Swahili-français*, Vol. I (1939), p. 42. On the other hand, Malagasy *afana* stands for a variety of rituals which are to provide "freedom from some witchcraft or charm," (Richardson, *Dictionary*, pp. 6–7, Abinal and Malzac, *Dictionnaire*, p. 6), sense which applies with precision to the possessed medium in the Sakalava *tromba*. In Malagasy, neither *afo* nor *afana* can be taken to mean ancestor or ancestral divinity, spirit. In this sense, one must go to the west African *afà*, "*la plus haute des divinités intermédiaires (chez les peuple Mina)*. . . . *Le culte d'Afà a été importé de la ville d'Ife*," in Roberto Pazzi, "Culte de mort chez les peuple mina," *Cahiers des Religions Africaines*, II/4 (1968), 257 and note 23.

[138] Cf. J. M. Vansina, "The Foundation of the Kingdom of Kasanje," *JAH*, IV/3 (1963), 355–374; and D. Birmingham, "The Date and Significance of the Imbangala Invasion of Angola," *JAH*, VI/2 (1965), 143–152, with a rejoinder by J. M. Vansina, "More on the Invasions of Kongo and Angola by the Jaga and the Lunda," *JAH*, VII/3 (1966), 421–429.

[139] See N. Chittick, "The 'Shirazi' Colonization of East Africa," *JAH*, VI/3 (1965), 275–294; C. H. Stigand, *The Land of Zinj* (1966, reprint of 1913 ed.), pp. 1–131; and Mathew, "East African Coast," in Oliver and Mathew, *History*, pp. 94–127; and G. S. P. Freeman-Grenville, *The Medieval History of the Coast of Tanganyika* (1962).

[140] In *COACM*, Vol. I (1903), pp. 120–126 and 460–462. Thévet's description is dated 1575, Megiser's 1609. See Sakalava Chapter for more extensive mention.

north from the southwest. What is even more telling, by 1717, there was hardly any trace left of Bambala's Bantu-speaking populations.[141] In this same area, not even a linguistic substratum pointing to Africa was noticed until early in this century, when Emil Birkeli began to investigate the living speech of the Vazimba and their kin Mikeha and Behosy, the sole ethnic "relics" still found among very diverse groups bearing the political name of Sakalava.

When well-documented, cohesive, and substantial African colonies in a 300-mile coastal belt could disappear within a mere century, it is easy to perceive that many cultural Africanisms elsewhere in the vast island would go out of style by the 1800s, when ethnographic descriptions begin to accumulate. To be of use, comparative ethnographic data must be of fairly high quality, as already defined. The shortcomings of Murdock and Deschamps would force almost any subsequent researcher into a far less imprecise endeavor. Prevailing distrust of many anthropologists for a deliberate chasing of traits and the historian's own predilection for sound data on which to base and make comparisons also serve to bridle an enthusiasm that could "excavate" African survivals even when these cannot be substantiated. All of these restrictions are necessary, and they narrow the range considerably by demanding a high degree of probability for every Africanism in Madagascar.

The hope of finding evidence in the earlier written sources remains, but it, too, is dimmed by the fact that these are neither abundant nor usually oriented toward an ethnographic description that one would be apt to expect from a trained twentieth-century anthropologist. For a few sections of the endless Malagasy coast, there is wealth of detail. This is particularly true of the southeast, a number of sources having come down through the French settlement at Fort-Dauphin (1643–1674).[142] These coastal sources sometimes provide even a glimpse into the Malagasy interior, but the number of Europeans known to have penetrated inland prior to the 1770s can be counted on the fingers of one hand. The Malagasy oral traditions are themselves of uneven historical and ethno-

---

[141] Drury, for example, visited Menabé in this period, *ca.* 1717, and found only that some Vazimba were bilingual; see also Kent, "Sakalava."

[142] *ANSOMCM*, Carton I, Pieces 1–29 (1642–1674; E. de Flacourt, *Dictionnaire de la Langue de Madagascar* (1658), in *COACM*, Vol. VII (1910), pp. 206–394, *Histoire*, *COACM*, Vol. VIII (1913), and *Relation de ce qui s'est passé en Ile de Madagascar depuis l'année 1642 jusqu'en 1660* (Paris, 1661), reprinted in 1920 as first section of Vol. IX of *COACM*; Du Bois, *Voyages* (1674); Carpeau du Saussay, *Voyage de Madagascar* (1722); Souchu de Rennefort, *Relation du premier voyage de la compagnie des Indes Orientales en l'isle de Madagascar ou Dauphine* (1668) and *Histoire des Indes Orientales* (1668); F. Martin, *Memoires*, 1665–1668, in *COACM*, Vol. IX (1920), pp. 429–633; and F. Cauche, *Relations*, 1651, in *COACM*, Vol. VII (1910), pp. 24–191. These are among the principal sources.

graphic quality. Finally, it is necessary to introduce at least one other aspect to be taken into account, namely the *linguistic* taboo (Malagasy, *fady*).[143] In one form or another, this *fady* was common to many old Malagasy societies. It has a complex and important bearing on the subject of external as well as internal borrowing. The few examples that follow as simple illustrations are supplemented in the Appendices.

The Malagasy linguistic *fady* could affect a single-word change or encompass a local vocabulary segment. For example, in the nineteenth century, a minor Sakalava chief named *Jiro* passed away and the term *jiro* (candle, light) was replaced with *fanaovanimazava*, or that which gives forth clarity.[144] This is the most common type of single-word *fady* —namely, the religious one affecting elders, chiefs, and kings whose names were tabooed upon death. It was also the most rigidly observed one since a violation of such a *fady* involved severe punishment and often the death penalty itself.

In western and southern Madagascar, a posthumous appellation (*fitahina*) for deceased monarchs would be immediately coined as a praise name, following a standard formula. Its stationary components were the prefix *andria*, meaning lord in the broadest sense, and the suffix *arivo*, or thousand, thousands in Malagasy. To these would be added then a key infix that normally depicted some noteworthy personal feature or the way in which the departed was appreciated by his subjects. Thus the *fitahina* (posthumous praise name) of Sakalava monarchs would come out as *Andriamandresiarivo* or *Andriamananiarivo*, Lord who conquered thousands and Lord lamented by thousands. At times, a living ruler could change his own name, as in the instance of *Andriamamba*, who became *Andriavoay*—the *mamba* and *voay* being synonyms for crocodile. Or, he could decide to retain his name but taboo the qualifier. A ruler named *Ramboa* (Noble Dog), for example, decided that *amboa* (dog) must be changed to *alika* (dog) or yet *fandroaka* (the chaser) and *famovo* (the barker).[145] A female Sakalava ruler named *Taosy* banned from the local vocabulary several words that appear to have merely resembled her name: *antetsi* (old) became *matoe* (ripe); *mataoatsi* (frightened) became *matahore* (afraid); *vosi* (lop off) became *manapaka* (cut); and *nosi* (isle, islet) became *vario* (rice area), which implies surrounded by water.[146] And, as the French explorer L. Catat

---

[143] As an idea, *fady* applies to what must never be done, what can be done under special circumstances, what should not be done, and what can be done without general approval. Penalties usually revealed the appropriate category.

[144] P. Lapeyre, *Dialectes hova et sakalava: essai d'etude comparée* (1891), p. 3. The term *jiro* applied in parts of western and southern Madagascar to a pole (without bark on top) used in circumcision ceremonies.

[145] A. Van Gennep, *Tabou et totémisme à Madagascar* (1904), p. 105.

[146] *Ibid.*, p. 111.

lamented while trying to map Madagascar, many Malagasy place-names were those of nearby rulers and when one of them died, the place would be renamed after his successor.[147]

There were also the so-called dual vocabularies for nobility and commoners or what Bloomfield sees as higher and lower languages. The dual vocabularies appear to have been restricted also to the peoples of western and southern Madagascar with the exception of the central-highlands Betsileo, who can serve as an example. Their commoners, in referring to their own house, children, dead, old, and eye, used *trano, kilonga, maty, antitra*, and *maso*. If these belonged to Betsileo nobility, the terms transformed into *lapa*, or court and house of nobles, *anakova*, or noble children, *folaka*, or noble who had fallen, who became broken and not dead, *masina*, or noble who is sacred not old, while the eye of a noble became a *fanilo* (torch). Similarly, the head of an ordinary Betsileo, the *loha*, would become *kabeso for nobility*.[148] While the linguistic *fady* and the dual vocabulary reveal the sacred quality of those who govern, in life and even more in death, the *fady* could also be placed on several unrelated words, banned by fiat of the state. Eight such words, for example, were tabooed in 1890 by a Sakalava king and had to be immediately replaced.[149] Among them was the Bantu-Malagasy compound for manioc, *bala-hazo*, which became *majera* (Malagasy, long root). It is interesting to note that some words in both Betsileo vocabularies appear to belong, as if by random linguistic chance, to Malagasy and Bantu idioms. This is the case of *maso* (eye, eyes) and *ana* (children, the young of). And each of the two vocabularies contains one word that turns out to be Bantu-derived, namely *kilonga* and *kabeso*.[150]

The word changes and dual vocabularies permit the extraction of an important rule. Political elites in Madagascar, no matter what their origin might have been, yielded sooner or later to the Malagasy linguistic matrix, which, having secured an early primacy, could not be dislodged by subsequent arrivals into the island. Ethnographic and historical data still to be presented in the body of this work confirm this linguistic

[147] L. Catat, *Voyage à Madagascar, 1889–1890* (1895), pp. 341–342.

[148] Cf. J. Sibree, "Curious Words and Customs Connected with Chieftainship and Royalty Among the Malagasy," *JAI*, XXI (1891), 223–224. See also Appendix below.

[149] A. and G. Grandidier, *Ethnographie*, Vol. III (1917), p. 358, n. a, from the ms. *Notes* of Alfred Grandidier.

[150] The royal term *kabeso*, found alone among the Betsileo highlanders, has puzzled a number of students. It is a replica of the Portuguese term for head or headman, and yet it *cannot* be a Portuguese loan. Actually, it derives from a very widespread Bantu term for divinity, root *-eza*, found in two related forms in Africa, *kabeja* and *kabezya*, cf. Alexis Kagame, "La Place de Dieu et de l'Homme dans la Religion des Bantu," *Cahiers des Religions Africaines*, II/4 (1968), 219. No less interesting, the Malagasy *folaka* and Bantu *voloka* have the same meaning, cf. W. Holman Bentley, *Dictionary of the Kongo Language* (1887), pp. 451 and 452.

process. They show that no royal lineage involving outsiders could emerge anywhere in Madagascar *before* sufficient kinship ties developed with the pre-existing populations. These ties invariably formed through intermarriage with indigenous and Malagasy-speaking women, a social process that seems to have required a minimum of one human generation. The ensuing linguistic change arrested the spread of foreign loans, reversed the borrowing, and flooded out the ostensibly higher idiom of the outsiders.

The most certain proof of this change sequence is to be found in the Anteimoro manuscripts, the *Sora-bé*. Alone in Madagascar, the Anteimoro—whose foreign origin is beyond dispute—developed a scribal tradition and preserved their own written annals in Arabico-Malagasy. The *Sora-bé* show that what has been retained is not the original Arabic dialect but rather the Arabic *script*, for which no substitute could be found in Malagasy. The living speech of the Anteimoro has been for a long time simply another Malagasy dialect. Thus, the general linguistic rule for intimate borrowing from a higher to a lower language seen in terms of local realities in Madagascar transforms the Malagasy into the higher language.

If an original idiom, belonging to "outsiders" managed to survive at all, it did so *only* as a "secret" and religious one, used in special rites by sacerdotal persons. Such secret languages have indeed been reported and even inferences have been made as to its family without knowledge of a single vocabulary item.[151] The sole exception is provided by the secret language of the Ankara, an Anteimoro priestly clan, reproduced and studied by Gabriel Ferrand. Ferrand found that Malagasy had made its impact on it as well but that a high percentage of Arabic words remained.[152] The Arabic influence in Malagasy is attested mainly in fields of specialized knowledge like astrology, calendar, and divination. To all of these, the Anteimoro made a lasting contribution, if not the only one.[153]

The purpose of dual vocabularies in Madagascar has been to differen-

---

[151] For example, two west-coast French *colons*, Estèbe and Edmond Samat, had reported to Alfred Grandidier in the nineteenth century an "unknown" and "completely strange" language employed only in Sakalava *dady* (ancestors) prayers. From this Grandidier adduced an Indian language, since no one could verify the language.

[152] G. Ferrand, *Les Musulmans à Madagascar et aux Iles Comores*, Vol. III (1902), pp. 5–39. Of the 247 "old" Ankara words, roughly 55 percent were Arabic loans.

[153] The best essay on this subject is L. Dahle's "The Influence of the Arabs on the Malagasy Language, as a Test of Their Contribution to Malagasy Civilization and Superstition," *AA*, I (1876), 75–91; to be supplemented with his "Sikidy and Vintana," *AA*, III (1886, 1887, 1888), 218–234, 315–327, 457–467. The Tantara of Imerina bear out the analysis of Dahle with specific references to the Anteimoro (see Merina Chapter 6).

tiate a noble of any rank in everyday life from those considered beneath him. Through acculturation, vocabularies of outsiders came to reflect sooner or later the dominant linguistic matrix or common Malagasy only to be amended by way of both the religious and secular word *fady*. The more refined speech of Malagasy political elites centered around the new monarchies was hence nothing more than a selectively borrowed vocabulary, consisting of superlatives and less pointed terms found in common Malagsy. This is the reason why the "elite vocabularies" reported in widely divergent parts of Madagascar tended to resemble one another. A ruler could not be *maty* (dead) but only *folaka* (broken). A seventeenth-century king in the central highlands or his counterpart in the deep south was an *Andria* (lord in Malagasy), whatever infixes or infixes and suffixes followed the prefix itself. His residence was not the simple *trano* (house) but a *lapa* or *lonaka* instead, and the king never gazed at anyone with his *maso* but rather with his *fihena* or *fanilo*. It is, therefore, not surprising that many students of Madagascar were apt to conclude either that a single dynastic origin must be attributed to the Andriana or, if not, that all of them somehow managed to swim ashore from chronologically convenient shipwrecks and became the Andriana in Madagascar.[154]

This process of elite-language leveling is not of recent date, but it has been accelerated since about the turn of the nineteenth century, and it also involves the transformation of hitherto political elites into educated and literate ones. As soldiers, officials, expatriate settlers, petty traders, and itinerant craftsmen of the precolonial conquest period (1810–1870), the Merina were able to loan out many of their own words and expressions to other Malagasy dialects. Missionaries serving the Merina monarchy, both Europeans and European-trained Merina Christians, taught school in the "bush" and used the Merina dialect. During the colonial period itself, Merina was taught in provincial schools while most of the lower-echelon administrators were recruited in Tananarive.[155] This is, in essence, how Merina became the official language of Madagascar through natural and induced expansion in the course of the last 150 years. And, among the non-Merina, the propensity for the word *fady* was certainly assisted by the readily available Merina substitutes. In this case of dialectical borrowing, the rule of loan movement from higher to lower language works well since the movement itself reflects imitation of the politically and hence culturally dominant idiom. The Betsileo example is perhaps the most revealing. The vocabulary of Betsileo nobility is closer to the Merina idiom than the language of Betsileo commoners, and there

---

[154] See Chapter 1 and R. K. Kent, "Alfred Grandidier," *BM* (1968).

[155] See R. K. Kent, "Malagasy Republic," in H. Kitchen (ed.) *The Educated African* (1962), pp. 249–266.

is no doubt that the origin of this goes back to the second half of the eighteenth century, when the Betsileo came under strong political and cultural influence of the Merina.[156]

The Bantu loans in Malagasy, retained to this day, do reveal something about how they were borrowed. They consist of two distinct clusters, an old or Afro-Indonesian one and a more recent or pure Bantu one. The earlier loans were intimately borrowed on the mainland *before* the mixed group crossed over to Madagascar. This prefiltered acceptance of Bantu loans by Indonesian speakers accounts for the fact that most of them have been retained in Malagasy. They occur in greater numbers than suggested so far.[157] Conversely, the more recent loans that still survive can only be accounted for in terms of fairly substantial numbers of Bantu settlers in Madagascar capable of diffusing them by the time the settlers themselves were physically and culturally absorbed by the Malagasy. It is, nonetheless, easy to see how linguistic taboos forced some of the Bantu loans, both old and recent, out of one or more dialects: *mamba = voay, amboa = alika*, and *bala-hazo = majera*.

It is now appropriate, after listing the restrictions and impediments, to turn to several types of African survivals that are both widely diffused and of high quality. Significantly, these are found in the realm of non-material culture and the Malagasy grammar provides a good start. It would be least susceptible to alien influences, and if some of these are still to be found, they must be attributed to intimate borrowing in Madagascar.

Many writers from Europe have long known it to be much easier to transpose certain Malagasy verbal formations into their own languages than to keep qualifying them. For example, instead of writing *le pays du peuplade Merina*, or the land of the Merina tribe, the Malagasy construct *Imerina* will do the same while saving four words in French and five in English. Any contemporary map of Madagascar on the scale of 1:500,000 will reveal a large number of Malagasy place-names with the *I-* prefix (Ihosy, Itasy, Ifangoavana). In *Imerina* itself (*I + Merina*), the prefix is both locative and augmentative. Sometimes, this augmentative role is strengthened by the addition of terminal *bé* (great, large), as in *Imandabé* or *Ivohibé*. Finally, the *I-* prefix is found also as a personal

[156] Callet, *Tantara*, Vol. IV (1958), pp. 866–869; V. Malzac, *Histoire du Royaume Hova* (1912), pp. 117–127; and G. Grandidier and R. Decary, *Histoire Politique et Coloniale*, Vol. V, Tome III, Fascicule 1 (1958), pp. 1–19.

[157] It has not been possible as yet to do sufficiently detailed work on Malagasy dictionaries from that of Webber (1853) to that of Hoffmann (1940–1948) but at least for the animal kingdom, a recent article lists ninety Malagasy words that are African loans, among them words for lion (*simba*) and camel (*angamia, angamira*), animals that have not existed in Madagascar.

pronoun (singular), often to convey some form of respect. Thus, *Iboto* translated would be "a Mr. Boto," the *I-* being less "noble" than *Ra-* and *Andria-* but still a mark of respect. In all four aspects, the Malagasy *I-* is a pure Bantu classifier.[158] Malagasy place-names beginning with *I-* are receding but they were once quite widespread. What follows the *I-* in Malagasy toponymy is usually a Malagasy description or name but the "habit" of *I-* prefix forming has remained, and in a few instances it occurs with African place-names as well.[159]

Another Bantu prefix in Malagasy is *ki-* and it will at times denote a diminutive form. This prefix is found in many words which are more or less pure loans to this day: *kitrele, kibana, kibory, kinoly, kibobo, kiady, kianja, kianjo, kibaha, kibango, kidoro, kifoka, kilenga, kilety, kinanga, kiso, kitamby, kitapo.*[160] And like the *I-*, it has passed into Malagasy cognates. Both simply confirm that some important African influences in Madagascar cannot, under any pretense, be explained through diffusion without people or to intimate borrowing from "slaves." Otto Dahl has also seen a number of other, if slightly less striking, African influences upon Malagasy grammar *and* phonetic patterns.[161]

The terms that, in common Malagasy, designate the social institutions of joking relationship and tattooing or *ziva* and *tomboka* have already been reported as Bantu loans. No less interesting are the prefixes *zara* and *zafi* encountered in the first chapter in connection with royal lineages in southern Madagascar: *Zafi* Manely, *Zafi* Raminia, *Zafi* Manara and *Zara* Behavana. *Zafi* comes from the Bantu *zaa* and *zara* from Bantu *ijara* (phonetics, *i-zara*), both with contextual meanings appropriate to the Malagasy prefixes.[162] It will be seen, in the actual case studies, that at least two cognates that follow the *zafi* and *zara* prefixes are unmistakably Bantu and provide in addition not only precise connections but meanings that are cross-confirmed by other types of evidence. To go a step further, the common Malagasy *foko* (phon. fūkū) for clan, family,

---

[158] See Torrend, *Bantu Languages*, pp. 327–328, for various entries for *I* in his Index. Curiously, this *I* prefix has not been discussed in Madagascar except in connection with whether or not it is less polite than *Ra-* or more. Cf. R. Baron, "The Personal Article I in Malagasy," *AA*, III (1886), 216–218; and G. Mondain, "Note sur le préfixe personnel malgache 'i,' " *BAM*, IV (1905–1906), 127–129.

[159] Isaka is also a site on the east African coast as is *Isango*, both reported in old sources (Flacourt, 1661) and Mariano (1613–1617).

[160] See Richardson, *Dictionary*, pp. 330–347, who gives Swahili etymins for many of these. Others are in Sacleux, *Swahili-français*, Vols. I and II (1939–1941). Several of the cited terms will reoccur in the Sakalava and Anteimoro chapters.

[161] O. Dahl, "Le Substrat bantou en Malgache," *NTS*, 343–360; also C. Tastevin, "De l'africanité de quelque phonèmes auxiliaires considérés a tort comme préfixes en Malgache," *Ethnographie*, No. 45 (1947–1950), pp. 178–202.

[162] So noted by Richardson, *Dictionary*, pp. 793 and 796.

tribe, community, comes from Bantu *ifuko*.[163] The same can be said of the *Vezo* and *Masikoro* terms generally used to identify the coastal fishermen of western and southern Madagascar and the pastoralists who once occupied much of south-central Madagascar.[164] These are far from being the only high-quality loans. Many others occur in more limited contexts from which, by our own rules, it does not seem useful to isolate them simply to provide one instance of concentrated quantity. So far, the stress has been mainly on ethnolinguistics.

If one turns to comparative ethnographic data, a good case can be made through a single general illustration. In discussing what they call the "cultural area" of southern Congo, Baumann and Westermann write:[165]

> At all of the courts, even those of the most absolute kings, the princesses had the privilege of selecting their temporary spouses at will. . . . An entire chain of rite and of custom, centering on a king identified with god and his posterity, gave a specific coloring to this civilization of nobility. Thus, the king is everywhere sacrosanct, he lives [often] in seclusion. . . . Whenever possible, his death is kept secret and a state of anarchy prevails . . . until the successor takes over. The so-called enforced death of the king . . . has been reported. . . . Certain parts of the royal body, especially the cranium, are preserved and become objects of a cult; everywhere the burial of chiefs is accompanied by human sacrifices. . . . What is called, in the cultural area of Zambezi, the *fangane* custom, based on the idea that the king transforms after death into a body worm first and a beast of prey afterward, [is present] although here it did not develop as fully [but] special preparations of the royal corpse, like the drying-up [of its humors], reflect [the same] idea.

The counterparts in Madagascar are not hard to come by.

The temporary-spouse prerogative was fairly widespread in Madagascar, under two typical forms. It could be restricted to males of noble birth (Antanosy Zafi Raminia, Andriana Merina), generally with success because violations would lead to exclusion from the family tomb (*very faty*). Or else, no caste restrictions applied (Sakalava). When a Sakalava princess "sees a man of ordinary station and wants to marry him, she takes her *Biby*. The man has no right to refuse. . . . It is the princess who feeds and clothes her *Biby* and discards him when no longer needed."[166] Most of the southern Malagasy (Mahafaly, Bara, Antandroy,

---

[163] *Ifuko* in Bisa; *mukoa* in Ila; *mu-kowa* in Bantu-Botatwe, *inter alia*.

[164] A. V. Hartnoll, and N. R. Fuggles Couchman, "The Masokora Cultivations of the Coast," *TNR*, No. 3 (1937), 35; in Ila, fisherman is *mu-zezhi*; in Bisa *mu-wesi* means one who oars.

[165] Baumann and Westermann, *Les Peuples*, p. 185.

[166] V. Tsarovana, "How the Sakalava Obey Their Kings: A Dialogue . . . (with) . . . Nabé Dadinidimasy" (translated title), in *Notes sur les Sakalava*, unpublished manu-

Masikoro) followed the Sakalava custom. The Anteimoro represent the only certain case of abstention from this prerogative.

Most of the kings in Madagascar became divinities posthumously, sometimes as part of special state cults. While alive, most were regarded as *masina* or quasi-divine, and extreme cases of this regard are not unknown (Betsileo, Sakalava, Merina). Many kings ate in isolation, at times literally alone. Attendants preset their personal utensils along with food and drink.[167] On the eastern coast, at certain periods, some kings ate with their slaves only. Elsewhere, if other persons were allowed to be present while the monarch ate, they could not share his meal, move, speak, cough, or spit.[168]

The kings' personal belongings, often property in transit, were also regarded as being *masina*, and not a few kings had officials at court charged with the task of being their food-tasters.[169] Gift objects, presented by the seventeenth- or nineteenth-century Europeans to the west-coast kings, had to be purified first or tasted by the giver himself, if edible or potable.[170] Among the Bara, for example, family heads ate alone and their wives could not watch the consumption of food.[171] At different periods, again, only invited guests—usually Europeans—could share a monarch's meal among the Merina or Antanosy.[172] In short, variants of

---

script, Notebook 173 (1912–1913), Collection of the Human Sciences Department, University of Madagascar. The quote is from page 18 of the manuscript.

[167] See discussion of the *olom-pody* (royal attendants) among the Betsileo in Chapter 6. This practice was prevalent in much of Madagascar excepting the upper east coast, where kingdoms formed only in the eighteenth century, under Europo-Malagasy chiefs, the Zanamalata (*zana, zanaka*=child, children+malata=mulatto).

[168] Notably among the Sakalava, cf. A. and G. Grandidier, *Ethnographie*, Vol. III (1917), p. 221, n. 2.

[169] James Hastie, "Le Voyage à Tananarive en 1817," *BAM*, II (1903), 243, observed that the Merina king Radama I (1810–1828) never drank water before it was tasted by an attendant. The Betsileo *olompody* also tasted food. According to the Merina oral traditions, *tsimandoa-mamy* was the name given to domestic slaves of Betsileo kings whose principal duty was to taste food.

[170] In 1719, Dutch gifts to the Sakalava king of Menabé were screened by royal relics and the head priest before being accepted, see the account of *Barneveld* in *COACM*, Vol. V (1907), pp. 25–26. In 1613–1614, Father Mariano noticed a north-western Malagasy kinglet who administered poison to a slave before entering into any relations with the Portuguese, cf. *COACM*, Vol. II (1904), p. 67. In the early 1850s, French Jesuits in Menabé presented gifts that were so "screened" before being accepted by the Sakalava king. In the late 1860s, Alfred Grandidier was himself subjected a number of times to the prior tasting of wine or food while visiting the Sakalava kings Vinany and Toera.

[171] A. and G. Grandidier, *Ethnographie*, Vol. III (1917), p. 221, n. 2. Their personal utensils were *fady* (forbidden) to anyone else, cf. H. W. Little, *Madagascar* (1884), p. 221.

[172] Cf. Flacourt, *Histoire*, *COACM*, Vol. VIII (1913), pp. 160–161; and Ida Pfeiffer, *Voyage à Madagascar* (1881), pp. 226–227 (Imerina).

the custom noted by Baumann and Westermann could be found in Madagascar at the level of ordinary freemen (*vohitsa*) and at the table of kings. The same can be said of seclusion due to certain *fady* days, weeks, or months, periods of mourning, or disease. Sometimes royal seclusion was the will of high priests, and the Mahafaly may well owe their national name to a protracted seclusion of an early Maroserana king.[173]

The state of anarchy did not follow the death of every monarch in Madagascar, and interregnums were at times quite brief. The Antandroy, on the strength of what is known about their past, do not appear to have generally waited more than three days to put the new king on the throne.[174] Secrecy concerning royal deaths was, however, more a rule than an exception. It was not unusual, for example, among the central-highlands Betsileo to withhold announcement of a royal death as long as eight months or a year.[175] The Bara held it secret for three months and the successor *organized* a period of total anarchy, perpetrated by his soldiers before the defunct king could be buried.[176] As in Africa, when the throne was being disputed by two or more pretenders, the Merina used to exile or kill the loser and all of his kin as traitors.[177]

In one period, among the Boina Sakalava, moribund kings were ritually killed by strangulation to "facilitate" the departure of "last breath."[178] Ritual killings of chiefs only were reported early in the nineteenth century in the vicinity of Vangaindrano (Mananjary district).[179] Among the Anteimoro, kings have been deposed and sometimes killed when a natural disaster or severe crop failure appeared to be connected with royal incapacity.[180] Certain parts of a dead monarch's body (hair, nails, occiput

[173] According to a Mahafaly tradition, one of their early kings had a *kola* (yaws) and was, therefore, confined to total seclusion by his priests (*ombiasa*); the subjects, who could not see their king, then named the land *Maha-faly*, or that which is forbidden (*fady*). For seclusion of the Bara kings, see G. A. Shaw, "Rough Sketches of a Journey to the Ibara," *AA*, I (1876—reprint), 235. J. Richardson and A. Davidson noted the same for the Tanala in "Tanala Customs, Superstitions and Beliefs," *AA*, I (1876—reprint), 221.

[174] E. Defoort, "L'Androy," *BEM*, XIII/2 (1913), 217. However, it is known that the funeral of at least one Antandroy king lasted three months.

[175] A. Dandouau, *Moeurs, coutumes et croyances betsileo* (ca. 1924), manuscript, in *BDP*, p. 130, on kind loan to me.

[176] See Bara Chapter 4 below, text and note 131.

[177] Related to G. Grandidier, *Histoire politique et coloniale*, Vol. 5, Tome 1 (1942), p. 47, n. 2, notule a.

[178] According to the Grandidiers (*Ethnographie*, Vol. III [1917], p. 10), there was no strangulation but, rather, the dying ruler's throat was cut with a special ceremonial knife.

[179] William Ellis, *History of Madagascar*, Vol. I (1838), p. 422; and J. Sibree, *The Great African Island* (1880), p. 303.

[180] G. A. Shaw, "The Arab Element in Southeast Madagascar," *AA*, V (1894), 209, states that the Taimoro had a "general" custom of "hurrying the dying into death." Cf. also B.-F. Leguével de Lacombe, *Voyage à Madagascar et aux Iles Comores,*

bone, kneecaps, beard, teeth, spine rings) were preserved as cult objects, the most developed case being that of the Sakalava. These particular parts of a royal body do not appear to have been preserved in southeastern, central, and much of eastern Madagascar, where, equally, no pertinent cults have been reported. The preservation of royal craniums have been reported among the eastern Tanala and southwestern Mahafaly as well as among a migratory group of Manambia, half-Bara and half-Tanala.[181] The cranium of the founding Maroserana king is still to this day the cult object for the Mahafaly.

Human sacrifices were neither uncommon nor limited to a single group, which is not too well-known. Specific instances in connection with royal funerals have been reported among the Mahafaly, Sakalava, Antanosy, Antandroy, and Betsileo, while even the *Tantara* of Imerina have been suspected of hiding from Europeans a practice that did exist before oxen were substituted for human victims.[182] Sakalava funerary rites associated with royalty suggest massive borrowing from mainland Africa, like the enveloping the body in hide of a royal bull, collection of humors into jars (*kisingy*), human sacrifices involving either royal slaves or maidens of the special *Jangoa* caste, slaughter of royal cattle, specialized funerary attendants (*Sambarivo, Marovavy, Antankoala, Bahary*), grave structures, types of regalia buried, time spans between death and burial, mourning practices for commoners and for nobility.[183]

The collection of putrid liquids from the royal corpse (the "drying up" of the body) was a practice common to a number of Malagasy groups—the Antankarana (among whom the task was left to the

---

1823–1830, Vol. I (1840), p. 230. As an actual observer, de Lacombe is not to be trusted unless other types of evidence are available as well since he did not in reality visit most of the places and peoples described but used oral reports of his compatriots in eastern Madagascar as his own.

[181] D. Jakobsen, "Note sur Andriamaro," *BAM*, I (1902), 50–52; A. and G. Grandidier, *Ethnographie*, Vol. III (1917), pp. 399–400. See also Bara Chapter 4 below.

[182] Reported as follows: *Antanosy*, Reverend Tau (1891), two slaves buried with the *mpanjaka* (chief); Alfred Grandidier (1882), also two slaves buried with the *mpanjaka* of migrant Antanosy. *Antandroy*, A. Grandidier (1899), four slaves buried with a king. *Sakalava*, Father Lacomme (1874), four slaves interred at Nossy-bé; construction engineer Guimet (1891), two slaves buried at Boina; Captain Defoort (1899), one slave at Ambato-Boeni. *Mahafaly*, A. Grandidier (1889), five females, wives of a king. *Betsileo*, several late nineteenth-century reports involving both slaves and royal wives. *Merina*, the oldest son of the last Merina prime minister made human sacrifices once a year; during the construction of royal tombs in the late 1600s or early 1700s; and, on a similar occasion, during the rule of Queen Ranavalona I (1828–1861). This note concerns only some of the specific cases reported.

[183] Ch. Guillain, *Documents sur l'Histoire . . . de Madagascar* (1845), p. 158; F. Pollen, "Un Pèlerinage d'un roi antankara au tombeau de son père," *BSSAIR*, (March 9, 1866), 73; and Dandouau, "Coutumes funéraires."

would-be Arab Onjatsy), Betsileo, Betanimena-Betsimisaraka, Ranomena, Tanala, Antanosy, and the west-coast Vazimba. In some, but not
all, of the cases the Sakalava collected the humors from defunct Maroserana. There is some evidence also that Merina nobles practiced this in
secret.[184] The liquid was sometimes buried or tossed into lakes or the
sea. Attendants, in certain cases, anointed their own bodies with it.[185]
The *fangane* custom (Malagasy *fanany, fanano* for snake or serpent,
usually a large one), associated with the first worm to come from a
decomposing royal body and growing into a serpent, is best documented
for the Betsileo.[186] The *fanany* was usually a boa, analogous with the
python or *fangane* of several groups from the Zambezi Valley to the
Interlacustrine kingdoms. Although something that points to serpent
transformation of a royal ancestor appears in one instance among the
Sakalava,[187] their prevalent belief has been that notables become crocodiles after death. This particular belief has also been noted in the northeast, east, and south, as well as parts of central Madagascar.[188] It is
confirmed also by the fact that the crocodile has managed to survive
mainly in those areas of the Great Island where this particular belief has
made him a *fady* animal that cannot be killed.

The sacred quality of rulers, expressed in a variety of forms, is not a
feature confined to Indonesia and Africa. The preservation of their crania
and human sacrifices associated with their burials are features common
to both Africa and Indonesia. Indeed, the duplication of many features

[184] A. Jully, "Ethnographie de Madagascar," *RM*, VIII (1906), 1034.

[185] Notably among the Sakalava-Boina and among the Onjatsy.

[186] L. Catat, *Voyage à Madagascar* (1895), pp. 295–296; Sibree, "Remarkable
Ceremonial," 198; J. Richardson, "Burial Customs," *AA*, I (1875—reprint), 73–77;
G. A. Shaw, "The Betsileo," *AA*, I (1878—reprint), 411; Father A. Abinal, *Vingt
Ans à Madagascar* (1885), pp. 242–246; Dandouau, *Moeurs*, pp. 146–150; H.-M.
Dubois, *Monographie des Betsileo* (1939), pp. 716–718. See also Appendix below
for an account from the *Tantara* of Imerina.

[187] J. Faublée, *Récits Bara* (1947), p. 184; and E. Birkeli, "Folklore sakalava
recueilli dans la région de Morondava," *BAM*, VI, New Series (1922–1923), 232–
233. Both authors find *fanany* survivals among the Bara and the Sakalava. The
instance referred to concerns the *do* (snakes) that moved around royal tombs in
Menabé and that were either feared or treated with respect.

[188] Dr. Louis, in *Mémoire sur les moeurs et coutumes des peuplades nord de
Madagascar* (unpublished typescript of 48 pages, dated 1950, in *AAM*), notes the
crocodile ancestors of two lakes, the first near Anivorano village at 60 kilometers
from Diego-Suarez and the second (Green Lake) at 5 kilometers from Vohémar. The
Sihanaka of Lake Alaotra and the Sakalava of Marovoay in Iboina have their own
crocodile ancestor cults. Marovoay means, in effect, "many crocodiles (*maro*=many+
voay=crocodiles). For the Bara, see J. Nielsen-Lund, "Travels and Perils Among the
Wild Tribes in the South of Madagascar," *AA*, III (1888), 441. For the Betsileo, see
J. Sibree, *Madagascar Before the Conquest* (1896), p. 146; and for the southeast,
see L. de Lacombe, *Voyage à Madagascar. . .* , Vol. II (1840), p. 223.

in these two broad geographical areas, a subject hardly touched by detailed investigation, poses some of the most intriguing problems, given that ancient contacts between Indonesia and Africa hardly belong to the realm of fantasy. Here, the importance of Madagascar is potentially enormous, and the present work will not fail to accentuate it. The subject of concentration, however, is not "culture" in its broadest sense, but mainly one aspect of it—the advent and diffusion of early kingdoms. In this more restricted realm, the problem of determining which of the two possible loaning areas has been paramount in Madagascar encounters two basic and simple points of departure. First, the advent of kingdoms in Madagascar occurs a *very long time after* the Indonesian-speaking element became established in the island and is completely disconnected from its protoculture or cultures. This is, moreover, a time when intercourse between Africa and Madagascar appears to be at its peak, when the European overseas expansion induces economic and political convulsions on the mainland, convulsions that throw forth human exiles who settle in Madagascar and stimulate an interplay between tradition and innovation in government, religion, and society. There is nothing particularly mysterious about this process and its timing, as the early kingdoms will show. Second, a convergence of features reveals that more meaningful prototypes are to be noted in nearby Africa than in distant Indonesia.[189] Yet, these two points of departure lead into an ultimate line of inquiry that is beyond the scope of the present work but one that will be opened as widely as possible for subsequent research. State building within the Great Island (as well as the very fact of its success) cannot be explained, in the final analysis, without a strong predisposition toward receptivity by the peoples already indigenous to Madagascar. This receptivity will emerge from the historical, linguistic, and ethnographic materials. And, it will force us into a reconsideration of the much older interconnections between Indonesia, Africa, and Madagascar.

[189] Comparative data from Africa on this subject will be found in Chapter 7.

chapter 3 THE ANTEIMORO:

A Theocracy in Southeastern Madagascar

> Because of their knowledge of Arabic script, the Antai-
> morona alone have been able to transmit . . . an outline of
> their early history and ancient beliefs which will permit us
> perhaps to reconstruct the origins and the basic elements
> for one segment of the old Malagasy society.
>
> Gabriel Ferrand (1891)

From at least two points of view, the Anteimoro[1] have had a rather
special attraction for students of Madagascar. They represent the last of
the overseas migrants to settle in Madagascar; hence their history does
not belong to deep antiquity. It is also a matter of established convention
in dealing with the Islamized Anteimoro to hold that the art of writing
in pre-1800 Madagascar belonged exclusively to them. In a strict sense,
however, this is not true. The ancestral Anteimoro, who settled between
Farafangana and Mananjary, were not the sole colony of Moors to take
root in the island. With much older counterparts in northwestern and
northeastern sections of Madagascar, they formed Arabico-Malagasy
communities known collectively as Antalaotra, or overseas people, from

---

[1] Various spellings have appeared in print besides the prevalent Anteimoro, namely
Antaimoro, Antaimorona and *Anteimahuri*. The prefix *Ant* and the infix *I* simply mean
people of in Malagasy. *Morona* stands for coast in Malagasy (*Antaimorona*=people
of the coast). Flacourt mentions *Imours* in 1661, but this does not accord with anything concerning the Anteimoro. Rather, early European accounts mention them as
Matitanes or *Matitanais*, from the Matitana River (*mati*=dead+*tana*=hand, so
named because the river dried up in one area), the center of early Anteimoro
settlement. There is no connection between *Imours* and Moors, while the *morona*
and *mahuri* etymologies remain unsatisfactory. For a discussion of *mahuri*, see note
110 below and text.

the Malay term *antay-laut*. In the southeast itself, the Anteimoro were preceded by other Antalaotra—the Antambahoaka of Mananjary—whose own migrants gave the Antanosy of Fort-Dauphin their ruling lineage of Zafindraminia (descendants of Raminia). All the Antalaotra colonies in Madagascar had their own scribes. A twelfth-century Arabic inscription has been found near Vohémar, principal site of an important culture complex.[2] Even the non-Muslim Sakalava rulers of Menabé used Antalaotra scribes, at least since the eighteenth century.[3] Nevertheless, no other Malagasy group can claim a scribal tradition, developed and preserved since antiquity by generations of "book-men" (*kitabi*),[4] nor yet the ability to manufacture paper, without which an isolated Muslim enclave would have had no means to produce its manuscripts. Nearly three generations ago, and in contrast to other Malagasy, the Anteimoro thus appeared extremely promising for study because their Arabico-Malagasy manuscripts could "reconstruct the origins and basic elements for (at least) one segment of the old Malagasy society."[5]

This promise was justified by the fact that, while precious few manuscripts have come down to us from all of the other Antalaotra, those of the Anteimoro run into hundreds.[6] The Anteimoro manuscripts, of which many copies have been made, can be divided into two categories or types. Both are generally known as the *Sora-bé* (Great Writings, or Sacred Books).[7] The older type consists of religious and cabalistic formulas. The oldest of these, manuscript Number 7 of the Bibliothèque Nationale in Paris, appears to have been composed late in the sixteenth century.[8] At

[2] Cf. P. Gaudebout, and E. Vernier, "Notes sur une campagne de fouilles à Vohémar," *BAM*, XXIV (1941), 91–114.

[3] Cf. "Vente le 22 aout 1732 par S. M. Adrian Baba, Roy de Seclaves, de l'Ile-Morotte à la compagnie des Indes," copy in *BGT*. Original is in French with Arabic signatures, certified by Bellier on May 26, 1750 and deposited in the Réunion Archives at St-Denis, Fonds de la Compagnie des Indes, Serie C°.

[4] The Anteimoro actually use the term *katibo*, but since this is a metathesis of the original Arabic, *kitabo* (sing.) and *kitabi* (pl.) will be used in the text here.

[5] G. Ferrand, *Les Musulmans à Madagascar et aux Iles Comores*, Vol. I (1891), pp. 16 and ii.

[6] It is impossible to estimate how many exist in various public and private libraries. As recently as 1965 the *Sora-bé* were still turning up in such divergent places as Stavanger, Norway, and Ambositra, a Betsileo township in central Madagascar. Jacques Faublée is translating those from Ambositra. It is believed that the Vatican and several German archives harbor an undetermined number of the *Sora-bé* as well. The Académie Malgache has a fine collection.

[7] *Sora* is from Malagasy *sóratra or writing*. J. Richardson, *A New Malagasy-English Dictionary* (1885), p. 589, however, lists two etymons or Malay *soorat* and Arabic *surat*, along with Swahili *sura*. Otto Chr. Dahl, *Personal Communication* (February 8, 1969), states that *sóratra* is an old Indonesian term.

[8] This manuscript was acquired probably between 1600 and 1650, for it contains an interlinear Latin translation of the period. Cf. E. Jacquet, "Mélanges malays, javanais et polynésiens," *JA*, 1st series, XII/3 (1833), 100; G. Ferrand, "L'Elément

some point in time, it now seems certain, the Anteimoro had decided to record contemporary events on paper, and this could have been no simple

arabe et souahili en Malgache ancien et moderne," *JA*, 2nd series, II/3 (1903), 451–452 and n. 5; and his "Texte arabico-malgache du XVI° siècle," *Notices et extraits des Mss. de la Bibliothèque Nationale* (Paris), XXXVIII/2 (1906), 450–576.

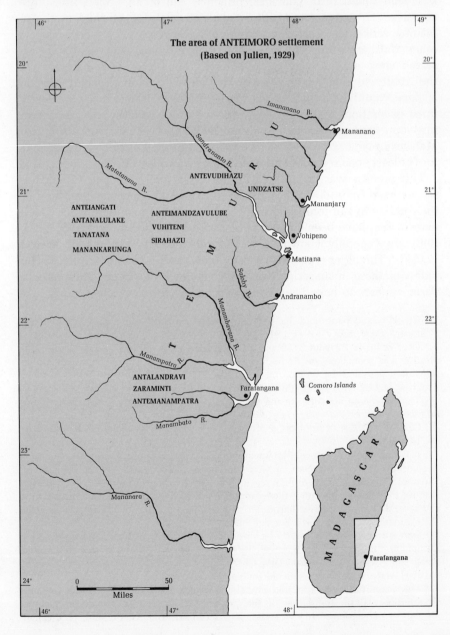

The area of ANTEIMORO settlement
(Based on Julien, 1929)

accident. Along with explanations of dreams came accounts of internal struggles, a list of amulets was followed by genealogies, and divination (*sikidy*) formulas went along with origins of the aristocratic clans.[9]

In a very real sense, the fact that the internal content of Anteimoro *Sora-bé* underwent this change has a historical significance that must be noted. Gradually, oral tradition could be recalled only within certain marginal families. Concern for events affecting the Anteimoro became instead a duty of royal scribes who wrote official history, while the commoners, or *ampanabaka*, drew apart from the living past much as the priestly and noble clans began to stand aloof from the freemen. In addition, the Anteimoro *kitabi* incorporated into the *Sora-bé* those aspects of the Antambahoaka past that could serve their own rulers, and most notably the legend of common descent from Raminia. It is thus soical change, broadly conceived as state formation, that revised the records. If a few surviving oral traditions, retained by rote, could not be changed with a stroke of the pen, written texts were altered all the time, as is confirmed by linguistic evidence.[10] Some of the available manuscripts were copied from unseen *Sora-bé* "originals," with which the *kitabi* would not part. Others were dictated to colonial administrators from memory alone. But, in terms of actual composition, few of the known historical *Sora-bé* can be said to antedate the 1860s.[11]

[9] This sequence is revealed in two ancient *Sora-bé* purchased by Alfred Grandidier at Vatomasina and Mahasoa, *ca.* 1870, namely Nos. 1 and 2 of the Bibliothèque Grandidier-Paris. They remain to be dated, but No. 2 relates events up to 1664. The oldest manuscript in this library, No. 3, which is extremely old and worn out, does not contain any historical data. Cf. G. Grandidier, *Bibliographie de Madagascar*, Vol. I, Tome 2 (1906), p. 729.

[10] G. Mondain, "Complément à la note sur l'emploi de l'écriture arabico-malgache," *BAM*, VI (1922–1923), 85–89.

[11] The more important ones are: (a) G. Mondain, *L'Histoire des tribus de l'Imoro au XVII° siècle d'après un manuscrit arabico-malgache* (1910). It consists actually of three manuscripts, designated as MS A, MS B, MS C, Arabico-Malagasy texts, annotations, and comments by Mondain. The MS A was originally sent by General J.-J. Gallieni to the Ecole des Letters in Algiers. One section that Mondain did not translate will be found in E.-F. Gautier and H. Froidevaux, *Un Manuscrit arabico-malgache sur les campagnes de La case dans l'Imoro, 1656–1663* (1907). MS B was prepared from oral accounts collected by the district head of Vohipeno in 1902 and has been called, after him, the "Vergely Commentary." (b) G. H. Julien, *Pages arabico-madécasses*, in four separate extracts (1929–1933) from the *Annales* of the French Academy of Colonial Sciences, totaling 283 pages, with photocopies of the *Sora-bé*, Arabic script texts and interlinear French translations, digests, annotations, and control commentaries. The first chapters of the *Pages* duplicate considerably two Anteimoro traditions, collected earlier and orally by Felix Guénot at Vondrozo in 1912 and summarized by Julien in "Notes d'histoire malgache," *BAM*, IX (1926), 2–13. These two will be referred to as *Hassani MSS* 1 and 2, after the informant. (In our footnotes below, we shall refer to those appearing in the *Pages* as, for example, *Hassani MS*, No. 1, *Pages* [1929].) (c) Manuscript 13 of the Bibliothèque Nationale in Paris, deposited there in 1899 by the traveler J.-B. Rolland de Kessang. This

It could be misleading to use a synchronic model with which to outline the Anteimoro social structure. The relative position of their noble clans changed at certain points in time long before the nineteenth century. Between about 1850 and 1892 there were several *ampanabaka* revolts, and these ultimately ended some aristocratic privileges.[12] The nobility–commoners–slaves triad obtains no longer, since the colonial period, too, blurred some of the older features; but, through traditional prestige, religion, and endogamy, the aristocratic clans retain much of their identity.[13] There are two noble phratries, those of the Anteony and Antalaotra, each with four principal clans. The Anteony include the *Ankazimambobé, Antemahazo, Anteisambo*, and the *Anteoni*, from whom the collective name derives. There seems to have been a fifth Anteony clan at one time, but its founder, Rambo, migrated with some followers shortly after the Anteimoro began to form.[14] The Antalaotra clans are those of the *Ankara*, renowned for the strictest endogamy rule and for possession of a secret language;[15] the *Antetsimeto*, religious specialists for agriculture and construction; the *Zafimbolazy*, now frequently *kitabi*; and the *Anterotri*, who had lost their specialized functions long ago but who retain Antalaotra status.[16] Finally, the *Onjatsy*, of whom less

---

manuscript is in four parts. Sections 2 and 3 contain only religious material. Historical accounts for the Anteony, Antalaotra, and Zafindraminia are in 1 and 4. (d) *Sora-bé* reproduced in Ferrand's *Musulmans* in three volumes: Vol. I (1891), Vol. II (1893), and Vol. III (1902). These will be referred to as *Ferrand MSS*, Nos. 1–8, while retaining the pagination of the *Musulmans* (namely, *Ferrand MSS* No. 6 in *Musulmans*, Vol. II (1893), p. 71). This is necessary to distinguish reported manuscripts from Ferrand's own text and interpretations.

[12] *Ferrand MSS*, No. 3, in *Musulmans*, Vol. II (1893), pp. 33–34. It would appear that first signs of an *ampanabaka* revolt manifested themselves around 1850, in the wake of the invading Merina army.

[13] A colonial decree of June 1896 abolished slavery in Madagascar and was implemented by Gen. Gallieni before 1905. This eliminated the *andevo* (slaves) among the Anteimoro without altering, however, the rest of their structure. A manuscript report, entitled "Anteimorona of Vohipeno" (1915), pages 1–4 (Archives of the Académie Malgache), reveals that the Anteony and Antalaotra were still regarded as rulers.

[14] The Zafirambo, or Afferambous, are mentioned between 1668 and 1670 as "inhabitants of high Matitana" in two French documents drafted at Fort-Dauphin (Archives Nationales, Paris, Section Outre-Mer, Correspondence Madascar, Carton I, Items 16–17, 25). Hubert Deschamps places the flight of Rambo about the sixteenth century, *Histoire de Madagascar*, 2nd ed. (1961), p. 110.

[15] Ferrand was able, after protracted residence among the Anteimoro, to examine this "secret" language. It was in reality an archaic Ankara idiom that revealed that roughly 54 percent of its words were Arabic. Cf. Ferrand, *Musulmans*, Vol. III (1902), pp. 5–39.

[16] Originally commoners, rewarded for successful mediation in a local war, the Anterotri lost this advantage as a result of strong Zafikazimambo opposition. Cf. *Ferrand MS*, No. 6, in *Musulmans*, Vol. II (1893), pp. 69–72.

than 1000 remain, form an outside kinship group with privileges that place them above the *ampanabaka* if not quite within the two phratries.[17] As could be expected, most of the known Anteimoro history revolves around the eight aristocratic clans.

A single Anteimoro arrival on the littoral roughly between Mananjary and Farafangana is not supported by any known source. In addition, it could not possibly accord with their historical formation in southeastern Madagascar. If we follow the Anteimoro accounts, Ramakararubé, great ancestor of all the Anteimoro and first Anteony chief, came to the mouth of the Matitana River with one of the Antalaotra clans, the Antetsimeto. It was Ranaha the Tsimetu who advised Ramakararubé not to settle initially at Matitana, "for the place here is bad, people plant the cane."[18] Ramakararubé went next to Manankara, but he found famine there and settled at Andrambi instead. He then married into the local lineage of Laniranu and fathered Andrianalivuaziri (Ali the Noble Vizir).[19] The second group of Anteimoro to land was led by Hamadi, known as Great Mohadjer of the Antalautra.[20] Hamadi himself is better known to the Anteimoro tradition as Andriambuaziribé, and he also took a spouse among the original inhabitants (*tompontany*) known as Antemanam-patra. Some years later, Hamadi was joined by new arrivals headed by Andriabakara Imaruvahini.[21] At the time of these three overseas migrations, local power was still in the hands of the more numerous *tompontany*. The Anteimoro recall thirteen *tompontany* groups between the Matitana and Manampatra.[22]

The puritanism of an adviser, Ranaha, is clearly meant to explain a mistake of the great ancestor who cannot be wrong, namely the unfortu-

[17] There are also a small number of "outcasts." The Anteimoro themselves call them *Antevolo*. They are considered untouchable, a group apart. The Antevolo simply include individuals rejected by their clans and they are by no means "untouchable" in the Indian sense of the term. See: "The Juridical Anteimoro Customs," in *Inquests*, Center for the Study of Local Custom, Law Faculty, University of Madagascar (April 6, 1961), p. 10, informant Tatahafa Dama.

[18] *Hassani MSS*, No. 1, in *Pages* (1929), pp. 21–22. The cane planting is an allusion to alcoholism.

[19] *Ibid.*, p. 23.

[20] *Ibid.*, pp. 27–28. The etymology of Mohadjer is *al-Muhadjirun*, migrants who followed Muhammad from Mecca to Medina in the *hidjra* (flight).

[21] *Hassani MSS*, No. 2, in *Pages* (1929), p. 29. *Bakara* is bull in Arabic. A small clan of Andrebakara was reported in July 1901 as residing in three villages of the Farafangana province.

[22] Anteiangati, Anteikiti, Anteimandzavulubé, Antanalulake, Vuhiteni, Tanatana, Sirahazu, Anteviduhazu, Antalandravi, Zaraminti, Antemanampatra, Undzatse (Onjatsy), and Manankarunga. The last have already been noted in connection with the Bara article, R. K. Kent, "Madagascar and Africa. I, The Bara Problem," *JAH*, IX/3 (1968), 387–408. The *Undzatse* spelling is phonetically correct without following the standard orthography, a general problem in European texts concerning Madagascar.

nate choice of *vavy* (wife) made by Ramakararubé. The Laniranu were a lineage, but there is little doubt that the Antemanampatra constituted a powerful local clan, with a river named after it, and one in alliance with Hamadi through his spouse. With the coming of Andriabakara a three-sided struggle developed. One, between Ali Vizir and Hamadi, was over dynastic rights without a kingdom in sight. The other was a natural outcome of the Antetsimeto fear of being displaced by the more recent migrants. Finally, Andriabakara's men, possessing no local kinship ties, began to fight the *tompontany*. The tradition recalls this development as a "seven-headed monster snake," the *fananimpitulaha*, which "came out of the sea" to plague local inhabitants.[23] After a protracted struggle, Ali won by taking away Hamadi's spouse and by slaying the *fanani*. He thus secured the correct alliance, overcame the Antalaotra with *tompontany* help, restored peace, and began to form a kingdom. In one tradition, Ramakararubé emerges as mediator between the Ali and Hamadi factions.[24] In another, he leaves Madagascar shortly after fathering Ali, now installed at Matitana.[25] In either case, Ramakararubé is beyond reproach, because only a common ancestor and his unblemished memory could minimize local conflicts. The relative status of each Anteimoro clan was yet to be defined, and all the Anteimoro were by no means present in southeastern Madagascar.

Ali had two sons, Ramusafotsy and Ramasomari. They, too, fought over the same *vavy*, in this instance Ravahininia, a Zafindraminia of the Antambahoaka. Marriage to an Antambahoaka princess had two advantages. To Ali, a *Silamo* (Malagasy, Islamic) kingdom without the nearby Antambahoaka meant mainly trouble in this formative stage. For the two contenders, a Zafindraminia spouse could, therefore, decide the issue of an appointed heir to Ali. Ramasomari displaced his brother in the contest but "had no children with Ravahininia." He married a *vadikeli* (second spouse), "Ratandramasi, an Onjatsy renowned for [magical powers in the] arts of construction."[26] Their son, Ramarohala, had seventeen sons in turn. Two of them became ancestors of the Anteisambo and Antemahazo. The *vadikeli* triggered a war between the Anteoni and Zafindraminia chiefs of the Antambahoaka. The "fall" of the *vadibé* (main spouse) brought about a territorial dispute, since the Zafindraminia were

[23] On this, see G. Julien, "Le Fananimptulaha ou monstre heptacéphale de Madagascar," *Comptes Rendus* (Académie des Sciences Coloniales), VIII (1926–1927), 205–212.

[24] *Hassani MSS*, No. 2, in *Pages* (1929), pp. 50–66.

[25] MS A in Mondain, *Histoire*, p. 51, and *Ferrand MSS*, No. 5, in *Musulmans*, Vol. II (1893), p. 57, also return Ali and Hamadi to Mecca after a sojourn of 48 years in Madagascar.

[26] MS A in Mondain, *Histoire*, p. 57.

no longer willing to be incorporated into the new Anteimoro state. The essence of these accounts is that the Anteoni-Anteimoro could not successfully merge with the older Zafindraminia for the sake of local legitimacy, while the patrilineal descent tradition of Anteimoro arrivals clashed with the matrilineal one to which both the Silamo Zafindraminia and the non-Silamo *tompontany* were firmly wedded. This particular problem would generate local conflicts well into the eighteenth century.

The last Anteimoro group to enter local history shortly after a state came into being is known as the Zafikazimambo. Written genealogies and texts turn Andriankazimambobé (great ancestor of the Zafikazimambo) into one of Ramarohala's seventeen sons.[27] This is inaccurate but logical because the rapid primacy gained by the most recent migrants meant that at some point they had to be given an Anteony origin. It was a task to which the *kitabi* were no strangers. A Zafikazimambo tradition claims even that all of the Anteony issue from their great ancestor, Andriankazimambobé.[28] But the transfer of retroactive events on paper did not obliterate the entire Anteimoro past from local memory. The chronicle obtained orally by administrator Vergeley is a definite statement of a separate Zafikazimambo line.[29] Etienne de Flacourt, an independent European source, also shows that the Zafikazimambo were the last of the Anteimoro to arrive in Madagascar and that they derive their name through a *tompontany* intermarriage. It was Casimambo, daughter of a powerful *tompontany* chief, who gave her name to the Zifikazimambo, as "is the custom in the south."[30] Nor does Flacourt leave any doubts as to why the Zafikazimambo were able to acquire a dominant position in the Anteimoro society and state almost from the outset. They were "all," he writes, "*Ombiasses* [priests] and scribes."[31]

The Zafikazimambo do not appear to have had much difficulty in qualifying first for the role of king-makers. But, in having a say as to who

[27] *Ibid.*, p. 59. Significantly, Andriakazimambobé is preceded here by a "brother" named Andriakatibofotsy (noble white *kitabo*), a high sacerdotal person judging by the name alone (p. 63); also Julien, *Pages* (1933), pp. 7–8.

[28] *Ferrand MSS*, No. 6, in *Musulmans*, Vol. II, pp. 69–71. This *Sora-bé* holds, at the same time, three conflicting views: (a) that the Zafikazimambo are an Anteony clan deriving from Andriamarohala; (b) that Andriamarohala and Andriamarozato are both the ancestral *pater* of the Zafikazimambo; and (c) that it was a son of Andriamarohala who fathered Antakazimambo. The *Ferrand MSS*, No. 5, in *Musulmans*, Vol. II (1893), pp. 57–62, makes no connection between Andriakazimambobé and Ramarohala.

[29] Genealogy in MS *B* (Vergely Commentary), appended to the end of Mondain's introduction, and pp. xlix–1 of the *Histoire*.

[30] E. de Flacourt, *Histoire de la Grande Ile Madagascar* (1661), in *COACM*, Vol. VIII (1913), p. 40. For a proposed *Mambo* connection, see the Bara article, *JAH*, IX/3 (1968), 404.

[31] Flacourt, *Histoire*, *COACM*, Vol. VIII (1913), p. 39.

the *Andrianonilehibé* (king of all Anteimoro) would be, they did not differ significantly from the other Anteimoro noble clans. The Zifikazimambo supremacy came from another source. This was the status of the Anteony, who could alone provide candidates for the throne. They earned it by settling the Anteoni-Zafindraminia conflict in a manner that accords with a zealotic group. They made war on the Antambahoaka, sparing only "children and women to whom certain islets and some fields were given to dwell in."[32] From this moment in time, the Zafindraminia are no longer significant in local Anteimoro history, but they do survive as an important ruling lineage among the Fort-Dauphin Antanosy.[33]

Until the Zafikazimambo attained control over the Anteimoro state, they contracted *tompontany* alliances, following the classic formula of all Malagasy Antalaotra who came to the island at various epochs and without their own women. At the time, the relatively recent Anteimoro kingdom was still a secular state in which the *tompontany* occupied an honorable place of *vohitsa*, or freemen. The Zafikazimambo changed radically both the nature of the Anteimoro state and this *vohitsa* position. The freemen were gradually reduced to serfdom and "treated like . . . dogs." "If a Lord [accidentally] fell, the serfs too had to prostrate themselves on the ground at once; if he travelled by dugout with serfs and fell overboard, they had to jump into the water as well; and the serfs had to pay heavy duties and were in [constant] debt as a result, to mention only some of the injustices."[34] Moreover, Islamic purity, which had once been strictly a social and religious matter—an individual way of life— became a criterion of *right* to rule. The former and uncomplicated division between royal Anteoni and other Anteimoro gave way to a new and fluctuating hierarchical clan struggle. These changes are confirmed by subsequent history.

The Anterotri were downgraded because they would not accept an exclusive Zafikazimambo right to the *sombili* (slaughter of all domestic animals).[35] Prior to the Zafikazimambo arrival, the Ankara considered themselves as guardians of Islam; but, as long as Islam remained outside the political arena, they accepted the Zafikazimambo as their "religious masters." Now, however, they claimed equal political power with the

[32] *Ibid.*, p. 40.
[33] Alfred Grandidier gives 1625 as the approximate date of the final Zafindraminia migration into Antanosy. There is no doubt, however, that it must have occurred much earlier, since the Zafindraminia *rohandriana* (chiefs, kings) were well established among the Antanosy by the time of Father Luis Mariano's visit in 1613–1614. In effect, the first Zafindraminia penetration of the Antanosy antedates even the Anteimoro arrival in Madagascar, as can be deduced from a Portuguese report of 1508.
[34] *Ferrand MSS*, No. 3, in *Musulmans*, Vol. II (1893), p. 33.
[35] *Ibid.*, p. 72.

Zafikazimambo on the grounds of being pure Silamo too. The main support for the Zafikazimambo came from the Antemahazo, with whom they are sometimes confused.[36] For about two generations, those of Andriankazimambobé and his heir Rabésirana, the Zafikazimambo maintained their supremacy. As Rabésirana grew old, most of the Antalaotra clans united behind Andriamasi, an Anteoni.[37] This gave the Ankara an advantage that they sought to hold by supporting Andriamasi's heir Andriamarofotana. Still, for a time, the Zafikazimambo-Antemahazo managed to regain much of the lost ground through the efforts of Andriamarofotana's rival, Andriapanolaha. Andriapanolaha was visited in 1638 by François Cauche, who called him the "greatest prince of the Matetanes,"[38] the name by which the Anteimoro were designated in the seventeenth century by the French residents at Fort-Dauphin. This toponymic tendency was common to Europeans of the epoch, and it obscured tribal names until well into the nineteenth century.

It is probably to Andriapanolaha that doctored genealogies and concern for historical events in the *Sora-bé* should be attributed. Through a comparison of two manuscripts, G. Mondain was able to discover that this must have been the time when "traditions began to alter . . . the writing doing injustice to truth."[39] But the return of the Zafikazimambo to power was cut short as a result of external causes. They were badly defeated between April 1659 and March 1660 in two military campaigns undertaken by Major La Case of Fort-Dauphin against the Anteimoro.[40] These expeditions were essentially punitive, although this factor has not been stressed. Primarily because of unfavourable terms of trade, Andriapanolaha was regarded as an enemy of the Fort-Dauphin settlement. The Anteimoro, a "nation of *Ombiasses*," as Flacourt called them, were generally credited by coastal Europeans with being the political and religious manipulators of the surrounding Antanosy near Fort-Dauphin. Once again, Flacourt provides the background behind La Case's expeditions against the Anteimoro.[41]

The *Ombiasses* here . . . are wonderously feared by the people . . . and [the unfriendly Antanosy chiefs] employed [their services] against the French. . . . They sent near the French Fort baskets full of papers with printed symbols and writings on them, eggs . . . with [the same], unbaked

---

[36] Cf. Gautier and Froidevaux, *La Case* (1907), 11.

[37] Mondain, *Histoire*, pp. 83–129.

[38] F. Cauche, *Relation du voyage . . . à Madagascar* (1651), in *COACM*, Vol. VII (1910), p. 57.

[39] Mondain, *Histoire*, p. xlix.

[40] Gautier and Froidevaux, *La Case*, pp. 11–12. For an outline of La Case's life and activities in Madagascar (1656–1671) see Deschamps, *Madagascar*, pp. 73–75.

[41] Flacourt, *Histoire*, *COACM*, Vol. VIII (1913), pp. 243–245.

earthen pots with writings inside and out, small coffins, dugouts, oars . . . all covered with symbols, scissors, tongs. . . . In short, there is hardly anything they did not try, even the poisoning of [our] water-wells . . . all of which gave the French something more than mere headache . . . forcing me to bring the [main] well closer to the Fort. . . . All of the local *Ombiasses* [here] are instructed by those from the land of Matetane.

It can be equally pointed out that Flacourt himself learned to read Arabico-Malagasy manuscripts because the *kitabi* could serve more than one master.[42]

E.-F. Gautier and H. Froidevaux depict the Antemahazo, following the defeat of the Zafikazimambo, as conquered but faithful subjects of La Case,[43] and it is apparent that the Antemahazo did supply La Case with men to help the declining fortunes of Fort-Dauphin. La Case's system of alliances collapsed, however, with his death in 1671, and three years later the Fort-Dauphin settlement came to an end. From the 1670s onward, the Ankara would face no serious competition among the Anteimoro. The "Tsimeto, Zafikazimambo, and Anteoni permitted them to take over religious power, source of riches, influence, and the right to provide chiefs for all the Anteimorona."[44] Thus, in the second half of the seventeenth century, the politicoreligious issues long dominant in local history were settled in favor of the Ankara. Dynastic squabbles continued mainly within the framework of descent.[45] From about the 1680s until the 1830s, the rice and slave trade with the Europeans and wars with the Tanala and the Antaifasy would dominate Anteimoro history.

La Case's expeditions into Imoro are confirmed by contemporary French sources. It is thus possible to gain some chronological control of Anteimoro history by working backward. Andriamarofotana was replaced as *andrianoni* (king) by another pretender in 1660.[46] Although eclipsed part of the time by Andriapanaolaha, Andriamarofotana had an extremely long, if nominal, rule before being succeeded by his grandson. Andriamarofotana became *andrianoni* after the deaths of Rabésirana and Andriamaso. Rabésirana was himself quite old when Andriamaso took over. Andriakazimambobé lost his life in a battle.[47] His importance suggests that the ruling span was not short. Ramarohala, on the other hand, man-

[42] "It was Dian Radam, *Ombiasse*, who . . . taught me how to read and write the Arabic letters"—E. de Flacourt, *Relation de la Grande Ile Madagascar* (1661), in *COACM*, Vol. IX (1920), p. 135.

[43] Gautier and Froidevaux, *La Case*, pp. 11–12.

[44] G. Gravier, *Madagascar* (1904), pp. 40–41.

[45] Julien, *Pages* (1933), pp. 7–31: MS A in Mondain, *Histoire*, pp. 83–119.

[46] Gautier and Froidevaux, *La Case*, p. 12.

[47] *Ferrand MSS*, No. 6, in *Musulmans*, Vol. II (1893), p. 71. It is possible to interpret this text in two ways: (a) Andriakazimambobé was assassinated by an Anteony; or (b) he lost his life in a war against "strangers."

aged to sire seventeen sons. Between the "slaying of *fanani*" (enthronement) and the nod given to Ramasomari, Ali was in power for a good
generation. Ramasomari's rule, however, was short because of the
vadikeli issue. Thus, it is possible to assign some very tentative spans as
follows:

> Andriamarofotana and Andriapanolaha, 1630–1660
> Andriamarofotana alone, 1615–1630
> Rabésirana, 1580–1615
> Andriakazimambobé, 1565–1580
> Ramarohala, 1540–1565
> Ramasomari, 1535–1540
> Ali, 1510–1535

Taking into account different sites of settlement, Ramakararubé could
have been in southeastern Madagascar as early as about 1490. The
Zafikazimambo might have arrived several years before 1565, possibly
by the late 1540s, to end the Anteimoro-Zafindraminia conflict started by
Ramasomari. Thus, the mid-sixteenth century is suggested as the time
when Islam became a political issue. There is another way of dating the
Anteimoro settlement in southeastern Madagascar, but this can best be
considered under the problem of origins.

The Anteimoro do not only represent the last overseas settlers to reach
Madagascar as a group. The Anteimoro, and particularly their principal
clans, were also unlike any other Malagasy. The Ankara, Tsimeto, and
Zafikazimambo—priests and king-makers with astute political training,
good Silamos, and zealots—grew not only in numbers but in ambition,
for which less and less room could be found locally. At Matitana and
Vohipeno, Farafangana or Mananjary, this unsettling talent found slight
outlets, and it sent forth something more than ripples in the tide of
political change affecting much of the late sixteenth-century Madagascar.
As a local state, the Anteimoro kingdom never amounted to a great power
in the island, unlike those of the Sakalava and Merina. Its energies, particularly before the eighteenth century, were directed inward. But the
kings' men, *mohadjers* and *kitabi*, *ombiassa* and *mpisikily*, found ample
opportunities elsewhere.

If the Anteimoro genealogical tree allows for some reasonable speculation in respect to an initial settlement, the Portuguese chronicles are less
imprecise. In 1507–1508 some months apart, two Portuguese captains
visited Matitana while looking for silver, cloves, and ginger. Neither of
them mentioned a possible colony of Moors at Matitana. One of the two,
Ruy Pereira, reported, however, that the local inhabitants were no
strangers to external trade, having brought silver and beeswax to his ship,
but that communication with the Portuguese was limited to sign lan-

guage.[48] According to Barros, Periera's information pointed to the avail-
ability of cloves and ginger as well as of silver. Moreover, Tristão da
Cunha, admiral of the Portuguese fleet in the western Indian Ocean, was
able to find at Mozambique a Moor named Bogima who had previously
been to Matitana, and who assured him that ginger was definitely present
there.[49] Eight members of the crew belonging to the second Portuguese
vessel confirmed that all kinds of silver ornaments could be seen, but
nothing else beyond the sugar cane and fish seemed worthy of note.
Their captain, Gomes d'Abreu, had visited the local chief and had eaten
with him in local fashion shortly before dying at Matitana.[50]

A more sober statement on commercial resources at Matitana came
from Diogo Lopes de Sequeira. He went there in October 1508. According to him, the cloves were not of indigenous origin. Rather, a single
load of cloves had once been salvaged from a shipwrecked Javanese
vessel, and the "natives, having seen in what esteem the Moors who
traded with them held the clove, began to collect fruits . . . similar to
laurel, the taste of which recalls the clove."[51] As for the silver ornaments,
"Blacks from the interior" did wear them, but the "Matitanais ignore
where this silver, impure at that, comes from."[52] Mainly because of
ginger, in 1513 Lisbon sent Luis Figueira to establish a small fort and
factory at Matitana but, by that time, "Matitana [was] a town densely
inhabited by Moors." At the end of a stay that lasted six months, Figueira
had to abandon his factory because, prodded by the "Moors," the "natives
attacked to get hold of his merchandise."[53] Another Portuguese attempt
to establish a factory at Matitana took place in 1521 without success.[54]
Thus, it is safe to say that the first Anteimoro colony *at Matitana* formed
between 1509 and 1512, and that Moors on the African mainland knew
about Matitana and traded occasionally with it before the Portuguese
discovery of Madagascar in 1506.

According to Figueira, the Matitana Moors were from Malindi.[55]
Other Europeans, not one a contemporary of Figueira, are divided on this
question. A tireless researcher, Ferrand could never decide whether the
Anteimoro came from the Arabian peninsula or from east Africa.[56] On

[48] Fernan d'Albuquerque, *Commentarios* (1557), in *COACM*, Vol. I (1903), p. 18.
[49] Barros, *Da Asia* (Decade II), in *COACM*, Vol. I (1903), p. 24.
[50] H. Osorius, *De Rebus Emmanuelis* (1574), in *COACM*, Vol. I (1903), pp. 48–49.
[51] Barros, *Da Asia* (Decade II), *COACM*, Vol. I (1903), pp. 48–49.
[52] *Ibid.*
[53] Barros, *Da Asia* (Decade III), in *COACM*, Vol. I (1903), p. 53.
[54] *Ibid.*, pp. 55–56.
[55] *Ibid.*, p. 52.
[56] After compiling three volumes on the subject, Ferrand could only conclude that
he was willing to call the Malagasy Muslims "Arabs" but "in the widest possible sense

the strength of some dubious linguistic inferences, Alfred Grandidier argued that they were Arabs from Arabia, but allowed them to reach Madagascar by way of east Africa instead of by a direct route.[57] Grandidier, however, would not concede that this passage made the Anteimoro *culturally* anything less than pure Arabs, or that it might have been of such long duration as to eliminate the Arabian peninsula altogether as a meaningful point of origin. In the 1650s Flacourt wrote that the Zafikazimambo claimed to have been sent by the "Caliph of Mecca" to "instruct" local inhabitants. At the same time, they were considerably "darker" than other Anteimoro "but, nonetheless, their undisputed masters."[58] As no Caliph had resided at Mecca for centuries and since Hūlāgū ended the Baghdad caliphate in 1258, this statement of derived religious authority shows how far removed the Zafikazimambo had been from the mainstream of Islam. In 1773 Charpentier de Cossigny, who spent some time at Antongil Bay, learned that the east-coast Arabs descend from "twenty-four families from the coast of east Africa" and had been present in Madagascar for at least two centuries.[59] Since, in the sixteenth century, the Portuguese also paused at Vohemar and discovered Malindi "Moors" there as well,[60] it is difficult to determine if the Vohemar and Matitana colonies were related or independent of one another, or even which of the two should fit de Cossigny's firsthand information.

Indeed, the presence of several Silamo colonies on the eastern shores

---

of the term," *Musulmans*, Vol. III (1902), p. 114. Although many pointed references are scattered in the three volumes, there is actually no evidence that Ferrand wanted to be concerned with the problem of origins before presenting all of the primary sources he could find. Ferrand's private library was sold in Leiden before World War II and with it some of the *Sora-bé* not published before went into unknown private hands.

[57] A. Grandidier, *Ethnographie de Madagascar*, Vol. I, Tome 1 (1908), pp. 143–157 and notes, and Vol. I, Tome 2 (1908), p. 639, n. 139; A. and G. Grandidier, *Ethnographie de Madagascar*, Vol. IV (1917), p. 508. Taken together, these segments begin with admission that the Anteimoro could have been from east Africa, progress to "many hypotheses could be advanced," and terminate in 1917 with the assertion that the "Tsimeto are descendants of Sunnite Arabs while the Ankara, Anteony, and Zafikazimambo descend from the Alides."

[58] Flacourt, *Histoire*, COACM, Vol. VIII (1913), p. 40. Flacourt also states on the same page that the Zafikazimambo have been in Madagascar "only 150 years"; since the first edition of Flacourt's *Histoire* came out in 1658, the date of arrival would be 1508.

[59] Charpentier de Cossigny, *Mémoires* (January 1773), cited in A. Grandidier, *Ethnographie*, Vol. I, Tome 2, p. 635, n. 8. On de Cossigny, see R. Coupland, *East Africa and Its Invaders* (1965 reprint), p. 76, n. 2.

[60] Barros, *Da Asia* (Decade III), COACM, Vol. I (1903), p. 53; and Diogo do Couto, *Da Asia* (Decade VII), in COACM, Vol. I (1903), p. 99.

of Madagascar, from Vohemar (Iharana) in the northeast to Fort-
Dauphin in the southeast, has produced a body of literature in respect
to their interconnections. Suggestions have been made that the Zafindraminia and the Iharanians are the same people.[61] Some of the Anteimoro texts claim or imply descent from Raminia.[62] To complicate matters
there exists an Antevohimaro clan among the Anteimoro.[63] The Onjatsy,
too, can be found today both in the area of Vohemar and in Matitana, as
has been reported in older sources.[64] There is, however, no serious evidence extant to permit a confusion of the Anteimoro and Zafindraminia-
Antambahoaka. The Zafindraminia antedate the Anteimoro in Madagascar by at least two centuries. Although a Shirazi origin has been
proposed for Raminia,[65] the most plausible hypothesis by far is that of
Ferrand, who saw him as an Indonesian Muslim accompanied by the
famous Wak-Wak (Antambahoaka), and residing for a time in east
Africa before going to Madagascar.[66] The account of Ibn al-Mujāwir
assumes some importance here.[67] Moreover, one of the Paris manuscripts

---

[61] The earliest is by A. Jully, "Ethnographie de Madagascar," *RM*, VIII (1906),
1025–1054; and the most recent by R. Cornevin, *Histoire de l'Afrique* (1962), Vol.
I, pp. 386–389. Cornevin implies that he is following Deschamps, who is less cate-
gorical on this subject.

[62] Manuscript 13 of the Bibliothèque Nationale in G. Ferrand, "La Légende de
Raminia," *JA*, 9th series, XIX/2 (1902), 225–230. Following this tradition, the
Anteimoro issue from Raminia's daughter Ravahininia and an unknown father at
Matitana. Conversely, a Tanala oral tradition claims that the Anteimoro gave birth
to the Zafindraminia (cf. Col. Ardant du Picq, "L'Influence islamique sur . . .
[les] . . . Tanala," *RTC*, XXVI/207 (1932), 266–269.

[63] This can be explained by Zafindraminia connections or by those of the Onjatsy
as people (originally) from Vohémar.

[64] The earliest written mention of Onjatsy at Vohémar, given as Anzatci, is in an
anonymous manuscript of 1816, Carton 11/99, Archives des Fortifications des
Colonies. Sakalava oral traditions refer to them as Hounzati in Iboina. The Anteimoro
Sora-bé mention them at Matitana several dozen times.

[65] A. Grandidier, *Ethnographie*, Vol. I, Tome 1, pp. 130–131, and notes. This origin
was suggested first in a letter by Abbé Charles Nacquart to Vincent de Paul, February 5, 1650, partially reproduced in *Mémoires de la congrégation de la mission
des Lazaristes*, Vol. IX (1866), p. 60.

[66] "Les Voyages des Javanais à Madagascar," *JA*, 10th series, XV/2 (1910), 302–
303, 330; "Le Pays de Mangalor et de Mangatsini," *T'oung-pao* (Leiden), 2nd series,
X/1 (1909), 1–16.

[67] Ibn al-Mujāwir, *Tārīh al-Mustabsir* (*ca.* A.D. 1223), pertinent passage in
Arabic and French reproduced by Gabriel Ferrand in "Le K'ouen-Louen," *JA*, 11th
series, III/3 (1919), 473–477. An English translation will be found in F. M. Hunter,
An Account of the British Settlement of Aden in Arabia (1877), pp. 183–196. The
hypothesis that the proto-Zafindraminia may have been Indonesians who occupied
coastal Aden for a while, moving first to east Africa after an invasion of the
"Barabar" is clearly supported by Ibn al-Mūjawīr's account. Through Islam and
Arabic writing, however, the proto-Zafindraminia could have acquired some Persian
borrowings while in east Africa.

contains an interesting and reasonably detailed statement of Raminia's journey to Madagascar. With companions divided into the Silamo and Kafiry—the Mofia, Antevandrika, and Masianaki—Raminia traveled fifteen days to reach Vinandratsy (dangerous river). Madagascar was sighted in another fifteen days. The migrants landed first at Harana (Iharana, old name for Vohemar). A division—probably a violent one— took place, and some of the men continued their journey. Raminia lived at Harana for "three years." With only the Zanak-Onjatsy left behind, he went south, pausing another "three years" at Ivondrona. He finally settled at Mangoro, bringing with him a "sacred jug."[68] This *sinibé vato* (great stone jug) has indeed been discovered near Ivondrona.[69] Another find attributed to Raminia is a 170 x 115 centimeter "elephant" carved in soft schist, and known as the *vatolambo* (stone boar).[70] The schist of three-legged Iharanian jugs and that of the *vatolambo* appear to be identical. Soft-schist carving techniques are generally seen as the most characteristic feature of Iharanian culture. Thus, there is some basis for the assumption that the Zafindraminia and the Iharanians were no strangers.

However, the Iharanian *culture* cannot be claimed for the Zafindraminia because the polished stone and building crafts of Iharana did not migrate south. The earliest Iharana date indicates that the Iharanians were there before the Zafindraminia. An early nineteenth-century Malagasy-French dictionary, composed in Mauritius and found in the British Museum, states that the Zafindraminia left Vohemar only after a "great war."[71] In 1831 a French source reported that an ancient population of Vohemar, known as *Henesouastes*, originated in the isle of Mozambique.[72] This term seems to apply to the Zanak-Onjatsy, whose gradual spread south, along the eastern littoral, is no cause for surprise. The Onjatsy also migrated among the Iboina Sakalava, where a nineteenth-century tradition reports them as having reached Madagascar

[68] Ferrand, "Légende," 224 and n. 3.

[69] A. Grandidier, *Ethnographie*, Vol. I, Tome 1, pp. 132 and n. 3, 133.

[70] *Ibid.*, pp. 133 and n. 1.

[71] Anonymous, *Mémoire sur Madagascar*, British Museum, Department of Manuscripts, Add. Manuscript 18126, pp. 45–46. It is inserted as a supplement to the *Grand Dictionnaire de Madagascar*, compiled early in the nineteenth century at Mauritius by B. H. de Froberville. The approximate date of this *Mémoire* is 1750, but it appears to be based on field notes made thirty-five to forty years earlier. Cf. Jean Valette, "Madagascar vers 1750 d'après un manuscrit anonyme," *BM*, XIV/214 (1964), 211–258.

[72] Th. Fleury, "Quelques notes sur le nord de Madagascar," *Bulletin de la Société de Géographie Commerciale de Bordeaux* (April 5, 1886), 203; based with three additional articles on the manuscript notes of French naval doctor Charles Bernier, dated September 27, 1834, or about three years after his visit to northeastern Madagascar. Cf. *ANSOMCM*, Carton XVII, Dossier 8, pp. 1–136. *Henesouastes= Hundzatse=Onjatsy* or Zanak-Onjatsy has been the proposed etymology.

originally from Malindi.[73] Most of the Onjatsy are still to be found, however, among the Antankarana, people who today inhabit the region of
Iharana. In effect, the Iharanian material culture is unique to northeastern
Madagascar, since it diffused nowhere else within the Great Island.[74] It
slowly declined, disappearing by about 1650 because the survival and
prosperity of Iharana depended on external commerce within a Moorish
trade empire, to which the European overseas expansion administered
a series of more or less important blows. Moreover, ethnographic data
collected over the past one hundred years will show in a moment that
the Anteimoro and Antambahoaka as well as Onjatsy cannot be given
a common origin.

Attempts to date approximately Raminia's migration into the Great
Island have had an unfortunate and completely unnecessary by-product.
In 1613, Father Mariano was informed by Tsiambany, main ruler of the
Antanosy, that the Zafindraminia advent "goes back to remote times for,
in direct line, he counted seventeen generations on one side and fourteen
on the other."[75] This is an often quoted passage, confirmed moreover
some four decades later by Flacourt who names Tsiambany's seventeen
ancestors.[76] Thus, the arrival of Raminia to Madagascar *itself* could be
placed around A.D. ±1300. It does not follow, as some writers have
claimed without historical necessity, that the birth of the Antanosy
dynasty coincides in time with the arrival of Raminia in Madagascar. The
report of Mariano is not obscure on this point: Tsiambany's ancestors
arrived first in northeastern Madagascar and took a long time to reach
Antanosy. It is known that some type of chiefdom existed very definitely
before the Zafindraminia became established among the Antanosy. Their
early chiefs were called *antibobaka* and their tombs still exist at Itap-
erina.[77]

The past of southeastern Antalaotra has been confused too often not

[73] "When the Sakalava reached Boueni (Boina) . . . around 1700 . . . the northwestern coast was occupied . . . by the *Hounzati* . . . whom the tradition reports as
having come from Mélinde" (Vincent Noel, "Recherches sur les Sakkalava," *BSGP*,
3rd series, I [1844], 410).

[74] Despite some speculation that such a diffusion might have gone toward the
Lake Alaotra region, recent excavations do not confirm it. Cf. René Battistini and
Pierre Verin, "Vohitrandriana haut-lieu d'une ancienne culture du Lac Laotra," *CM*,
I/1 (1964), 53–90.

[75] L. Mariano, *Relation . . . 1613–1614*, in *COACM*, Vol. II (1904), p. 49. The
Portuguese text was first published in *BSGL*, 7th series, No. 5, 313–354.

[76] Racoubé=Maaszoumare=Dian Alive=Rahomado=Dian Bahohac Ragomma=
Dian Savatto=Dian Pangharen=Dian Roamasso=Dian Pangarzaffe=Dian Bohits=
Dian Missaran=Dian Ravaha=Dian Nong=Dian Arrive=Dian Raval=Dian Massin-
pelle=Dian Bevoulle=Dian Tsiamban (Andrian Tsiambany), cf. Flacourt, *Histoire*,
COACM, Vol. VIII (1913), pp. 86–87.

[77] A. and G. Grandidier, *Ethnographie*, Vol. III (1917), p. 538.

to require an examination of a would-be common descent. The Antambahoaka themselves claim parentage with the Anteimoro *only* through
marriage, as is attested by the *vadibé* role of Ravahininia. Whereas Ferrand discovered almost 55 percent of Arabic words in the old Ankara
vocabulary, the ratio in an analogous Antambahoaka one decreased by
some 22 percent in comparison. This could mean two different degrees
of linguistic Arabization, or that the Antambahoaka had been in Madagascar *much* longer because of word loss. In either case, the common
descent is not sustained, and marriage rules in the two groups argue
strongly against it. The Anteimoro practice both tribal and clan endogamy, which is strictly observed, and have genuine castes.[78] Exogamy
is, on the other hand, the general Antambahoaka rule, excluding only
associations with the Antevandrika and Antevolo, while castes do not
exist as could be expected.[79]

In features associated with funerary ritual, the two groups have certain
similarities. Both wash their dead, shave the hair and beards of the
deceased, tend to bury at night, and share with contiguous groups of the
Anteifasy, Anteisaka, and some Tanala the *kibory*, the name given to
communal graves.[80] The Antambahoaka *kibory* are, however, open on all
sides while the Anteimoro place hangarlike constructions over them and
add palisades around, allowing access through a single door.[81] Women
cannot enter the Anteimoro *kibory* except when aged and even then only
to perform certain specific tasks.[82] The Antambahoaka have no such *fady*.
Moreover, according to Shaw, their old women used to "expedite" those
about to pass away by suffocation, a custom unknown to the Anteimoro.[83]
Also, the Antambahoaka bury their dead in coffins, piled on top of one
another. The Anteimoro make no coffins and wrap their dead in mats and

[78] Compare, for three different time periods, Flacourt, *Histoire, COACM*, Vol. VIII
(1913), p. 42; the account of pirate Nathaniel North's stay at Matitana in 1709, in
COACM, Vol. III (1905), p. 586; and Gabriel Gravier's statement that aristocratic
endogamy was the principal cause of the 1878 Ampanabaka revolt, in *Madagascar*,
p. 41.

[79] H. Deschamps and S. Vianès, *Les Malgaches du sud-est* (1959), pp. 19–24.

[80] For a general discussion of the *kibory* (Anteimoro, Antambahoaka, Anteisaka,
Antaifasy), see Raymond Decary, *Le Mort et les coutumes funeraires à Madagascar*
(1962), pp. 175–195. For added materials on the Anteimoro *kibory* alone, see Charles
Poirier, *Notes d'ethnographie et d'histoire malgaches* (1939), pp. 21–28, published
as Volume XXVIII of the *MAM*.

[81] J. Sibree, "South-East Madagascar," *Notes of a Journey Through the Tanala,
Taimoro and Taisaka Countries in June and July 1876* (1876), pp. 57, 62. Booklet
of 81 pages.

[82] Th. Lord, "Jottings of a Journey to the South-East Madagascar," *AA*, IV (1892),
471.

[83] G. A. Shaw, "The Arab Element in the South-East Madagascar," *AA*, V (1894),
209.

lambas. It has been reported that the Ankara of the Anteimoro once believed that the humors of deceased kings produced a seven-headed monster snake, the *fananimpitulaha,* a belief most incompatible with Islam.[84]

The communal *kibory* do not appear to have been introduced into southeastern Madagascar by the Anteimoro as similar types of graves occur in northern sections of the littoral where no Anteimoro influence can be claimed and where the communal graves are much closer to the Antambahoaka model, including the use of coffins. Among the older funerary features of the Anteimoro, at least two should be noted. At one time the Tsimeto buried their dead individually in huts, a practice that survived into the nineteenth century only for royalty. The use of stone pillars in conjunction with burial sites, while uncommon among other Malagasy, is not only an old custom but also possesses some distinct features in that the *tsngambato* (commemorative stone pillars) are placed at some distance from the graves, always to the east, and in groups of unworked phalli. Royal Anteimoro tombs were marked usually by a stone pillar in the shape of a pyramid, 3 to 4 meters high, while their capital is itself called *Vatomasina,* or sacred stone. The Anteimoro very definitely withheld the announcement of royal death.[85] If the Antambahoaka ever had kings, no historical record survives to show this to have been the case. Unlike the Anteimoro and Antambahoaka, the Zafindraminia Antanosy fed their dead.[86] Like the Zafindraminia and Merina kings, those of the Anteimoro were buried with silver.[87] The Tsimeto and Onjatsy, unlike the Anteony, did not place on the feet, hands, and around the necks of their dead any of the Quranic verses.[88] In the 1870s, an Anteimoro king was poisoned by the Tsimeto, on Ankara orders, for committing "public impropriety" with his prospective wives.[89] Such puritanism emerges nowhere in the Antambahoaka past.

It was Flacourt's firsthand observation that two parallel societies existed among the Antanosy, one of the *"blancs"* and the other of the *"noirs,"* the former being Zafindraminia and the latter known collectively as Marinh:[90]

---

[84] A. and G. Grandidier, *Ethnographie,* Vol. IV (1917), p. 15 and n. 3.

[85] Mondain, *Histoire,* p. 151. After the death of a minor *Andrianony,* Andriamanoro, who filled the office very briefly between Rabesirana and Andriamarofotana, there was an interregnum of just under one year.

[86] For eight to fifteen days, wrote Flacourt, "the kin of the deceased send their slaves with food for him . . . as if he were alive," *Histoire, COACM,* Vol. VIII (1913), p. 147.

[87] De Mondevergue, "Extracts," 1668, *ANSOMCM,* Carton I, Section II, pieces 13 and 17; A. and G. Grandidier, *Ethnographie,* IV (1917), 40 and n. 2.

[88] A. and G. Grandidier, *Ethnographie,* IV (1917), p. 18 and n. 5.

[89] *Ibid.,* 477 (a).

[90] Flacourt, *Histoire, COACM,* Vol. VIII (1913), pp. 25–27; also pp. 78–81, where two interesting and pertinent details are added, namely that all Antanosy

The Zafindraminia . . . divided into three . . . estates: Rohandrian, Ancandrian, and Ondzatsi; the Rohandrian are those from v·hom they get their king or principal chief, called Ompiandrian or Dian Bahouache, while they themselves have the rank of princes; the Ancandrian are those who issue from a Rohandrian and a woman who is of the blacks or else of the Ancandrian or Ondzatsi; . . . the Ancandrian, like the Rohandrian, have the right to cut the throats of animals; the Ondzatsi . . . can only cut the throat of fowls. . . . The blacks of this province . . . are divided into four, namely the Voadziri, Lohavohits, Ontsoa, and Ondeves; the Voadziri are the highest among the blacks and are chiefs of the lands, being descendants of the (original) masters of the land before submitting to the whites; and when they are too far from the whites and there is no Rohandrian or Ancandrian in their villages, they have the authority to cut the throat of animals. The Lohavohits are those who descend from the Voadziri and who are also high among the blacks but with the difference that the former command over lands while the latter commands only his people and only in his village, with the right to cut the throat of animals when he wants to eat. . . . The Ontsoa are below the Lohavohits; the Ondeves are worst of all for this word Ondeve means "a man lost."

Some rather important aspects emerge from this description. It tells us distinctly that those to be supreme rulers, or *ompiandrian* (Malagasy, *ompiana + andriana* or 'those groomed to be rulers'), among the Antanosy came from the nobility of Antambahoaka origin, or *Dian Bahouach* (*andriana + bahoaka*, the missing infix *ant* or *anta* being simply people and the *mb* being reduced to *b*). At the same time, the basic sociopolitical structure was clearly *not* imported from the Antambahoaka by the Zafindraminia. Rather, they duplicated the one pre-existing among the Marinh, fact easily explained by the adoption of exogamy among the *rohandrian*. In this way, a kinship base for authority was acquired organically while the expanded structure reflected a model already familiar to the *tompontany*. Two new features, nonetheless, were introduced into the local Antanosy society, the idea of kingship, with supreme ruler presiding over chiefs and nobility, and *sombily* (exclusive right to slaughter domestic animals), which clearly was to sustain the pre-eminent position of the Zafindraminia as a collective aristocracy. Yet, the *sombily* prerogative was by no means rigidly applied, and the introduction of kingship did not produce a centralized state. This is all in great contrast to the Anteimoro, who managed to retain and superimpose much of their sociopolitical structure on the *tompontany* of Matitana and

---

"estates" (Ancandrian, Ondzatsi, Voadziri, Lohavohits, and Ontsoa) excepting the Zafindraminia *rohandrian can* be reduced to the status of slave (*ondevo*); equally, the three upper estates among the Marinh participated actively in the selection of successor to a dead "Grand" or "Roi."

who did not yield their *sombily* rights to the Ampanabaka, or commoners, until the bloody revolts of the nineteenth century. It is thus safe to state that while some important internal divergences can be noted among the aristocratic Anteimoro clans and while all of the southeastern Antalaotra were profoundly affected by the different *tompontany* with whom they merged in language and kinship, there are no longer any grounds for confusing the Antalaotra as mere branches that can be traced back to the same original ancestor.

One could dismiss all of the already reported statements which link the Anteimoro with Africa. The Portuguese, for example, were too prone to assign to all the Moors of Madagascar a Malindi origin. The Anteimoro, if only for obvious religion-induced reasons, have themselves claimed "Meccan origins," using the term *antampasemaka* or (people of the Meccan sands).[91] In a chapter on Malagasy religion, Flacourt wrote that the Zafindraminia legends of origin mention a great flood from which only four mountains were spared, the Zaballicaf, Zaballicatoure, Zaballiraf, and Zaballibazani.[92] In his annotations to the Flacourt text, Alfred Grandidier transliterated *zaballi* as Arabic for mountain (djebel), with Mounts Kaf, Sinai, and Arafat corresponding to the first three in Flacourt.[93] However, several years earlier, Grandidier used the same transliteration idea for a text of an Anteimoro chronicle acquired in 1901 by a colonial administrator of the Farafangana province named Marchand. The pertinent text is as follows:[94]

> The inhabitants of eight villages near Maka left together in search of a new land of their own as a result, say the Anteimoro, of internal quarrels. The chronicle preserves the names of these villages . . . *Zobaly-Zobaly, Zobaly rafay, Zobaly faramaseko, Zobaly faradabaitry, Alimokadosy, Zobaly marohazomamoa, Zobaly kafo, Zobaly alifo;* and their tombs at *Marovany,* and their fountains at *Sinamo.*

It is a matter of considerable obscurity as to how Grandidier was able to identify the Zaballicatoure of Flacourt *and* the Zobaly faradabaitra of Marchand as Sinai. There is no doubt that the two texts are in themselves very different, not to mention the fact that they belonged to two distinct Antalaotra groups and that one was reported around 1650 and the other at the turn of the twentieth century. The important question is, to what extent can the Marchand text be taken to point to Arabia?

---

[91] "Ontampasemaka," according to Flacourt, "because they are Arabs from the Red Sea," *Histoire, COACM,* Vol. VIII (1913), p. 40. See also Van Gennep, *Tabou,* p. 130.

[92] Flacourt, *Histoire, COACM,* Vol. VIII (1913), p. 94.

[93] *Ibid.,* 94 and n. 1–3. The notes are not Flacourt's.

[94] Marchand, "Les Habitants de la province de Farafangana," *RM,* III (1901), 484.

There certainly is nothing improbable about the Anteimoro belief that Arabia had *once* been the ancestral home. Yet, if their traditions are read carefully, the ancestral Anteimoro seldom came directly from Maka. The crucial document in this connection is an Anteimoro genealogy, now lost, that revealed that Ramakararubé was at best the *tenth* successor of a line that had fled Maka.[95] The Anteimoro *tsangambato*, or commemorative stone pillars, placed east of the common graves (*kibory*)[96] are extremely suggestive of the northeast African *menhir*.[97] The sixteen-pattern *sikidy* (divination) of the Anteimoro, which their *ombiassa* diffused in much of Madagascar, was traced long ago by Grandidier *himself* to Africa rather than Arabia.[98] There is still another and extremely important feature of Anteimoro society that not only sets them completely apart from all other Malagasy, but that can be traced without mistake to the African mainland, namely the *age groups*. These have been adequately described in their contemporary setting by Hubert Deschamps and Suzanne Vianès.[99] Earlier authors, however, hinted at their presence,[100] while an unusual agricultural productivity in old Anteimoro society points to an institution of considerable antiquity and one that only *they* could have brought into the Great Island.[101] It was Julien who first saw the possibility that the term Anteimoro (phonetics, *Temūrū*) might not be at all Malagasy but African. He saw it as deriving from *Mahūrū*, "*métis d'Africaines et d'Arabes de la partie occidentale des Iles Comores, dans certains cas aussi des originaires de la côte d'Afrique et îles voisines.*"[102] By inference at least, there is no plausible alternative to the African mainland as the Anteimoro point of origin.

The Anteimoro neither minted nor used coin. Their older tombs are

---

[95] A. Grandidier, *Ethnographie*, Vol. I, Tome 1 (1908), pp. 148 and n. 5, 156; A. Jully, "L'Origine des Malgaches," *BAM*, I/1 (1902), 18.

[96] For a reproduction of *tsangambato*, see photograph 9, planche II, in Deschamps and Vianès, *Les Malgaches du sud-est*, following p. 115.

[97] These stone phalli appear to be most widely present in southern Ethiopia, "averaging around 12 feet in height," G. P. Murdock, *Africa* (1959), p. 198.

[98] A. and G. Grandidier, *Ethnographie*, Vol. IV (1917), pp. 500–503. At least seven of the sixteen patterns "carry in all Madagascar the same nomenclatures as in Darfur and North Africa" (p. 503). Cf. Mohammed es-Zenati, *Khatt er-Ramel*, summarized by A. B. ben Choaib in *Revue Africaine* (1906), pp. 62–71.

[99] Deschamps and Vianès, *Malgaches du sud-est*, pp. 55–57.

[100] H. D'Escamps, *Histoire et géographie de Madagascar* (1884), p. 414; A. S. Huckett, "Southeast Madagascar," *CLMS* (August 1887), 352; and Ferrand, *Musulmans*, Vol. I (1891), p. 9.

[101] A number of early sources reported high population density and unusually large quantities of rice among the Anteimoro. In the 1870s, for example, rice granaries in some villages outnumbered the dwellings three to one. In the period 1644–1645 two sloops made seven voyages to Matitana to obtain rice for Fort-Dauphin.

[102] Julien, *Pages* (1929), p. 75.

without inscriptions. They built no mosques, unlike the Swahili-influenced Antalaotra of northwestern Madagascar and the Comoro Islands.[103] Although Anteimoro Islam allows for the same type of syncretism observed on the east African littoral, merging the traditional and intrusive religions, it is nowhere nearly as evolved as Islam of Swahili urban centers.[104] It is beyond doubt that the Anteimoro term for communal graves, *kibory* (phonetics, *kibur'*, with barely audible terminal vowel) derives from *khabura/makaburi*, the most common word for graveyards on the Swahili coast (used in both cases as plural *and* singular).[105] Yet, there is no indication that this term was introduced in southeastern Madagascar by the Anteimoro. In effect, linguistic research has turned up only one other Swahili loan in the Anteimoro idiom, while a comparison of their Arabic script with those of Zanzibar and the Comoros has yielded only one common letter.[106] The Anteimoro "standard" script is actually devoid of standard Arabic orthography, "some words having been written in 216 different ways, 54 of which could be approximately called correct."[107] It does include twenty-six punctuation symbols, which appeared at first so unusual and distinct as to suggest a means with which to discover the original center of diffusion.[108] Unfortunately, similar corruptions and symbols appear to have plagued much of the Arabic calligraphy in the post-Caliphate period.[109] *Mahūrū*, moreover, seems to

[103] The Lulungane mosque was first reported in 1506. On northwestern ruins, see Charles Poirier, "Terre d'Islam en Mer Malgache," *BAM*, special issue (1954), 71–116. In 1916, at Ngazidja (Grande Comore), there were 168 mosques, the oldest of which (at Tsauéni) goes back to the first Muslim arrivals—cf. M. Fontoynont and E. Raomandahy, *La Grande Comore* (1937), p. 23.

[104] J. S. Trimingham, *Islam in East Africa* (1964), pp. 53–75; Deschamps and Vianès, *Malgaches du sud-est*, pp. 70–71; Ferrand, *Musulmans*, Vol. I (1891), pp. 15–41. A comparison of the Ferrand and Deschamps–Vianès passages shows that considerable dilution of Islamic survivals occurred in the last seven decades (1891–1959), the opposite of the gains Islam made in Africa under colonial rule. This is almost certainly due to a total isolation of the Anteimoro from outside contacts; there is no doubt that Islamic roots were much stronger in the earlier centuries.

[105] Cf. A. H. J. Prins, *The Swahili-Speaking Peoples of Zanzibar and the East African Coast* (1967), p. 106.

[106] *Mozinga*, for cannon, appears to be the only one of Swahili loan-words. The common letter is for *ng* transliterations. A. Grandidier, *Ethnographie*, Vol. I, Tome 1 (1908), p. 129, notule 2c; and Ferrand, *Musulmans*, Vol. III (1902), p. 115 (table).

[107] G. Ferrand, "Notes sur la transcription arabico-malgache," *Mémoirs de la Société de Linguistique de Paris*, XII (1902), 164; and A. Grandidier, *Ethnographie*, Vol. I, Tome 1 (1908), p. 153, n. 2.

[108] Julien, *Pages* (1929), pp. 113–114.

[109] I am indebted to David Flattery of the University of California, Berkeley, for discovering this general trend. The Hassani manuscripts as well as those of Mondain reveal a good number of Anteimoro words that appear to belong to some African languages, a matter currently being researched.

have applied in the Swahili idiom with some precision to emancipated slaves.[110] This could perhaps apply to some of the ancestral Anteimoro but certainly not to their principal lineages and clans. In short, the Swahili coastal belt and nearby islands, as well as the Comoros, must be excluded as possible points of origin. This is all the more certain since the Anteimoro knowledge of paper manufacturing does not appear to have been a known feature of the Swahili culture.[111]

There are no grounds for seeing *Temuru* either as a Malagasy name or as a corruption of one alien to the Malagasy dialects, particularly since the Anteimoro did not trickle into southeastern Madagascar as individuals. As related groups of migrants who reached southeastern Madagascar a short time apart, the Anteimoro could not have parted with their name. And, given the dynamic nature of the Anteony and Antalaotra, one would expect to find some trace of the *Temuru* in their former homeland. Such a trace has been found by Enrico Cerulli in the epic song of Ethiopia's *negus Yeshak* (1414–1429). It mentions a subsequently vanished people named Temur (Semur/Temur) in connection with the Somali (Sumālē).[112] Even more interesting, the *Temur* and *Sumale* survive as archaisms in the living speech of the inhabitants of Harar and are recalled as close kin.[113]

It is certainly the vast Somali hinterland and part of eastern Ethiopia, with their desert and semiarid environment, that suggest themselves as repositories of zealotic and fossilized Muslim communities, one or more of which ultimately sired the Malagasy Anteimoro. For a long time before

---

[110] Trimingham, *Islam in East Africa*, pp. 148, 185.

[111] Either the Anteimoro brought the technical knowledge with them, possibly from contacts with such Red Sea commercial centers as Zeila and Berbera, or else they took it over from the pre-existing specialists serving the Zafindraminia. Flacourt reported in his *Histoire, COACM*, Vol. VIII (1913), pp. 279–280, that the beaten-bark technique was employed in paper manufacturing, and that the bark itself came from the *avoha* (*Dais Glaucescens*) *tree*. D. Hunter, in *Papermaking: The History and Technique of an Ancient Craft* (1947), pp. 29–47, attributed the beaten-bark technique (*tapa*) to the Pacific islands in general. Yet, Flacourt was certain at the time that the Anteimoro paper "is made almost in the same manner as in France with the exception that [the Anteimoro] do not have the same tools . . . nor as many machines," *Histoire*, p. 279. A useful English summary of Flacourt's description in respect to how the paper was made will be found in Samuel Copland's *A History of the Island of Madagascar* (1822), p. 105. This work is, to a large extent, a translation of Flacourt, transposed uncritically into the nineteenth century. It is worth noting that the Anteimoro words for paper, ink, and pen represent Arabic loans in Malagasy.

[112] E. Cerulli, *Somalia, scritti vari editi ed inediti*, Vol. I (1957), p. III. According to Julien, Hassani, "*auteur de notre copie et conservateur du texte original*," was uncertain whether Anteimoro should come out phonetically *Temuru* or *Tamaru*. As for its etymology, "*il prétend qu'il s'agit d'une ville d'Arabie. S'agirait-il de Tamara, près Berbera?*"—cf. *Pages* (1929), p. 61, n. 1.

[113] Cerulli, *Somalia*, Vol. I, p. III.

1500 this area—running south to north from the borderlands of Kenya to the Red Sea—had been a cul-de-sac for a great variety of *wadads* and *Imams*, a home for dissenters and heretics who generated their own strife, of fragmented political systems and religious conflicts, doctored genealogies and social structures almost duplicated by the Anteimoro. Since cattle were not present at Matitana in the sixteenth century, the reference to *bakara* (بقر) in Andriabakara indicates a previous pastoral environment. The old Ankara vocabulary also contains a tell-tale term for king or *solitani* (ساطلان),[114] unknown to Malagasy languages,[115] but used in northeastern Africa, while the title of *mohadjer* has been reported as common only to one area of northeastern Africa, namely eastern Ethiopia.[116] The Anteimoro age groups are not at all analogous to those of the Bantu-speaking peoples. Rather, they reproduce in Madagascar such a system as, for example, the *gada* one of the Conso, while the Conso *mehrin* differ from the Anteimoro *tsangambato* neither in function nor in kind, but only in height.[117] The term *Vatomasina* (sacred stone) for the "holy capital" of the Anteimoro equally points to an older association with megalithic culture. Nor are the likely causes of Temur exile from northeastern Africa absent—namely, internal religious strife and the Galla expansion, the date of which remains imprecise but not too far removed from the turn of the sixteenth century.

If one returns to the curious Marchand text, the term *zobaly*, which occurs eight times, cannot be transliterated on *linguistic* grounds as *djebel* (Arabic, mountain), while the text itself refers very clearly to dwelling sites and not to any mountains. The Malagasy equivalent of *dj*/phon. *dz* would be the *j* and not the *z*. The Malagasy *o*, followed by consonants, is without exception *u* (*oo*), while the terminal *y* can stand for any vowel or to stress the letter preceding it. On the other hand, as many of the early written sources show, the *z* in Madagascar interchanged most readily with *s*: *Zada/Sada/Çada*, *Andriamazoto/Diamasuto*, *Zolimas/Solimas*.[118] These examples are from different parts of Madagas-

---

[114] Ferrand, *Musulmans*, Vol. III (1901), p. 26.

[115] From this must be excepted the *sikidy* formulas, which contain sultan in the slot for king. Cf. Ardant du Picq, "Etude Comparative sur la Divination en Afrique et à Madagascar," *Bulletin du Comité d'Etudes Historiques et Scientifiques de l'Afrique Occidentale Française*, XIII/1 (1930), 9–25, particularly 13.

[116] H. A. R. Gibb and J. H. Kramers, *Shorter Encyclopaedia of Islam* (1953), p. 390; and Fr. Buhl, *Das Leben Muhammeds* (1930), p. 109, cited as reference in the translation by Schaeder.

[117] Cf. Ad. E. Jensen, "Elementi della cultura spirituale dei Conso nell' Etiopia meridionale," *Rassegna di Studi Etiopici*, II/3 (1942), 217–258; Murdock, *Africa*, pp. 201–203. The *menhir* photograph in Jensen shows them to be somewhat shorter than the *tsangambato*.

[118] *COACM*, Vol. II (1904), p. 28, for *Diamasuto*; *COACM*, Vol. II (1904), p. 49, for *Solimas*; *COACM*, Vol. I (1903), p. 37, for *Zada*. The areas are those of Ranobé,

car, and the last one is linguistically most telling because it was examined and explained. It derives from *Islam/Islamos/Silamos* who then become *Zolimas/Solimas*. In Malagasy, *z* may also change into *ts*, but as both Ferrand and Grandidier (elsewhere) have shown the Arabic *dj* (voiced affricate) would be equivalent to Malagasy *g* as in *Ragibourail* (from Arabic, *Ra-Djebril*).[119] It is in the old term *Sumālē* (for present Somali) that Zobaly (*Subale*) finds the nearest kin. The presence of *b* instead of *m* in Malagasy version poses no serious problem because *mb* combinations in this idiom are common (*mamba, zomba, simba, sambo, fomba*), particularly in cases of verified or suspected African loans, and sooner or later either the *m* drops out in favor of *b* or (more rarely) the reverse loss takes over.

No less interesting, the Marchand text includes, besides some Malagasy words, also others which decidedly are not. Thus, *fara* is Malagasy for descendants of, or offspring, while *rafay* (in Zobaly *rafay*) is simple metathesis of *fara*. There are other Malagasy terms as well in the text.[120] But, at least two, *Alimokadosy* and *Sinamo*, mean nothing in Madagascar. It would be tempting to see in the first *ahl-I-Mukadishu* (Arabic, people of Mogadisho) and connect the abandoned fountains of *Sinamo* with the Sidama area (or even *kafo* in the Marchand text with Kafa), but this would be to retrogress into the kind of etymological chase which even Turgot had rejected in the eighteenth century. Still, the effort of Grandidier to transform the Marchand text into a proof of Arabic origin of the Anteimoro cannot be accepted.

A most unusual narrative history of the Anteony has been uncovered.[121] Penned around 1933 by an Anteimoro, former subgovernor of his province, it is based on two apparently ancient *Sora-bé* entitled *Volampotsa* (from Malagasy, *volafotsy*, or silver) and *Ilovango* (*ilo + vango*, or stroke of light) never made available to European students of Arabico-Malagasy

---

Antanosy, and Anorontsangana (northwest). The first two were reported early in the seventeenth century and the third early in the sixteenth century.

[119] Cf. G. Ferrand's "Tableau de transcriptions en caractères arabes des lettres equivalentes dans les dialectes bantous de Zanzibar et des Comores et le dialecte antaimorona," in *Musulmans*, Vol. III (1902), p. 115; and the Grandidier transliteration in Flacourt, *Histoire, COACM*, Vol. VIII (1913), p. 90.

[120]*Maro*, for example, is many; *hazo*, tree or trees, collectively; *mamo*, discouraged or downhearted. *Marovany* could be the climbing plant *Mimulopsis sp.* or else a composite of *maro* (many) and *vany* (notch, joint, pillar shaft). The *ma-* in *maseko* appears to be Malagasy adjectival and verbal prefix but *seko* is not found in the local vocabulary, and the same applies to *dabaitry* (in *fara-dabaitry*).

[121] J.-P. Rombaka, *Tantaran'drazan'ny Antemoro Anteony* (ca. 1933). There exists a French translation by Mrs. Ramaroson and Miss Raharijaona, but this could not be obtained. A resumé, however, was found in a typescript communication to the Académie Malgache, presented at the session of December 15, 1949, by the late M.-M. Colançon, "Note sur un manuscrit arabico-malgache," pp. 1–8.

writings. The completely novel information, insofar as it could be gathered from a summary by M.-M. Colançon, consists of two major points. The less complicated one is that the Anteimoro did pause at *Iharambazaha* (Vohémar) before settling in the Matitana area, and that two of their great ancestors came together in two ships. This would confirm that the Anteony and Anteimoro Antalaotra were kinsmen as well as that the Anteimoro presence in southeastern Madagascar, prior to the main settlement at Matitana, was fairly close to the suggested date of ±1490. In essence, the Anteimoro were a cohesive group that imported its own sociopolitical and religious structure into the island.

The second and more surprising point is the claim that the followers of the two great ancestors were of different origins, from southern Spain, Morocco, southern Algeria, Tizzi Ouzou, Kabyle, and from eastern Africa. Colançon reacted by lampooning this statement, and, on first glance, it does seem to make slight sense. It is possible and even likely that some of the overseas Anteimoro were not related ethnically to others. More aptly, however, it would appear that the *ethnic* origin of the "followers" plays no role at all. The statement could either refer to connections with 'Alid dynasties which ruled in Spain and Africa[122] or else it is an enumeration of various subbranches of an important Muslim religious order, *tarika*, that spanned both the Maghrib and northeastern Africa. Such an order could only have been the Qadiriyya. It could also incorporate both the 'Alid and Qadiriyya aspects since these are not necessarily to be seen as incompatible. Judgment must, of course, remain suspended somewhat until the two older *Sora-bé* can be compared with the 1933 one. There is still no valid reason to dismiss the probability that the Temur and the Qadiriyya may have been intimately linked in the fifteenth century. There are, equally, grounds for suspecting that the Anteimoro *ombiassa* sought to extend and perpetuate a Muslim religious order in Madagascar. According to Flacourt, the "*ombiasses* have several ecclesiastical offices . . . the *Male* . . . an apprentice writer; . . . *Tibou*, a kind of subdeacon; *Mouladzi*, a deacon; *Faquihi*, a priest; *Catibou*, a bishop; *Loulamaha*, an archbishop; *Sabaha*, a pope or kalif."[123] This organization had disappeared by the nineteenth century, but it does point to a religious order. The *ombiassa* could not maintain it in a culturally new and highly fragmented island that absorbed and diluted all external tendencies to create a single center of culture and of authority.

[122] Under "'Alids," see H. A. R. Gibb and J. H. Kramers, *Shorter Encyclopaedia of Islam* (1953), pp. 32–33.
[123] Flacourt, *Histoire, COACM*, Vol. VIII (1913), p. 244. These offices can be brought closer to the etymons: *Male/Mallam*; *Tibou/Thaleb*; *Mouladzi/Mawlā* (used with various suffixes); *Faquihi/Fakih*; *Katibu/Khatib*; *Loulamaha/'Ulamā*; *Sabaha/Sahaba* (?), or companion of the Prophet, roughly the equivalent of *Muhādjirūn*.

The inner political life of the Anteimoro state is marked by more or less continuous instability and ferment that prevented its territorial expansion while producing an endless stream of expatriates, most of whom were *ombiassa*, or magico-religious specialists. A number of institutions adopted by other Malagasy[124] attest beyond doubt the wide impact of itinerant Anteimoro *ombiassa*, but no one can convey better an appreciation of this impact than the Anteimoro themselves. To quote an Anteimoro manuscript dealing with Merina conquests in the nineteenth century:

> With the Ankara, [King] Radama warred against the Ambalika and won. With the Ankara, he warred at Ambositra and won. At Tamatave, he subjugated the Red King. The Ankara followed Radama at Vohibato and Efandana and he won; at Midongy and he won; at Mahabo and he won; against the Antsihanaka and he won; at Vohemar and he was the victor; at Mahalaza and there was victory; at Mongoro and there was victory. . . . This is the good the Ankara did for the Twelve Kings until now, O ye men and women, thus spoke the Ankara and Zafetsimeto.[125]

No one could say that the Ankara *ombiassa* did not cultivate a very fine appreciation of history. And, if there is slight doubt that the Anteimoro were upon arrival in Madagascar an Afro-Arab people, the attested presence at Matitana of bow and arrow[126] (weapons which disappeared by the mid-nineteenth century), and of a pre-existing group of *Manancarunga*, the adoption through intermarriage of title *kazi-mambo*, and the faint echoes of a royal *fanany* cult at Matitana more than suggest some earlier connections of the Malagasy *tompontany* of the southeastern littoral with the Bantu-speaking Africa and more particularly with the Rhodesian culture area. These connections will be reinforced in the course of the ensuing chapters.

---

[124] The most important of these are the Arabic calendar, with impressive impact on agriculture and astrology; the open assembly or *kabary*, a major political institution; and the art of divination (*sikidy*), which intersects virtually every aspect of human activity. Cf. L. Dahle, "Sikidy and Vintana," *AA*, III (1886–1888), 218–234, 315–327, 457–467; G. Ferrand, "Note sur le calendrier malgache et le Fandruana," *REES* (1908), 93–105, 160–164, or *Extract*, pp. 1–33; G. Julien, *Institutions politiques et sociales de Madagascar*, 2 vols. (1908–1909). The *ombiassa* also influenced certain specific institutions in at least three Malagasy societies, but these are not discussed here.

[125] *Ferrand MSS*, No. 2, in *Musulmans*, Vol. I (1891), pp. 123–129. The military events related belong to the first quarter of the nineteenth century. They involved conquests among the Betsileo, Sakalava, Betsimisaraka, Antankarana, and Sihanaka. The reference to Twelve Kings is meant to pay tribute to the twelve national amulets (*sampy*) of the Merina, ostensibly destroyed in 1869 when their state officially adopted the Protestant religion. The Red King was the Zanamalata ruler of Tamatave, Jean René, who became a vassal of Radama I.

[126] MS A, in Mondain, *Histoire*, p. 105.

chapter 4 THE BARA:

"Africans" of Madagascar

In the great Bara family . . . it is impossible . . . to find in
any two clans the same opinion even on the most minute
historical point . . . some legends alter daily under the pen
of those who transcribe them and evoke the most acute
astonishment among the old Bara questioned on their past.

Boin and Mouveaux (1897)

Why question the old men! They can tell you nothing of a
past which is of no interest to them. . . . It is not the same
for me and my kin, for we like to find in the traditions
passed on from generation to generation the bases for our
authority.

Impoinimerina, king of the Bara Imamono,
to Captain Du Bois de la Villerabel (1900)

The Bara have no Arabico-Malagasy manuscripts, although their calendar and divination show Anteimoro influences.[1] They are an inland
people, and by 1890 only a handful of European explorers and missionaries had ventured into Ibara.[2] Their historical traditions are few in
number and have been collected almost at the last minute. In 1887, there

[1] Cf. C. Le Barbier, "Notes sur le pays des Bara-Imamono, région d'Ankazoabo,"
BAM, III, N.S. (1916–1917), 92–96; and J. Faublée, *Récits bara* (1947), p. 290, n.
[2] Richardson (1877), Cowan (1880), Nielsen-Lund (1887), Catat and Maistre
(1890). Alfred Grandidier skirted Ibara in 1868 and again in 1870. A few nameless
missionaries of the London Missionary Society probably ventured into Ibara, a few
miles south of Ihosy, after the 1850s. This is implied by R. Baron, "The Bara," *AA*,
II (1881), 82–84, which appears to be based on an earlier London Missionary
Society report.

were "not fewer than forty so-called kings" among the Bara and they fought with each other very frequently.[3] A decade later, General Galliéni's officers in the south found no ruler who could control more than one of the four major Bara groups.[4] Events still recalled by aged Bara in the 1890s, as well as changes in family names and cattle markings, imply that this political mosaic evolved from a single Bara state about the 1820s.

Some of the Bara resisted European conquest and, later, European administration, along with other forms of influence. This did not endear the Bara to students of the Malagasy past. "Warlike and prone to pillage, less civilized than the eastern Malagasy and especially those of the center,"[5] the Bara "have been in reality true barbarians."[6] Some fifteen years after the annexation of Madagascar, a journey to Ibara was still considered a difficult, if not hazardous, undertaking.[7]

According to Alfred Grandidier, the name *Bara* is of relatively recent origin, *ca.* 1800.[8] A history of Madagascar written in 1822 does not mention it.[9] A former sea captain who lived in southeastern Madagascar between 1823 and 1837 made no reference to the Bara as such in a report on the different provinces and the degree to which the new Merina power controlled them.[10] It was the Reverend William Ellis who in 1838 mentioned the Bara for the first time.[11] His map of Madagascar, although inaccurate in many respects, placed them approximately in the right area. Nevertheless, a number of maps drawn in the second half of the nineteenth century failed to note the Bara as such. The etymology of the term Bara has hardly been explored, but "it may derive from the root *bara*," which implies the "idea of rudeness and barbarity."[12] Another suggested translation is "simple, naive."[13]

The legendary past of the Bara has been discussed in connection with

[3] J. Nielsen-Lund, "Travels and Perils Among the Wild Tribes in the South of Madagascar," *AA*, III (1888), 443. Translated from the Norwegian.

[4] J. J. Galliéni, *La Pacification de Madagascar: opérations d'octobre 1896 à Mars 1899* (1900), pp. 291–298.

[5] A. Grandidier, *Ethnographie de Madagascar*, Vol. I, Tome 1 (1908), p. 277.

[6] G. Grandidier and R. Decary, *Histoire politique et coloniale*, Vol. V, Tome 3, Fascicule I (1958), pp. 166–167.

[7] W. D. Marcuse, *Through Western Madagascar in Quest of the Golden Bean* (1914), pp. 99–100.

[8] A. Grandidier, *Ethnographie*, p. 279.

[9] S. Copland, *A History of the Island of Madagascar* (1822).

[10] A. Dargèlas, "Notes," (December 26, 1837), manuscript, pp. 1–12, in *BGT*. On Dargèlas see Leguével de Lacombe, *Voyage à Madagascar et aux Iles Comores, 1823–1830*, Vol. II (1840), pp. 352–355.

[11] Wm. Ellis, *History of Madagascar*, Vol. I (1838), p. 62.

[12] A. Grandidier, *Histoire de la géographie de Madagascar* (1892), p. 186, n. 1.

[13] Capt. Vacher, "Etudes ethnographiques," *RM*, V (1903), 404; and G. Kling, "La Toponymie malgache," *BM*, VII (1957), 806.

two themes, the advent of the Zafimanely dynasty and the origins of the Bara themselves. This historical discussion leaves a great deal to be desired. To Alfred Grandidier, the Bara along with their Zafimanely rulers appeared as descendants of an Indian shipwreck on the southeast coast who migrated north to settle between the Ionaivo and Itomampy rivers.[14] Jacques Faublée, for nearly two decades the only student of the Bara, had them coming from southeast Asia with iron weapons.[15] Others, in contrast, did not hesitate to link the Bara with Africa. In the 1880s it was already suggested that the Bara came as a group directly from Africa to Madagascar.[16] African traits in the island were found to be most pronounced among the "Bara clan of Manambia."[17] A similar conclusion was reached through the measurements of eleven Bara skulls.[18] An early anthropologist detected levirate survivals among the Bara and hinted at an Ethiopian connection.[19] The African *Mbara*, living west of Lake Nyassa, were also seen as possible ancestors.[20] A colonial administrator, who lived among the Bara for several years, provided a solution that has been something of a classic in explaining almost anything African in Madagascar: the Bara "looked African" because of an infusion of "Makoa slaves."[21]

In the late 1950s, southeast African antecedents were claimed for the Bara on two distinct and novel grounds. A comparative study of the Bara and Caffres of Mozambique showed that they "match in 12 out of 14" physical traits, establishing thus "for the first time . . . an obvious kinship."[22] Secondly, Louis Michel, a sociologist who did some field work among the Bara, was told that the "Bara lived once in southeast Africa . . .

---

[14] A. Grandidier, *Ethnographie*, p. 278; and Grandidier and Decary, *Histoire politique*, pp. 167–168.

[15] Faublée, *Récits bara*, p. 485.

[16] Cf. D. W. Cowan, "Geographical Excursions in the Betsileo, Tanala and Bara Countries," *Proceedings* of the Royal Geographical Society (June 1882), 521–537; and his brochure *The Bara Land: A Description of the Country and People* (1881), mainly on the Imamono.

[17] L. Catat, *Voyage à Madagascar, 1889–1890* (1895), p. 359.

[18] R. Verneau, "Note sur les caractères céphaliques des Bara," *L'Anthropologie*, XXXIII (1923), 503–505.

[19] Zaborowski, "Comments" at the 850th Session of the Société d'Anthropologie de Paris (July 18, 1907), *BMSAP*, VIII/4 (1907), 398–399, following a brief report by administrator Sallè.

[20] G. Ferrand, "L'Origine africaine des Malgaches," *JA*, 2nd series, XI/3 (1908), 426–427. Ferrand found the *Mbara* in J. Torrend's *A Comparative Grammar of the South African Languages* (1891), p. 9.

[21] Le Barbier, "Bara-Imamono," 71.

[22] M.-C. Chamla, *Recherches anthropologiques sur l'origine des Malgaches* (1958), p. 191. Published as Vol. XIX, No. 1, series A, of the *Mémoires du Museum National d'Histoire Naturelle*.

a thousand men and women [having] crossed the Mozambique Channel to land between Morondava and Tuléar," on the west coast.[23]

Of all the Malagasy groups, the Bara alone found wide support for an African origin. The characteristic feature of claims regarding Bara origins made before the last decade is opinion and, with the sole exception of Alfred Grandidier's, expressed as such without scientific pretensions. Regarding exclusively the Bara, M.-C. Chamla's recent anthropometric contribution is no vast improvement over earlier work by R. Verneau. At best, it is limited by the small number of samples on both sides of the Mozambique Channel.[24] The conclusion is not only premature, but far too bold as well. Until Michel, no one has been able to report a Bara tradition that clearly states what has hitherto only been suspected by some early writers. Geographical expressions like southeast Africa or Mozambique Channel simply do not exist in traditional Bara texts. Michel nowhere identifies his informants or the manner in which the information was imparted. To document the entirely novel thesis that

[23] L. Michel, *Moeurs et coutumes des Bara* (1957), p. 15. Published as Vol. XL of the *Mémoires de l'Académie Malgache*.

[24] Chamla, *Recherches*, pp. 79–80 and tables, *passim*.

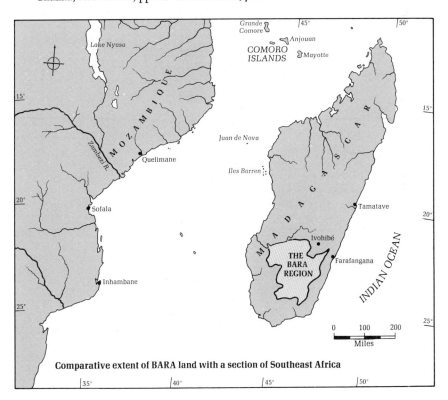

Comparative extent of BARA land with a section of Southeast Africa

the Bara landed on the western coast, he claims to have searched among other groups in the south and southeast for traditions of Bara passage noted in earlier sources and to have found no trace of them.[25] Again, such a passage has never been attributed to the southern Antandroy or southeastern Antanosy sources, but only to *some* of the Bara texts.[26] Michel also holds that the kinship of the Bara and Bantus is confirmed by "religious principles which hardly differ,"[27] while the Bara "skin is frankly black and impregnated with the strong odor characteristic of the Bantus."[28]

According to Michel, the "first Bara chief who came from Africa" was Rabiby, "father of Ndriamanely (Andriamanely),"[29] himself the founder of the Zafimanely dynasty. He then lists five rulers subsequent to Andriamanely, the last of whom died—as is known—in 1909.[30] If we assume that no other oral or written evidence exists, it would follow that the Bara arrived in Madagascar toward the middle of the eighteenth century. The only problem is that the son of Rabiby was Andriamanely II. He appears in both Bara and Betsileo traditions as a contemporary of the Betsileo jester king, Andriamanalina I, who died in 1790, and the Merina king Andrianampoinimerina (1778–1810). Moreover, if the Bara had come from Africa to Madagascar as late as 1750, their original language or a substantial part of it would have to have been manifest some twelve to fifteen decades later. Dramatically, Michel presents a comparative word list of forty-nine words for the Merina and Bara dialects without discussion or analysis.[31] The implication would be that because, in forty-

---

[25] Michel, *Bara*, p. 15.

[26] For example, Impoinimerina, the last great king of the Bara-Imamono (d. 1909), held that in remote times of the first Bara ancestor, *Ravatoverery*, Fort-Dauphin was the home of his subjects, called Tanala (forest people), according to E.-J. Bastard, "Mémoires d'un roi bara," *RM*, VI (1904), 391. Another Bara tradition states that they lived first somewhere between Fort-Dauphin and Cape Sainte-Marie, southernmost tip of Madagascar, probably near the mouth of Mandrare River—cf. Du Bois de la Villerabel, "La Tradition chez les Bara," *NRE*, VI (1900), 263. By way of contrast, an Antaisaka tradition places one of the early Bara ancestors at Tafiatsara, in Menabé, on the western coast—cf. H. Deschamps, *Les Antaisaka* (1936), p. 163. These points of landing have played a huge role in the thinking of most *Malgaschisants* about the points of origin. When one takes into consideration the nature of the seas and hazards of early navigation, such relationships cannot be taken seriously any longer.

[27] Michel, *Bara*, p. 59, n. 3.

[28] *Ibid.*, p. 15.

[29] *Ibid.*, p. 17.

[30] *Ibid.*, pp. 23–24. For the date of Impoinimerina's death, see Grandidier and Decary, *Histoire politique*, p. 178.

[31] Michel, *Bara*, p. 16.

nine instances, the Bara and Merina employ different nouns and verbs with identical meanings, *"il n'existe qu'un pas facile à franchir."* The Merina typify the purest form of Malagasy language. Therefore, the Bara must be a Bantu-speaking group.

It is certainly possible that ancestral Bara spoke a non-Malagasy tongue, but the Bara of 1957 or 1967 did not. One has only to consult the

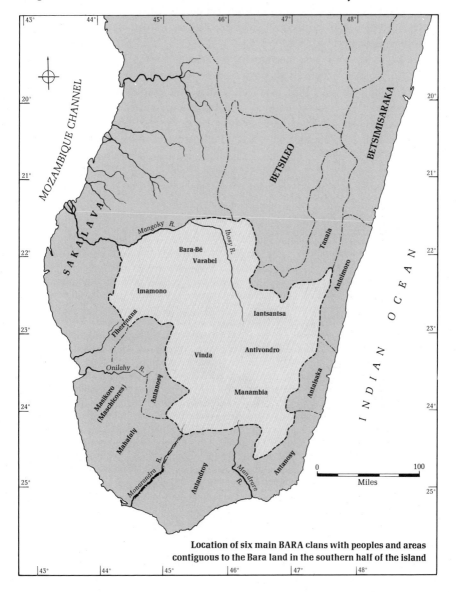

Location of six main BARA clans with peoples and areas contiguous to the Bara land in the southern half of the island

poems and folktales of the Bara reproduced integrally by Michel himself,[32] or the more extensive texts collected by Faublée,[33] to see that they speak a Malagasy dialect. Moreover, a comparison of forty-nine words identical in every respect for both groups—an easy task—would show with equal drama that no divergence exists at all.[34] Even a random-sample examination of words listed by Michel could never sustain the conclusion he forces the uninitiated reader to draw. Thus, for manioc, Michel gives *mangahazo* and *kaza* as the Merina and Bara equivalents. In the compound version, *hazo* is a general Malagasy term for tree, while *manga* stands for manioc in *ki-Bondei, ki-Nyika, ki-Sambara,* and *ki-Zigua,* among others.[35] The African connection is clear in the Merina case, but not in the Bara one. Actually, the prevalent Bara word for manioc is not *kaza* but *balahazo,* and *bala* is indeed the term for manioc in a number of central African languages.[36] The unhappy nature of Michel's word juxtaposition can be illustrated even better by *gaga* (Merina) and *tserika* (Bara), which stand for surprised, astonished. *Tserika* is, in effect, a general Malagasy term for situations of surprise,

---

[32] *Ibid.,* pp. 171–173, 175–177.

[33] Faublée, *Récits bara,* pp. 23–475.

[34] In this respect, two simple generalities should be noted. The Merina words are usually longer, involving an extra *na* ending. Also, the following are phonetically interchangeable without slightest alteration in meaning: v/b, mb, d/l, r/l, p/f, j/z, h/k, tr/ts, t/ts, ao/o, and terminal "y" (introduced by European orthographers) with any of the five vowels. Examples can now be given, all meanings being identical and with a Bara/Merina sequence. (1) Identical orthography examples: aka/aka, androany/androany, any/any, bodro/bodro, boroka/boroka, feo/feo, iva/iva, kely/kely, koa/koa, kisinto/kisinto, mena/mena, nonky/nonky, omaly/omaly, maty/maty, rano/rano, reny/reny, tompo/tompo, tony/tony, tovo/tovo, tsena/tsena, vala/vala, vola/vola, vony/vony. (2) The l/d interchange: aly/ady, faly/fady, haly/hady, lia/dia, lily/didy, sikily/sikidy, valy/vady, vily/vidy. (3) The ts/tr and t/ts interchanges: laitsy/laitra, mahihitsy/mahihitra, sambotsy/sambotra, potsitsy/potsitra, raty/ratsy, tihy/tsihy, vaty/vatsy, vitika/vitsika. (4) Miscellaneous interchanges: mbela/vela, abo/avo, bay/vay, baventy/vaventy, laja/laza, laha/raha, saky/sahy, andafi/andafy, heniky/henika, bariky/barika, folaky/folaka, kabaro/kabary, ombe/omby, pohy/fohy. (5) Added endings: lala/lalana, heritao/heritaona, hamba/hambana, vitra/vitrana, vita/vi(n)tana (mute middle "n"), velo/velona, sakoa/sakoana, saro/sarona, le/lena, mitsanga/mitsangana, fanjaka/fanjakana, mahata/mahatana, tomby/tombina, levy/levina, lamosy/lamosina, teny/tenina, taheja/tahezana, vojo/vozona. (6) Examples of doubling and inversion: vao/vaovao, kibo/kobobo, jalahy/zazalahy, lehitovo/tovolahy, talahaka/tahalaka.

Compiled from O. Jensenius "Dictionnaire bara-hova," *BAM,* VII (1909), 167–194.

[35] Ch. Sacleux, *Dictionnaire swahili-français,* Vol. II (1941), p. 501. The Swahili synonym is *muhogo.*

[36] Under *manioc/bala,* see W. H. Bentley, *Dictionary and Grammar of the Kongo Language* (1887).

while *gaga* is limited to Merina.[37] There is also a Bara noun *gaga*. It means something quite different—namely, raven, crow, or blackbird in general.[38] The Merina equivalent would be *goaika*, a very close phonetic relative of the southeast African *dyogoa-wika* for birds and roosters.[39]

The most that can be said for the forty-nine-word list is that the Bara and Merina express the same meaning through different nouns and verbs, but that each one must be studied on its own terms. Some of the ethnographic data assume considerable value when isolated from the rest of Michel's work. Difficulties with the Bara past are great. They can be appreciated through the web of tradition.

As princes and subjects, for one reason or another, left the political matrix, the great Bara *raza* (family) tradition broke into small pieces as well. New units, with their own family trees, called *tarika*,[40] took root. Grandsons were often named after their grandfathers. Their own descendants skipped generations as a result. The classic case in Bara history involves Andriamanely I and Andriamanely II, and it will be seen how the two are confused. Some of the Bara rulers had three names. One ruler had four names. One name, *Rehandry*, repeated itself for three consecutive generations.[41] The new *tariki* themselves were usually renamed. The resettlement patterns were extremely complicated. The Andraramanga, subclan of the Bara Antambahy, changed settlements six times before settling near Bekily. Faublée has shown graphically how a Bara *raza*, that of the Tambi, fragmented into nine branches—each with its own cattle earmark—and forgot their common origin.[42] Loss of tradition and blurred kinship enhanced incest, which was less often purified through special rites (*tandra*) than by expulsion or departure from the *raza*. The savanna, which covers the vast Bara plateau, and the cattle-

---

[37] J. Webber, *Dictionnaire malgache-français* (1853), p. 712.

[38] Jensenius, "Dictionnaire bara-hova," p. 172. The Merina *gága* and Bara *gagá* appear to have different stresses. The Bara *gagá* and Merina *goaika* (like the Sakalava *koáke* for "crow") could be instances of onomatopoeia, according to Otto Dahl, *Personal Communication* (February 8, 1969). This is not an easy question to resolve given that there is a relatively large number of Bantu loans in Malagasy for many species of the animal kingdom, including birds.

[39] Sacleux, *Swahili-français*, Vol. I (1939), p. 191, and Vol. II (1941), p. 1023.

[40] Etienne de Flacourt mentions in 1661 *tareche* in connection with a *sikidy* formula and translates it as "road," *Histoire de la Grande Ile Madagascar* (1661), p. 173. Dahl, *Personal Communication*, holds the Bara *táriky* as having the stress on first syllable, not on the second as in the Arabic term for way, which is found in Malagasy *sikidy* formulas. Hence, *táriky* should be Indonesian-Malay *tárik*, or drawn.

[41] Rehandry I became Lehimanjaka; his son, Kely, became Rehandry II, changing to Impoinimerina when enthroned; and his son Iatahara became, in turn, Rehandry III. The three Rehandry span the ±1838–1924 period.

[42] J. Faublée, *La Cohésion des sociétés bara* (1954), pp. 57–61.

based economy of the Bara, were hardly impediments to fragmentation.

At the end of the nineteenth century there were three large, two intermediary, and over two dozen lesser Bara clans.[43] Of the three, the *Bara-bé* occupied the heartland, or the Horombé Plateau; the *Iantsantsa* were in the east; and the *Imamono* in the west. The intermediary *Vinda* were in the southwest, and the *Antivondro* settled to the east of the Ionaivo River. The centers of the three kingdoms were, respectively, the middle valley of Ihosy, Ivohibé, and Ankazoabo. The Vinda capital was at Benenitra, near the Onilahy River. The Vinda formative period goes back to the sons of the Bara king Raikitroka (Ratsileondrafy upon enthronement and Andriantompoinarivo posthumously), believed to have ruled between 1804 and 1817.[44]

According to one account, three of Raikitroka's sons could not agree on the rights of succession and asked the Merina king Radama I (1810–1828) to arbitrate.[45] One son, Ramasoandro (known also as Ratsimamo, Rasoky, and Tsimamatoa), remained at the head of Bara Iantsantsa. Tonanahary (also Raselea) and Ratsimivily (also Andriamanalina) went westward and founded the Bara-bé and the Bara-Imamono.[46] A fourth son, Ramifoky, appears as founder of a lesser Bara clan, the Mananatana. The foundation of the Vinda is variously attributed to a fifth son of Raikitroka, to one of Tonanahary's sons, and even to a grandson of Andriamanely I. According to a recent text, succession had nothing to do with these formations. The three sons of Raikitroka had known no disputes, and Tonanahary and Ratsimivily left of their own accord while the father was still alive and were never to have any differences.[47] Faublée has argued that the grazing lands of the "nuclear" Bara territory, between the Ionaivo and Itomampy rivers, could not sustain all the cattle on hand and that, therefore, a "search for more cattle and new grazing lands impelled the Bara toward western prairies." Various Zafimanely princes and their followers thus left the elder branch, which retained the name Vinda, while the junior branches became known as the Bara-bé, Bara-Kunda, or Bara-Imamono among others. Moreover, this westward

---

[43] Among them: Ambilony, Imandabé, Vohitovo, Vohilakatsoka, Vatolava, Sahamasina, Tambavala, Antandramena, Zafinala, Beampongo, Manonga, Menamaty, Mandronarivo, Mananatana, Mandrapaka, Manambonarivo, Manievy, Antimaraha, Zafindrendrika, Zafimarovola, Zafindrianabo, Zafimitovo, Andrafasy, Andriambé, and Tanamilaza. Cf. Capt. Vacher, "Etudes ethnographiques," *RM*, V (1903), 401–408; and A. Grandidier, *Ethnographie*, pp. 283–285.

[44] These dates come from a newly discovered manuscript, based on Bara and Betsileo traditions, collected by J. Rabemanana (p. 94). See text and note 65 below.

[45] A. Grandidier, *Ethnographie*, p. 279 and n. 2.

[46] *Ibid.*, 278, n. 3a.

[47] Michel, *Bara*, p. 18.

migration "was accentuated by pressure from the Merina, who undertook military expeditions in the southeast."[48]

There is little doubt that one Zafimanely—Tonanahary—did travel to the Merina capital of Tananarive to secure an alliance against his two brothers and that he was killed there during a second visit.[49] This is confirmed by A. Dargèlas' manuscript of 1837, which mentions a Ratunhaar (Ratonanahary) who "betrayed his own family" in order to control his province, situated "northwest of the valley of Amboule," or geographically in the direction of eastern Baraland.[50] As for the Merina pressure on the Bara, it did not yield much by way of conquest beyond a rather precarious military outpost at Ihosy. It is quite true that Merina traditions claim great victories over the Bara.[51] The generals who led Merina troops into Ibara on two occasions were unofficial husbands of Queen Ranava-

[48] Faublée, *Sociétés bara,* p. 139.
[49] De la Villerabel, "Tradition," 269.
[50] Dargèlas, "Notes," p. 3.
[51] See Father Malzac's *Histoire du royaume hova depuis ses origines jusqu' à sa fin* (1912), p. 251. Malzac points out that these victories had "no lasting results."

Bara chief Androrehana, West Betroky.

lona I. Similar victories, notably over the Sakalava, were announced, without any basis in truth, by gun salutes in Tananarive for other court officers with new generalships. In 1894, just before the collapse of the Merina monarchy, its official documents did not even list Ibara as a tributary province.[52] Only a few years later, difficulties encountered in the south by French commanders confirm that control over the Bara, even with modern weapons and military organization, required a protracted effort.

The invulnerability of the Bara is further attested by the ethnographic data collected by Captain Vacher. It shows a huge influx of groups fleeing the Merina from the east, southeast, and north of Baraland. Its human geography underwent a radical change roughly between 1850 and 1890. The Merina pressure thus served mainly to augment the subjects and vassals of the Zafimanely. Uninhabited regions, like those of Imanombo, Bekily, and Mahaly, were settled successively around 1850, 1875, and 1890.[53] Some of the new arrivals into Ibara had abandoned traditional rulers because of alliances with the Merina, made to bolster internally weak positions. Others were led by chiefs unwilling to face war or even accept the status of Bara vassals too long. Most of the migrants found the Zafimanely preferable to Ranavalona I. In turn, the Zafimanely used these new Bara against their own recalcitrant subjects, and many of the latter promptly left to form independent *tariki*. The detailed, and for the most part quite accurate, notes of Vacher, an almost contemporary observer, offer thus an entirely different picture.

The speed with which social and political change could take place is worth illustrating. The Manambia, a mixture of eastern Bara and Tanala long under the local Zafipanolahy dynasty, fled from the Merina troops in the 1850s, contracted settlement alliances with three successive Bara clans, moving on each time until the Vinda at last accepted them. Later, they fought the Vinda too and left to settle finally at Tsivory. Here, they were joined by the Antanosy fleeing from the Fort-Dauphin area, and together they created an independent if small kingdom.[54] Within a single generation, the Manambia lost their state, migrated over fairly long distances, and rebuilt it with a group with which no previous kinship ties were known.

[52] H. Berthier. *Notes et impressions sur les moeurs et coutumes du peuple Malgache* (1933), p. 137; and Michel, *Bara*, p. 28, n. 1.

[53] Vacher, "Etudes ethnographiques," 385, 390, 394. In 1912, for example, around Ivohibé alone, there were nine minority groups in addition to Antivohibé and Zafimanely: Tambovala, Sahamasy, Kimoso, Ambiliony, Tisarsaivo, Manampy, Chanampy, Antsahampindra, and Vohilakatra, according to an anonymous report, "Renseignements sur les Bara," (1912), manuscript, pp. 1–5, in BGT.

[54] Vacher, "Etudes ethnographiques," 412.

The argument that the nuclear Bara had too many head of cattle and, at the same time, sought to increase their herds, seems to be a conflict between two aspects of unrefined determinism. Equally, succession was the root cause of struggles involving Raikitroka's sons. It cannot and does not account for the entire political history of the Bara. There are too many incongruities, in traditional texts and elsewhere, to accept the existing ideas about Bara formations. The first problem, therefore, concerns the *fariti* or tribal and clan names.

Following Le Barbier, Michel translates Iantsantsa as sharks (*antsantsa*) and Imamono as those who kill. The selection of shark is curious because the Iantsantsa have no memories of ever having been a coastal group. As for the Imamono, this name is an abbreviation of *Tsimamonolongo*, by which the western Bara were known to earlier settlers of the area in the 1860s.[55] In this original context it means those who do not kill their friends. *Tsy* is a general negative, while *longo* means friend, or ally, apparently from the Bantu *lungo/lunga* (to unite). In actual Bara speech, Imamono comes out as *mamūnu*. It is clear that a phonetically convenient loss has affected not only *tsy* + *longo* but also the *I* prefix for place or person. As Michel would have it, the western Bara were in a constant state of war with groups of the Fiherenana Valley, and hence "Ratsimivily honored them with the name Imamono." This would explain the present understanding of *mamóno* (to kill), but it has little to do with the etymology of the name reported almost a century before Michel undertook fieldwork in western Ibara. As will be shown, the Bara who came westward were not known to themselves as Tsimamonolongo.

It is equally quite incredible that the Bara-bé, or Great Bara, would develop as a mere branch of the sharks (Iantsantsa) because Tonanahary began with "a handful of followers" but came to rule "over a large and prosperous group."[56] All Bara traditions, except the one reported by Michel, regard Tonanahary as a most unpopular ruler because the Merina invasions were attributed to him. His actual reign was, moreover, quite brief.

Faublée translates *antsantsa* as lizard.[57] There are lizards in Ibara, but they tend to concentrate in the drier western section of the Imamono. Some of the Bara regard the lizard as a *fady* animal.[58] While his transla-

---

[55] A. Grandidier, *Ethnographie*, pp. 279, 282. It is possible to accept either that earlier settlers created this name or that the Bara migrants so named themselves. Although Alfred Grandidier published this traditional data only in 1908, it is based on notes made between 1869 and 1870.

[56] Michel, *Bara*, p. 18.

[57] J. Faublée, *Les Esprits de la vie à Madagascar* (1954), p. 115.

[58] E. Bensch, "La Faune dans le sud de Madagascar," *RM*, IV (1902), 147. *Fady*=sacred, forbidden.

tion is different, Faublée does not depart from the idealized account of Bara formations, and his account is by no means satisfactory either on linguistic or historical grounds. As given by the only existing dictionary for all Malagasy dialects, the general meaning of *antsantsa* is *"faute ou malédiction très ancienne qui persévère sur les descendants."*[59] There can be no dispute about its accuracy. According to Bara tradition, Renitsira, a nephew of Andriamanely I, was disinherited by his father Diamandana because Renitsira had incestuous relations with his own mother.[60] The Bara say *"ny Zafimanely ny anabaviny rai raika nefa reny samy hafa dia mpiandry sy ny vadin'ny rainy afatsin'ny terekazy dia azony lilena."*[61] It means that even among the Zafimanely rulers, "who can copulate with sisters of two beds," as well as with their "fathers' wives," one's own mother, is the true "exception." In Bara folklore grave incest leads automatically to rejection and disinheritance.[62]

On his deathbed, continues the tradition, Diamandana asked "his brother" Andriamanely I to execute Renitsira. The uncle, at first, wanted no part in the killing, and "sent Renitsira into war against the Tanala, hoping that death would find him, but this was not to be." Andriamanely then "paid one hundred head of cattle to a subject" who speared Renitsira to death. "I have struck Renitsira," reported the anonymous subject, "but it is you who must withdraw the spear from his body." As the spear came out, Andriamanely's feet and hands caught a few drops of blood. "A few days later, the *angama* (leprosy) began to spread over these extremities. . . . Since this terrible lesson, a Zafimanely never kills close kin, even after the gravest of insults."[63] It can be noted in passing that *angama* will not be found in Malagasy dictionaries. The nearest equivalent is *kwanga*, or *leucoderma* (white leprosy), in the Ki-Amu of east Africa. *Balanga* is another term used for leprosy.[64] Also, Renitsira may

[59] Webber, *Dictionnaire*, p. 59.

[60] De la Villerabel, "Tradition," 265.

[61] Quoted from *Bara texts*, collected in 1924 by an anonymous writer. The orthography reveals that they were taken down by a Bara who had gone to school and learned the official language. The original typescript bears the docket number 664 of the Bibliothèque Charles Poirier, acquired in 1965 by the University of Madagascar. I am indebted to Mrs. J. Poirier of the university for making the document available to me.

[62] Faublée, *Récits bara*, pp. 23–35 and *passim* thereafter.

[63] De la Villerabel, "Tradition," 265.

[64] Sacleux, *Swahili-français*, Vol. I (1939), p. 88, used all along the eastern littoral of Africa and adjacent islands. Charles Sacleux translates *balanga* as *"tache blanche de fausse lèpre, généralement confinée aux mains et aux pieds."* The Merina term for leprosy is *habokana* (*boka*=leper). In other dialects, however, *boka* is the equivalent of false, for example, *mpanjaka-boka* is a false or illegitimate king or chief.

well not be a personal name. It is composed of *reny* (mother), *tsy* (not), and *ra* (blood) and means literally, not of mother's blood.

The corroborating tradition is a mixture of fiction and historical data, which can be disengaged with profit. The Andriamanely who did have leprosy was called *Dutana* (mutilated hand) as a result. New evidence has come to light to show that Dutana was the second Andriamanely, and not the original founder of Zafimanely. Northern Bara traditions, collected early in this century by J. Rabemanana and bequeathed to the Académie Malgache in manuscript form, reveal that this leper king was a contemporary of the Betsileo king Andriamanalina I who, as indicated earlier, died in 1790.[65] It is also known from written European sources that Andriamanely I died in 1653.[66] The would-be murder of Renitsira is a fiction, which explains the *angama*, and a lesson is added to affirm the traditional belief that spilling of noble blood constitutes high crime. The confusion of two periods, one in the middle of the seventeenth century and the other some thirteen decades later, hides the really important aspect of tradition: dynastic change. The future Iantsantsa were, in effect, "not of mother's blood," Diamandana's descendants "disinherited," not by the progenitor, but by a new ruler, Andriamanely I.

The eastern Bara were not known in the 1650s as Iantsantsa but as *Antikondra*. When, considerably later, Ramasoandro arrived to take over the eastern Bara, it was easily recalled that they were *antsantsa* without right to rule. The Antikondra predate Ramasoandro by about two centuries. There had to be a parent unit for them as well. Rabemanana's informants clearly indicated that all subsequent divisions among the Bara derive from the Bara-bé. If Le Barbier is read carefully, as should be done by all who collected Bara texts, various units took new names in distinction from the Bara-bé.[67] Le Barbier is also quite specific about the Imamono, formerly a group of Iantsantsa and Mananatana, who migrated westward.[68] This is fully attested by Charles Guillain, who acted as a mediator in the first dispute between the *Masikoro* of the Fiherenana Valley and the Iantsantsa mentioned by that name some two decades before the adoption of Imamono or, more accurately, of Tsimamono-longo.[69] The foundation of Ankazoabo, the Imamono capital, has been

[65] J. Rabemanana, *Le Pays des Kimoso et son histoire: depuis les origines jusq'à l'an 1820*, manuscript of 99 in-folio pages without date, in the Archives of the Académie Malgache. The document is without an assigned number and appears to have been composed around 1912. The reference page is 88.

[66] Flacourt, *Histoire* (1661 ed.), p. 40.

[67] Le Barbier, "Bara-Imamono," 66.

[68] *Ibid.*, 66–67.

[69] Ch. Guillain, *Documents sur l'histoire, la géographie et le commerce de la partie occidentale de Madagascar* (1845), 311.

dated quite accurately as 1838.[70] The Imamono are thus fairly recent; the Iantsantsa are much older, but underwent a change of name from earlier Antikondra at the turn of the nineteenth century; while the Bara-bé are nothing short of the parent unit for all Bara.

Until now, it has been firmly contended that the Bara-bé can be found nowhere in the old European sources. This is demonstrably false. Etienne de Flacourt, who lived at Fort-Dauphin between 1648 and 1655, wrote that some 110 years before his time, around 1550, seventy or eighty Portuguese transporting a great deal of gold were killed by the Malagasy.

[70] Grandidier and Decary, *Histoire politique*, pp. 170–171.

Bengita, great Sakalava chief.

He gave two versions of this incident and an explanatory note. In the first, the "massacre" took place after a "feast" near a site called Imours. The Portuguese brought along all of their gold to be "entertained" by "two brothers" named Dian Missaran and Dian Bohits, who came with 500 or 600 men.[71] In the second version, the Portuguese were in dispute among themselves over the gold. The captain and those who sided with him came to a site named *Varabei*. Their hope was to be able to use the forces of Dian Missaran and Dian Bohits against the other Portuguese, "established near Manghafia" (Manafiafy), but the captain and his men were "betrayed" and eliminated in turn.[72] The explanatory note states that the Malagasy involved in this massacre were the Zafikazimambo,[73] aristocratic clan of Anteimoro whose state was along the southeastern littoral, bordered by the Tanala, eastern Ibara, Antaifasy, and Betsimisaraka.

A century after the massacre, on January 14, 1655, Flacourt was visited by a "son of Dian Mitouve," ruler of Icondre (Antikondra), along with representatives of other regions. They asked him to prevent his own French irregulars, then in the land of *Manamboule*, from siding with the sons of Dian Panolahe and thus altering the local balance of power. In dispute was the land of Ionghaivou. A territorial settlement was reached whereby the western half of Iongaivo Valley went to Dian Mitouve and Dian Raval of Icondre, and the eastern half to the "nephews and issue of Dian Panolahe."[74] The Dian Panolahe in question was Andriapanolaha, ruler of the Zafikazimambo. The valley of Manambolo, a river which is joined by the Iongaivo, was his western frontier. The Flacourt arbitration took place on the eve of La Case's expeditions, which would remove the Zafikazimambo as competitors for their own *andrianony* (king). Dian Panolahe's "sons and nephews," the *Zafipanolahy*, ruled over the southern Tanala. The son of Dian Mitouve was a *Zafimitovo*, a Bara clan then in its formative stage. In effect, around 1655, Andriamitovo headed the Antikondra together with Dian Raval, a name which will recur.

The *v/b* and *b/v* phonetic conversions are legion in Malagasy, and *Varabei* can readily be recognized as Bara-bé. The gold taken from the Portuguese was never found. Perhaps this gold was never in Portuguese possession. It did, however, exist. An informant, whose parent group remains unknown, told Flacourt that five rulers, among them Dian Panolahe, shared "twenty *sines* or urns full of gold, each *sine* easily con-

[71] Flacourt, *Histoire* (1661, ed.), p. 32.

[72] *Ibid.*, p. 33.

[73] *Ibid.*, pp. 18–19.

[74] E. de Flacourt, *Relation de la grande isle Madagascar* (1661), in *COACM*, Vol. IX (1920), p. 392.

taining from ten to twelve pots . . . four strong blacks being needed to carry one of the *sines*."[75] This gold was collectively known as *marofeh*. A free translation would be great heritage, and it may reflect a political alliance of the five rulers. The *volamena*, or gold, is of great importance in the history of southern and western Malagasy: political alliances were contracted with it, blood covenants were made on it, wars could be stopped by it, justice could depend on trials by ordeal involving gold, a dynastic branch could be called Volamena, and kings were buried with this metal.

Two Portuguese crews, some 600 men in all, are known to have attempted a crossing of Madagascar in the late 1520s, from the southwest to the southeast coast.[76] Four survivors, rescued in 1530, reported that most of their Portuguese compatriots were dispersed in the interior. "Black Portuguese" were found some seven decades later by the Dutch at Manafiafy, or St. Luce Bay, on the southeast coast.[77] There was a Portuguese fort, the *tranovato* (stone house), built on one of the two islets in the Fanjahira River, which flows through Antanosy. There is no agreement as to when it was constructed, but estimates range from 1528 to 1578. It was first described by the ubiquitous Father Mariano.[78] The Antanosy king Tsiambany could not recall to Mariano whether the *tranovato* was constructed during the time of his father or his grandfather. Of the Portuguese associated with this fort, some had left Madagascar, others had taken part in wars, or had married locally. Some of his own chiefs and wives, said Tsiambany, were half-Portuguese by descent.[79] The caves of Mount Isalo are also sometimes attributed to the Portuguese. These caves are on the rim of westernmost Bara-bé land. They are a tourist attraction despite difficult access. Apart from the old *tranovato*, they have no architectural analogy in the entire south-central Madagascar. The pillars of a small cave and the well-preserved outer wall of the largest one are of cut white sandstone.[80]

[75] *Ibid.*, p. 374.

[76] *COACM*, Vol. I (1903), pp. 58–59, 63–76. Manoel de la Cerda and Alexis d'Abreu commanded the two shipwrecked vessels.

[77] *Ibid.*, pp. 265–267. The Dutch crew, once in Bantam (Java), told a Portuguese missionary there that the Malagasy-Portuguese of Manafiafy had asked for priests from Portugal. Eventually, this missionary reported the information to the Archbishop of Goa. A group of missionaries, on the way to Mwene Mutapa, were told to look into the matter, but no action was taken in the end.

[78] L. Mariano, "Relation . . . 1613–1614," in *COACM*, Vol. II (1904), pp. 41–43. Some maps continued to show the Portuguese Fort at Fanshere (Fanjahira River) well into the eighteenth century.

[79] *Ibid.*, p. 50.

[80] See Faublée, *Récits bara*, pp. 163–164, note, for a brief but succinct description. Much ink has been spilled on this subject, but nothing of substance has been added.

Bara warriors, early 1900s.

"Dian Missaran," or *Andriamisara*, and "Dian Bohits," or *Andrian-bohitra*, present an even more interesting aspect. In a Zafindraminia genealogy given by Flacourt and reported in the previous chapter, Andriamisara appears as the eleventh descendant of the original ancestor (Rakouba) while Dian Bohits is listed as Andriamisara's father. However, both of the "massacre" versions claim that Dian Bohits and Andriamisara were brothers. While investigating the contemporary Bara, Michel discovered a hitherto unreported small vassal clan of the Iantsantsa called *Ndriamisara*. What surprised Michel was not the discovery itself, but rather that some of the Bara "accord to the descendants of Ndriamisara . . . the quality of a noble caste." This, he states, is not possible because all Bara nobles were "created" by Ndriantompoinarivo (Raikitroka) and he never "gave such a rank to the Ndriamisara."[81] Andriamisara is also a great cult name for all the Sakalava. According to the manuscript notes of Alfred Grandidier, written in the 1860s while he lived among the Sakalava, Andriamisara even left a mark of his presence in the Ihosy Valley, where he made a blood covenant (*fatidra*) with "Sangazy, chief of the Antanandro" and, after a feast, "promptly massacred the entire ruling hierarchy."[82] Grandidier places Andriamisara at Ihosy around 1650. Flacourt mentions him at Varabei around 1550. Moreover, Flacourt notes in the massacre version that both Dian Bohits and Andriamisara were Zafikazimambo and hence Anteimoro. Elsewhere in his work they both appear, as we have already noted, in a Zafindraminia genealogy.

All of this points to what should have been discovered long ago. The *Noble Misara* (Andriamisara) crosscuts a number of local ethnicities and reoccurs in different chronological periods. The Zafikazimambo have him, as do the Zafindraminia. A Dutch source mentions a chief named *Misara* at Saint-Augustine Bay in 1663.[83] Sakalava traditions, except in the case of Andriamisara, have never given the same name twice for any of their Maroserana rulers. But, Andriamisara appears and reappears as high priest, king, or priest-king. Andriamisara *efa-dahy* (forefather) figures in Sakalava divination (*sikidy*) formulas although the Maroserana have disclaimed an early knowledge of divination.[84] Even a northeastern

[81] Michel, *Bara*, p. 21.

[82] A. Grandidier, *Notes de Voyage* (1869), manuscript, p. 688, cited by Guillaume Grandidier in the unfinished *Essai d'histoire des Malgaches de la région occidentale* (not dated), pp. 4–5_{b1s}, n. 1, private library of Hubert Deschamps.

[83] *COACM*. Vol. III (1905), p. 312; account by Joachim Blank of the vessel *Waaterhoen*, based at the Cape of Good Hope (1663).

[84] One of the Grandidiers was told by unnamed Maroserana that their ancestors did not bring the *sikidy* with them to Madagascar, *Ethnographie*, Vol. III (1917), p. 495, n. 1. In this statement, they saw "another proof" of the Indian origin. There is no necessary connection between the absence of *sikidy* and the claim that this demonstrates an Indian origin. Quite the contrary argument obtains from what is

coast *sikidy* cites Andriamisara as divine authority.[85] In the spoken language of the Sakalava *tromba* (spirit possession) the voice heard most often is that of Andriamisara. According to a Sakalava informant, cases have been known when this voice spoke in the Menabé dialect way up in northern Boina by mediums who had never left their native villages.[86] Even among the Merina of central highlands, a student of local past reported that some of his informants held Andriamisara to have been an Anteimoro.[87] The Zafindraminia genealogy cited by Flacourt came from a *Sora-bé*, drafted by the *ombiasses* from Matatane, or Anteimoro priests, one of whom had taught him how to read the Arabico-Malagasy script.[88] The discovery of an Ndriamisara clan among the eastern Bara by Michel makes it clear that we are dealing with itinerant priests, perhaps a religious order, forming just about the time of the Zafikazimambo advent in southeastern Madagascar. The most dramatic piece of evidence in this connection is a linguistic one. *Isara* is an Arabic term for divination, used also in eastern Africa.[89]

The earliest mention of Barabé is thus found in a mid-seventeenth-century document. This century-old tradition reported by Flacourt does not mention Bara-bé as a people, but as a site. At some point in time thereafter an ethnic adoption of this name must have taken place. The process itself at least is not a historical mystery. The principal Bara version of Zafimanely genealogy states that Andriamanely I was fathered by Andriamena, Andriamena by Rapapango, Rapapango by Andriankeho-heho, Andriankehoheho by Rabaratavokoka, and Rabaratavokoka by Ravatoverery.[90] *Bara* thus appears as part of an early ancestral name. With five ancestors behind Andriamanely I, Rabaratavokoka would fall somewhere in the sixteenth century. On one point, Bara traditions are hopelessly confused: were Rabaratavokoka and Ravatoverery two rulers,

---

known, namely that the Indian merchants were part of the same Muslim culture that included Arabs from Arabia, "Arabs" from Persia, or "Arabs" and "Moors" from Africa itself.

[85] F. Raphael, "Ny Famohazan'ny Sikily," (Awakening of the *sikidy*), manuscript pp. 1–5, in *AAM*. In this formula, Andriamisara is both a lower divinity and a high sacerdotal figure addressing greater divinities (*izany ny Zanahary nampijotsoany Andriamisara*, or gods to whom Andriamisara addresses his prayers).

[86] R. K. Kent, *Field Notes* (1965), informant—Charles Betoto.

[87] Rainitovo, *Tantaran'ny Malagasy Manontolo*, Vol. II (1932), pp. 174–180; cf. Deschamps, *Anteisaka*, p. 163 and note.

[88] Flacourt, *Relation*, *COACM*, Vol. IX (1920), pp. 135, 179–180; cf. his *Histoire*, *COACM*, Vol. VIII (1913), pp. 243–256 for information which could not have come from any other sources. According to the universally overlooked statement of Flacourt, it was "Dian Radam, ombiassa who . . . had taught me to read and write the Arabic characters" in *Relation*, p. 135.

[89] Sacleux, *Swahili-français*, Vol. I (1939), p. 307.

[90] De la Villerabel. "Tradition," 263–264.

or two names for the same ruler? An identical problem plagues the traditions of Sakalava and Mahafaly concerning the founder of the *Maroserana*, Madagascar's most durable and, until the nineteenth century, most successful dynasty. The Sakalava-Mahafaly problem also involves Rabaratavokoka and the name of Andriamandazoala, which may easily have been his posthumous one (*fitahina*).[91]

The literal translation of *Andriamandazoala* is "Lord who causes the forest to wither." That we are clearly dealing with a royal *title* is confirmed in the already noted name of Dian Raval (*Andriandravala*), ruler of Icondre. While the root words are Malagasy (*ála* = forest; *ráva* = destroyed, demolished; *lazo* = wither, fade; and *ála* again), the title itself is analogous to the "Crusher of Trees," one of Mwene Mutapa's own.[92] Titles are among the most arbitrary items of culture; it is therefore difficult to imagine anything less than a case of loan-translation. Some very interesting problems emerge also from such great ancestral names as *Rabaratavokoka* and *Ravatoverery*, both of which are closely associated in the oral tradition and may well have belonged to the same great ancestor. Much depends on how the first of the two compounds is reduced to its component parts.

If *bara* in *Rabaratavokoka* is *not* a root word, then the correct translation of this name would be "bent-noble-reed" (*Ra* = noble + *bararata* = reed + *vokoka* = bent, a term often used to refer to a ruler who died, in an indirect way). A great ancestor conceived as a "reed" is not an idea found in other Malagasy ethnic cultures. It is, however, deeply imbedded within parts of Bantu-speaking Africa and notably among the Zulu. According to Reverend Callaway, "in the Amazulu traditions . . . 'nations' broke off from *uthlanga*," term which "strictly speaking" means reed, "capable of stooling, throwing out offsets." "It thus comes, metaphysically, to mean a source of being; a father is the *uthlanga* of his children, from which they broke off." Callaway concludes that the original meaning of this tradition was that men spring from the reed but that the word alone came down "whilst the meaning was lost."[93] If, on the other hand, *bara* is a root word, the compound associates it with a *tavo* (any type of large

---

[91] All Sakalava kings received a *fitahina*. In some cases, only the *fitahina* survives, particularly since it was forbidden to mention the former name after the death of each monarch. The *fitahina* came into use quite early in Sakalava history, but it may not have been a rigorously observed substitute until the second half of the seventeenth century.

[92] *Matyoremiti*, see D. P. Abraham's "The Early Political History of the Kingdom of Mwene Mutapa, 850–1589," in *Historians in Tropical Africa*, Proceedings of the Leverhulme Inter-Collegiate History Conference, September 1960 (1962), mimeographed p. 68.

[93] C. Callaway, *The Religious Systems of the Amazulu*, London, 1870, pp. 2–3 and note.

container) and *koka* (any long trench, crevice, ditch).⁹⁴ In this sense, it is further associated with *Ravatoverery*, "great-noble-stone-without-peer" (*Ra* = noble + *vato* = stone + *ve/bé* = great + *rery/irery* = alone, without equal). What is thus conveyed amounts to a link between the founding ancestor or ancestors and some site marked by a most unusual rock formation.

A kraal called *Baramazimba*, ruled by *Umgabe*, "dynastic name of a petty chief whose territory includes the Zimbabwe ruins," was found by J. T. Bent on August 6, 1892, in the heart of the old Mwene Mutapa empire. It was adjacent to "a huge split rock, just a square block of granite eighty feet high split into four parts, so that narrow paths led from each side into the heart of it. It was one of the most extraordinary natural stone formations I have ever seen."⁹⁵ It is known from the Bara folklore that their ancient sacerdotal persons, or *mpamoha*, were possessed by ancestral spirits called *Angabé*, spirits representing the departed rulers in much the same manner through the Shona *Masvikiro*.⁹⁶ In 1844, moreover, it was reported that the Bara capital "is a great village called *Monongabé*, consisting of 700 to 800 solidly constructed dwellings."⁹⁷ *Given* as "spirit," the term *Angabé* would seem to derive from Malagasy *angatra* (spirit). Yet, there is another Malagasy variant from which it could derive just as well, namely *rangàhibé/(i)ngàhibé* which means "great elder" or "great father." In the old days, when one Malagasy ruler acknowledged another as his "father," this meant submission to a greater or more powerful ruler. Today, *ngabé* is heard in many parts of Madagascar as an honorific title, a form of addressing an elder. The title thus of the Shona petty chief, or *umgabe* (and it is very probable that this word can be found in other Bantu languages), allows a parallel with the Malagasy *ngabé* whether in the religious or political sense or both since these often tend to merge anyway. But, if the rock itself along with *umgabe/ngabé* analogy and the presence of the word *bara* in the African kraal may be attributed to coincidence, this is not the case with two other items.

According to Bent, the principal people of the area in question were the Makalanga, famous *Mocarangas* of early Portuguese sources. In Madagascar, an Anteimoro manuscript relates that the first Anteimoro to

---

⁹⁴ Webber, *Dictionnaire*, pp. 389, 660.

⁹⁵ J. T. Bent, *Ruined Cities of Mashonaland* (1893), pp. 65–66, 85.

⁹⁶ The *mpamoha-Angabé* relationship disappeared from Ibara precisely because the Bara had no unified kingdom under the Zafimanely. In contrast, under the name of *tromba*, it survives among the Sakalava, where it took the form of state religion through which defunct monarchs could express their will in public.

⁹⁷ H. D'Escamps, *Histoire et Géographie de Madagascar* (1884), p. 523. This work was published originally in 1846 under the pseudonym Macé-Descartes. The statement is identical in both editions. The prefix *Mo-* (Mu- phon.) does not appear to be Malagasy.

arrive in the land of Matitana discovered there an important coastal group named *Manankarunga*.[98] Even more precisely, Flacourt wrote that the *Manancarongha* are "at present subjects of the Chiefs of Matatane and they had been frequently at war with one another."[99] In the 1650s, when Flacourt came into possession of this datum, the "Chiefs of Matatane" (Anteimoro kings) were still the Zafikazimambo. It could hardly be a matter of coincidence to find the Rozvi-Karanga title for chiefs, or *mambo*, reproduced so clearly in Malagasy *Zafi-kazi-mambo*, rulers of the indigenous *Manankarunga* whose own group name is, again clearly, non-Malagasy and also a near-duplicate of the Karanga, people of the Zimbabwe. In this connection, it is also worth reporting that a single Malagasy tradition places the suffix *tsimibaby* after *Rabaratavokoka*.[100] If it means anything in Malagasy, *tsimibaby* would be a person or object which (or who) "is not carried." One should not, however, dismiss entirely the possibility of phonetic kinship with *zimbabwe*. In effect, one finds in all of the linguistic items mentioned above an unusual degree of Afro-Malagasy duality, partly hidden by the delicate problem of loan-translations and at times rendered even more difficult by a multiplicity of ways in which a Malagasy compound can be understood. Yet, it is probable that further and more detailed research precisely in this field of endeavor will some day permit us to find a number of fundamental answers on both sides of the Mozambique Channel.

"After endless wars which troubled and ravaged his land, in Africa, Ndretsileo left for the unknown. By dhow, together with Ndramandetahoho, he arrived in Madagascar, at the mouth of Menarandra, where Marosirana gave him the land of Manambovo."[101] This is not a Bara, Sakalava, or Mahafaly tradition. It comes from the Antaifasy, group wedged between the Anteimoro and Antaisaka[102] further southeast. While "Africa" would not appear as such in the traditional texts, these are left, however, to speak for themselves, and one can only regret the absence of an explanatory note as to how this point of departure was

[98] In G. H. Julien, "Pages Arabico-Madécasses," *AASC* extract (1929), p. 24.

[99] Flacourt, *Histoire, COACM*, Vol. VIII (1913), p. 18. Flacourt also states that the *Manacaronha* (also spelled *Manacarongha* on page 15) gave their name to a whole section of the area which became land of the Anteimoro. In explaining how the title-name of Zafikazimambo came into being, Flacourt pointed out that the Anteimoro adopted it through intermarriage with a local princess.

[100] Sgt. Firinga, "La Dynastie des Maroserana," *RM*, III (1901), 664.

[101] M. Fontoynont and E. Raomandahy, "Les Antaifasy: origines et guerres avec les tribus voisines," *BAM*, New Series, XXII (1939), 1.

[102] The *ei* or *ai* in Anteimoro or Antaisaka are a matter of relatively arbitrary choice. When pronounced, for example, Antaisaka sounds in English like "Tehshak" (*Téšak'*). This is simply an old problem of orthography and spelling resolved as yet by no firm rule or convention.

conveyed. Antaifasy tradition calls Marosirana "king" at the same time of Andrevola-Mahafaly and of the Bara-Sakalava. This is, of course, a statement that all four groups had Maroserana rulers. It is interesting to note that the same tradition calls Ndriamandetahoho a "Zafimanely." The Zafimanely could not antedate Andriamanely I. The Antaifasy use of this name is an anachronism, but it does pose a problem of fundamental political transition in Bara history. According to Flacourt, Andriamanely I died in 1653. Flacourt calls him a Mahafaly king, a statement to which a strong objection has been made.[103] It cannot be sustained, for two reasons: It would close the door to further investigation, and, moreover, Flacourt had very definite knowledge of Andriamanely I.[104]

Early in June [1649] came twelve blacks from Mahafalles, on behalf of Dian Manhelle, lord of the land, to ask me for Frenchmen who would go to make war against Dian Raval, his enemy. . . . I ordered Sieur Le Roy to go and find Dian Manhelle with fourteen Frenchmen and some of our own blacks. The secret understanding was that all won in that war would be equally divided, half going to the French and half to Dian Manhelle and his blacks. Arriving at Mahafalles, they assembled two thousand blacks and, after marching for twelve days, entered enemy territory where they won ten thousand head of cattle . . . and over five hundred slaves.

Dian Manhelle died in 1653. . . . [His] land is richer in cattle than any other in this Island and he increased his wealth through theft and pillage inflicted on the Lords of Machicores, once his masters. . . . He and his brothers possessed over forty thousand head of cattle . . . apart from the gold and silver he held. . . . They [at this moment] have no fixed abode . . . [and roam] over some 35–40 leagues [inland].

In western and southwestern Madagascar today the *Masikoro* (Machicores) are considered as either Sakalava or Mahafaly. No one knows the origin of the term Masikoro, but it has been taken to mean people of the interior as opposed to the Vezo, or people of the coast, also considered now as Sakalava or Mahafaly.

Flacourt's account shows that Andriamanely (Dian Manhelle) was beginning to build a cattle empire in the 1640s and that, in the 1650s,

---

[103] Grandidier and Decary, *Histoire politique*, pp. 182–183. The authors cite as supporting document a letter written from Fort-Dauphin by Abbé Nacquart on February 9, 1650. The pertinent passage reads: "The French made war upon Andriandravalo, a Mahafaly chief, together with Andriamanely, who complained to have been wronged by him" (n. 2, pp. 182–183). The passage actually fails to state that Andriamanely was *not* a Mahafaly ruler, and it is extremely doubtful that the good Abbé was as well informed as Flacourt. See also text and note 111 below.

[104] Flacourt, *Relation*, COACM, Vol. IX (1920), p. 263; *Histoire*, COACM, Vol. VIII (1913), p. 40.

his brothers—the Zafimanely properly speaking—were spreading into the interior. The ashes of the once powerful Masikoro state were all around them:[105]

> The entire land of Machicores is ruined by wars; some time ago, its King, Dian Baloualen or "master of hundred thousand cattle-pens," was Lord of all these lands of Machicores, Concha, Manamboulle, Alfissach, and Mahafalles, even today the people say so . . . but, after his death, his sons warred against one another . . . ruining themselves, each one on his own [while] Dian Manhelle and the Zaffe-enrenavaoulles [Andrevola] grew rich at their expense.

Among those so ruined, Flacourt mentions Dian Raval.

A tradition has been recorded concerning the formation of Masikoro. One of Rapapango's brothers, "with those of the Bara who followed him," brought under his authority the "Manarilava, whose huts stood on the Isalo escarpment, the Mikeha, people of the plains, and the Voazimba of the rivers and the sea. From this union . . . came the Masikoro."[106] The Andrevola were founded by this Bara noble and became the ruling Masikoro family. Apparently, the Bara were too few to impose their name on the Manarilava, Mikeha, and Vazimba. Actually, the term Masikoro itself does not appear to have been either invented by the Andrevola or transferred from one ethnic group to several. Much of the intermediary plateau of southern Madagascar contained a secondary growth of scrub forest, its characteristic feature. In Tanzania, in the extensive hill area behind Dar es Salaam, such a scrub forest "is known to the natives" as *mashokora*.[107] Therefore, it is possible to suggest that the term Masikoro in southern Madagascar applied to the inland peoples who lived in the *mashokora* environment. This is probably the main reason why the Bara were not known by that name to the seventeenth-century coastal Europeans. Of the French settlers at Fort-Dauphin, only two—Claude Le Roy and Sieur Foucquembourg—are known to have made journeys into the Bara interior, but no accounts have been found to throw light on its ethnography. Le Roy was killed in Madagascar by the Zafimitovo.[108] Foucquembourg was killed near Paris by a common thief.[109] From 1642 to 1646 Foucquembourg was second in command at Fort-Dauphin. He had extensive private papers, but they were never

[105] Flacourt, *Histoire*, COACM, Vol. VIII (1913), p. 44.

[106] De la Villerabel, "Tradition" 264.

[107] A. V. Hartnoll and N. R. Fuggles Couchman, "The 'Mashokora' Cultivations of the Coast," *TNR*, No. 3 (1937), 35.

[108] Flacourt, *Histoire*, COACM, Vol. VIII (1913), p. 13.

[109] *Ibid.*, 210.

found.[110] Gradually, Masikoro came into use as an ethnic name and, in this narrower sense, designated the subjects of Andrevola.

The Andrevola evolved from the Bara, although this is naturally minimized by their own nineteenth-century tradition, because the Masikoro and the Imamono were frequently at war.[111] Flacourt states that Andriamanely I (Dian Manhelle) and Andriandravala (Dian Raval) of Antikondra (Icondre) were "mortal enemies" but that they were also "brothers."[112] What the Zafimanely genealogy hides—and it was the only one available among the nineteenth-century Bara—is that descendants of Andriamanely I, himself a Maroserana ruler of the Mahafaly, simply grafted him on to the Bara one. This was not a difficult task since the Zafimanely and the Bara had the same great ancestor in Rabaratavoka. The Bara line began with Rapapango's father, attained its apex with Andriamena, and lost control with Diamandana's death. The posthumous name (*fitahina*) of "master of hundred-thousand cattle pens" must have been Andriamena's. Flacourt notes that the oldest son of this ruler was Dian Mandreandanghits and that he was put to death by Andriamanely I (Dian Manhelle), the same fate that befell Andriandravala (Dian Raval).[113] It can now be clearly seen that *Dianmandreandan* and *Diamandana* are one and the same, that the execution of Andriandravala is associated with the myth of Renitsira, and that both myth and history attest to dynastic change in the seventeenth-century Ibara.

It seems useful to reproduce here an oral version that illustrates some of the conflicts, the connections with other groups through marriage, and the role of gold in settlement of feuds—a version which also addresses itself to the founding of Bara Vinda, a clan left out of the general discussion.[114]

> [Manely's] three sons, Diamanofotsy, Ratsimive, and Diamaranhetsy, did not live in peace. The oldest son established his residence at Ranotsara, a day's march south of Ivohibe; the second withdrew to the banks of Ionaivo but quickly regretted his departure and resolved to chase his brother away. Diamanafotsy, beaten in a decisive encounter, fled to the Tanala, people of the same tribe to which his mother, Vohilakatsy, belonged . . . and who received him well. One of his sons was killed in the battle. His wife, Rambahira, could find no consolation. Seeking to avenge the death of her son, she went to look for Ramitongoa, another son of

[110] *Ibid.*, 213.

[111] Capts. Toquenne and De Thuy, "Etude historique, géographique et ethnographique sur la province de Tuléar," *NRE*, V (1899), 103. The links were stressed *only* through women.

[112] Flacourt, *Relation*, COACM, Vol. IX (1920), p. 340.

[113] *Ibid.*, 44.

[114] De la Villerabel, "Tradition," 266–267.

Diamanofotsy, then at Makaiky, near Ihosy, and addressed him in a manner which would do away with indifference: "How can you support with patience the outrage against your father? I, who am Sakalava, have a heart full of anger. Go to my people to get warriors since yours are dead." They left and did not fail to return with a large number of men whose main leaders were renowned for their exploits. There were among them many heroes whom the Betsiriry still recall in their song: Garamanalataka, Mitsangasivelo, Voamianary, Retahinalika, Repapa, and others, no less renowned. Ratsimive fought against them with courage but was wounded and abandoned by his men; he then sat on an anthill to await death. The Sakalava surrounded him and Ramitongoa came close. "Kill me," said Ratsimive, speaking to him, "the warriors with you are nothing but slaves without right, except in direct combat, to touch a *mpanjaka*." Rambahira, seeing that Ramitongoa hesitated and fearful that her revenge would not come to pass, cried out in anger: 'If you do not strike the murderer of my child and of your father, I will consider you as his accomplice!' Then Ramitongoa, moved by fear, speared the wounded [Ratsimive] through. . . . After this battle, in which Ratsimive lost his life, one of his sons went with 200 warriors to the Ionaivo. He is considered as the founder of Bara Vinda, now found on the left bank of Sakamare River. For a long time, relations with other Bara were hostile, then hatreds began to subside and, one day, the *mpanjaka*(s) exchanged the *volamena*, covenant by gold.

It may be noted in passing that among the Sakalava warriors hired for the battle, one of the names celebrated in the Betsiriry song, *Garamanalataka*, contains the Swahili term *gharama* (Swahili, expense; Malagasy, hire, wages).[115] The infix -*na*- is a conjunction for forming indefinite pronouns and adverbs while *lataka* comes from *latsaka* (Malagasy, fallen down). An idiomatic translation of this name would be, mercenary who does not fall down (in battle).

Andriamanely I died before all the Bara could be brought under a single authority. The Zafimanely imposed themselves gradually, in the absence of any pre-eminent local family. Until Raikitroka, some fifteen decades later, the different Zafimanely kinglets were in continuous internal struggle for control of Ibara. Raikitroka unified most of Ibara by the turn of the nineteenth century, but he lived to see the start of new subdivision. There is no doubt that the once powerful state, which stretched from Mount Isalo in the west to the Manambolo River in the east, and which reduced the Mahafaly to vassal status, was a Bara one. Of this state, next to nothing is known. It was almost certainly a multi-ethnic one, encompassing such groups as the Kimoso, Tambahy, Maroen-tana, Antandrona (sometimes called western Betsileo), some southern Betsileo, part of the Tanala, and northern Antandroy. Thus, contrary to

[115] J. Richardson, *A New Malagasy-English Dictionary* (1885), pp. 211, 317.

previous belief, there was an early Bara state. It formed sometime in the second half of the sixteenth century and lasted until about 1650. This is somewhat longer than Raikitroka's subsequent experiment with an all-Bara state, one which so altered traditions that no two subgroups could agree on the smallest historical point by the end of the nineteenth century. The Bara political history, moreover, did not begin with the Zafimanely. Their advent in Ibara represents a hitherto unsuspected dynastic change, unsuspected both because traditions were altered and because the time depth is much greater. With relative ease, the nine-teenth-century Zafimanely could thus find, in the traditions, the grounds for their authority.

Toward the beginning of Andriamena's rule there "started the trade for rifles, imported by the English, 14 to 16 head going for one of them."[116] Another tradition reduces the number of cattle by half.[117] A number of English vessels visited southwestern Madagascar between 1607 and 1614 but not for some years after the last date.[118] An exchange of firearms for cattle in this particular period is not, on the whole, supported by the English accounts, which will be examined in some detail in the following chapter. More than likely, however, some firearms found their way into the interior via a shipwrecked crew[119] or by way of intermediaries on the coast able to salvage some of them.[120]

Whether they come from European sources or from collected oral traditions, epitaphs to Dian Baloualen, Andriamanely I, and Raikitroka read like a well-rehearsed script; children always devour the work of their fathers. Pastoralism and open spaces have already appeared as pillars of a deterministic *vintana* (fate, inevitable destiny) theory. These forces of nature apply equally to the Sakalava or the Mahafaly, whose political experience has, nonetheless, been different. One only has to see the huge clouds of dust that follow a sea of cattle all along the western plains to perceive that *vintana* is not the answer.

The military men and administrators who collected Bara traditions

[116] De la Villerabel, "Tradition," 265.

[117] See the first Bara tradition in the Appendix.

[118] Davis (1607), Koeling (1608), Middleton and Downton (1610), Marlowe and Davy (1612), Newport and Peyton (1613), and Downton, Pring, and Elkington (1614).

[119] Middleton and Davis were told in 1607 that, some six weeks before their arrival at Saint-Augustine Bay, a ship of unknown flag "was wrecked on this coast and from it came large numbers of armed men who dispersed well into the interior . . . [and] after having at first treated the local inhabitants with humanity, there was a bloody war in which, they too lost a lot of men." *COACM*, Vol. I (1903), p. 404.

[120] At least two Dutch ships were lost on the Antandroy coast early in the seven-teenth century. François Martin, on the whole a reliable source, claimed to have seen in this area some local men armed with blunderbuses and pistols.

after 1896 came to attribute major clan formations to the sons of Raikitroka. They reported what could be learned from the Zafimanely. Both parties were, in essence, after the same principle of historical legitimacy but with two different ends in mind. The French believed that it could be found in the study of the past and that its discovery

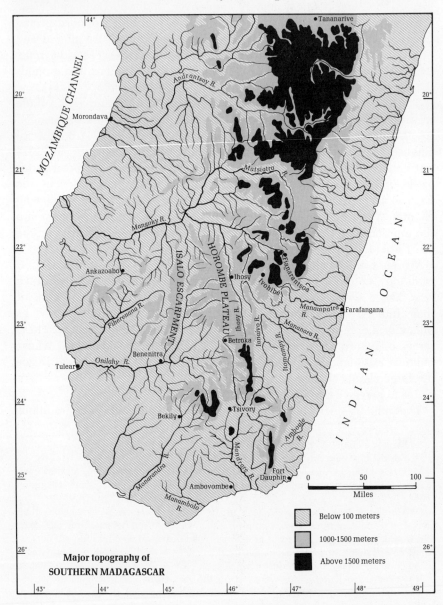

Major topography of
SOUTHERN MADAGASCAR

would help bring all of the Bara under a single system of administration.[121] The Zafimanely kings thought mainly in terms of improved control within their own clans.[122] It would appear, from what is known, that the major clan has been the classic political unit of the Bara.

There is considerable historical interest in comparing the notes of two men who, some fifty years apart, sought to describe the rudiments of Bara political system. The models are those of Le Barbier (1917) and Michel (1957); one difference should be pointed out immediately. Le Barbier was among the Bara when old institutions were in retreat but still quite visible. Impoinimerina, a provincial governor at the time, died in 1909. His son, Rehandry III, tried to rule the Imamono like Rehandry II and could refer constantly to his father. Le Barbier, who knew him, provides a description of the Imamono system of government and justice that is both contemporary and that refers to the times of Impoinimerina and Lehimanjaka (Rehandry I) before him. Michel, on the other hand, faced the ungrateful task of depicting shadows.

According to Michel, the Bara king is an absolute ruler in theory only. Succession is strictly direct; primogeniture is law. The king is assisted by a council of ministers, the *tandonaka* being its individual members. They are four in number and are chosen by the king from the nobility. Appointed for life, the *tandonaka* are succeeded by their own sons. The ministers live at the royal court. They travel frequently on the king's behalf and act as his ambassadors in foreign and domestic areas. They become military chiefs in wartime, but Michel found that general wars are very rare. They receive a fixed income from the people and not the king.

Next in line are the governors of the king's provinces, the *manandranomay*. Also four in number and selected by the king, they have no fixed income. They may or may not be of noble descent. Any Bara, as long as not of *andevo* (slave) origin nor a female, can qualify for this office. In wartime the *manandranomay* are next in command after the *tandonaka*. Provincial governors are assisted by their own councils of ministers, usually elders or *ionaka*. Village chiefs are elected by their own communities (*fokonolona*). Slaves among the Bara—a unique feature says Michel—always came from outside groups. Debts which are not honored or inability to pay an imposed fine do not lead to enslavement, but to expulsion from the village and sometimes from the clan. There is

[121] Marshal Lyautey, *Lettres du sud de Madagascar, 1900–1902* (1935), pp. 253, 300. Lyautey believed that if the past and the present ensuing from it were known to the military, "*on eut pu réunir en un seul bloc tous les groupes Bara sans exception . . . sous l'autorité d'un seul chef de la caste Zafimanely*" (p. 300). This reasoning, however, was not applied only to the Bara (see pp. 271 and 251).

[122] Du Bois de la Villerabel, "Etude sur le secteur des Bara Imamono," *NRE*, V (1899), 526.

a class of royal slaves, the *tsimandos*. The term itself is of Merina origin. The king has his own guard of ten young nobles. They are called *tsimanata*. In war they shield the king. High crimes are tried by the king, and death penalties are carried out by the *tsimanata*. Although a primitive people, the Bara never practiced trial by ordeal. Most of the justice is rendered below the king.[123]

According to Le Barbier, the *mpanjaka-bé* (king) is an absolute monarch except in three instances: when being "ratified" as successor, when war is to be declared on an outside group, and when a calamity, like famine or epidemic, strikes. He can negotiate treaties, make alliances and blood covenants,[124] or take a spouse from a non-Bara group without consulting anyone. Direct-line succession or the right of the oldest son to the throne is honored as often as not and has no force of customary law. Any *one* of the king's sons or brothers with the most partisans can succeed him. The king owns everything and nothing. He has no income from taxes of any kind. His income comes from two principal sources: the spoils of war[125] and from judicial penalties involving confiscation of property.

The Bara hierarchy includes the *mpanjaka-kely* (kinglets), *mpanjaka* (great chiefs), *olobé* (notables who are not of noble class), village chiefs (*tana-bé* or *tana-kely* chiefs depending on the size of their village), and the *mahombé* (royal slaves). The majority of Bara are *vohitsa* (freemen), while the *andevo* (nonroyal slaves) come from other groups. Only the king can reduce a Bara *vohitsa* to slavery when debts and fines cannot be paid. A *vohitsa* so reduced becomes, however, a royal slave, not a private one. Some of the *mahombé* are personal attendants and confidential royal servants.[126] The *mahombé*, unlike the *vohitsa*, are permanently subject to royal levies and have no electoral voice. The *vohitsa* carry great weight with royal successors, for they provide the numbers and therefore ratify the successor. The *olobé*, although appointed by the king, embody the *vohitsa* will. They are men of the people, a kind of gerontocracy, a council of elders. The *olobé* office is nonhereditary. In theory, an *olobé* is never appointed for life. In practice, they are seldom recalled.

The king also appoints village chiefs, who can be recommended by others or selected entirely by the king. The great chiefs, on the other hand, come through their own clans or subclans and the king seldom

---

123 Michel, *Bara*, pp. 34–51.

124 See the Bara Appendix below for *fatidre* (blood covenant).

125 See the first text of the Bara Appendix below.

126 The *mahombé*, writes Faublée, "formed a kind of royal bodyguard, men of confidence, attached to the king like the slaves attach to their master" (*Récits bara*, p. 49). The word resembles closely the old Shona-Rozvi *mutupo* of *mhumba*, or heart, cf. Abraham, "The Early Political History," pp. 61, 76, n. 8.

fails to accept them. In their own domains (*faritany*), the *mpanjaka* (chiefs) exercise the same kind of authority that the *mpanjaka-bé* has over the entire Bara unit he rules. *Razzias* and limited or localized wars, or reprisals involving another Bara group or an external one, fall within the domain of the *mpanjaka*. A declaration of general war must be approved both by the *olobé* and the great chiefs who carry out the mobilization and who become generals if war is declared.[127] Le Barbier does not explain the role of *mpanjaka-kely*.

"Before our arrival," adds Le Barbier in past tense, the "king alone held the right to justice, high and low, civil or repressive: his competence was absolute and his jurisdiction extended over the whole area under his administration."[128] The king and the great chiefs had the same right in custom, but crimes involving the death penalty could be tried only by the *mpanjaka-bé*. A Zafimanely, a royal wife or concubine could also be tried by no one else. Adultery by a king's female was punished by upper-lip mutilation or by severance of an ear.

Capital punishment was carried out in secret but all trials were public. False testimony (*kitomboka*) was taken for granted, one party neutralizing the other. For minor infractions, the rights of *mpanjaka* were delegated. Settlement was generally immediate either by *sasalia* (damages with interest) or through *tsarampilongoa* (amicable solution). Since trials were public and contesting parties often had equally strong cases, the *mpanjaka* avoided difficult decisions by resorting to impartial means of trial by ordeal. The Bara did not administer *tanghin*. They had five other varieties: by gold (*tange volamena*), by muzzle-loader (*tange ampinga-haratsa*), by boiling water (*tange ranomay*), by a swim across a croco-dile-infested river (*tange rano misy voay*), and by physical contact with a dead ancestor (*tange lolo*).[129] *Tange ranomay* was restricted to women,

---

[127] Le Barbier, "Notes," 97–100, 105.

[128] *Ibid.*, 100.

[129] *Ibid.*, 100–104. In the *voay* variant, the accused had to swim across a crocodile-infested river; the *ampingaharatsa* trial involved the firing of a muzzle-loader without any unusual follow-ups (protracted smoke, strong backlash, chip off the piece) so that the amount of powder put into it would make the difference; in the *tange volamena*, a gold piece was placed in a *finga* (bowl) filled with water, and the accused drank his share. He was then locked up in a hut for twenty-four hours, and if there were no signs of a swollen stomach or excessive urination, guilt would be dismissed; for the *tange ranomay*, a large vessel full of boiling water and with a small stone in it was placed next to a *sajoa* (jug) containing cold water. The accused female had to retrieve the stone in a single plunge of the hand and transfer it into the cold-water jug. If the hand showed no trace of burn, she went free. The *lolo* was predicated on the fear of the dead. It would appear, from the various readings on the subject, that the use of *tanghin* prevailed in Madagascar in the east, center, and west-northwest; of boiling water, in the southeast and southwest; of the *voay* or *mamba*, in the southeast; of the red-hot iron (passed over the tongue), in the south

tange lolo was for both sexes, and the remaining three were limited to men. An arbiter (*mpititiky*) had to be present at each type of trial. The *mpanjaka* could not attend those of the *lolo* and the *voay*.

Although it mixes notions about the past with present-day survivals, it is clear from the 1957 account how the Bara system evolved. In return for an end to slavery, monarchical absolutism, war, and old ways of rendering justice, the royal family was perpetuated through a guaranteed succession by first-born sons, while the Zafimanely were insulated against decline in status. Traditional authority and administration were thus incorporated into the new system, leaving the impression of two parallel governments.

The changes as much as features of the older model provide ample testimony as to why the nineteenth-century all-Bara state had a short life span. Monarchy was not a source of stability but of tension. Without fixed income, the amount of wealth, mostly cattle, a king could accumulate depended on war and judicial cases serious enough to reach his jurisdiction. Major wars, except in cases of outside attack, could not be waged without going through an elaborate machinery of approval. The type of war sanctioned by custom involved redistribution of wealth in cattle among the *vohitsa* themselves. The king did no more than adhere to it on a more lavish scale. Thus, in one crucial respect, the distinction between ruler and subject disappeared with disastrous consequences.

Various forms of treason, attempted regicide, adultery with wives of a king absent from his capital, refusal to obey royal orders, murder and arson—all crimes to be judged by the king and leading to loss of life and confiscation of cattle—increased precisely when Zafimanely monarchs took cattle from each other's subjects. In a Bara kingdom that brought under one authority two or more major clans the monarch could not loot his *own* subjects. The greater number of relatively independent *mpanjaka* made it even more difficult to secure approval of foreign wars.

Paradoxically, therefore, the more powerful a kingdom became, the greater grew its *mpanjaka-bé's* difficulties in maintaining the court and the harem. The answer to this flaw in political machinery was the single major-clan kingdom. The central importance of mobile wealth (cattle) explains why territorial acquisition was of slight importance to Bara kings. The continuous multiplication of the *tariki*, as can now be clearly seen, was a response of the more or less wealthy Bara families not to any lack of grazing lands but to the instability fostered by great clan kings, all related as Zafimanely.

---

and southwest. The *lolo* variant of trial by ordeal seems to have been relatively rare, since it has been reported only among the Bara and associated with northern Antandroy. The whole subject is worth a comparative study far beyond anything attempted so far.

One particular institution among the Bara attests to the loss of distinction between ruler and subject: the *andrahufiki*. Originally, the *andrahufiki* came into being as religious specialists who presided over Zafimanely circumcisions and who acted as funerary attendants of dead kings. In time, however, the *andrahufiki* assumed the role of high priests whose principal duties were no longer religious but political. They could grant asylum, intervene in justice, veto royal acts, and stop wars between the Zafimanely.[130] In no other Malagasy group can such a transition be noted for the secondary nobility of funerary attendants.

The mention of *tandonaka* in 1957 but not in 1917 is interesting. Those known by that name had quite a different function in earlier Bara history. When a Bara king died, his body was secretly taken to the nearest mountain by a group of soldiers. Three months later it would be announced that the king is *folaka* (broken) and that a new one was "elected" to take his place. The dead king could not be buried after this announcement until the soldiers pillaged and killed throughout his domain.[131] The length of this organized period of anarchy depended on the successor's own will. It thus served a triple function: (1) to augment possessions of the departing king, (2) to speed up ratification of the incumbent, and (3) to prevent regicide by fear of consequences.

Antandonaka was the name given to the royal soldiers, the *tsimanata* recalled in 1957. An even closer link would be the *fanalolahy* of Manambia. This was a royal guard composed of renowned warriors and headed by a military chief called *talay*.[132] Royal soldiers called *antandonaka* too existed among the Antanosy, and they doubled as funerary attendants for the Zafindraminia.[133]

To what degree, it can now be asked, were the Bara culturally distinct from other southern Malagasy and to what extent does ethnographic data support the pre-Maroserana and post-Mahafaly dynastic changes?

A number of features have been advanced as being distinctly Bara: levirate, a wrestling sport called *ringa*, esteem for smiths, a special hair style, a unique form of addressing nobility, a dance called *papango*, a particular aspect of *bilo* (curative trance), *fady* against sheep and goat raising, a sacrificial knife called *vy lava*, inhospitality to strangers advertised by *kiady* (a stick implanted in front of Bara huts, a "keep-out" sign), and belief in the *helo* (earth spirits). The list could be extended, but even this brief accounting reflects that most of its components came from the single-group type of studies.

---

[130] Faublée, *Cohésion*, p. 138; his *Récits bara*, pp. 219–222. In the Bara folklore, says Faublée, the *andrahufiki* are sometimes confused with the *Mahumbé*. This is, perhaps, not an accident.

[131] A. and G. Grandidier, *Ethnographie de Madagascar*, Vol. III (1917), p. 521.

[132] Vacher, "Etudes ethnographiques," 414–415.

[133] A. and G. Grandidier, *Ethnographie*, p. 38.

Bara folklore reveals that levirate was once widespread, and its survival has been attested by Faublée.[134] The same can be said of the Bezanozano of east-central Madagascar.[135] European seventeenth-century documents, for example, report levirate among the Antanosy.[136] *Ringa* is also Mahafaly.[137] It is preceded by provocations, and the victor must pin the shoulders of his opponent to the ground. The term *ringa* is found, with the same generic meaning, in three southeastern Africa areas.[138] Esteem of smiths among the Bara was connected with the making of weapons, particularly muzzle-loaders without the possession of which, it seems, a Bara could not be sure of his manhood. The banning of firearms in the first half of this century may be the cause of an uneven attitude toward the smiths today.

Although the Bara nobles were *andrina* (*andriana*), they were addressed as *osa* (pronounced *ousha*). In Malagasy, *osa* is a general term for weakling or coward. In Gi-kunya and Ki-tikuu, *mwosa* applies to those who attend the dead.[139] Part of the Bara secondary nobility gained this status by attending dead kings and the meaning of *osa* would be closer to the east African rather than Malagasy definition.

The Bara *papango* (falcons noted for graceful and sustained flight) dance appears to be similar to the *golika* of the Mahafaly.[140] The *kiady*

---

[134] Faublée, *Récits bara*, pp. 70–71; and his *Cohésion*, p. 23 and *passim*.

[135] Kent, *Field Notes*. Communicated by Jean Poirier of the University of Madagascar, who has been studying the Bezanozano. On this group, see: Captain Noël, "Le Pays Bezanozano," *NRE*, II (1897), 1–27; and Vallier, "Etude ethnologique sur les Bezanozano," *NRE*, III (1898), 65–84. Historical knowledge on the Bezanozano is extremely poor and quite contradictory.

[136] Father d'Almeida, Mariano's companion, wrote that "what is most deplorable" among the Antanosy "is that they even marry the widows of their brothers and of their fathers," *COACM*, Vol. II (1904), p. 197.

[137] E. Mamelomana, *Les Mahafaly* (not dated), unpublished typescript of 78 pages (unnumbered), No. 141 of *BP*, under *ringa*. Various forms of man-to-man combat existed outside the Bara. *Ringa* and *moraingy* (Betsileo) seem to be analogous, with the difference that the nape of the neck must be pinned down in the latter; elsewhere (and curiously), wrestling is called *balahazo* (a term also for manioc), which may be suggestive of its origin; several types of boxing go under the terms of *toranga* and *mandao toranga* (northwest), or even *totohondry*; there were, or are, also forms of combat that involved the use of one leg or leg-hand or two legs combinations (*diamanga*), or nails alone (*antsefaka*). Cf. Ch. Bénévent, "Etude sur le Bouéni," *NRE*, II (1897), 70–71; R. Decary, *Moeurs et coutumes des Malgaches* (1951), 175–177; and A. and G. Grandidier, *Ethnographie*, p. 135.

[138] Sacleux, *Swahili-français*, Vol. II (1941), p. 777 (Vanga-Rufiji, Cazi-Kilifi, and Rasini Island, opposite coast as well); also *linga* in his Vol. I (1939), p. 475. *Linga* implies balance and harmony.

[139] *Ibid.*, Vol. II (1941), p. 653.

[140] Mamelomana, *Mahafaly*, under *golika*. The chief difference seems to be in the more acrobatic execution of the middle and last-dance sequences.

were used by the Anteimoro to forbid entry into cultivated fields.[141] The sheep–goat *fady*, now on the way out, was common to the Bara, Vazimba of Menabé, Antaisaka, and the majority of the Sakalava.[142]

The *vy lava* (long knife), passed on from father to son, has its roots in early Sakalava history as a royal symbol and will be noted in that connection. It appears, however, as a royal symbol only among the Sakalava and the Bara clan of Manambia. Elsewhere in the south and west, as well as parts of the interior, noble families had sacrificial knives. Some knives had quite intricate designs.[143]

The *bilo* ceremony[144] is fairly widespread in the south under the same name and elsewhere under different ones. The Bara innovation seems to consist of two life-size statues, representing a man and a woman, that are placed near the residence of the "tormented" person who will take the *bilo* cure. Similar representations appear among the Antandroy and the Sakalava-Menabé but not in connection with the *bilo* or the *tromba*. This innovation may be recent, and it could come from a famous family of Bara sculptors from Iakora.[145] The *helo* subdivide into several categories.[146] They can cause the need for *bilo* or else become protectors of individual Bara. The Antanosy also had the *helo* but used an additional name: *baleka*. In southeast Africa, *leka* (imperative of *eka*) means not to be touched or do not touch! In earlier times the Zafimanely were regarded as intermediaries between the *helo* and the *vohitsa*.

Clearly, it is difficult to isolate any number of features and assign them uniquely to the Bara, since cultural cross influences have been at work a long time. Nonetheless, some have thought that the Bara possess one feature shared with no other group. "It is the manner in which Bara set

---

[141] G. Mondain, *L'Histoire . . . de l'Imoro* (1910), p. 135 and n. 1.

[142] A. and G. Grandidier, *Ethnographie*, p. 597 (218).

[143] See, for example, the booklet *Madagasikara regards vers le passé: exposition 10–20 novembre 1960* (1960), photographs on page 68 and explanatory notes on page 62 for exhibit items F. 30–34; photographs on page 67 and explanatory notes on page 62. All the knives are Bara. The most arresting ornamented knife was seen in Menabé (owner does not wish to be identified).

[144] There are many descriptions of the *bilo*, some of questionable value. What seems to be a reasonably authentic one is taken from Mamelomana, *Mahafaly*, and given in the Bara Appendix below although it applies to the Mahafaly.

[145] Deriving from the first sculptor, Manjanivo, this family from Iakora is now in its fifth generation. It appears to be the only such *family* known in Madagascar. An entire village among the Tanala-Zafimaniry has taken up sculpture as a means of livelihood, but this is due to a period of famine.

[146] *Helu atumua, helu mena, helu mena panjaka* and *helu meti*, cf. Faublée, *Esprits*, pp. 29, 34–35, 38–39, 63. *Atumua* applies to a person stricken by *helo* (*helu* is Faublée's spelling), the other types—red and dark are extrapersonal. The Antanosy appear to have been familiar with *helo*, as well, but more in connection with haunted tombs.

their hair," wrote a late nineteenth-century observer, "that distinguishes them from other southern Malagasy."[147] The Bara, wrote another, "have a unique hair style: they make a kind of crown on top of their heads by rolling the hair into round clumps, all equidistant and of the same thickness; to achieve this . . . they add a mixture of lard and ocher which has a repugnant odor [but] this is on the way to extinction."[148] This *billes-de-billard* style has been noted among the Tanala, Mahafaly, and southern Sakalava.[149] In the seventeenth century, the Antanosy Roandriana made "their hair into a crown" with beeswax, a "bizarre" form of hairdress to Flacourt.[150] Perhaps—for the last century—the conclusion of Faublée is apt: the Bara "society is also that of other southern Malagasy."[151]

Certain additional conclusions can, nonetheless, be drawn. The Mahafaly, Sakalava, and Antanosy analogies seem to occur with some frequency even when distinct Bara traits are mentioned. The *dady* religion, common knowledge of the *Tantara*, and the same dynastic family from the beginning to the end mark the Sakalava-Boina until the 1840s and the Sakalava-Menabé until the 1890s. The sole link of this kind among the Bara, after about 1650, consisted of the Zafimanely. Historical data, legend, and an analysis of the Zafimanely political system show that they took over the Bara from outside, not from within. The Zafimanely themselves held that they are distinct from the Bara on the grounds of *futi nunu* (white breast, white origin)[152] and the *helo* force. Their own association with the *helo* shows an attempt to provide religious underpinnings for an unfavorable interplay between nature and political ingenuity. The king and the priest, however, could not merge because the Zafimanely were incapable of holding a unified Bara state long enough.

The Bara monarch was quasi-divine. The *vohitsa* could not look at his face while the king traveled.[153] An English missionary was almost killed

[147] Captain Lefort, "Mission dans le Sud," Part II, *NRE*, III (1898), 274.

[148] De la Villerabel, "Etude," 525.

[149] Toquenne and de Thuy, "Etude historique," 104.

[150] Flacourt, *Histoire*, *COACM*, Vol. VIII (1913), p. 120.

[151] Faublée, *Cohésion*, p. 138. Toquenne and de Thuy wrote in their "Etude historique," p. 105, that neither in dress nor in the physical traits could anyone determine beforehand to which tribe an individual belongs.

[152] That is, according to Faublée's translation of the phonetic words (in standard orthography *fotsy nono*). But, the Bantu *futi* means kneecap, which was indeed a Maroserana relic (see Sakalava chapter), while *nununa* is Bantu for brothers. Hence, what the Zafimanely were really saying was that they are of Maroserana descent (brothers of the kneecap) and not whites ruling blacks.

[153] G. Mullens, *Twelve Years in Madagascar* (1875), p. 87.

merely for having spoken to a king's female.[154] Words were made *fady* after the king's death.[155] Among the Manambia, his office regalia included the *vy lava* as symbol of life and death over the subjects, sometimes called *jama*.[156] His residence alone could form a stockade, except for the Imamono who built forts (*manda*) with rifle openings (*kobo manda*) against attacks of the ethnic Masikoro.[157] On the other hand, king cults did not develop among the Bara for their Zafimanely kings. In an island where the dead surpassed the living in importance, this fact alone shows amply that Bara esteem for the monarchy of Zafimanely kings could not have been great. Moreover, the Bara royal funerals were not followed by orgies, a practice common to most Malagasy groups.

The term *jiny* among the Mahafaly of today applies to the spirit which torments a person in need of *bilo* cure.[158] But, in *Andriamaro*, the name given to the cranium of their founding Maroserana king, the Mahafaly had the equivalent of a *dady* cult. *Andriamaro* protected all Mahafaly against outside enemies and a high-priest medium interpreted his will.[159] The nearest analogy, in Madagascar, was to be found in the *Andriamarosivy*, the cranium of the southern Tanala, with whom the Manambia were heavily intermixed. There was one crucial difference. While *Andriamaro* demanded Mahafaly prayers and cattle offerings, *Andriamarosivy* had to have marrow from the spine of human victims, with which it was anointed from time to time.[160] The Mahafaly anointed—with bullock lard—their tomb stones and the Bara their mortuary coffins. Only in the northwest, in Boina, did royal coffins have to be lubricated with fat from breasts of the human female.[161]

[154] Cowan, *Bara Land*, pp. 61–62.

[155] *Ibid.*, pp. 70–72; Baron, "The Bara," 82–84; Catat, *Voyage à Madagascar*, pp. 341–342.

[156] Vacher, "Etudes ethnographiques," 415–416; Sacleux, *Swahili-français*, Vol. II (1941), p. 1036, notes that among other meanings *Zama* is the equivalent of being submerged.

[157] Bastard, "Mémoirs d'un Roi Bara," (1904), 404, and (1905), 322, gives *manda* as fort and *kobo-manda* as *nombrils du fort*. Sacleux, *Swahili-français*, Vol. I (1939), p. 428–429, defines *koboa* in connection with *mato* (*koboa mato*) as *"sortir les yeux de leurs orbites, avoir les yeux très granda paraissant comme sortier de leurs orbites."* *Manda*, on the other hand, implies fortification, *"planche disposée horizontalement en bas de l'encadrement de la porto de la case, en avant et du coté intérieur,"* Sacleux, *Swahili-français*, Vol. II (1941), p. 501.

[158] Under *jiny*, see Mamelomana's *Mahafaly*.

[159] D. Jakobsen, "Note sur Andriamaro, idole célèbre chez les Mahafaly," *BAM*, I (1902), 50–52.

[160] Vacher, "Etudes ethnographiques," 516.

[161] See A. Dandouau, "Coutumes Funéraires dans le nord-ouest de Madagascar," *BAM*, IX (1911), 171; and *Jangoa* in the ensuing Sakalava chapter.

The fact that the Bara had no *dady* supports the proto-Maroserana split. The cranium cults, at two extremities of Ibara, could not be imported either on a limited scale by the Manambia, who claim triple descent (Zafipanolahy–Zafimanely–Maroserana),[162] or on a larger one by the Zafimanely. The stormy nineteenth-century passage of the Manambia, from the eastern to the western rims of Ibara, may well have had something to do with *Andriamarosivy*. The Zafimanely could and did alter the old Bara genealogy. In so doing, however, they could not offer Manely's skull as a *dady* of Bara origin. The Mahafaly political system was also erected over groups of *tompontany*,[163] with a dominant chief, in this case Tsileliky. Down to the absence of royal taxes, the Mahafaly political system hardly differs from that of the Bara-Zafimanely.[164]

The Mahafaly had *Andriamaro* and two other safeguards. The Maroserana married into Tsileliki's own family first and then imposed their rule. This local family was then given the right to slave levies, it could not be punished for most types of transgression, and its members did not have to shave their heads after the death of a Maroserana king.[165]

The migrants who came with the Maroserana and the favorite former subjects of Tsileliky, together with his own family, were incorporated into the *Renilemy* (castes of five mothers), analogous to the *hova* Betsileo or Andriana in Imerina. The Maroserana always took wives from the *andriantsileliky*. Subjects (*vohitsa* Bara, *Hova* of Merina, *olompotsy* of Antanosy, who belonged with the former noble castes) became the *valohazomanga*, and all outsiders settling among the Mahafaly were grouped into the *folahazomanga*.[166]

From the start, thus, dynastic change among the Mahafaly was no simple imposition of external rule in the absence of traditional authority. Local potentates were incorporated into the privileged segment of the population and their daughters were given the status of Maroserana. Outside settlers were not used against the Mahafaly, a practice fol-

[162] Vacher, "Etudes ethnographiques," 408–410.

[163] *Inter alia:* Antangola, Foloamby, Antimitongoa, and Koneky. According to Rakotonavalona, "Mahafaly: Tableau" (1916), manuscript of three pages in *BP*. The Renilemy were considered as *tompontany* by this time.

[164] The Mahafaly political system is briefly described in Grandidier and Decary, *Histoire politique*, Appendix XXXI, pp. 235–236.

[165] Under *Andriantsileliky*, see Mamelomana, *Mahafaly*.

[166] Under *Renilemy, Valohazomanga*, and *Folahazomanga*, see Mamelomana, *Mahafaly, passim*. The *hazomanga*, a kind of family, clan, or national altar for prayers and sacrifices is common to the south, southwest and west. Some *Malgachisants* have used the *hazomanga* to distinguish between religions of the western-southwestern populations and those of the center. But, this is questionable. The Anteisaka, under Muslim influence, had it in the southeast but called it by a different name, *fototra*. The *hazomanitra* of Imerina appears to have the same function.

lowed by the Zafimanely among the Bara. The Mahafaly *razzias* were directed, on the whole, against other groups, the Masikoro, Antandroy, Bara, and even Sakalava. Thus, while the Zafimanely invasion into the interior of southern Madagascar may account in part for the collapse of the old Bara state, and while the Zafimanely could draw on the Mahafaly political system, something else was missing.

The Antanosy-Zafindraminia influence seems to have spread in two directions, toward the Antandroy along the southern coast and in the direction of eastern Bara. Sometime late in the sixteenth century, the *tompontany* of future Antandroy—Karimbola, Manambovo, and Mahandrovato—obtained an initial dynasty of Zafimanara. The Zafimanara claim descent from the Andrevola of Masikoro and the Tsienimbalala.[167] The Tsienimbalala are of Antivondro origin.[168] They formed, by migrating from eastern Ibara into northern Antandroy, some decades after the Andrevola became rulers of the ethnic Masikoro. The Antaifasy tradition, cited earlier, shows that the land of Manambovo was a Maroserana fief. This accords fully with what the Zafimanara say of their own parentage since the Andrevola founder was a grandson of Rabaratavokoka, from whom the Maroserana derive. The Zafimanara did not rule alone over the *tompontany* too long. Migrants from the east and from the west came in great numbers and submerged the *tompontany*, except the Karimbola.[169]

The Antanosy influence came with the eastern migrants. Kings in Antandroy became Roandriana and alone had the right to cut the throat of animals.[170] Moreover, early in the eighteenth century, one of the four Antandroy dieties was named *Dean Antemoor*.[171] The title of Roandriana survived, but kings in Antandroy gradually lost the exclusive right to slaughter animals. This was not due to an Ampanabaka type of revolt, as among the Anteimoro, but rather to the new migrants who introduced a tithe tax for the Roandriana and annual tribute from vassals (*fahenza*).

[167] Vacher, "Etudes ethnographiques," 327.

[168] *Ibid.*, 327, 509.

[169] The Karimbola, who appear in the earliest European accounts, claim to have had no history of migration. While many *tompontany* seem to have been given fictitious names (Fonoka, Koneky), the Karimbola, along with the Kimoso and the Vazimba, represent an existing and, apparently, old group. Defoort believed that the Karimbola long ago were a group of Bantu-speaking peoples but gave no reasons or evidence to support this belief, cf. his "L'Androy," *BEM*, XIII (1913), 156.

[170] R. Drury, *Madagascar or Robert Drury's Journal* . . . , edition of 1729 reproduced in French translation, in *COACM*, Vol. IV (1906), pp. 149, 165, 175. I worked with this edition in French and also with the previously cited English edition of 1890, at different times, as both are scarce. Drury was among the Antandroy around 1710 and is the first European to set this name on paper.

[171] *Ibid.*, pp. 209–210, 218, 307.

The Antanosy influence in eastern Ibara was, it would seem, cultural, and it can be deduced from two items that are not recent introductions. One is the *hazomboto*, or circumcision pot, and the other consists of granaries *a pilotis axial*. Both are identical only among the eastern Bara and the Antanosy of Fort-Dauphin.[172]

There was, very probably, another reason for the fall of the early Bara state. Andriamanely I began his ascent in the late 1630s or early 1640s. A decade or two before him, a substantial Sakalava migration passed through Baraland. Led by Andriamisara-Andriamandresiarivo, it was on the way to the east coast where it would become known as the Anteisaka.

The name *Saka* appears twice on Flacourt's map of 1661 and once in the text of his history. The two Saka sites appear approximately where the Anteisaka did, in fact, settle. Since the relatively uncharted western portion of Flacourt's map does not show the Sakalava or any site named Saka, Grandidier was able to argue that the west-coast Sakalava must derive from the east-coast Antaisaka.

As both Marchand and Hubert Deschamps have shown, after several years of residence among the Antaisaka and the study of oral tradition down to the family level, not a shred of evidence bears this argument out. All of the Antaisaka traditions contend that their migratory movement was from west to east.[173] Conversely, no known Sakalava tradition reports a migration of the Antaisaka from the east coast. The case becomes even stronger when it is recalled that the birth of Menabé belongs, as will be seen, in the second decade of the seventeenth century although the presence of Maroserana goes further back in time. The foundation of Menabé was not attained in peace; therefore, there is a good reason for an early seventeenth-century migration of a losing Sakalava faction.

This migration did not cross Baraland in a single movement. It took approximately two generations to get to the east coast. Andriamandresi led the Sakalava eastward but it was his grandson, Behava, who founded the Zarabehava, Antaisaka dynasty.[174] By 1650, at the time when the Zafimanely began to take over Ibara, the movement was over. It had led across the Bara plateau into what is known as the Bara-Tanala Valley. This valley has one exceptional feature: "it is the only point in the island where the basins of the west and the east-coast rivers connect without obstacle."[175] The Antaifasy passed through this valley somewhat later. The first Antaifasy-Anteimoro war took place in the 1680s. This approxi-

[172] Faublée, *Cohésion*, pp. 125, 128.

[173] Marchand, "Les Habitants de la province de Farafangana," *RM*, III (1901), 485–486; and Deschamps, *Anteisaka*, pp. 162–164 and *passim*.

[174] Marchand, "Les Habitants," 489; and Deschamps, *Anteisaka*, p. 165.

[175] E.-F. Gautier, *Madagascar: essai de géographie physique* (1902), p. 126; cf. Deschamps, *Anteisaka*, p. 14.

mate date can be advanced because this first of the many wars cost the life of Anteimoro Andriamilafikarivo.[176]

It is difficult to say precisely how the two migrations affected the Bara. Antaifasy texts report many battles but none with the Bara.[177] According to Antaisaka sources, Andriamandresi was killed among the Bara but not by them.[178] On the other hand, Grandidier's own notes, written among the west coast Sakalava in the 1860s, attest to the struggle between Andriamisara-Andriamandresiarivo and the *tompontany* of Ibara before the advent of Zafimanely. As for the Bara, their tradition gives a curious account of the separation of two brothers, Rapapango, who succeeded Andriankehoheho, and Rakouba, or Ratuba, who founded the Andrevola dynasty.[179]

There is a very strong case to be made that the Sakalava passage eastward and the disintegration of the first all-Bara state occur in the same time period—±1620–1640. What is both certain and telling, neither the title name of the founding Anteisaka rulers, the *Zarabehava*, nor the toponymic term *Saka* (phonetics, *Shaka*) belong to the basic Indonesian vocabulary of Malagasy idioms. On the contrary, *zara* derives from Swahili *i-jara* or division, while *behava/behewa* is Swahili for inner court.[180] The Antaisaka founders were thus a branch of the Sakalava who "divided from the inner court." The linguistic items here confirm what the tradition holds anyway. But, one can go further. To students of the east African past, *Šaka/Shaka*, at some four miles east of the old Ungwana, is a well-known site. As J. Kirkman has written, "Shaka is the scene of the Swahili legend of Liongo, an Arab-Pokomo or Arab-Galla hero."[181] *Shaka*, as both a site and capital of the Ozi Kingdom in east Africa, has been reported long before 1661 (earliest mention of *Saka* in Madagascar

[176] Mondain, *Histoire . . . de l'Imoro*, p. 73.

[177] Fontoynont and Raomandahy, "Antaifasy," 1–28.

[178] Deschamps, *Anteisaka*, p. 164. See the ensuing Sakalava chapter for confirmation from west-coast sources.

[179] De la Villerabel, "Tradition," 264: "Before dying, Diakehoheho did not take care to name one of his two sons as heir to authority, but the wisdom of the two sons repaired the oversight of their father. Rakuba, the older, said to his younger brother, Rapapango: "if we engage in a struggle for supremacy, what will become of our descendants? They will transform into salt (*manjary sira*) or into a whirlwind (*manjary talio*). Let us therefore swear to eternal amity through a sacrifice . . . to fulfill this, they bent the heads of the seven spears which the Tanala had sold to them, and they killed dogs with the seven muzzle-loaders which the Antanosy gave them; then these weapons thus rendered inoffensive, they sacrificed two oxen: one white with red spots, for Rakuba, and the other black with white spots, for Rapapango. After this ceremony, the older (of the two brothers) . . . left."

[180] Sacleux, *Swahili-français*, Vol. I (1939), p. 102.

[181] J. Strandes, in *The Portuguese Period in East Africa* (1961—German ed. 1899), p. 334.

by Etienne de Flacourt),[182] so that the problem of anachronism does not pose itself. The case is, however, even more interesting. Events in east Africa associated with Liongo have been dated as late as the 1600s and as early as the tenth century. As Bernard Vlekke reports, there are Javanese traditions as well about a legendary prince and hero of culture, *Aji Saka*, who was to have introduced into Java the "first social and political organization. He was "believed to have taught the people of Java the art of writing and to have given them their chronology."[183] In Java, in east Africa, and in Madagascar, thus, *Saka* appears as something important. But, whereas in the case of Java and east Africa the provenance of *Šaka* may have been *directly* from Asia, this does not hold for Madagascar, where *Šaka* could only have been introduced by way of the African mainland.

---

[182] Cf. J. S. Trimingham, *Islam in East Africa* (1964), p. 13; Strandes, *Portuguese Period*, pp. 214, 217; and R. Oliver and G. Mathew (eds.), *History of East Africa*, Vol. I (1963), p. 105 and n. 1.

[183] B. Vlekke, *Nusantara* (1943), p. 14.

chapter 5 THE SAKALAVA:
Origins of the First Empire in Madagascar

> In every place visited among the Sakalava we found events and names recalled by tradition still living in the memory . . . we have heard the Sakalava invoke these names in all important activities of their social life and recall with pride these events . . . and, in the presence of testimony thus given by an entire people, it became difficult to remain completely skeptical.
>
> Charles Guillain (1845)

Apart from the Merina, no other Malagasy society was as rich in oral traditions as the Sakalava (Šákkállava) of western Madagascar. As one observer reported some twelve decades ago, "the Sakkalava, kings and subjects alike, are ruled by oral traditions . . . often called *fitera*, or customs, and *n'antoaniraza*, or ways of the ancestors . . . and these include history, mythology, and poetry."[1] The analogy ends, however, when the *Tantara* of Imerina are considered as a model.[2] These traditions were compiled by a single man, as dictated by informants within a relatively small geographical area that saw the birth of the Merina monarchy.[3]

---

[1] V. Noel, "Recherches sur les Sakkalava," *BSG*, XX (1843), 285, 292–293.

[2] F. Callet, *Tantaran'ny Andriana* (1873–1902), five volumes in two different editions. Translated into French by G. S. Chapus and E. Ratsimba as *Histoire des rois* (1953–1958), in four volumes. The *Tantara*, as these texts are popularly called, constitute both a great classic of the Merina idiom and an early monument to oral tradition. Subsequent reference here will be to *Tantara*.

[3] Father François Callet collected most of the *Tantara* at six historical villages, including Alosara (the nucleus of Merina monarchy) and Ambohimanga (Merina Necropolis). See the discussion of the *Tantara* in the ensuing chapter.

Together with other important Merina traditions,[4] the *Tantara* were obtained when the Merina monarchy was at the peak of its power. The Sakalava traditions were compiled under different circumstances.

When Captain Charles Guillain[5] explored the west coast of Madagascar, in 1842–1843, and began to collect Sakalava oral traditions along with his contemporary, Vincent Noel,[6] the old Sakalava empire had collapsed after nearly seven decades of disintegration. Iboina's last important ruler, Andriantsoli, had fled to the isle of Mayotte and his land was rapidly coming under Merina control. Menabé, the southern part of Sakalava land, had only a few Merina outposts at the time, but it was divided among several more or less independent kings and kinglets. After Guillain and Noel, others would continue to gather Sakalava traditions over a vast stretch of territory between Analalava in the northwest and St. Augustine Bay in the southwest. Thus, there was quite a historical and geographical contrast, between the Merina and Sakalava, and it is not surprsing that one west-coast resident could find no oral traditions among the Sakalava,[7] while another could contribute two monographs of unusual merit.[8] The fragmentary nature of collected Sakalava oral texts made it possible, perhaps even necessary, to suffuse them with purely theoretical speculations about the early past. In turn, these were often reproduced as traditional sources by writers who simply rewrote what they read, sometimes without acknowledgments. No one, however, duplicated the work of Callet on the *Tantara* of Imerina or brought the Sakalava *lovan'tsofina* (heritage of the ears) into a single body of tradition.

The Sakalava can be defined through a combination of five features. One is dialect. A comparison of several dictionaries and vocabularies

---

[4] These include the very important *Merina Manuscripts* (2 volumes, 370 pages) written between 1864 and 1866 by a high priest of Queen Ranavalona I; *Tantara sy Fomban-drazana* (Ancestral History and Custom) (132 pages), written in 1896 by Rainandriamampandry; and *Early History of Imerina to 1838* (in three manuscript in-quarto volumes) written in English between 1838 and 1862 by Raombana, who had been educated by the London Missionary Society. Together, these sources have made possible two important histories of the Merina that were written subsequently by Europeans.

[5] Captain C. Guillain was the author of the most important monograph on the Sakalava—*Documents sur l'histoire, la géographie et le commerce de Madagascar* (1845). Under the same basic title, Guillain also published three volumes and an atlas dealing with the eastern African coast.

[6] On Noel, see Guillain, *Documents*, pp. 10, n. 1; 18 n. 3; 353 and n. 1; 354–355.

[7] "Of the history of ancestors, no traces. The *lovan'tsofina* or legends orally transmitted . . . and the *angano* or history, fables, tales are but few," wrote P. Lapeyre, *Dialectes hova et sakalava: essai d'etude comparée* (1891), p. 4.

[8] E. Birkeli, *Marques de boeufs et traditions de race: documents sur l'ethnographie de la côte occidentale de Madagascar* (1926), and *Les Vazimba de la côte ouest de Madagascar* (1936).

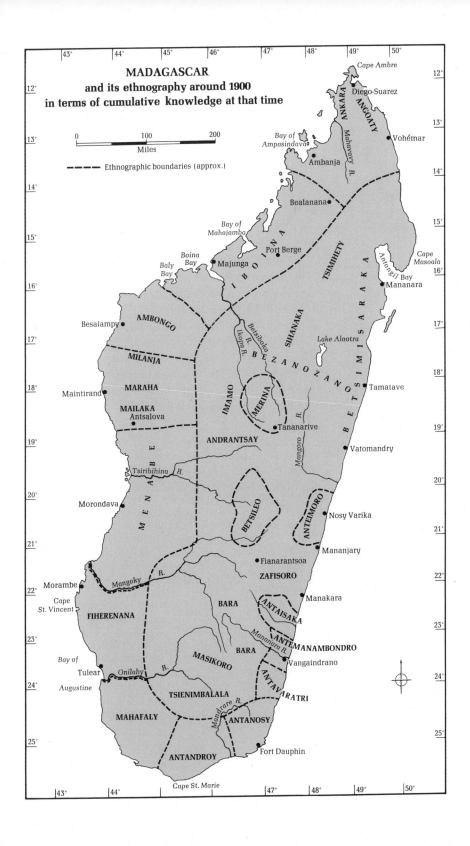

MADAGASCAR
and its ethnography around 1900
in terms of cumulative knowledge at that time

0   100   200
Miles

- - - - Ethnographic boundaries (approx.)

Cape Ambre

ANKARA

ANGOATY

Diego-Suarez

Vohémar

Bay of
Ampasindava

Ambanja

Mahavavy R.

Bealanana

TSIMIHETY

Cape
Masoala

Bay of
Mahajamba

Antongil Bay

Port Berge

Mananara

Boina
Bay

Majunga

BETSIMISARAKA

Baly
Bay

I B O I N A

Besalampy

AMBONGO

SIHANAKA

Lake Alaotra

MILANJA

B E Z A N O Z A N O

Betsiboka R.

Ikopa R.

MARAHA

IMAMO

MERINA

Tamatave

Maintirand

MAILAKA
Antsalova

Tananarive

Vatomandry

ANDRANTSAY

Mangoro R.

M E N A B E

Tsiribihina R.

BETSILEO

ANTEMORO

Nosy Varika

Morondava

Mananjary

Fianarantsoa

Morambe

Mangoky R.

ZAFISORO

Cape
St. Vincent

Manakara

FIHERENANA

BARA

ANTAISAKA

ANTEMANAMBONDRO

Mananara R.

BARA

Vangaindrano

Bay of

MASIKORO

Tulear

Onilahy R.

TSIENIMBALALA

ANTAVARATRI

Augustine

Mandrare R.

MAHAFALY

ANTANOSY

Fort Dauphin

ANTANDROY

Cape St. Marie

compiled between about 1850 and 1945,[9] reveals that the Sakalava dialect contains the greatest amount of Swahili and other Bantu loan-words.[10] It is also worth noting that while linguistic taboos occur in other Malagasy societies, they do not appear to have been as intense and widespread as among the Sakalava.[11] The second feature is the *dady* cult. *Dady* means grandparent or, by extension, ancestor. All Malagasy share, in a broad sense, the cult of ancestors, but what makes the Sakalava *dady* rather special is that they are *Ampagnito-bé* (*phonetics, 'mpanitúbé*) or great royal ancestors, represented by carefully preserved relics.[12] External decorations and casings are not identical for every *dady*, but all of them envelop bits of occiput bone and right patellae, teeth, nails, and hair of the Sakalava kings.[13] Their importance can be understood best by recalling that no ruler could assume office without being in possession of the *dady*. Twice in the nineteenth century Sakalava political obedience was secured by outsiders with help of the *dady*—by the Merina through capture of the *dady* and by the French through their return.[14] The ceremony of the royal bath has been observed in only three Malagasy societies— Sakalava, Merina, and Anteimoro. The Sakalava *Fitampoha*, however, applied and still applies to the *dady*, not to living rulers, as was some time ago the custom among the Merina and Anteimoro in their annual *Fandroana*.[15]

The powerful nature of royal ancestors emerges also through the *tromba*, or spirit possession, as it is often called, and the *tromba* can be private or public. For the Sakalava as a group, the public *tromba* has been of considerable importance. Through royally appointed mediums, a

[9] Cf. J. Webber, *Dictionnaire malgache-français* (1853); Abbé Dalmond, *Vocabulaire malgache-français pour les langues sakalava et betsimisara* (1844); J. Richardson, *A New Malagasy-English Dictionary* (1885); A. Jully, *Manuel des dialectes malgaches; hova, betsimisaraka, betsileo, tankarana, taimorona, tanosy, sakalava-mahafaly et du souahely* (1901); and B. H. Hoffmann, *Vocabulaire français-hova-sakalava-tsimihety* (*ca.* 1945), unpublished typescript of 218 pages, owned by the University of Madagascar.

[10] This was first noticed by the Norwegian missionary and linguist, Lars Dahle, in his analysis of "The Swaheli Element in the New Malagasy-English Dictionary," *AA* (1885), 99–115. Richardson in his *Dictionary* lists the appropriate words as either Sakalava or "provincial." Also consulted were the unpublished manuscripts of the Académie Malgache entitled *Enquêtes sur les dialectes malgaches* (1909–1912).

[11] Arnold Van Gennep, *Tabou* et totémisme à *Madagascar* (1904), pp. 104–119.

[12] Charles Poirier, *Notes d'ethnographie et d'histoire malgaches* (1939), pp. 13–18. See also his Planche II, photo 2, on which nine *dady* are visible.

[13] Jean Valette and Suzanne Raharijaona, "Les Grandes Fêtes rituelles des Sakalava du Menabé ou 'Fitampoha,' " *BM*, IX/155 (1959), 294.

[14] See "Restitution des reliques des rois sakalava à leurs familles," *JOM* (March 12, 1902), 7183.

[15] Cf. G. Razafimino, *La Signification religieuse du Fandroana ou de la fête du nouvel an en Imerina* (1924); and C. Collins, "The Fandroana or annual festival of the Taimoro," *AA* (1898), 149–151.

deceased Sakalava monarch spoke to the people to express his will, usually to initiate a particular activity.[16] The *tromba* and the *dady* have been intimately connected with the fourth feature, the dynastic family of the Maroserana to which the *Ampagnito-bé* belonged.[17] The creation of the Sakalava states of Menabé and Boina, which controlled western Madagascar in the eighteenth century, coincided with the extension of Maroserana power. In turn, all four features blend into traditional history, which envelops and defines the Sakalava. The essential outline of this history—the advent of the Maroserana, their initial contact with the Sakalava, followed by the foundation of Menabé, and later of Boina— was perceived most clearly by Noel and Guillain, the two earliest students of the Sakalava.

To Noel, who worked in Iboina, it seemed futile to look for the Sakalava origins, lost in the mist of time. They became historically important only "from the rule of *Andrian-dahe-foutsi* (White King) whose ancestors had been shipwrecked on the Mahafaly coast," which, according to his Iboina informants, stretched from Feherenga (Fiherenana River) to Faridifai (Fort-Dauphin) or roughly twice the area of the present-day land of the Mahafaly. Prior to its conquest by Andriandahifotsy, Menabé was known as Ansakuabé.[18] This king founded the *Zafivoula-mena* (sons of gold) branch of the Maroserana dynastic family, which ruled Menabé since about 1650. Around 1690, Andriandahifotsy died and received the *fitahina* (posthumous and usually prize name) of Andrian-hanninga-arrivou (king mourned by thousands). The conquest of Iboina was accomplished by one of his sons.[19] It is not surprising that oral texts collected by Noel in the north, far away from Menabé, attribute to a single conqueror king not only the foundation of this early kingdom and of the legitimate, or golden (*Volamena*) dynastic branch, but also the advent of the Sakalava themselves.

It was Guillain who pointed out for the first time that while the well-known 1661 map of Etienne de Flacourt[20] did not mention the Sakalava, this "does not mean that they were not already present on the western

---

[16] The standard, if unevenly written work on this subject is Henri Rusillon's *Un Culte dynastique avec évocation des morts chez les Sakalaves de Madagascar: le "Tromba"* (1912).

[17] For an accessible Maroserana genealogy, see H. Rusillon, "Notes explicatives à propos de la généalogie maroserana zafimbolamena," *BAM*, new series, VI (1922–1923), 169–184 and table.

[18] The core area of the Sakoambé seems to have been the hinterland of Morondava, which harbors their tombs, decorated with wood carvings of birds and humans.

[19] Noel, "Sakkalava," 290.

[20] Although published only with the second edition of Etienne de Flacourt's *Histoire de la Grande Ile Madagascar* in 1661 (1st ed. 1658), this map was based on geographical data gathered by Flacourt between December 4, 1648 and February 12, 1655.

coast." Flacourt designated a part of Menabé as Lahe Fonti (Andrian-dahi-fotsy), "clearly the name of this Sakalava ruler, mentioned (also) by Drury and by the tradition."[21] In the Naval Archives, Guillain found a 1668 document that revealed that some chiefs of the St. Augustine Bay area had gone all the way to the French settlement at Fort-Dauphin to ask for help against "Laheuefouchy."[22] Southern Menabé may thus have been founded close to 1650 but the "Sakalava tribe must have been in existence for some years when [Lahefoutsy] assumed command."[23]

Guillain reported two versions concerning the proto-Maroserana. In the southwest, the prevailing tradition was that a group of whites came from the eastern interior under their leader, Andrian-Alim-bé. Within a short time, he gained control over the southwestern lands, which became known as *Mahafaly*, "a site sacred, respected, fortunate, in allusion to the glorious destiny augured by the arrival of the White Chief."[24] But, the western or purely Sakalava traditional version held uniformly that the group of whites was of overseas origin, having landed one day on the southwest coast at Tolia-Maeva (Tuléar of today) and that the local inhabitants "elected" one of them, *Andriamandazoala*, as their leader. It was he who founded the Volamena dynasty "whose members still rule in independent sections of Sakalava land."[25] One of his sons, *Andria-misara*, decided to settle on the banks of the *Sakalava River* and named his village after the river. This name was gradually adopted by all those who recognized Andriamisara as their ruler.[26] Andriandahifotsy was his son. Many years after Guillain, a French infantry officer stationed in Menabé reported that the oldest known Sakalava ruler was *Rabaratavo-koka* (a name which other traditions give to founder of the Bara and even as the pre-*fitahina* of Andriamandazoala). His kingdom "extended from the Isalo massif to the Manambao River and from Midongy to the sea . . . some 6000 square kilometers . . . with an effective control over a much more limited area."[27]

[21] Guillain, *Documents*, p. 8.

[22] *Ibid.*, p. 8 and n. 3. See also text below and footnote 156 for the significance of this document.

[23] Guillain, *Documents*, p. 9.

[24] *Ibid.*, p. 10. The interpretation of *mahafaly* (*faly=fady*) as sacred site is supported by some traditions, as noted in the preceding chapter, but without any allusion to the White Chief or glorious destiny.

[25] *Ibid.*, 10–11.

[26] *Ibid.*, p. 12 and n. 1. Guillain implies that the Sakalava River, affluent of the Mangoky (or Saint-Vincent on some older European maps), obtained its name from another river further north.

[27] Lt. Thomassin, "Notes sur le royaume de Mahabo," *NRE*, VI (1900), 397. The boundaries of Menabé were never precise. At its peak, this kingdom seems to have encompassed all lands south-north from the Fiherenana to the Manambao Rivers and from the coastal line to the massifs of Isalo, Midongy, Lava, Tsara, and Bongo.

Alfred Grandidier, who spent some time on the western coast of Madagascar in the late 1860s, held that the earliest historical mention of the Sakalava appeared in the account of Robert Drury, who called them *Saccalavour*.[28] This particular spelling was attributed to Drury's cockney

[28] A. Grandidier, *Ethnographie de Madagascar*, Vol. I, Tome 1 (1908), p. 215 and n. 5; cf. R. Drury, *Madagascar or Robert Drury's Journal . . .* , 7th ed. (1890), pp. 234, 256, 259–260, 264, 266, 272, 274–275. The spelling in this seventh edition of the 1729 original is *Saccalavour*.

Sakalava warrior, from a late 18th-century(?) painting.

since his transliteration of other Malagasy words and proper names show a consistent pattern.[29] While, as will be seen, the Sakalava are mentioned in sources which antedate Drury's original edition of the *Journal* (1729), Grandidier was indeed the first to assert that the key to Sakalava origins could be found in the name itself. He dismissed some earlier interpretations given by European missionaries in the island.[30] In 1872 he argued that the Sakalava must be taken to mean people of Saka who dispersed over long stretches of land (*lava* = Malagasy, long). By adding *Ant/Ante* (people) and *I* (place of) to *Saka*, he obtained *Anteisaka*, a name which does designate a distinct group in southeastern Madagascar. Through the Sakalava of Menabé, Grandidier was also able to establish a claim of their kinship with the Anteisaka[31]—but *not* which of the two was the actual parent group. In none of his extensive writings, including an unpublished biography and manuscript notes made among the Sakalava,[32] did Grandidier allude to or reproduce a Sakalava tradition that supports an Anteisaka origin. As noted in the opening chapter (see text and notes 76–77), both Deschamps and Marchand have shown in some detail that the founders of Anteisaka came from the Sakalava of western Madagascar. According to oral texts collected by Joel Boto, a Betsimisaraka chief of Vatomandry told him early in the 1920s that the present land of Anteisaka was founded "by two brothers who were Sakalava warriors named Faniliha and Behava, then at war with the Bara . . . [and] their descendants became Zanafaniliha and Zarabehava (Anteisaka ruling lineage)."[33]

[29] For example, the Mahafaly king Hosintany became *Woozington*; the term *vazaha* for foreigner came out as *verzarhar*; *mena*, or red, as *maner*; Mahafaly itself as *Merfaughla*; *soa*, or good, as *suer*; and so on. Compare Drury's "Vocabulary of the Madagascar Language," *Journal*, pp. 319–335, with comments by Reverend Richardson at the end of the volume.

[30] *Inter alia:* long cats from inverted *lava+saka*; defiant ones from *sakaray*; people of long plains from *sakany*. While this position by Grandidier is on solid ground, he also dismissed a more plausible statement by Reverend Jorgensen, namely that the Sakalava tribal name may obtain from a "native (Malagasy) corruption" of a foreign word, in his "Notes on the Tribes of Madagascar," *AA*, III (1885), 53.

[31] Quoted in G. Grandidier, unpublished *Essai* on the Sakalava, typescript p. 4, n. 8, from his father's *Notes* (1867), pp. 1–10. See also note 32 below.

[32] A. Grandidier, *Notes et Souvenirs* (1917), manuscript of 413 pages, particularly pp. 98–213, in the Archives of the Malagasy Republic. The manuscript *Notes* of Alfred Grandidier made among the Sakalava in the 1860s and the 1870s are now in undisclosed private hands. However, lengthy extracts fortunately have been reproduced in both printed works and in Guillaume Grandidier's unfinished *Essai d'histoire des Malgaches de la région occidentale: les Sakalava* (not dated, but composed between 1945–1955), typescript of 78 pages with extensive notes, now in the private library of Hubert Deschamps, Paris. I am indebted to Professor Deschamps and to Jean Valette, Director of the National Archives of the Malagasy Republic, for their kind permission to consult the two unpublished originals.

[33] J. Boto, "Tradition relative à l'origine des Betsimisaraka-Betanimena," *BODE*, XXV (1923), 252–253. Jan Vansina has shown the importance of cross-checking the

Although Grandidier's Anteisaka hypothesis, "hooked-up" as it has been with the "Indian" origin of the Maroserana, has won general acceptance among students of Madagascar, a number of his own contemporaries did look toward Africa rather than India. Colonel Prud'homme, for example, allowed for the possibility that the whites mentioned in Sakalava traditions as the proto-Maroserana might have been Arabs, but he argued that Sofala had been their home and that they left it for the west coast of Madagascar "with their allies, the Mozambiques."[34] Captain Aymard saw Cafres in the Sakalava and speculated that "they are therefore Southern Africans who had crossed, some centuries ago, the Mozambique Channel and settled in Madagascar on the coast directly opposite and nearest to the point of departure."[35] Gabriel Ferrand pursued the idea of the tribal name Sakalava being related to origins but, unlike Grandidier, sought the answer overseas. In Father Mariano's account of Menabé in 1616, he spotted a group named *Suculambas*. To him, this represented a corruption of the Bantu tribal name *Machoukoulombe/Mashukulumba* or even *Shukulumbue* of the High Zambezi Valley, a name that became Sakalava in Madagascar.[36] While there is no doubt that the Suculambas of Mariano and the Sakalava of later sources are an identical group, the association with the Ila-derived Shukulumbwe of northwestern Rhodesia was far too bold—not only because single-feature associations, out of context, are risky at best, but also because the 1616 date in Madagascar requires at minimum an even earlier confirmation of Shukulumbwe on the mainland. This can be done, for example, in the case of the *Sakoambé/ Sakuambé/Sakumbé*, a people who were once important enough in western Madagascar to give a part of it their name. According to Dos Santos (1609), there indeed was a kingdom of Sacumbe on the Zambezi River, at some distance upstream from Tete and at a point marked by a cataract that impeded navigation for some twenty Portuguese leagues.[37] Dos Santos described it as a "rugged, fortified hill honey-combed with copper workings." But, there is nothing comparable to suggest that the Shuku-

---

traditions of one group with those found among contiguous ones. Indeed, an anonymous manuscript recently acquired by the University of Madagascar, dealing with the *Anteisaka of the Andarezo District* (1915), states that the oldest informants among the Rabehava and Zanafanilaha "say their ancestors came from Menabé and were Sakalava."

[34] Lt. Col. Prud'homme, "Considerations sur les Sakalava," *NRE*, VI (1900), 9. As far as can be determined, Prud'homme applied the term empire to the Sakalava before anyone else. It is both well-chosen and valid but only for the period of ±1690–1775.

[35] Capt. Aymard, "Le Pays sakalava," *BSGT*, XXVI (1907), 98–99. Aymard was a French captain serving in Sakalava land.

[36] G. Ferrand, "L'Origine africaine des Malgaches," *JA*, 10th series, XI/3 (May–June 1908), 429.

[37] Cf. E. Axelson, *Portuguese in South-East Africa, 1600–1700* (1964), pp. 5, 37.

lumbwe formed as a people and state late in the sixteenth or early in the seventeenth centuries.

As in the history of the Anteimoro, Bara, and Mahafaly aristocracies, there is oral recall among the Sakalava-derived traditions of the process by which the ruling elite formed. While details vary as well as provide some interesting data, the fundamentals are not significantly different. Prud'homme's own Sakalava interpreter, Sergeant Firinga authored an

Sakalava warrior, Bay of Mahajamba, late 1800s.

account that has been largely neglected.[38] In essence, he states that whatever their origin might have been, the proto-Maroserana and their immediate descendants failed to build any lasting states or political structures because they could not attract a sufficient local following. This situation changed only through an indigenous family, the *Analamahavelona,* so-named after a forest near which it resided. This family incorporated the intrusive migrants and provided the kinship base that ultimately led to the emergence of Maroserana power and political success.[39] Firinga also stresses the importance of local priests, or *moasy,* in facilitating the extension of Maroserana power.[40] This is also a thread that runs through Malagasy traditions connected with kingship and the innovator priest will soon reoccur in some telling ways for the Maroserana Sakalava.

It is fair to say that the basic ethnography of Sakalava land remained virtually unknown until the first decade of this century. Its geographical limits, north–south, are the Bays of Ampasindava (13° 42′) and St. Augustine (23° 35′). Inland depth varies anywhere from 50 to 250 kilometers. Fiherenana, Menabé, and Iboina provide the main and very broad divisions. The Fiherenana area begins at the Onilahy River, which empties into the St. Augustine Bay, and terminates at the Mangoky River (21° 20′). Menabé continues from the Mangoky to the Namakia River (18° 36′). Iboina ends at the Bay of Ampasindava, while southern Iboina is subdivided into four smaller provinces that are sometimes mentioned separately: Mailaka, Maraha, Milanja, and Ambongo (18° 36′ to 16°). The Sakalava, thus, were usually refined as the Antifiherenana, Antimena (Antimenabé), Antimailaka, Antimaraha, Antiambongo, and Antiboina. These are, however, geographical names simply prefixed by the term for people (*Ant/Anti*). They do not reveal an ethnic composition. The all-inclusive term Sakalava sheds hardly any light on the subject.

Some of the missing detail came from Alfred Grandidier, who sought to find out where the *tompontany* (masters of the soil, original inhabitants) could be located and which groups arrived either with the Maroserana or subsequently. Among the *tompontany* of Fiherenana, he listed the Tentembola, Antanandro, Mikeha, Antambaha, Andrifengo, Voroneoka, Sakoambé, Tsiveta, and Vezo. The Antanandro, Mikeha, and Sakoambé were also *tompontany* in Menabé, along with the Antanala and the Vazimba. In the four smaller provinces the Antanandro and Vazimba reoccurred. The additional *tompontany* were given as Behosy, Kazemby, and Sandangoatsy as well as Vezo. In essence, all of these excepting the

---

[38] Sgt. Firinga, "La Dynastie des Maroserana," *RM*, III (1901), 658–672. Firinga was a Sakalava from Nossi-bé. The genealogy, as arranged by him is, however, full of chronological errors.

[39] Firinga, "Maroserana," 662–663.

[40] *Ibid.*, 665–667.

Vezo were also Vazimba subgroups, and one of them—the Sandangoatsy —also resided in Iboina, together with the Manandabo, Behisotra, and more of the Antanandro. Over thirty groups came with the Maroserana or after.[41] The general conclusion would be that the Antanandro had spread from Iboina to Fiherenana, that the Vazimba and Sakoambé were concentrated in Menabé and Fiherenana, along with the Vezo, and that the migratory direction of "newcomers" was south-to-north with a previous east-to-west pattern, since the Maroserana came from the eastern littoral of Madagascar.

Hardly anything appeared in print concerning the early Sakalava between 1914 and 1924. Guillain and Noel belong to the time when Baron de Mackau, the minister of state for the navy and the colonies, and de Hell, governor of Bourbon (Réunion), sought to rebuild French influence in the western Indian Ocean.[42] The conquest and requirements of the first administrators in western Madagascar account in good measure for a flurry of historical literature between 1897 and 1907. By 1912, it had thinned out, and the war in Europe almost put an end to it. The Maroserana were finally rediscovered in 1922 by Henri Rusillon, who knew the northwestern Sakalava well.[43] His main concern, however, was not with Maroserana origins, but rather with their genealogy and particularly with the "Andriamisara problem." There were, he pointed out, actually *two* Andriamisara. The first was fathered by Rabaratavokoka together with Andriamandresi, father of the great Andriandahifotsy. The second Andriamisara was Andriandahifotsy's high priest, credited by tradition as the creator of the *dady*. Rusillon saw two reasons why Andriamisara II, who was not even of "royal blood," came to be regarded as the Maroserana founder, an honor which rightly belonged to Andriamandresi:[44]

---

[41] A. Grandidier, *Ethnographie*, pp. 217–227. Among them: the Andrevola, Andrabala, Tohitohy, Antamby, Zazaboto, Andrasivy, Vongovato, Zafinitsara, Tsiboka, Sangoro, Andrasily, Anaivo, Iritsy, Tsitompa, Jangoa (actually not an ethnicity but rather a Sakalava-Maroserana funerary caste), Andraramaiva, Andratsoka, Vatobé, Manendy.

[42] A letter of February 16, 1843, Document 61 of the Bibliothéque Grandidier at Tsimabazaza-Tananarive, has revealed a *De Hell Plan* for conquest of Madagascar by a march directly from the Bay of Bombetock to Tananarive. Fifty-three years later, this plan was made operational. Thus, even in the early 1840s, the Sakalava were to be won over for an eventual conquest of Imerina.

[43] In addition to the monographs already noted, Rusillon published *Un Petit Continent: Madagascar* (1933), and gave a typescript of 248 pages, *Le Boina-Madagascar: essai de géographie humaine* (1926), to the Library of the Société des Missions Evangeliques, Paris.

[44] Rusillon, "Zafimbolamena," 172.

Because Andriamisara II was more directly under Muslim and semi-Arab influences . . . and because the royal *moasy* (priest) had, in the eyes (of the Sakalava), a power which was special (and) divine and which transformed him into a supra-natural being to whom Andriandahifotsy owed his success. The idea is found all along the history of the Volamena dynasty, and their kings were always accompanied by a *moasy* when they were not *moasy* themselves.

Sakalava-Vezo, region of Tuléar.

Rusillon suggested, again following Grandidier,[45] that Maroserana meant many ports and was a title that indicated control of the coast. The history of Iboina, founded by Andriandahifotsy's son Andriamandisoarivo, was one "of family struggles."[46]

Guillain and Grandidier made some use of early European accounts for the western coast of Madagascar. Others did not go that far. Oral tradition, on the whole poorly collected, could offer slight "control." The problem was one of method. Here, the only real innovation came from the pen of a Norwegian missionary, Father Emil Birkeli, a source of uncommon interest. He conceived of studying cattle markings, the symbols of property carved on the ears of cattle, to find in this way the pattern of migrations and thus determine to what extent new evidence could control oral tradition and be, in turn, controlled by it. Every group used its own markings, wrote Birkeli, the "one on the ear prevents any possible confusion (and) is an official document of primitive society . . . of crucial interest to historical and ethnographic studies."[47] It took Birkeli sixteen years to collect the data. He worked in Fiherenana and in Menabé, from Tuléar to Maintirano, roughly between the 24th and 18th degrees latitude south.

Birkeli was able to reduce the markings to four basic categories— namely, angular, open triangle, closed triangle (spearhead), and the square. The ethnostatistical findings of Birkeli can be outlined in a single synoptic quote:[48]

> The first category was patterned after the fishtail (*ohimalane*) and the spoon (*sotro*) which ended in fishtail (*ohintsotro*). *Ohimalane* was the marking of coastal fishermen, the Vezo. Groups of the forest and interior, the Mikeha, used the *ohintsotro*. Collectively, the fishtails included 18 groups. *Tsieningea*, the open-triangle marking, belonged to strangers and liberated slaves, 13 groups in all. One of them—the Vazimba— were subdivided into five groupings. The closed-triangle or spearhead (*mandranidroe*) was the marking of Fiherenana and Menabé conquerors. It included 11 groups, among them the Maroserana. Finally, the *tsakazo*, or square marking, included 20 groups, among them the Andrevola whose cattle were not marked. Of the 18 fishtails, 15 recalled a north-to-south migration, coming from above the 18th degree of latitude south, and 3 recalled east-southeast to west-southwest migrations. The Vazimba apart, *tsieningea* markers recalled north-to-south migrations in 4 cases, east-to-southwest in another 4, while 1 had moved from south-to-north and 3 had

[45] *Ibid.*, 173, n. 1; and A. Grandidier, *Ethnographie*, p. 214, n. 3. This etymology is useless.

[46] Rusillon, "Zafimbolamena," 174.

[47] Birkeli, *Marques*, pp. 5–6.

[48] *Ibid.*, pp. 9–48.

no recollections of movement. Of the five Vazimba subgroupings, 3 had been north-to-south migrants and 2 east-to-west. Among the spearheads, 7 came from east-to-west and 4 from south-to-north. Among the squares, 8 could not remember any migrations, 5 had moved from south-to-north, 5 from east-to-west and 2 from north-to-south.

In view of the previous findings and theories of Grandidier, the more extensive and precise data of Birkeli turn out to be rather unexpected. Of the total sixty-five groups,[49] the largest number, or twenty-four, came to Menabé and Fiherenana from the *north*. Ten came from the opposite direction, while ten more could recall no migration, eight of these in Fiherenana alone. Twenty-one arrived from the interior to the west coast, but the Maroserana were *not* among them. Their special marking, *tsimirango*, diffused from south to west, or from the land of the Mahafaly. In his *Journal* of 1729, Drury connects the Maroserana with this marking by noting that the king of Menabé had his cattle marked "with a mark called *Chemerango*,"[50] and it will be seen how this relates to the problem of Maroserana origins. No less important, some of the enumerated groups claimed *themselves* to have been of overseas origin.

The Besakoa and their kin, Antemangoro, both with fishtail markings, recalled that two of their ancestors came from a faraway island and were settlers in the north, or Antavaratse (from *Ante-varatra*, people of the north).[51] These, in turn, held that their ancestors were originally from Maka but lived at Anora (?) before coming to Madagascar. Indeed, the names of the two ancestors, Darikipetuali and Faidabé, are alien to Malagasy and suggest both Arabic and Arabico-Swahili etymons.[52] The Antavela and their kinsmen Firorobia said they came from Angodza (either Zanzibar which is locally called Unguja, or Ngazidja, one of the Comoro Islands), where the "Antavela are still to be found," and their great ancestor was a "renowned smith."[53] The Vazimba of the Tsiribihina River said they had fled from the central highlands of Madagascar but their ancestors spoke "Makoa," a term that is synonymous in Madagascar with Africans. The Vazimba of the nearby Morondava area said they had migrated southward from Iboina and were "Makoa on the maternal side (only)." The Vazimba of Tuléar remembered that they once lived in the Tsiribihina delta. Vazimba settlers at the Mangoky, however, recalled

---

[49] *Ibid.*, pp. 7–8 for enumeration.

[50] Drury, *Journal*, p. 271.

[51] Birkeli, *Marques*, pp. 11–12.

[52] *Faida* is a widespread Arabic term for profit or gain, the *bé* being Malagasy for great, much, or many. In Swahili, *daraka* stands for responsibility; *petua* for return and up-turn, cf. Sacleux, *Swahili-français*, Vol. I (1939), pp. 164, 169, 213–214; and Vol. II (1941), p. 746.

[53] Birkeli, *Marques*, p. 14.

an overseas migration from Kasomby.[54] The Mikeha could remember their north-to-south migration only because long ago they had been

[54] *Ibid.*, p. 25. At least two other terms point to the same king-making and state-building group in central Africa, and so it might not be far fetched to imagine that Kasomby may be a recollection of the expansion of Lunda Kazembe. On the other hand, *ka-* is a Bantu diminutive prefix, while *omby* is a Bantu loan in Malagasy for cattle.

Sakalava-Antalaotra, region of Majunga.

mpiziva (joking-relationship pals) with the Vazimba back north. At one time the Mikeha did not mark cattle; they carved property symbols on the forest lemurs. The old Mikeha spoke even in Birkeli's time "a language radically different from Malagasy."[55] Two centuries before him, Robert Drury spent six months among the Vazimba of the Tsiribihina delta and noted the same fact, suggesting also bilingualism in that the Vazimba spoke a Malagasy language as well.[56] The writer of Drury's preface, claiming that Drury himself supervised the printing of entire book, held that the "Verzimbers, indeed, by their woolly Heads must come from the more Southern Part of Africa."[57] But, Drury himself left us nothing to indicate what the Vazimba idiom was at that time.

It is well-known from the *Tantara* of Imerina that the Vazimba were the early inhabitants of the central highlands, that they were partly absorbed by the Hova or expelled, and that many of them fled to the western coast of Madagascar.[58] Much ink has been spilled on the problem of Vazimba origins. Mainly on linguistic grounds, Grandidier argued that the Vazimba had been of Melanesian Negroid stock and that hence the Andriana who founded the Merina state simply came among a less sophisticated but still kindered speech group. At the same time, suggestions that the Vazimba came from Africa have been rejected both in and outside Madagascar on the dubious argument that they are unrelated to the famous Zimba of the east African littoral.[59] To deny such a kinship is entirely correct, for neither the chronology nor the customs of the Zimba and Vazimba agree.[60] Tribal names, however, are rarely useful *alone* for postulating relationships. The Vazimba reports given to Birkeli, reports of one or more overseas migrations and of being either entirely Makoa (African) or *only* on the "maternal side," point to the more obvious possibilities of several transplants from the mainland, which one could perceive as being various admixtures of Afro-Malagasy. The prefix *va-/wa-* is decidedly non-Malagasy. The stem *zimba* does not necessarily relate to any particular ethnic group. But, one could note here with much profit that Drury saw the Vazimba as the most important pottery-makers

[55] *Ibid.*, pp. 15–16.

[56] Drury, *Journal*, pp. 265, 280.

[57] *Ibid.*, p. 34.

[58] Callet, *Tantara*, Vol. I (1953), pp. 7–29, 442–456 *inter alia*.

[59] Cf. R. Avelot, "Les Grands Mouvements de peuples en Afrique: Jaga et Zimba," *Bulletin de Géographie Historique et Descriptive*, XXVII (1912), 75–216; and Alfred Grandidier, "Notes sur les Vazimba de Madagascar," *MSP*, special issue (1888), 155–162, also translated into English by James Sibree as "The Vazimba," *AA* (1894), 129–135.

[60] Cf. Fr. João dos Santos, *Ethiopia Oriental*, Vol. II (1891—1st ed. 1609); Callet, *Tantara*, Vol. I (1953), pp. 19–28; and Savaron, "Contribution à l'histoire de l'Imerina," *BAM*, new series, XI (1928), 61–81.

in Madagascar,[61] and that pots and jugs retain the Bantu terms *nongo* and *zinga* in current Malagasy. The same terms can be found in the older Merina dialect as well.[62]

Obviously, the Swahili and other Bantu loan-words in the Sakalava dialect cannot be of Indonesian origin. The *dady* and the *tromba* find fairly precise analogies in Africa. The royal *tromba* medium among the Sakalava corresponds to the Shona *svikiro*, while the function and context of the institution offer close parallels with the Shona *mhondoro*.[63] Cults of royal relics, which include parts or the whole cranium, nails, and other segments of a royal body, have been reported in central and southeast Africa by both older and more recent sources, to indicate only a few at this moment.[64] In previous chapters we noted that the Mahafaly and the Tanala (eastern neighbors of Ibara) have had cranium cults. Moreover, reliable data describing the funerary rites given to Sakalava kings suggest nothing less than massive borrowing from the mainland, to indicate again only a few features and sources.[65] All of this cannot be

---

[61] Drury, *Journal*, p. 280.

[62] A. Abinal and V. Malzac, *Dictionnaire malgache-français* (1888), pp. 417–418 and 808–809 (Merina); Callet, *Tantara*, Vol. I (1953), p. 129. The *Tantara* state that no one could recall the origins of pottery as the "Vazimba had it."

[63] D. P. Abraham, "The Early Political History of the Kingdom of Mwene Mutapa, 850–1589," in J. M. Vansina, R. Mauny, and L. Thomas (eds.), *Historians in Tropical Africa* (1962), mimeographed, pp. 62, 67, 77, n. 13 also for works by Posselt, Bullock, and Gelfand on the same subject. The Sakalava mediums, known sometimes as *vaha* (from *vahavahana* or informed beforehand, and also *famahavahana*, manifestation), do not appear, however, to have had a role in matters of succession, like the Masvikiro.

[64] In the widest sense, H. Baumann and D. Westermann, *Les Peuples et les civilisations de l'Afrique* (1962), pp. 154, 169, 185, 223, 249–250, 531–537 (for bibliography of older primary accounts). In a more limited way, De La Croix, *Relation universelle de l'Afrique*, Vol. III (1688), pp. 364–365, saw the taking of hair and nails from the dead as a general custom in Loango kingdom. More specifically, Clement Doke, in *The Lambas of Northern Rhodesia* (1931), pp. 187–189, reports that the Lamba even had an official with the title of Nail (*Lyala*) who kept the teeth, nails and toes of deceased chiefs.

[65] *Inter alia:* enveloping of body in hide of royal bull and collection of humors into jars (*kisingy*), human sacrifices involving either royal slaves or maidens of the special caste of *Jangoa*, occasional strangling of moribund rulers, slaughter of royal cattle, specialized funerary attendants (*Sambarivo, Marovavy, Antankoala, Bahary*), grave structures, positioning of royal remains, types of regalia buried, time spans between death and burial, intense mourning practices for commoners and nobility. For accessible accounts: A. Dandouau, "Coutumes funéraires dans le nord-ouest de Madagascar," *BAM*, IX (1911), 157–172; Ch. Poirier, *Notes d'ethnographie* (1939), pp. 91–95, 105–114; R.-L. Cagnat, "Tombeaux royaux et mahabo du nord-ouest," *RM*, new series, VIII/30 (1941), 83–117; A. and G. Grandidier, *Ethnographie de Madagascar*, Vol. IV, Tome 3 (1917), p. 515 (Appendix 23, under Sakalava); and Chapter 2 of this work, text and notes 178–188.

attributed to slaves from Africa or to repeated invention in Madagascar. Anyone who has spent some time observing the Vezo fishermen and their outriggers on the western littoral of Madagascar would be forced to conclude, as I did, that the Mozambique Channel barrier belongs to European mythology.[66]

Since 1913 Birkeli had also been puzzled by the speech of Tsiribihina Vazimba. Phonetically, it reminded him of Mahafaly and Vezo, but the language itself was decidedly different.[67] As he collected the cattle markings, the Mikeha and Behosy idioms attracted his attention as well. In 1936, Birkeli published a monograph on this subject. The vocabularies were difficult to compile. He was most successful with the Behosy (a Vazimba subgroup), and he also sought similar words in some other Malagasy dialects. He found—in central Africa, particularly among the Bisa—the closest word relationship between Behosy and another tongue. What is equally and perhaps even more telling, at least four general Malagasy terms find Bisa correspondents in basic structure and meaning: *ziwa/isiwa* (joking relationship), *foko* (phonetics, *fūkū*)/*ifuko* (tribe, clan, community), *vezo* (phonetics, *vēzū*)/*mu-wesi* (one who rows, sailor), and *ombiasa* (phonetics, *ûmbiaš*), *moasy/mu-losi* (priest).[68] Taking into account dialectical variations, Birkeli found that several hundred Malagasy words had Bantu equivalents, with over 100 for Bisa alone, of which 55 corresponded with Sakalava words, 23 with Vazimba, 22 with Betsileo, and 12 with Merina.[69] There certainly are cases cited by Birkeli where links with Bantu languages are somewhat strained. The same is true for Ferrand. Nonetheless, the vast majority of these words as well as their number point firmly to the mainland. Many can hardly be said to represent "recent" borrowing. In effect, older works by Dahle and Ferrand and more recent work by Dahl make it possible to claim a Bantu substratum in one or more Malagasy idioms.[70]

[66] Again, the origin of this goes back to Alfred Grandidier, who held that *"les nègres d'Afrique . . . ne sont nullement marins, (ils) n'ont pas de bateaux capable de tenir la haute mer, (et ils) n'ont jamais colonisé volontairement des pays d'outre-mer. La traversée,"* moreover, *"de la côte Sud-Est d'Afrique aux îles Comores et à Madagascar est difficile à cause des courants qui sont contraires; elle est facile dans l'autre sens," Ethnographie*, Vol. I, Tome 1, p. 170 and n. 3. The patterns of current in the Mozambique Channel are infinitely less monolithic, a factor known in some detail at least since 1859, when Captain Ch. P. de Kerhallet published his *Considerations générales sur l'Ocean Indien* (see particularly pp. 86–87 and 104–108). The eastern African outrigger is certainly no "new" watercraft either.

[67] Birkeli, *Vazimba*, p. 7.

[68] *Ibid.*, pp. 63, 66. The *tromba* according to him has the Bisa equivalent of *ntembo* (prayer to spirits).

[69] *Ibid.*, pp. 63–65.

[70] Dahle, "Swaheli Element," 99–115; G. Ferrand, "L'Elément arabe et souahili en malgache ancien et moderne," *JA*, 10th series, II/3 (1908), 353–500; and O. Chr.

If one turns to the European accounts before 1650, some of which still remain to be found,[71] those already in print offer invaluable information about the west coast of Madagascar. In the far north, in a large bay "named Çada or Sada" (Anorontsanga, 13° 54′55″), the Portuguese in 1506 found an extremely dense population of "Cafres, for it is here that slaves of the town of Melindi, Mombaz, and Mogdicho take refuge." When the Portuguese, led by Tristan da Cunha, approached Sada, about 2000 Cafres armed with shields, spears, bows, and arrows grouped on the beach with the obvious intent to prevent their landing.[72] The Portuguese also found "important Arab towns" at the mouth of the Mahajamba River (15° 29′ 50″) and at Boina Bay, which they called Mazelagem (15° 47′ to 15° 48′ 20″). As in east and southeast Africa, the towns were located on islets, while their "plantations" stood on the larger land mass. The principal town on the islet of Nosi Manja, in the Mahajamba Bay, was called Lulungane, and it contained, according the Portuguese, Arabs or Moors from Malindi and Mombasa. At Lulungane there were large quantities of cloth, silver, and gold. "It was mainly to this port that dhows from Malindi and Mombasa brought merchandise from Africa and Arabia." Rice was the most important exchange commodity, and it seems that Madagascar had been for some time the rice basket for towns of the African littoral. "Not even twenty ships could have taken all of it away," reported the Portuguese in Lulungane. To a lesser extent, slaves, beeswax, and cattle were also exported. The Muslim population seemed "more civilized and richer" than any other on the western coast of Madagascar. "Their houses and mosque" were made of hard stone and limestone, "with terraces like those of Kiloa and Mombasa."[73]

According to a chronicle based on the account of Balthazar Lobo de Souza, whose men explored the northwest coast of Madagascar in two

---

Dahl, "Le Substrat bantou en Malgache," *NTS*, XVII (1953), 325–362. Suggestions of a Bantu substratum in Malagasy have been attacked recently in Tananarive by linguistic arguments that seem no better than those employed by Father Tastevin to prove that Malagasy is an African tongue. A Bantu substratum in Malagasy cannot, in effect, be "proven" any longer. But, this is not quite the same problem as one concerned with more *limited* substrata possibilities in Menabé and Ibara. This is a pregnant linguistico-historical subject, and doctrinaire positions in linguistics should enjoy no greater imunities than those in other disciplines.

[71] On the whole, the Portuguese National Archives and those of Goa, both secular and religious, remain to be researched in respect to Malagasy materials, particularly for the period 1506–1640. I have undertaken this in 1969 and 1970 with support from the John Simon Guggenheim Memorial Foundation, to which I am most grateful.

[72] Fernan d'Albuquerque, "Commentarios do Grande Alfonso d'Albuquerque" (1557), in *COACM*, Vol. I (1903), p. 22.

[73] *Ibid.*, pp. 15, 20–22, 26–31, 36–37.

fustas during 1556, the real name of Madagascar was *Ubuque*.[74] The
Malindi Moors still had two towns, ruled by Cheiks. One was at Boina
Bay, but the other stood on the opposite, or northeastern coast, at Bimaro
(Vohémar, Iharana).[75] The northwest coast, roughly between latitudes
14° and 16° south, contained five "states," but two of them were ruled by
chiefs as opposed to the others, which had kings. One king was named
Lingi. He controlled both banks of the river that emptied into Boina Bay.
From this bay to the Duria River (or present Sofia, 15° 5′) there was
another apparently minor king, but Duria itself traversed the lands of
Tingimaro, then "the most powerful king in the island . . . continuously
at war with his neighbors, one who sells prisoners to the Moors of
Lulungane." The Portuguese from Mozambique appear to have been the
principal buyers of these prisoners held by the Moors. This trade in slaves
between Mazelagem and the Portuguese, however, came to a temporary
halt in 1587, following a "revolt of the Moors," prompted not by local
Moors but by those who traded with them from Arabia.[76] It is worth
repeating that eastern Africans referred to the Malagasy as *wa-Buki* and
that *u-Buque/uBuke* is an old Bantu term for Madagascar. The term
duria is Swahili (*duru, duria*) conveying the action of something that
turns over or circulates, as in the case of rivers.[77] According to J. G.
Roberts, the royal ox of the Rozwi Mambo was called *gumbo tungamira*
(leading leg).[78] Sacleux defines *ṭūnga* as *"chasser, pousser ou poursuivre
devant soi, mettre en fuite."*[79] *Lingilingy*, in Malagasy, means elevated
but *līnga*, in Swahili, is to harmonize.[80] Afro-Malagasy links are certainly
suggested in the royal names of Tingimaro and Lingi, while the mixture
in shades of meaning for the Bantu and Malagasy terms is itself of no
small interest.

In 1613, two Jesuits from Goa arrived at Mozambique, Fathers
d'Azevedo and Mariano, to whom many references have already been
made. They were to proceed to Madagascar in search of converts and
work there, if necessary, for two years. Mariano made a total of four
visits to the western coast of Madagascar between 1613 and 1630, the

[74] Do Couto, *Da Asia* (Decade VII, 1616), in *COACM*, Vol. I (1903), p. 99.

[75] *Ibid.*, p. 99.

[76] *Ibid.*, p. 100 (for the states), 155–159 (for the revolt), which are based on three sources—Faria y Sousa, *Da Asia* (1675); João dos Santos (1684 translation in French by Charpy); and G. Cardoso, *Agiologio Lusitano* (1666).

[77] Sacleux, *Swahili-français*, Vol. I (1939), p. 176.

[78] J. G. Roberts, "Totemism, Zimbabwe and the Barozwi," *NADA*, No. 24 (1947), 51.

[79] Sacleux, *Swahili-français*, Vol. II (1941), p. 913.

[80] Richardson, *Dictionary*, p. 393 for Malagasy; and Sacleux, *Swahili-français*, Vol. I (1939), p. 475, for Swahili. It is obvious that there is no root *lingi* in Malagasy but only a redoubled adjective.

principal two being those of 1613–1614 and 1616–1617. He explored the coast from Boina Bay to the Onilahy River for over fourteen weeks, pausing briefly at various bays and river mouths: the Cassane (Sambao, 16° 36′ 30″), Sadia (Manambolo delta, 18° 55′–19° 1′), Mane or Mania (Tsiribihina delta, 19° 33′–19° 50′), Manaputa (Morondava delta, 20° 11′– 20° 20′), Isango (Bay of Belo, 20° 44′ 30″), Massimanga (Manombo, 22° 59′), and Unguelahi (Onilahy, 23° 34′ latitude south), among others.[81] Mariano also stayed four weeks at Sada (Monogarivo, 14° 8′), his northernmost point of exploration, six weeks at the Bay of Boina, and fifty-four weeks at Sadia, the heart of northern Menabé.[82] In all this time he converted no one and considered himself to have been a failure. It is only from another Jesuit, who wrote in 1620, that one learns of the personal prestige accorded Mariano from Manambolo to Monongarivo.[83] Mariano's accounts are of the utmost importance.

In the northwest, there was now a new Mazelagem (Mazelagem Nova), and Mariano used the term Boina (*Boena*) for the first time. Its king, Simamo, and all of new Mazelagem's 6000–7000 inhabitants were Muslims. The big slave buyers came from both east Africa and Arabia, but those with the greatest local influence were from Lamu, Pate, Mombasa, and Malindi.[84] It is clear that what had once been mainly an overseas enterprise for east African Moors was now in the hands of local Malagasy rulers, that Islam had gained many converts in Iboina, and that Lamu and Pate traders had joined those of Malindi and Mombasa. It also appears that slaves had superseded rice as Iboina's main export. The kingdom of Sada, north of Boina Bay, was under Tingimaro, still the most powerful and richest ruler. This suggests that *Tingimaro* was a title rather than a personal name. The capital of this king, Ankoala,[85] was four leagues inland. The king and "high persons" were strict Muslims, attending mosque every day. His subjects, in contrast to those of Simamo, were neither entirely Muslim nor pagan, but a "mixture of the two." Tingimaro was under "Arab influence," and continuously at war with new Mazelagem. One of his "vassal Moors" acted as the royal spokesman. To deter-

[81] Cf. L. Mariano's letters in COACM, Vol. II (1904), pp. 16–30, and Vol. III (1905), pp. 642–674, from which this composite itinerary and stays have been extracted.

[82] At Sada, June 6–July 6, 1614; at Bay of Boina, April 15–25, 1613, May 18–24, 1614, June 4–18, 1619, and two weeks approximately in 1620; at Sada, June 15–17, 1613, and June 10, 1616 to June 17, 1617, a full year.

[83] Father Gomes, *Letter* (1620) in COACM, Vol. II (1904), p. 333.

[84] L. Mariano, *Relation . . . 1614*, in COACM, Vol. II (1904), pp. 14–15; *Letter,* September 17, 1616, in COACM, Vol. II (1904), p. 213; and *Letter,* August 24, 1619, in COACM, Vol. II (1904), pp. 305, 312, 317.

[85] Curiously enough, the only explanation of *Ankoala* available in Malagasy is that this term applied to tall and lean cattle that came from the town of Ankoala.

mine Mariano's intentions, a king's slave was put through the "poison ordeal" but "fortunately survived."[86] According to Mariano and d'Azevedo, Tingimaro's subjects were not *Cafres* but *Buques* (Malagasy).[87] The story south of Boina was quite different.

The long stretch of western coast, from latitudes 16° to 21° south, was known as Bambala.[88] Virtually every bay or river mouth of any size had its own ruler, and some were densely populated. The kingdom nearest to Boina Bay, on the Cassane (Sambao) River, was under a non-Muslim ruler named Sampiliha. Its people were planters who cultivated millet and manioc. The southernmost "kingdom" Mariano visited on the west coast, at the Onilahy River mouth, belonged to Diacomena, a ruler who met the Jesuit father with an escort of 500 well-dressed men armed with spears.[89] The most notable state between those two points was Sadia at the Manambolo delta. In 1613, it had some 10,000 inhabitants, all "black with fuzzy hair," who planted millet and kept cattle. Direct trade with the Moors further north was slight, but Sadia did have some commercial relations with the Boina Bay inhabitants. A fleet of Sadian outriggers had once saved Boina from famine by bringing provisions. The king of Sadia was named Capitapa, a "man of ninety." He befriended Mariano and gave him his own son Loquexa as the Jesuit's guide for further coastal exploration.[90] Approximately two years later, on June 10, 1616, Mariano returned to Sadia and remained there one year.

Not long before Mariano's second visit to Sadia, two of Capitapa's sons were killed by a younger brother named Mananqui. He thus became heir presumptive, but his excessive cruelty forced him to leave Sadia and establish a new residence, at some two leagues distance. Mariano noted that he had taken along the bravest of men, called Suculambes, and among them were several of the king's own sons and cousins. The people of Sadia were called Ajungones. Mariano's own presence triggered a civil war. Mananqui assumed that his younger brother Loquexa would use Portuguese support and Mariano's "magic powers" to take over the throne after Capitapa's death, and so he promptly declared war.[91] The Ajungones and Suculambas fought a number of battles. Mananqui was killed in one, but a younger brother named Quissoa replaced him. Later, Capitapa's

[86] Mariano, *Relation, COACM*, Vol. II (1904), pp. 66–67.

[87] D'Azevedo to Superior at Goa, *Letter*, May 23, 1617, in *COACM*, Vol. II (1904), p. 249.

[88] Mariano to Madeiros, *Letter*, August 24, 1619, *COACM*, Vol. II (1904), p. 315, for definition of the Bambala coast.

[89] For Cassane and Sampiliha, see Mariano, *Relation, COACM*, Vol. II (1904), p. 17, and Vol. III (1905), pp. 659–661; for Diacomena, see *COACM*, Vol. II (1904), pp. 30–31.

[90] Mariano, *Relation, COACM*, Vol. II (1904), pp. 20–21, first visit.

[91] Mariano, *Letter*, July 1616, *COACM*, II (1904), 217–218.

own brother and one of Loquexa's sons were killed by the Suculambes. As a result of the warfare, Sadia decreased from about 1000 dwellings and 10,000 inhabitants to 600 dwellings and "no more than 3000 inhabitants." The old king, Capitapa, was hardly obeyed.

On his third visit to western Madagascar, Mariano heard that Capitapa had died in 1619. The Suculambes were then the most powerful group, in alliance with another—the Quisaju—and "some Buques."[92] As their language and customs show, wrote Mariano, the people of Sada "descend from Malindi Cafres." With some modifications, the "language is the same as that of Malindi coast." But, now that Mariano, and especially d'Azevedo, knew it better,[93] "it is less barbaric and far richer in words than we had previously supposed."[94] Mariano complained that in Sada sons married "their fathers' widows save their own mothers," while the fathers took "also the widows of their sons." They believed their dead could aid the living and constantly honored them. One of the local inhabitants "assumes the role of *Afo*[95] and, taking his name, tells of wars past and future or else incites those present to some enterprise." This is about as accurate a description of the monarchical *tromba* as Rusillon would provide three centuries later, although Mariano never used this term. Moreover, they had "ugly wooden images, ornamented with beads and other jewelry." Following the general custom, the "oldest son cut the beard and the nails of his father on the day of death and places these relics, most precious in local eyes, in the said wooden images and sometimes he carries them on a scarf." They have "many divinities," including "their dead, especially chiefs, notables, and those who die very old." The hair and nails of the deceased were also sewn into leather belts "guarded religiously as relics." The oldest sons of noble families enclosed the "relics in an ugly little box, carried along in wars and on holidays."[96] The cult of the *dady* was, thus, not only present in early seventeenth-century Sadia, but it was practiced by commoners and nobility alike, although in somewhat different ways.

[92] *Ibid.*, pp. 218–221; and Mariano, *Letter*, October 22, 1616, *COACM*, Vol. II (1904), p. 239 for population decline.

[93] Mariano, *Letter*, October 22, 1616, *COACM*, Vol. II (1904), p. 225; and *Letter*, August 20, 1617, *COACM*, Vol. II (1904), p. 252, in small print. In several pages, Mariano refers to d'Azevedo's superior linguistic knowledge. There is little doubt that Father d'Azevedo had written many letters to the superior of the Order of Jesus at Goa, but only two have been found so far. Internal evidence suggests also that other Jesuit missionaries visited the west coast of Madagascar from about 1580–1630.

[94] Mariano, *Letter*, August 20, 1617, *COACM*, Vol. II (1904), p. 256 (small print). Elsewhere, Mariano states that the language of the Bambala coast, taken as a whole, is "analogous with those . . . of Mozambique and Malindi."

[95] See footnotes 137 and 138 in Chapter 2 for problems connected with this term.

[96] Mariano, *Letter*, 22 October 1616, *COACM*, Vol. II (1904), pp. 226–229, 232–233 (*tromba* and *dady*).

Nothing was undertaken by local inhabitants without prior consultation of a witchcraft that had many forms, by using fruits of a tree (bananas very often) or by making signs in the sand with hot iron. For this "divination there is a priest whom they call here *Maganga*,"[97] a pure Bantu loan. Although his witchcraft and advice "are often wrong," as "we could ascertain," the Maganga "is held in extraordinary regard and everyone respects and fears him." As a rule, the Maganga who performed divinations was a highly placed person who had "an important role in affairs of government." The only form of political alliance "honored is the one when they open their veins and lick the blood."[98] Mariano concluded by saying that "all of the customs described apply to the west coast peoples, from Sadia to Mazelagem" and "all speak the same language."[99] This is reiterated several times by Mariano, who also informs us in a most telling statement that while in most other parts of Madagascar the language spoken is Ubuque (Malagasy), in contrast to the Bambala Coast, the Ubuques and the Cafres of the Bambala Coast seem to share many of the same customs. In November 1619, Mariano secured a "bull" from the Boina Bay ruler, written by a "Moor" and a revealing document in its own right.[100] This bull and a brief account by another Jesuit constitute the only published record of Mariano's third visit to western Madagascar.

The earliest account for the western coast of Madagascar below latitude 22° south comes from Nuno da Cunha, who landed on August 23, 1528 at San Iago Bay (mouth of the Mangoky River) to search for some Portuguese shipwrecks.[101] He found that the interior immediately behind the coast was densely inhabited by "blacks with fuzzy hair like those of Mozambique." After two days of trading, the local inhabitants brought to da Cunha the sole survivor of the previously shipwrecked crews. Da Cunha learned that the people of the Mangoky "live in small communities and have no great chief to lead them."[102] Almost seven decades later De Houtman (1595) and John Davis (1598) reached the southern

[97] *Ibid.*, p. 230.

[98] Mariano, *Letter*, August 24, 1619, *COACM*, Vol. II (1904), p. 307.

[99] Mariano, *Letter*, October 22, 1616, *COACM*, Vol. II (1904), p. 235.

[100] This "bull" authorized, in the name of the king, Luis Mariano and other Jesuit fathers to reside at Mazelagem. It was dated in the month of *Fungalo*, sixth day of the moon, in the year *juma atano molongo antini peti nerufi*, computed as November 4, 1619. It terminates: "I, Dadade, wrote [these words] on the order of Simamo and also [by permission of] Jombe Baqueli, Mandeishe Sabunda, Sangansa Hassani, Sangasa Malimu, Jombe Sabanda and by all the people of the land" and is signed "Simamo"—witness "Agilcouta." See *COACM*, Vol. II (1904), pp. 325–326. *Jumbe* has been the title of rulers on the Swahili coast and Comoro Islands.

[101] On this two-vessel shipwreck, cf. the accounts of Gaspar Correa, Diogo do Couto, and João de Barros in *COACM*, Vol. I (1903), pp. 58–59, 63–76.

[102] Barros, *Da Asia* (Decade IV, 1613), in *COACM*, Vol. I (1903), pp. 66–67.

extremity of Fiherenana, at St. Augustine Bay. De Houtman's men were delighted with the local terms of trade: a tin spoon fetched an ox or four sheep, along with some dried fish and milk. Silver spoons, however, were refused. Iron and red copper seem to have been in abundant supply, but no planting or harvesting was done by local inhabitants. The Dutch learned that, at some distance from the coast, there was "a great habitation named *Rango*."[103] John Davis, on his first visit to Fiherenana as pilot of a Dutch vessel, merely noted that the people there "are as black as coal."[104]

Payrard de Laval (1602), John Davis (1607), and William Finch (1608) have left limited accounts of the St. Augustine Bay area in the first decade of the seventeenth century. De Laval saw "women with shaven heads" and reported that several kings were at war at the time and that some of them "follow the laws of Muhammad and others do not."[105] On his second visit to the Onilahy, John Davis brought along a south African from an unspecified bay some 24 miles from the Cape of Good Hope (who should have spoken Khoisan rather than Bantu). The local inhabitants of Onilahy fled when Davis landed, but a boy of about 15, with a leg injury, remained behind. Davis could not communicate with him. His south African companion, however, was able to obtain a fair amount of detail from the lad about fresh-water resources further up the river and how the water could be secured and transported. The inland capital was named Rota. This was subsequently confirmed by a journey up the Onilahy. The language of this area of Madagascar, concluded Davis, was quite different from those of Africa, but resemblances could be noticed. Davis' stay was cut short by a local attack from which he brought back several bows.[106] Finch observed that the men around Onilahy wore their hair in a "curious manner," with braids and tufts, and that their spears were barbed.[107]

In the 1630s three men spent some months in the St. Augustine Bay area—namely, Richard Boothby, factor of the English East India Company; Walter Hamond, a doctor on one of Boothby's ships; and J. A. Mandelslo, diplomatic agent of the Duke of Holstein. All three were to paint essentially unreal pictures of southwestern Madagascar.[108] Man-

[103] "Premier Atterrissage des Hollandais à Madagascar," in *COACM*, Vol. I (1903), pp. 179, 182–196. This Dutch account was reprinted from De Constantin, *Recueil des Voyages*, Vol. I (1725), pp. 286–341.

[104] J. Davis, "Troisième Voyage des Hollandais aux Indes, à bord du navire le *Middleburg*," in *COACM*, Vol. I (1903), p. 255.

[105] Payrard de Laval, "De la Baie de Saint-Augustin," in *COACM*, Vol. I (1903), pp. 294, 299–300.

[106] Davis, "Troisème Voyage," *COACM*, Vol. I (1903), pp. 402–406.

[107] For Wm. Finch's account, see *COACM*, Vol. I (1903), p. 415.

[108] W. Hamond, *A Paradox Proving That the Inhabitants of Madagascar Are the Happiest People in the World* (1640), and *Madagascar, the Richest and Most Fruit-*

delslo's account was somewhat less misleading and certainly harmless, but those of Boothby and Hamond ultimately led to an ill-fated English colony at St. Augustine Bay and to the loss of more than one hundred English lives.[109] One item in Boothby's description and two items in Mandelslo's are, however, of some importance. For the equivalent of six head of cattle, Boothby purchased from a native priest a book examined subsequently by Master Henry Gouch of Trinity College, Cambridge.[110] Gouch found it to be written in hieroglyphics like those of the "ancient Egyptians." But, there is little doubt that the "book" was an Anteimoro *Sora-bé* containing cabalistic formulas.[111] As for Mandelslo, he alone reproduced and described the Malagasy bow in some detail. This is an important contribution because the bow, mentioned in early European accounts as a weapon, was no longer in use in most of Madagascar by 1800. After an apparently labored comparison, it was Alfred Grandidier who pointed out that the bow reproduced by Mandelslo was a duplicate of the Congolese bow.[112] According to Mandelslo, the Malagasy "bows are at least 5 to 6 feet long, with a rather loose cord," but this "hardly prevents the shooting of arrows with speed and dexterity."[113] He also reported that there were, in 1639, three local kings and that one of them was named Massar (Misara).[114]

The earlier European accounts of the west coast by A. Thevet and J. Megiser end with a strange and intriguing tale. Reported by Thevet in 1575 and summarized by Megiser in 1609, the story contains the following points. A "huge flood" of some "300 years ago" had devastated the west coast of Madagascar for a period of "three weeks." Months later, "when the lands became dry again," several ships with "merchants from Çefala," stopped at Madagascar by chance. They found a "dead land" and learned from some of the survivors what had happened. The news then "spread throughout eastern Africa" and:[115]

---

ful Island in the World (1643); R. Boothby, *A Briefe Discovery or Description of the Most Famous Island of Madagascar, in Asia, Near the East Indies* (1640); and J. A. Mandelslo, "Relâche . . . dans la Baie de Saint-Augustin," all four reproduced in French translation in Volumes II and III of the *COACM*.

[109] Of the English colony of 140, under John Smart, 128 died at St. Augustine Bay in 1644. One of the twelve survivors, Powle Waldegrave, answered Boothby five years too late. Cf. *An Answer to Mr. Boothby's Book of Description of Madagascar* (1649), in *COACM*, III (1905), pp. 221–258.

[110] See *COACM*, Vol. II (1904), pp. 434–435. Boothby was at the bay in 1630.

[111] The Anteimoro did not begin to set their own history down on paper before the 1630s.

[112] Reproduction of the bow in *COACM*, Vol. II (1904), p. 488$_{bis}$; Congolese bow analogy, A. and G. Grandidier, *Ethnographie*, pp. 187–188, n. 6, notule b.

[113] Mandelslo, "Relâche," *COACM*, Vol. II (1904), p. 490.

[114] *Ibid.*, p. 491. Mandelslo's visit was in 1639.

[115] See *COACM*, Vol. I (1903), pp. 120–126, Thevet (1575), and 460–462, Megiser (1609). There are certain differences between Thevet and Megiser, among

. . . the two kings of Çefala and Mozambique ordered their ships to transport to the island three or four thousand persons so that it can be repeopled. The captain of this fleet was a pagan, born at Çefala and named Albergra. . . . [Some 200 years later], the Kings of Magadoxo and coast of Adel left with a huge fleet, some 25 or 26 thousand men in all, in order to invade the rich island of Taprobane or Sumatra but a tempest threw them off course and they landed on the coasts of Albergra. . . . They remained for eight months (and) before leaving they erected at different points of the island eight pillars on which they engraved in Chaldean . . . "MAGADOXO" . . . name which later, by corruption, became Madagascar.

Thevet, who visited Arabia and eastern Africa but not Madagascar, hints that he had heard all this from a Sofala resident encountered in Arabia. Grandidier considered Thevet as a "cardinal liar," and, indeed, many passages in Thevet belong in the world of fantasy. On the other hand, Malagasy oral traditions recall that the sea had flooded the western coast more than once. Some rather large river floods have taken place, islets have disappeared, waterways have changed courses. Also, tablets containing symbols no one has as yet deciphered have been found in at least one part of Madagascar, at Mailaka, on the northwestern coast.[116] A good case can be made, as Thevet himself held, that Madagascar is a corruption of Magadoxo/Madagoxo by metathesis. In addition, the two tales, one placed at ±1275 and the other at ±1475, would have the advantage of "accounting" for the advent of eastern and southeastern African colonies in western Madagascar *as such.*

If we turn from Thevet, we still can come to several important conclusions based on the data found in European accounts of the western coast before 1650. Political fragmentation was its only uniform feature, from Anorontsanga to St. Augustine Bay. Early in the sixteenth century, the Bay of Anorontsanga was dominated by a colony of Africans formed by *former* slaves of Malindi, Mombasa, and Mogadishu. Not far south, at Mahajamba and Boina, there were two centers of overseas trade conducted by "Moors" from Malindi and Mombasa. Rice was the most important export commodity at the time. Within a few decades, the overseas demand for Madagascan rice declined in favor of slaves in part, perhaps, because of rice production in eastern Africa. In turn, the demand

---

them the claim by Thevet that Sofala traders did not visit western Madagascar by chance since previous commercial relations did exist.

[116] This inscription is reproduced in Ch. Poirier, "Réflexions sur les ruines de Mailaka situées au fond de la Baie de Passandava, côte nord-ouest de Madagascar," *BAM*, new series, XXVIII (1947–1948), 97, n. 3. At least one of the Swahili chronicles suggests a considerable maritime excursion into the Indian Ocean lands beyond Africa itself by a local ruler or rulers.

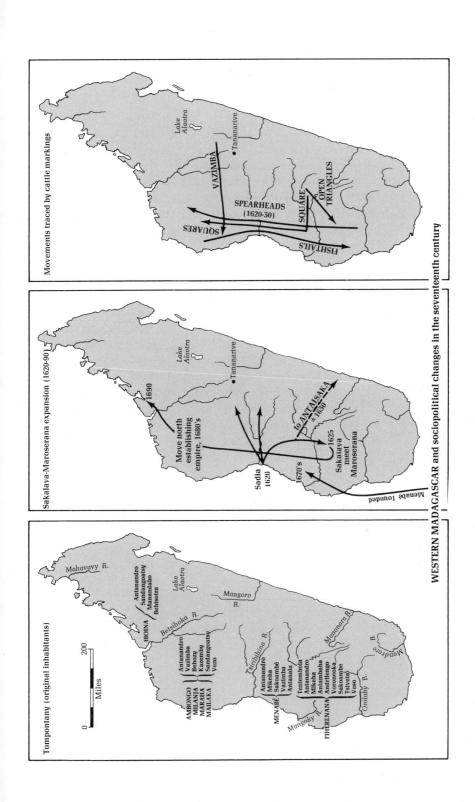

Tompontany (original inhabitants)

Mahavavy R.

IBOINA
Antanandro
Sandangoatsy
Manandabo
Behisotra

Betsiboka R.

Lake Alaotra

Mangoro R.

AMBONGO
MILANJA
MARAHA
MAILAKA
{ Antanandro
Vazimba
Behozy
Kazemby
Sandangoatsy
Vezo }

Tsiribihina R.

MENABE { Antanandro
Mikeha
Sakoambé
Vazimba
Antanala }

Mangoky R.

Mananara R.

FIHERENANA
{ Tentembola
Antanandro
Mikeha
Antambaha
Andrilemgo
Voromeoka
Sakoambe
Tsivetai
Veso }

Onilahy R.

Mandrare R.

0   200
Miles

Sakalava-Maroserana expansion (1620–90)

1690

Move north establishing empire, 1680's

Lake Alaotra

•Tananarive

Sadia 1620

1670's

to ANTAISAKA ± 1630

1625

Sakalava meet Maroserana

Menabe founded

Movements traced by cattle markings

Lake Alaotra

•Tananarive

VAZIMBA

SPEARHEADS (1620–30)

SQUARES

SQUARE

OPEN TRIANGLES

FISHTAILS

WESTERN MADAGASCAR and sociopolitical changes in the seventeenth century

for slaves led to the growth of a number of small local states in the northwest, mainly along river banks a few leagues inland. The rulers of these states raided the interior, going even as far as the central highlands, and sometimes they fought one another. Increasingly, the coastal Moors relinquished their exclusive control. They became intermediaries instead and, no doubt, still reaped the greatest benefits from a now intensified slave trade. At least three types of change came about as a result: demographic, political, and religious. By the early seventeenth century the Cafres (Africans) of the northwest were displaced by the Ubuques (Malagasy), whose own rulers controlled the slave trade. The nature of this demographic change is not very clear. Titles like *Tingimaro* and *Lingi*, toponyms like *Duria* and *Ankoala,* or even *Anorontsanga*,[117] would simply confirm the earlier African element, but the titles themselves might suggest its absorption rather than re-export to Africa through slave trade. On the other hand, the Islamized Moors of the Swahili coast were decidedly incorporated both as permanent settlers (Antalaotra) and as the most influential of the kings' men. Conversions to Islam appear to have been numerous as well in northwestern Madagascar.

The coast below latitude 16° south was not exposed to the same changes. It took no part in overseas trade. Its people were mainly engaged in agriculture, planting manioc and millet. The testimony of Mariano shows that the whole Bambala Coast, some 300 miles in length, was inhabited by Cafres and not Buques, and that their language belonged to the Bantu family. The *tromba* and the *dady* are described in all of their essential features. Linguistic reports by d'Azevedo remain to be found for the Bambala Coast, a matter being attended to at the time of this writing. Nonetheless, many of the place-names as well as the names given to rulers, nobility, and priests, and even three of the "ethnic" names are distinctly non-Malagasy. *Loquexa* parallels *Lukwesa* or Lunda Kazembe, the kings' title name repeated over the generations.[118] *Bambala* (*ba* locative prefix) is found in Mbala (Ambala, Bambala), peoples of the Kwango and Kasai, also found among the Ila of middle Zambezi.[119] The *Quisaju/Kisaju* (allies of the Suculamba warriors) could well derive this name from the old *Kisaju/Kisiju* settlement, "situated at about 80 miles south of Dar es Salaam."[120] *Capitapa/Kapitapa, Cassane/Kassane* and *Ajungones/Azungunes* mean nothing in Malagasy even if possible etymons are not easy to come by.[121]

---

[117] In Bantu idioms, *amatshangana* means people who have gathered together.

[118] J. Vansina, *Kingdoms of the Savanna* (1966), pp. 170–172; A. C. Pedroso Gamitto, *O Muata Kazembe*, trans. by I. Cunnison (1962). 2 volumes, passim.

[119] G. P. Murdock, *Africa* (1959), pp. 292–293, 365.

[120] James Kirkman in Justus Strandes' *The Portuguese Period in East Africa*, trans. by J. F. Wallwork (1961), p. 339.

[121] *Tapa*, of course, appears in Mwene mu-tapa. According to Baumann and

There is also no doubt that the Suculambes of Mariano are the Saka-lava, whose own *tromba* and *dady* cult would, in a relatively short time,

Westermann, *Peuples*, p. 219, *"dans le Ganda, de grands morceaux ornés de dessins faits avec de la boue, de magnifiques genres de tapa étaient réservés aux rois."* KAPA is "tortoise" in Makua-Lomwe. J. Stimson and D. S. Marshall, *A Dictionary*

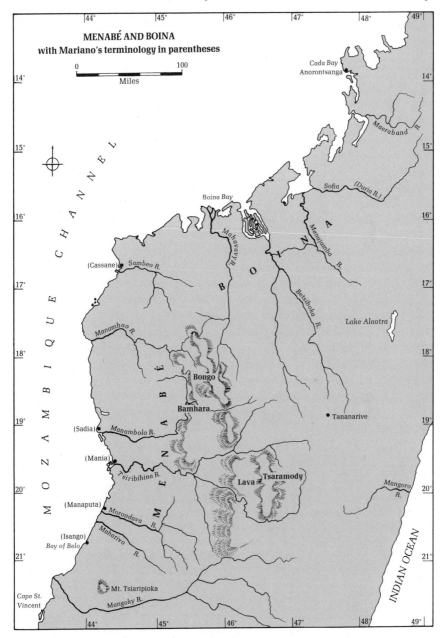

MENABÉ AND BOINA
with Mariano's terminology in parentheses

0   100
Miles

become the property of Maroserana rulers. By about 1620, the Sakalava had eliminated Capitapa's state and had secured alliances with the Quisaju as well as with some Ubuques.[122] They were then reported as the most powerful warrior group, raiding far and wide. The *Tantara* of Imerina, which contain numerous references to the Sakalava, recall that "in the very beginning of Ralambo's rule, the Sakalava besieged all of Androkaroka, north of Alosara, but were defeated by Ralambo."[123] Alosara was the nucleus of the early Merina state in the highlands. The site of Sakalava defeat was named Mandamako (or lazy) in memory of Ralambo's daytime attack, which found the Sakalava asleep since they only fought at night.[124] According to the most reliable estimates, the start of Ralambo's reign in Imerina falls into the early 1620s. In view of Mariano's own statement that the Ajungones fought only in the daylight and the Suculambes only at night,[125] the *Tantara* suggest a high degree of accuracy.

The coast below latitude 22° south again presents the aspect of political fragmentation, with some significant differences in comparison to Bambala and the northwest. Its peoples were mainly pastoralists who did not plant. Although black as coal and with fuzzy hair, suggesting to at least one observer connections with Mozambique, their language was not related to the Bantu family. It did, however, contain enough loan-words for a south African idiom-speaker to find out the nearest source of fresh water, how it could be transported, where the local capital was as well as the name by which it was known. The area where this took place, it is worth recalling, is the same one where eight out of ten local groups informed Birkeli that they had no memories of migration. In an area where cattlekeeping was the paramount economic activity, the word *Rango*, noted as early as 1595, points to the presence of Maroserana. Seven years later, de Laval saw "women with shaven heads," a distinct custom following the death of a Maroserana, one that did not exist further north until the foundation of Menabé. Conformity to this custom had indeed caused the Maroserana a great deal of trouble, from the lands of

---

of Some Tuamatuan Dialects of the Polynesian Language (1964), list under *kapi*, to be encircled, shut (in), and under *kapina*, denseness of population.

[122] Already in his *Letters* of July and October 22, 1616 (*COACM*, Vol. II [1904], pp. 218–221, 239), Mariano foresaw the fall of Sadia. The alliances are reported in his memorandum to Goa from Mozambique, August 20, 1617, *COACM*, Vol. II (1904), p. 258 (small print).

[123] Callet, *Tantara*, Vol. I (1953), p. 278. Some of the references to the Sakalava are discernible anachronisms but many others are placed in proper sequence and context.

[124] *Ibid.*, p. 278.

[125] Mariano, *Letter*, October 21, 1616, *COACM*, Vol. II (1904), p. 220.

Mahafaly in the southwest to Iboina in the north, where the formation of the *Tsimihety*, now an important group, took place as a result of refusal to submit to the Maroserana. In effect, Tsimihety means literally those who do not cut their hair. It might be recalled from the Bara chapter that, according to the Mahafaly oral traditions collected by Mamelomana, their ruling clan (Tsileliki) did not have to undergo the shaving of heads following Maroserana deaths only because they intermarried with this dynastic family. Moreover, against the ethnographic and linguistic materials brought together in the Bara chapter (see notes 92–100 and related text), it would be difficult to overlook that the term *Rota* (by which the inland capital was known) is the same one applied to Mwene Mutapa's royal scepter,[126] symbol of the high office.

The "book" acquired by Boothby attests, equally, to the presence of one or more Anteimoro religious specialists, the only ones who could have written a *Sora-bé*. This is further confirmed by Mandelslo's reference to a local chief as *misara* (*massar*), a term deriving from Arabic *isara* (or divination). The brief statement by de Laval shows also that political struggle at St. Augustine some three decades *before* Boothby's visit was already connected with Islam. This intrusive force could have reached the St. Augustine Bay by the turn of the seventeenth century only from the Anteimoro. All of this serves rather well to stress an important point. The "controversy" in Mahafaly and Sakalava oral traditions concerning the proto-Maroserana as having been *either* migrants from the eastern interior under Great Noble Ali (Andrianalimbé) *or* migrants from overseas under the Crusher of Trees (Andriamandazoala), is in essence no controversy at all. Both of the two basic traditions represent a valid recollection of distant past. The *historical* Maroserana were already an admixture of intrusive migrants and indigenous chiefly families. The *proto*-Maroserana, intrusive migrants who were *not* Malagasy and who attempted to build local states probably from the moment of their advent in Madagascar, made use of magico-religious specialists from the eastern interior, itinerant *ombiassa* or *misara* of Anteimoro provenance. As to the overseas origin of the proto-Maroserana (a subject on which more than a hint has been presented) and the manner in which the *misara* were used in state building, these are problems on which more light is certainly available.

The Iboina Sakalava appear to have once possessed an important historical manuscript. Sometime before 1907, Gautier and Froidevaux heard of the Sakalava *Annals*, written in Malagasy language and Arabic script, but they could not find this source.[127] This manuscript was indeed held

126 Abraham, "Mwene Mutapa," pp. 68, 86, n. 60.

127 E.-F. Gautier and H. Froidevaux, *Un Manuscrit arabico-malgache sur les campagnes de La Case dans l'Imoro, 1659–1663* (1907), p. 5.

by a Zafi Volamena princess and is now known to have perished in a fire.[128] There exists, nonetheless, an abridged version of the *Annals*, dictated from memory by *mpanjaka* (chief) Tovonkery.[129] No other traditional document has come from a higher official source. It states that the Maroserana came from Mijomby or Midzombi with a shipload of gold, landed at present-day Tuléar, and gained supremacy over local people very gradually.[130]

According to an old Sakalava oral historian from the islet of Nossi-bé, Bosaria, the Maroserana originated in Mahafaly at the time when the contiguous land of the Andrevola was known only as Masikoro.[131] In the older and unpublished primary sources that can be identified, Andriamandazoala and Rabaratavokoka appear alternately as Maroserana founders. [132] Among the Sakalava oral traditions recorded in 1965, those of Menabé recall Rabaratavokoka, while those of Iboina claimed that Andriamisara fathered the Maroserana family.[133] Andriandahifotsy, following the 1965 Iboina texts, never went beyond Menabé, and Iboina was

[128] Reported in Dreyer to Analalava province chief, *Letter*, December 9, 1915, appendix to Document 620 of the Charles Poirier Bibliothèque, now owned by the University of Madagascar.

[129] Tovonkery was the elder of all the *mpanjaka* (chiefs) of Maromandia and the principal guardian of oral tradition. He was entrusted with the key to the royal family tomb at Kapany. The "prodigious memory of Tovonkery," wrote Dreyer in the *Letter* of December 9, 1915, "the assurance with which he told me the kin links of different ancestors, make me believe that [his accounts] . . . are exact on the whole. . . . There is nothing extraordinary in all this once it is borne in mind that the *Joro* prayers of the Sakalava require the enumeration of the ancestors . . . along with the important events which go with each of them. . . . Some conserve . . . this memory religiously and this is precisely the case of Tovonkery. It is for this reason, and also because he is the elder of all *mpanjaka* of Maromandia, that they entrusted to him the key to the family tomb at Kapany."

[130] Tovonkery, *"Ory Mpanjaka Voalohany izay Fantatra Tantara araka ny Lovantsofina dia: Andriamandisoarivo,"* ("The first of kings whose history is known according to the heritage of the ears was Andriamandisoarivo"), in his *Lovantsofina Milaza ny Tantara Nihavian'ny Mpanjaka Sakalava Samy Hofa Eto Amin'ny Faritany Maromandia (Oral Traditions of the Sakalava Kings)*, submitted by the district head of Maromandia (1915), p. 7, Document 620, *BP*, University of Madagascar.

[131] Cited by R. De La Motte Saint-Pierre, *Nossi-bé 13° latitude South* (1949), unpublished typescript of the Académie Malgache, pp. 53–54.

[132] G. Grandidier, "Les Sakalava," unpublished typescript, pp. 1–3 and n. 8–9 (based on his father's *Cahiers* [1868–1870]); Abdallah, "Généalogie des Maroserana," (not dated), pp. 1–2, Document 629, *BP*; Ch. Betoto, "Histoire de la royauté sakalava" (1950), typescript, pp. 3–4, by kind permission of the author.

[133] *OTT*, Reel I (1965), at Mirinarivo-Majunga (Iboina). Informants: *mpanjaka* Nintsy, Mamory-bé, and Tsimanohitra Tombo. Mirinarivo-Majunga is the site of the *doany* that contains the Sakalava royal enclave (*Zomba*) and the Maroserana *dady*. Mamory-bé and Tombo are *ampitatara* (historians) and tomb guardians.

first penetrated by his son Andriamandisoarivo.[134] Andriamisara was with him.[135] At the time of the Sakalava conquests, the Manandabo were the largest single group indigenous to Iboina. Long before them, however, there was in the north the "rich kingdom of Borifotra."[136] Boina derives its name from a renowned "Arab," but the northwest was known since time immemorial as Bokiny (from Ubuque). The "real Sakalava," I was told with stress, do not exist anymore, for this name applied originally to conquerors from the south *only*—to the *Sakalava ny Sakalava* (*real* Sakalava by plural and redoubling). Not everyone "joined" them. The Tsimihety refused to shave their heads and fled into the far north. The Bezano (Bezanozano of today) and the Sihanaka (now people of the Lake Alaotra region) also fled from them into the interior. The Vazimba gave no resistance, while some of the Antanandro remained with the Sakalava and others fled.[137] The reason why the Maroserana came north from southern Menabé and Fiherenana was the pressure of the Andrevola and their subjects, the Masikoro.[138] The Vazimba and the Antanandro were of the same "Makoa" origin.[139] The *Sakalava ny Sakalava* attained their northern conquests with the help of three famous and feared *mososa*.[140]

[134] King-wronged-by-thousands—this *fitahina* alludes to a dynastic dispute between the sons of Andriandahifotsy. It was given to the younger one, Tsimanatona (see text below), founder of Sakalava-Iboina. In the older days, former kings could never be mentioned by their lifetime names but only by *fitahina*.

[135] *OTT*, Reel I (1965): informant—Nintsy. J.-C. Hébert, who knows the Iboina-Sakalava well, states that other well-informed *ampitatara* have been in complete agreement that Andriamisara was a sacerdotal companion of this Maroserana king, not a member of the royal family, while the term *misara* came to be applied to Maroserana kings. The proof of this, he writes, consists of the four Andriamisara whose *dady* are preserved at Majunga for, in reality, these *are* the Maroserana *dady*—personal communication, April 4, 1969. Hébert is one of the few Europeans to have actually visited the tomb of Andriamandisoarivo in the district of Mitsinjo, on the banks of the Mahavavy River. His *doany* at Bezavo is analogous to that of Mirinarivo-Majunga but has been eclipsed by the latter.

[136] *OTT*, Reel I (1965): informant—Tombo. This is most likely an allegorical recollection of the old Mazelagem of Portuguese sources.

[137] *Ibid.* The reference to an earlier Sihanaka and Bezanozano presence in western Madagascar is worth further investigation.

[138] *OTT*, Reel I (1965): informant—Mamory-bé. Cf. Birkeli, *Marques*, pp. 21, 26, 34–35.

[139] *OTT*, Reel III (1965), taped near Morondava, Menabé. The informant does not wish to be identified by name. In no way, however, is he connected with the Vazimba for whom he claims the same Makua origin. His association of the Antanandro with Africans (Makoa) is in harmony with what could be deduced without mistake from older European sources with which my informant had no contact.

[140] *OTT*, Reel I (1965): informant—Tombo. Father Webber, who spent some time toward the middle of the nineteenth century among the Sakalava, defines

As the foregoing reveals, Sakalava tradition is not concerned mainly with the proto-Maroserana origins. It stresses genealogy, succession, legitimacy, and events associated with the Maroserana-Sakalava kings. The reverse has often been true of late-nineteenth- and early twentieth-centry Europeans as well as of the Antalaotra Muslims of Majunga. This is the fundamental reason why the Maroserana turn out to have been "Arabs," "Indians," or "whites" with glorious destinies. With this back-ground in mind, the report of Tovonkery assumes particular value. In a very corrupted way, it may or may not refer to Mozambique (Midzombi) as the point of Maroserana origin. One can only note in this connection that some 250 years earlier, a French source familiar with southern Madagascar had held that the "blacks" of this Island were its "original" population but that the "whites came some time ago from Mazambique . . . having been expelled by the tyrant of Quiloe (Kilwa)."[141] But, even this is far less interesting than the firm connection of the Maroserana with *gold.*

The general finding of early Europeans who actually visited the Great Island concerning gold can be expressed through Mandelslo's statement that "it is said there are gold mines" in Madagascar but the "inhabitants do not use this metal and hence do not look for it under the soil."[142] In fact, the mining of gold in Madagascar is a late-nineteenth-century development fostered mainly by Europeans who sought and obtained concessions in Imerina where deposits of some importance have indeed been found. But, neither among the Merina nor among the Betsileo did gold become the metal of nobility, a role filled rather by *silver* and dating back to Vazimba times. While gold is now mined in Madagascar and silver is not, deposits of silver—contrary to the reports of a number of writers—do exist. For example, article 9 of the Merina monarchy's famous *Code of 305 Articles* specifically prohibited any extraction of silver. Early European accounts report silver ornaments among the Mala-gasy; however, these same accounts did remark about the inferior quality of the silver. Notwithstanding that there is the Indonesian term *bulau* (*Dayak*) for gold, which parallels the Malagasy *vola* (phonetics, *vūla*),

---

mososa as "one in contact with the demon, one who carries the *ody* (amulets, relics) and flags in expeditions"—*Dictionnaire,* p. 482. The root *osa* is also found in the hosana priests in Mwene Mutapa. I recall coming across *hosana* in connection with African religious expression in Brazil, attributed to men from west Africa and more specifically from Dahomey. Phillip Peek informs me that *Osa* is also a high Yoruba diety.

[141] Carpeau du Saussay, *Voyage à Madagascar* (1722). Although published in 1722, this work was actually written in 1663.

[142] *COACM,* Vol. II (1904), p. 488. For a more detailed statement, see A. and G. Grandidier, *Ethnographie,* Vol. IV, Tome 4 (1928), 189–199.

vola alone does not designate gold unless qualified by *mena* (red) or silver without *fotsy* (white). Linguistically, it is arguable which of the two metals was defined by *vola* before the qualifiers *mena* and *fotsy* became commonplace. The relative scarcity of silver in comparison to gold in Madagascar in terms of actual deposits does not lend itself to our own cultural ethnocentrism that relates *economic* value to the factor of scarcity. What one is dealing with in Madagascar is the politicoreligious role of the two metals in traditional societies. And, the vast political and religious (but *not* economic) role of gold in southern Madagascar, already presented for the Ibara case, can, therefore, be ill-explained as anything else but the product of influence gained by outsiders who brought a large quantity of this metal with them, namely the Maroserana. It is most significant to note that even the more common name for this dynastic family has been in effect *Volamena* (gold) or *Zafimbolamena* (descendants of gold). In fact, it is the term *maro* that appears twice connected with gold in old Madagascar, through the *Maroserana* and the great heritage of gold in Ibara called *Marofeh*.

The term *feh* could derive from *féhy* (bundle, tie), which fits descriptively the urns or bundles of gold reported. Less likely, it might point to *fehitra* for kin or family. As for *serana*, which the reliable Guillain recorded in southwestern Madagascar from local informants as meaning trace, traces, or paths, in connection with the Maroserana, it is given a different meaning by Abinal and Malzac "those who had many ports; name given especially to (Merina) princes whom Radama I sent as governors to different coastal ports where he established customs."[143] From this, it is often deduced that Maroserana was a title meaning those who control many ports. This is a pointed anachronism and transposition of Merina nineteenth-century institutions to other Malagasy. Moreover, no one could argue that the Maroserana kings controlled any ports much before the seventeenth century, long *after* this dynastic name had been around and indeed at the time when it was being replaced by *Volamena*.

There is no doubt that the nearest gold-bearing area in relation to Madagascar was the old empire of Mwene Mutapa in Rhodesia and it is also certain that the term for gold there was *mari*.[144] Hence, there is little left by way of a simpler or more reasonable explanation than to perceive the original compound as *mari + serana* or *gold + traces*, being composed of a loan-word for gold imported by the gold bearers themselves and of a Malagasy one with the *dialectical* meaning of traces.[145]

---

[143] Abinal and Malzac, *Dictionnaire*, p. 557.

[144] Abraham, "Mwene Mutapa," p. 68.

[145] If one were to accept the Merina dictionary version of *seranana* as ports, it would be necessary to explain why this meaning was not known in southwestern Madagascar in the 1840s.

Maro in Malagasy means many. The phonetic drift from *mari* to *maro* would seem hardly surprising in that it replaced something unfamiliar with something common, as much through the pull of the Malagasy part of the compound as for the purpose of emphasis. "Those who" once "made traces of *gold*" thus became "those who made *many* traces" by changing the *i* into *o* (*mari* to *maro*). I have encountered in older Malagasy texts such versions of Maroserana as *Mariserana, Marisirana,* and *Marosirana,* and Guillain even tells us, in no uncertain terms, that the "standard" *Maroserana* failed to yield any meaningful etymon from the most informed local elders in the very section of Madagascar where this dynastic family saw its birth. There was no adequate explanation, wrote Guillain in the early 1840s, beyond the *idea* of a title which, if literally translated into French, meant many parts or many traces.[146] And, having thus rather pointedly lost the loan-word and with it the sense of true meaning, Maroserana was gradually replaced by the Malagasy Volamena because gold itself was the important family mark. The exact ethnicity of the Maroserana founders will probably never be known. On the other hand, linguistic and ethnographic vectors converge at the gold-producing empire of Mwene Mutapa. This is the most that can be said in the present state of knowledge.

The Maroserana formed in Mahafaly ±1550. Some remained in the familial cradle; others migrated into the interior or further north along the coast. Because of a political consciousness developed outside of Madagascar, they became mainly state builders. Yet, their early kingdoms were either powerful and short-lasting (Bara) or else durable but far less impressive (Andrevola, Mahafaly). The contention of Noel and others that the Maroserana made the Sakalava historically important is, however, contrary to evidence. Without the Sakalava warriors, their *dady* and *tromba* as well as oral records of the past, there would have been no Menabé and Iboina, and no one would remember the Maroserana as such today. From about 1650, the political fortunes of Sakalava-Maroserana can be separated no longer. What remains unclear is the period of 1620–1650 and the manner in which the Volamena kings adopted the Sakalava politicoreligious institutions. Here, only partial and incomplete answers can be obtained at the moment, mainly from internal sources.

Because the southeastern Antaisaka, a branch of the Sakalava who migrated across Ibara to their final home in the 1620s, remember not only the distant Maroserana ancestors (Baratavokoka, Andriamandazoala) but also the conqueror king Andriandahifotsy,[147] it would appear that the Volamena and Sakalava were in contact by ±1625 and certainly before

146 Guillain, *Documents*, p. 11, n. 1.
147 H. Deschamps, *Les Anteisaka* (1936), pp. 163–164.

1640. Nothing is known about *how* the Sakalava accepted Andriandahifotsy as their leader and king, but old *Makua*, personal attendants of a northwestern Sakalava *mpanjaka*, reported the following history of how the *dady* became a royal cult:[148]

> The *dady* go back to Andriamandresi and Andriandahifotsy, who had subjected several villages in Menabé, extended and augmented their father's kingdom. They had a *moasy* of great renown. At the death of Andriandahifotsy, king of the warriors and the *moasy*'s master, the *moasy* cut his hair and his nails and pulled his teeth out, placing them together with his own *ody* [amulets]. Then he prepared a wooden box, ornamented with pearls, and placed the remains of the deceased monarch into it. The box came to be respected as much as the king when still alive. As the conquests went on, Andriamisara took the box along saying "the king's body is in here and those who do not obey me . . . take away the ancestral force from the box." The people submitted to the Zafinimena kingdom. No one could handle the *dady* as well as the *moasy*, Ndramboay who—after his [own] death—became Andriamisara. When he died and in accordance with the will of Andriandahifotsy, his own hair, nails, and teeth were placed in the box. He was thus greatly honored and considered as the king's son although this he was not, no more than being the king's father. Andriandahifotsy's son, Andriamandisoarivo, when sent by his older brother to conquer the north, would not leave without the wooden box. This is how the royal ancestors became the *Zanahary* [Gods]. It was a *vaha* [medium possessed by the *tromba*] in whom Andriamandisoarivo had great confidence, that got to carry this box and thus became the *mpiboha* [carrier]. As he went to conquer Iboina, Andriamandisoarivo arranged his hair exactly like Andriamisara. The *mpiboha* carried a cane exactly like Andriamisara's. And although the box contained the remains of the king and his *moasy*, it was Andriamandisoarivo [himself] who gave it the name of Andriamisara. In time, there were four main *dady*.

This is the most descriptive and detailed traditional account known to exist.

It tells us that the incorporation of a conqueror king into the *dady* was intended to facilitate the acceptance of the Volamena. This innovation is attributed to the sacerdotal person (*moasy*) of Ndramboay (noble crocodile, from Andria-voay). Indeed, Ndramboay appears in numerous traditions that are associated with either Andriamandazoala or Andriamandresi, one regarded as the founder of Maroserana in Menabé and the other in Iboina. As in the detailed tradition above, it is the *coming into power* of the Maroserana that receives an association with Ndramboay.

[148] Anonymous, "Niandohan'ny Fivavahan'ny Sakalava," ("Origins of the Sakalava Religion"), manuscript notebook, Document 2238/2, Académie Malgache, pp. 1–7, set down on paper *ca.* 1908.

In other traditions, however, he is credited with two other innovations: human sacrifice of the favorite royal spouse and the creation of a new symbol for Sakalava royalty—the *vy lava*, or long ceremonial knife.[149] The old *Makua* appear to have been better informed on the Andriamisara problem than anyone else. The *moasy* was posthumously awarded the status of royal ancestor as well as the *fitahina* of Andriamisara. Since the *misara* were in essence chiefs with magico-religious powers in the far southwest, similar to the *moasy in Menabé*, the case is one of dialectical borrowing through royal fiat, and not any dynastic mystery, as Rusillon believed that he had discovered. In turn, of course, with the passage of time the *dady* could no longer be controlled. They became the Ampagnito-bé and *zanahary* (gods) of the Volamena and west-coast peoples who came under their rule and assumed the political and "national" name of Sakalava. Until 1926, both Andriamandresi and Andriamisara were buried at Bengy, but the remains of Andriamisara have since been moved to Majunga. Like the people, it is the tradition itself that elevates the *misara* to the status of *andriana* and confuses the priest with the king, a confusion that applies mainly to the very beginnings of Maroserana dynastic power, a period almost beyond recall.

The foundation of Menabé was certainly a momentous event in Malagasy history. It involved long years of warfare. It produced radical changes in human geography and economy. It led to an empire not only in control of the west coast from the Onilahy River to Boina Bay, but also one that exacted tribute from peoples of the interior as well. In the early 1660s Andriandahifotsy was still conquering lands south of Menabé. By 1696, a Dutch slaver found his son Tsimanatona (by *fitahina* Andriamandisoarivo) as ruler of the Bombétoke Bay, just south of Boina.[150] European sources shed light on the period 1660–1670. The ensuing two decades, marked by the conquest of northern Menabé and southern Iboina, can be outlined mainly from oral tradition.

In 1663, twenty-four years after Mandelslo's visit to the Bay of St. Augustine, a Dutch quartermaster named Joachim Blank reported that its chiefs (one of whom was about to be succeeded by his brother *misara*) were then at war with their northern neighbors, belonging to a "nation" called *Lohafuty*.[151] In 1666, another Dutch quartermaster, Jacob Granaet, landed in the same area. The "three principal chiefs," he wrote, "with

[149] Cf. R. K. Kent, "The Sakalava: Origins of the First Malagasy Empire," *Revue Française d'Histoire d'Outre-mer*, LV/199 (1968), 161–162; and Bernard, "Notice sur le *Vy Lava*" (not dated), manuscript pp. 1–3, Document 623, *BP*.

[150] Reported by Captain Holm of the *Soldaat*, in *COACM*, Vol. III (1905), pp. 381–382.

[151] J. Blank, "Voyage de la flute Waaterhoen," in *COACM*, Vol. III (1905), pp. 307–309.

whom Mr. Blank had traded in 1663 were killed by the *Lapahoutis*."[152] On his famous map of 1661, Flacourt had already noted *Lahe Fonti*, a land rich in cattle, *south* of *Terra del Gado*, the Portuguese name for Menabé. Flacourt, who lived in southeastern Madagascar (1648–1655), never traveled to the west coast, but other Europeans in and around Madagascar were hearing a great deal about Lahefouty (Andrianda-hifotsy) and his men, Lapahoutis (Sakalava warriors).

On October 28, 1666 François Martin spoke to the first mate of a French vessel that had just returned to Fort-Dauphin from an exploration of Terra del Gado.[153] He learned that all land north of the St. Augustine Bay was under "Lahe Foutchy." Southern Sadia of Mariano's time, the heart of Menabé, appears to have been conquered by 1666 because a party of forty-five French sailors left the vessel at latitude 19° 18' south and made contact with Lahefouty's men. Martin could not recall whether only some of the French were lost on the field of battle, having joined the king's warriors in a local conflict, or whether all forty-five were killed by Lahefouty's men.[154] In 1669 an embassy from Andriandahifotsy reached Fort-Dauphin. Its leader astounded de Mondevergue and de Faye, then in charge of the French colony, with "an adroit speech which lasted two hours."[155] This was a bid for a treaty of friendship to prevent possible French aid to chiefs south of the Onilahy, which would force the Volamena king to commit his army along the southern border lands and abandon conquests in the north.[156] A glimpse at this army is provided by Sieur Desbrosses, a trader of Fort-Dauphin, who journeyed approximately 150 leagues to reach Andriandahifotsy.[157] He was sent in 1671 "as much to assure him of continued friendship as to trade for cattle, of which La Hayfoutchy had a great number." The king had just gone to war toward the east, but returned with some 12,000 men to meet Desbrosses "and had all of them do the *mitave*" (from *mitava ampinga*,

[152] J. Granaet, "Description de la Baie de Saint-Augustin," *COACM*, Vol. III (1905), p. 334.

[153] F. Martin, *Mémoire concernant l'Ile de Madagascar, 11 août 1665–19 octobre 1668*, in *COACM*, Vol. IX (1920), p. 514.

[154] *Ibid.*, pp. 479, 515–516.

[155] *Ibid.*, pp. 605–606.

[156] The 1668 document to which Guillain had referred in his account is actually dated February 22, 1670, and is entitled "Relation des remarques qui ont estes faites sur les principalles bayes, ances & havres de l'Isle Dauphine & Isles Adiaçantes," (*ANSOMCM*, Document C5AI/32). I am grateful to M. Laroche, the director, for permission to use the Archive materials. The document was prepared by the captains, pilots, and merchants of the vessel *Petit St. Jan*. On folio 4 of the text, it is stated that chiefs of the St. Augustine Bay area came to Fort-Dauphin early in February 1669 to ask its governor "for protection against La Heye Fouchy."

[157] In Du Bois, *Les Voyages faites . . . aux Isles Dauphine ou Madagascar, & Bourbon, ou Mascarenne, es annees 1669–1672* (1674), p. 108.

a dance with synchronized movement of shields) in his honor. Desbrosses saw over 26,000 head of cattle and acquired 200. To the governor of Fort-Dauphin, Andriandahifotsy sent a gift of fifty prime bulls.[158]

Historical traditions of Menabé mention various clans that came either with the Volamena kings or shortly thereafter.[159] They tend to lump, on the other hand, pre-existing populations into three units: (1) Vazimba, the sweet-water fishermen, (2) Vezo or coastal fishermen, and (3) Antanandro, agricultural peoples of the coastal hinterlands. There is wide agreement in oral texts that neither the Vazimba nor the Vezo offered any resistance to conquerors from the south. The Vazimba had no important chiefdoms or military organization; they had no plantations to defend.[160] With their swift river dugouts, they proved of immediate use to Sakalava warriors by taking their women and children downstream to safety during the conquests. [161] The serious opposition came from the Antanandro. They were more numerous at that time than any other group in Menabé, including the invading army. For many years, their chiefs were able to retard and even halt the Sakalava-Maroserana drive to the north. Two events preserved by oral traditions mark the turning point in favor of the Sakalava. One was the battle of the Midongy massif. According to one of Birkeli's informants, Andriandahifotsy "pushed the conquests as far as Midongy, a peak that could not be taken, [but] as the tide was turning [against him], his wife, Matseroke of the Sakoambé tribe, sent reinforcements and firearms obtained from the whites named Digasi and Dabadi."[162] The introduction of firearms by Andriandahifotsy into the wars against the Antanandro is no anachronistic tale. It is attested by the fact that the ten original flintlocks are preserved as Sakalava relics. Alfred Grandidier saw two of them at Mahabo and eight at Belo-on-the-Tsiribihina in 1870.[163] The other event was a blood covenant (*fatidra*) between Andriandahifotsy and the "Antanandro chief Sangajy," who was killed, along with his "notables" in the "orgy" that followed the covenant.[164] A number of traditions even associate the foundation of Menabé

[158] *Ibid.*, pp. 105–108.

[159] Kent, "Sakalava," 158–159.

[160] Drury, *Journal*, p. 280, wrote that he "could not find that ever they formed themselves into regular kingdoms . . . each town being a distinct and independent commonwealth." This was in contrast to their "superior ingenuity" in crafts and medicine (the Vazimba cured Drury's frambesia).

[161] G. Grandidier, "Essai," p. 3$_{bis}$, n. 7. "To the Maroserana and Sakalava chiefs they paid as tribute the *réré* or large river turtles, excellent food, along with sweetwater fish and bananas."

[162] Birkeli, *Marques*, p. 33.

[163] G. Grandidier, "Essai," pp. 4–5$_{bis}$, n. 3.

[164] *Ibid.*, pp. 4–5$_{bis}$, note 2.

(the Great Red) with a "ruse employed against the Antanandro," involving a red bull (*ombe mena*), an animal that became sacred thereafter and could not be slaughtered.[165] While the two events cannot be dated with precision, they must have taken place after Desbrosses' journey of 1671.

Sometime before 1703, the captains of two ships (belonging to the New York merchant Frederic Phillips) when sailing near the mouth of the Morondava River learned that *Andian Lifouchy* had died. The new ruler of Menabé was his oldest son *Timanongarivo* (Tsimanongarivo). Following the death of the old king, a younger brother named *Andian Chimenatto* (Andrian Tsimanatona) attempted to wrest power from Tsimanongarivo, but he lost out and went north, "where he had huge success in war against *Andian Methelage*" (ruler of Boina Bay). Twenty armed men from the crews hired by Phillips were left behind. Their mission was to secure a trade monopoly for Phillips by helping Tsimanatona to "subject completely to his authority the Antaylouts [Antalaotra] and the Vaujimbos [Vazimba]."[166] Andriandahifotsy seems to have died around 1685, and the conquest of Iboina began as a result of a dynastic struggle in northern Menabé. By the 1690s the ranks of Sakalava warriors had thinned out. Drury mentions that Tsimanongarivo had himself gone toward Messelage with no more than approximately 800 men.[167]

A French captain described Tsimanatona in 1708 as a man of about 40, "nearly all black." His throne was an ebony armchair with ivory ornaments. The king wore a large silver chain, filled "with all sorts of magic symbols and figures, considered by sovereigns as protectors against all accidents."[168] Only a few years later, Tsimanongarivo was seen by Robert Drury as a "terrible figure," laden with gold and silver. His capital was called Moharbo (Mahabo). Twenty or thirty houses formed the court enclave within the palisades of the town. Drury, who had spent more than a decade in southwestern Madagascar, wrote that this king "lived in a more grand manner than any I had hitherto seen." His subjects kneeled before him or prostrated themselves. Those of "high station" licked his knee, and the "meaner people" licked his feet.[169] Some three decades later, a description of the Iboina court at Marovoay would make

[165] First reported by Guillain, *Documents*, pp. 12–13.

[166] Pirate Cornelius, "Account" (1703), in *COACM*, Vol. III (1905), pp. 616–617. This is the first mention in print of both Antalaotra and Vazimba.

[167] Drury, *Journal*, p. 274.

[168] De la Merveille, "Récit," August 7, 1708, in *COACM*, Vol. III (1905), p. 620 (small print), reprinted from La Roque, *Voyage de l'Arabie heureuse en 1708–1710* (1715).

[169] Drury, *Journal*, pp. 261–262. Drury estimated Tsimanongarivo's age at around 80.

the accounts of the French captain and Robert Drury seem pale by comparison.[170]

The Dutch slave ship *Barneveld* visited Menabé in 1719. Armed once "only with spears, bows and arrows," these men—the "*Souklaves*"—are "now fully supplied with firearms (and) are the equal of any European in ability to use them."[171] The Souklaves (this is the earliest written source to use the spelling closest to present-day Sakalava) obtained firearms through slave trade, taking most of the exported slaves from "neighbors" in the interior. It is a well-known tenet of Malagasy history that the Sakalava began to make slave raids by sea on the Comoro Islands and along the east African littoral *late* in the eighteenth century.[172] The *Barneveld* account strongly suggests a much earlier beginning, around 1710. The Souklaves were "expert in navigation" and had outriggers as long as 30 to 40 feet, some 8 to 9 feet wide, and capable of transporting forty to fifty men. "These served as war vessels to raid the neighboring countries with."[173] By about 1710 the Sakalava were already in control of most of the western coast, from the Onilahy River to Boina Bay and even beyond it. The large outriggers, hence, could not have been put to any local use. All along the coast, there were port officials who would immediately board an incoming vessel, ask for its flag and type of cargo on board. By a system of fire signals, the king would be notified of its arrival. Within no more than three days, he would be in port, usually with about 2000 men. No one could remain ashore without his permission. Each province had its own governor. Because of the inland distances from the capitals of Menabé and Boina, "these governors sometimes take advantage . . . to proclaim themselves kings." Sooner or later, however, provincial revolts were suppressed and "all those who took part were sold into slavery."[174] In 1719, Menabé was ruled by a king named Romeny (Ramena) who had "absolute power over his subjects and whom they respect and worship . . . almost like an equal of God." Although regarded by their monarch as serfs and slaves, the inhabitants appeared "perfectly satisfied with their lot." Gifts presented to the king by the Dutch were first screened by "spirits of defunct kings." There were no standing armies

[170] For a brief outline of Sakalava kingdoms in the eighteenth century, see Hubert Deschamps, *Histoire de Madagascar*, 2nd ed. (1961), pp. 103–104.

[171] "Relâche du . . . *Barneveld*" (1719), in *COACM*, Vol. V (1907), pp. 22, 24.

[172] The best essay on this subject is still E. de Froberville's "Historique des invasions Madécasses aux Iles Comores et à la côte orientale d'Afrique," *AVG*, II (1845), 194–208.

[173] "*Barneveld*," *COACM*, Vol. V (1907), p. 35.

[174] "Séjour de Jacob de Bucquoy à Madagascar et moeurs de ses habitants," (1722), in *COACM*, Vol. V (1907), pp. 104–105, 132.

but the king could put into the field "as many men as he has among his subjects."[175]

Almost unnoticed in comparison with the military and political events has been the demographic and economic change in Menabé itself. It not only received an influx of migrants from the north (Antevaratra) and from the south in more recent times, but it also lost a majority of its earlier inhabitants (Antanandro). Except for a section of relatively inaccessible Ambongo,[176] the Bambala Coast and its immediate hinterland retained only the forest-dwelling Mikeha, Behosy, and some other Vazimba subgroupings as populations of any antiquity. Toponymy, one of the most conservative of linguistic elements, confirms this change. The Bambala Coast place-names reported by Mariano either disappeared from subsequent written sources and cartography or else were replaced.[177] Moreover, unlike the isolated Mikeha and Behosy, who avoided contact with strangers, most of the Vazimba gradually lost their cultural antecedents as well as their former and attested bilingualism.

The overrunning of the Bambala Coast is confirmed in no uncertain terms by yet another aspect of change. In the place of predominantly agricultural communities, there were, by 1700, mainly pastoralists who came from the south and the north to become Sakalava. But, in doing away with the older agriculturalists, the Sakalava were forced to find new subjects who could and would plant and harvest the food. By 1700, also, kingdoms of the interior of Madagascar, continuously exposed to Sakalava slave raids, had much stronger defensive systems, and neither annual tributes nor the increasingly unproductive raids into the interior could meet both the Sakalava demand for agricultural labor and the European demand for Malagasy slaves. It is in the general economic condition that the origin of sea raids on the Comoro Islands and on east Africa must be sought. These overseas raids were arrested in the 1820s through an Anglo-Merina alliance. Within a decade, however, the Sakalava managed to come up with a new way of doing business as usual. They now traded their excellent cattle for slaves from Africa, as a growing number of American and European merchants discovered new and profitable terms of trade: inferior firearms unacceptable to the Sakalava were

---

[175] "*Barneveld,*" *COACM*, Vol. V (1907), pp. 21–22, 25.

[176] Its very nature turned Ambongo into a refuge for dissident elements both from Menabé and Iboina. Both the Sakalava and Merina raided Ambongo several times in the eighteenth and nineteenth centuries. Cf. Nicolas Mayeur, "Journal de voyage au pays des Séclaves," 1774, *BAM*, X (1913), 64; Guillain, *Documents*, pp. 271–273; and *L'Iraka*, No. 91 (March 15, 1901), 735–736.

[177] Cf. A. Grandidier, *Histoire de la Géographie de Madagascar*, rev. ed. (1892), pp. 191–195.

exchanged in Mozambique for the Makua (a variety of Zambezi peoples) and, in turn, the Makua were traded on the Sakalava coast for prime cattle.

Numerically diluted in the vast domain which still bears their name, the *Sakalava ny Sakalava* disappeared as an ethnic group, having given by 1710 an empire to the Volamena kings. They came out of the Bambala peoples, who also exist no longer. Their mode of life and original language are relics of history. Others took their name. Their *dady* and *tromba* survive because victorious monarchs needed them for mundane ends. Many of the features belonging to the old African culture that vanished in western Madagascar penetrated Imerina in the central highlands. In time, the Merina empire displaced the Sakalava one and came to dominate two-thirds of the Great Island. On the whole, European students in Madagascar did not, or could not, perceive this broader reality. The contrast, by the 1830s, between a splendid Merina court in Tananarive and the lowly Makua slave was too great. And, yet, until the turn of the nineteenth century, the Merina were hardly an important power.

chapter 6 IMERINA AND
THE TANTARA

The feeling of wrong over their conquest brought about, in the Hova soul, a mixture of guilt and of fear, translated vaguely into the belief that the Vazimba will one day come back to reclaim the land of which they were robbed. It is here that the origin of the cult rendered to the Vazimba must be sought.

Ensign Dupré (1863)

In the *Tantaran'ny Andriana* (*Histories of Kings*) the Imerina nation has a written classic of its language and culture as well as a source without a peer in Madagascar. Even a century after its compilation the *Tantara* has been cited as a model for collecting oral traditions elsewhere.[1] These particular *Tantara* represent several years of labor by the Jesuit Father François Callet, who came to Tananarive in 1864. Within a few years, he was acknowledged as one of the most accomplished students of the Merina dialect. By luck or his own efforts, Callet was able to serve as a missionary at Ambohipo, Imerimandroso, Ambohijanahary, Imerinafovoana, Ambohimanga, and Alosara.[2] All of these places are connected with the early history of the people who are called today Merina. Three of the sites are particularly important: Alosara is associated with the first Merina king. Ambohimanga became the necropolis of Merina kings. In Ambohijanahary, Callet found something of a rarity. This was the

---

[1] Cf. J. M. Vansina, R. Mauny, and L. Thomas (eds.), *The Historian in Tropical Africa* (1964), pp. 165–166.

[2] A. Cadet, "Pages oubliées," *BAM*, I (1902), 125. Surprisingly little has been published about Father Callet himself. However, in 1969 I was informed from Tananarive that he is a subject of a dissertation to be printed.

Antehiroka clan, apparently the only concentration of people in Imerina who could claim direct descent from the Vazimba, early inhabitants of the central highlands and almost legendary beings by the 1860s.

Father Callet had a natural inclination to talk with the old men, "over a snuff of tobacco." It did not take him very long to become influenced by an environment in which the past lived in the present. He began his studies by jotting down oral texts after his conversations. However, he seems to have soon asked the old men to dictate directly to him so that their own words could be set down on paper. A small volume of the *Tantara* compiled by Callet was published in 1873. Three more volumes

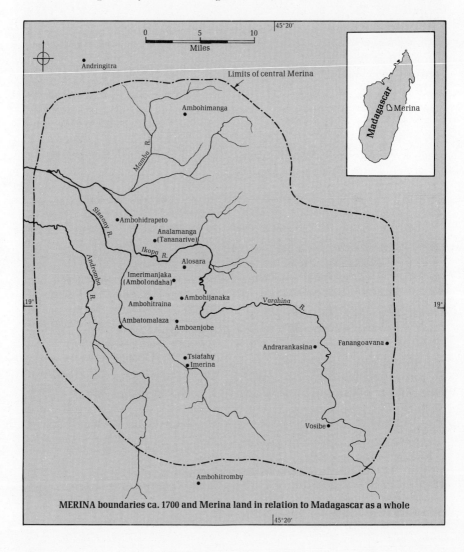

MERINA boundaries ca. 1700 and Merina land in relation to Madagascar as a whole

were published between 1875 and 1881. The limited number of copies were taken by local families, as literacy in Imerina was relatively high even then, and none of the printed *Tantara* "could be obtained from them at any price."[3] Printed materials in general are held in such high regard even today, and works relating to the Merina will be sold to a *vahiny* (foreigner who is at least partly acceptable) only when a local citizen is in dire financial need. The prices asked tend to exceed greatly those for which the same books could be obtained in Europe. Following the Franco-Merina war of 1883–1885, Callet transferred to Réunion and completed still another volume of the *Tantara*, shortly before his death in April 1885. This last volume was published in 1902.

The *Tantara* of Callet, "Le Roi incontesté des livres malgaches," had, until just a few years ago, two major drawbacks. One is extremely limited access, given that most of the *Tantara* were translated into French only between 1953 and 1958.[4] For some seventy-five years, thus, their contents could be read and discussed by a mere handful of non-Malagasy who had mastered the old Merina idiom, as spoken in the 1870s and one which even the younger Merina of today find difficult to understand.[5] Direct translations not only were few and concerned mainly a particular topic or chapter of the *Tantara*, but also the limited translations were not widely available.[6] Out of this condition grew an exclusive reliance of

[3] A. Boudou, *Les Jésuites à Madagascar au XIXe siècle*, Vol. II (1942), p. 159; and Cadet, "Pages," 126.

[4] F. Callet, *Tantaran'ny Andriana* (1873–1902), five volumes in two editions. Translated as *Histoire des rois*, Vol. I (1953), Vol. II (1956), and Vols. III–IV (1958), by G. S. Chapus and E. Ratsimba. A fifth volume is to be released by the Académie Malgache. All notes in this work refer to the *translated* volumes of texts collected by Callet as *Tantara*, followed by volume number and year of publication.

[5] The *Royal Merina Archives*, housed in Tananarive, contain several thousand documents that remain almost untapped. When I inquired about a large-scale team translation, I was told that only a handful of relatively aged persons in the capital could read, understand, and translate the contents today.

[6] These are: "*Ody et Fanafody*: extraits du *Tantara ny Andriana*," *BAM*, XI (1913), 151–218, trans. by B. Dandouau and M. Fontoynont; "*Tantaran'ny Andriana*: premier chapitre," *BAM*, XII/1 (1913), 21–114, trans. and annotated by M.-M. Colançon; and "Un Chapitre du *Tantara*: essai de traduction intégrale," *BAM*, new series, IV (1918–1919), 76–130, trans. by P. Soury-Lavergne. The Catholic bi-monthly, *Ny Iraka* (*The Messenger*), published many short extracts of the *Tantara* between 1897 and 1903. Only seventeen dealt with periods before 1787–1810. The "original" text, however, appeared in somewhat modernized Merina dialect with juxtaposed French translations. Issues of *Ny Iraka*, which was suspended on two occasions, are so scarce that even the Académie Malgache does not own a complete set. In addition, the entire first series of the *Bulletin de l'Académie Malgache* have been long out of print (along with the early volumes of the second series) and are seldom available outside Tananarive.

the interested public on the secondary and interpretative volumes of Alfred Grandidier and Father Victorin Malzac.[7] They advanced two different hypotheses about dynastic change in old Imerina.

Alfred Grandidier, as has been related in Chapter 1, contended that Javanese or Malays arrived in Madagascar toward the middle of the sixteenth century, that they left the eastern littoral and penetrated the central-highlands Vazimba around 1555, and that they founded a new dynasty of Andriana by Andriamanelo in 1590.[8] In support, he cited three types of evidence. One was documentary, consisting of two Portuguese accounts dating back to 1557 and 1559, accounts with which he took unacceptable liberties to create a group of Javanese shipwrecks. An alleged absence of "linguistic change" in old Imerina became proof that the Melano-Polynesian and Negroid Vazimba were speech kinsmen of their new Indonesian and Mongoloid rulers. Last but not least, the innovations of Andriamanelo as reflected in the *Tantara* completed the totality of evidence.[9] Cautiously at first, he credited Andriamanelo only with the introduction of rice and improvement of the iron-working and fortification-making techniques.[10] Citing, however, the *Tantara* as his source, Grandidier combined Andriamanelo with his successor, Ralambo, and attributed to them also the introduction of circumcision, divination, and astrology.[11]

To Malzac, Merina was simply another name for the Hova who had reached the central highlands long "before 1300," had intermixed with the Vazimba *tompontany*, and gained ascendancy with Andriamanelo, not in 1590 but half a century earlier.[12] According to Malzac, the very *lack* of linguistic change argued against new overseas arrivals possessing a different level of civilization. The Hova, since time immemorial, had been *"une portion notable de la population primitive immigré dans*

[7] A. Grandidier, *Ethnographie de Madagascar*, Vol. I (1908), pp. 72–82 in particular; V. Malzac, *Histoire du Royaume Hova depuis ses origines jusqu'à sa fin* (1912; reprinted 1930), particularly earlier sections. Father Victorin Malzac gave a summary of his thesis in "Les Hova, premiers habitants de l'Imerina," *NRE*, V (1899), 341–349, two years before Alfred Grandidier proposed his own in *L'Origine des Malgaches* (1901), pp. 66–92, 156–159. This work was incorporated in the first volume of his *Ethnographie* (1908), without substantial changes. The genesis, however, of views on this matter held by Grandidier *père* can be traced to three earlier articles: "Note sur les Vazimba de Madagascar," *MSP*, commemorative issue, (1888), 155–161; "Les Hova," *BCM*, I (1895), 113–125; and "Sur l'Origine des Malgaches," *RM*, I/6 (1899), 24–33.

[8] A. Grandidier, *Ethnographie*, p. 83.

[9] *Ibid.*, 81 and n. 1–2. Grandidier's "Javanese" theory and the evidence it was based on was discussed in Chapter 1.

[10] *Ibid.*, p. 83.

[11] *Ibid.*, pp. 79–80.

[12] Malzac, *Royaume Hova*, pp. 16, 30–31.

l'Ile."[13] Andriamanelo, "first king who gave prestige to the Hova nation," applied to royal issue the ancestral custom (*mentindrazana*) of circumcision, but in respect to the use of iron and to the idea of building fortified villages he was an original innovator.[14] Neither Grandidier nor Malzac disputed that a dynastic change took place with Andriamanelo or that racial traits of the Merina or Hova pointed to an Indonesian origin. The absence of linguistic change led them to opposite conclusions. But, if Grandidier had to manufacture his Javanese shipwrecks, how could Malzac account for the introduction of the use of iron and new fortification ideas as two "independent inventions" associated with the start of a *new* dynasty, all three features arising spontaneously within a group that had been indigenous to the Imerina? Moreover, the Merina calendar and astrology turn out to be Arabic while the sixteen-pattern *sikidy* is also their divination system.

Hubert Deschamps has attempted to "mellow" this problem somewhat by being less dogmatic. He points out that by 1400, at the earliest, the Hova reached Imerina, as could be estimated from seven to eleven "sovereigns" before Queen Rafohy, "herself generally placed toward mid-sixteenth century."[15] He allows the Hova their Andriana from the outset, conceding the probability of Indonesian shipwrecks along with the "mystery" that surrounds the Hova-Andriana arrival in Imerina.[16] Depending on the direction from which they came, their ancestral groups could be either the Zafindraminia (southeast) or the Iharanians (northeast).[17] Deschamps revives the old argument as well by holding *andriana* to be a "prefix of chiefly names or those given to the noble classes . . . among the Merina, Tanosy, Tandroy, Mahafaly, Sakalava, Bara, and Betsileo, or peoples who obtained chiefs from newcomers of the Medieval Era," and more specifically "Iharanians, Indians, or Indonesians."[18] In

---

[13] *Ibid.*, p. 16; and Malzac, "Les Hova," 342.

[14] Malzac, *Royaume Hova*, pp. 32–33.

[15] H. Deschamps, *Histoire de Madagascar*, 2nd ed. (1961), p. 57.

[16] *Ibid.*, p. 55.

[17] *Ibid.*, and n. 3.

[18] *Ibid.*, and n. 2. It is difficult to see how a *historical* argument can be made for this claim. As the bulk of the present work has already shown, by the time the Andriana (in the sense of title alone) dynasties develop, there are no "newcomers" to be talked about but, rather *Malagasy* who, in the cases of Maroserana and Anteony, retain some political ideas and features of their ancestors who at one time had been newcomers. The only instance—and it is still not entirely certain—of a non-Malagasy to have been "elected" supreme ruler by a local Malagasy group and its chiefs is that of Count Benyowsky, assuming he wrote the approximate truth. The title given him among the eastcoast Betsimisaraka was not *Andriana* but *Ampansacabé* (*Mpanjaka-bé* or Great Ruler)—Cf. Augustus Count de Benyowsky, *Memoirs and Travels*, Vol. II (1790), p. 268; and the critical work of Prosper Cultru, *Un Empereur de Madagascar au XVIII⁰ siècle: Benyowsky* (1906), pp. 162–164.

essence, the end result of this more eclectic explanation is a restatement of the Myth of the White Chief and the admission that since nothing can be ascertained, nearly everything is possible. Why would it take at least a couple of centuries for the "newcomers of the Medieval Era" to become the state builders of the sixteenth century? Would not their political ideas dilute rather than come to fruition after such a *long* passage of time? If the term *andriana* was applied to Indonesians, Indians, and Iharanians, this could only mean that it came from *common* Malagasy. It is, in no way, an argument for using *andriana* as an indicator for *external* origins of rulers and nobility. As Deschamps notes correctly in a different part of his volume, the Betsileo did *not* use the term Andriana at all.[19] The Bara accepted, at some point, *andriana* as a title prefix but (as was noted in Chapter IV) addressed their nobility as *Osa*. The Anteimoro, whose founding ancestors were beyond a shadow of doubt non-Malagasy, also used *andriana* and even their supreme ruler had the title of *Andrianonilehibé*. Finally, if *andriana* is absent from some groups in Madagascar, the *only* universal term for ruler in the island has been and is *mpanjaka*.[20]

Deschamps clearly holds that cultural influences and political change are inseparable and that both presuppose a fairly strong number of migrants. A Merina text that would even hint at a migration from the northeast into the central highlands has never been found. The Iharanian complex has failed to reveal a centralized political structure and bears no relation to the more recent Merina state. An Iharanian cultural influence may be seen in some of the Merina tombs and polished stone techniques. But, by their own accounts, these are very recent innovations.[21] Deschamps notes seven to eleven predecessors of Rafohy, a transitional Vazimba-Hova-Merina queen. A more careful reading of *Tantara*'s subsequent chapters and other sources as well reveals, as will be seen, only *four* ancestors of Rafohy, all from the same area of *Ampandrana*. Actually, the "sovereigns" in question were, at most, lineage heads. The most fantastic genealogy ever constructed in Madagascar is that of Malzac,

[19] *Ibid.*, p. 111.

[20] According to J. Webber, *Dictionnaire* (1853), pp. 338, 483, this is a composite of *mpan*, which designates someone in office, and *jaka*, which stands for gift or present. In many Bantu idioms, *anza* (root *anda*) is associated with chieftainship and means to start, to lead, to undertake—cf. Ch. Sacleux, *Dictionnaire Swahili-français*, Vol. I (1939), p. 69. The Malagasy *j* is the exact phonetic equivalent of *dz/z*, while the Malagasy ending *-ka* denotes an effect or consequence. In central Bantu idioms, *mapanzo* was the head cloth of chieftainship, cf. I. G. Cunnison, *Central Bantu Historical Texts*, Vol. II (1962), p. 27 (published as No. 23 of *RLC*). Mpanjaka/ mpanzaka is simply a modified Bantu loan, with the root surrounded by Malagasy prefix and suffix. And it is a loan of the highest social quality.

[21] J. Faublée (ed.), *Ethnographie de Madagascar* (1946), p. 127.

who placed the first Hova-Merina "king" in 1300, by assuming twenty-year generations and an unbroken line of succession.[22] Predecessors, contemporaries and successors cannot possibly be determined from the early-period accounts in Callet's *Tantara*, as there was no single family of rulers at that time. One *Tantara* version, for example, names eight "sovereigns" in five nearby villages.[23] It is only with Rafohy's son, Andriamanelo, that a reconstruction of Merina royal genealogy begins to make sense.

The Iharanians were no king-makers. The Javanese shipwrecks and the Indian arrivals belong to the world of sheer fantasy. In the sixteenth century, the Maroserana state building was confined to the southern half of the Great Island, while the Anteimoro were not fully formed much before mid-century. *If* a group nonindigenous to the Vazimba of future Imerina is to account for its new dynasty of Andriana and *if* major cultural and political changes go hand in hand, the sole remaining possibility in Deschamps' eclectic explanation would be an early Zafindraminia migration into the central highlands. But, this too, must be qualified. Such a migration should have been very gradual indeed, involving many settlements along the way from southeastern Madagascar, across Ibara and Betsileo. One would thus have to discover first some definite traces of such a population movement from south to north, show next who these migrants were and, *if* they turn out to have been Zafindraminia, end by making a sound case that they provided Imerina with its ruling dynasty of Andriana. Two traditions, one from Etienne de Flacourt and the other from a *Sora-bé*, allow for a reasonable degree of probability that the Zafindraminia ancestors did not confine their movement to the eastern and southeastern coast of Madagascar.

According to Flacourt, one of Raminia's sons named Racoube went into the interior from the east coast and, having crossed the land of *Anachimoussi* (Kimoso or Ibara), settled among the *Azoringhets* (Betsileo) and married the daughter of the "Grand du pays."[24] The Arabico-Malagasy Manuscript 13 of the Bibliothèque Nationale in Paris (see Chapter 3, note 9), published, translated, and annotated by Gabriel Ferrand, makes much the same statement but with three variants. The direct descendant of Raminia turns out to be a female—Andriandrakova. She

---

[22] Malzac, *Royaume Hova*, pp. 28, 30–31. "At the time when the Malays came to Imerina," wrote Alfred Grandidier, "its inhabitants were, like those of the rest of Madagascar, grouped into small independent families, each following its *chef naturel*, and not into nations, more or less important, under authority of kings . . . we could even go as far as to say that (the would-be kings of early Imerina) belong in the realm of mythology," *Ethnographie*, pp. 76–77.

[23] Callet, *Tantara*, Vol. I (1953), pp. 10–11.

[24] E. de Flacourt, *Histoire de la Grande Ile Madagascar* (1661), in *COACM*, Vol. VIII (1913), pp. 85–86.

arrives in *iMerina* (the term is actually used), near the *iKopa* River (Tananarive of today is not far from the Ikopa), and learns from the local Vazimba that it would take "two months of walking to get to the sea."[25] In the Flacourt version, Racoube eventually leaves the interior and returns to the coast. These two traditions, one picked up toward the middle of the seventeenth century by Flacourt at Fort-Dauphin and the other appearing in an Anteimoro *Sora-bé* composed toward the end of the nineteenth century, are sufficiently independent to place at least a few Zafindraminia into the Vakinankaratra (or southern section of Imerina). The "remigration" of Racoube claimed by Flacourt, who was closer in time to the subject at hand, suggests strongly that the Zafindraminia made hardly any political inroads by way of state building among the *tompontany* (original inhabitants). Clearly, then, the extent of southeastern influences in Imerina needs to be determined with some regard for chronology and only after two more basic problems have been dealt with—namely Imerina before the advent of Hova and their own migration into it.

As regards the sources—hardly a minor question—the *Tantara* of Callet can now be worked with directly *and* with other traditions as well. Some of them, from a collection of Merina manuscripts until recently in private hands, appear in a volume published by Guillaume Grandidier.[26] Others are contributed by C. Savaron.[27] Savaron depended on Callet's *Tantara* to some extent. The oral texts he himself collected between 1887 and 1927 are rather heavily edited. The great merit of Savaron was that he did notice and he did follow up with completely new materials the second major weakness of the *"roi incontesté des livres malgaches."* When it comes to the *fony Vazimba ny tany* (epoch when earthly power was held by the Vazimba), Callet's *Tantara* are generally vague and often contradictory. Yet, they give admirably detailed accounts of social, re-

---

[25] G. Ferrand, "La Légende de Raminia," *JA*, 9th series, XIX/2 (1902), 228–229; and his "Les Voyages des Javanais à Madagascar," *JA*, 10th series, XV/2 (1910), 320–321.

[26] G. Grandidier, *Histoire politique et coloniale*, Vol. V, Tome 1 (1942), *passim.* These manuscripts are subdivided into seventy-seven topics and are listed in sequence in his *Bibliographie de Madagascar*, Vol. I, Tome 1 (1906), pp. 730–733. They were written between 1864 and 1866 by the last head priest of Ranavalona I and consist of two in-folio volumes with a total of 371 pages.

[27] C. Savaron, "Notes sur le Farihin-dRangita," *BAM*, X (1912), 373–377; and "Contribution à l'histoire de l'Imerina," *BAM*, new series, XI (1928), 61–81, and XIV (1931), 57–73. As collector of gold levies for the Merina monarchy, Savaron went to northern Imerina in the 1880s. Some years later, he traveled extensively in the Imerina province of Antankaratra, in the south. The first part of his "Contribution," published in 1928, is of major importance but cannot be understood until *after* one has managed to understand the whole subject.

ligious, political and economic events that span three generations of Andriana or those of Andriamanelo, Ralambo and Andrianjaka, two of whom *still* belong in this Vazimba epoch. To supplement Callet, Savaron, and the Merina Manuscripts, two unpublished sources for other *Tantara* are added. One is from *northern* Imerina, the region of Anjozorobé, and was dictated by Rabozaka, Merina governor who fought the French in the "Rebellion of 1896."[28] The other, covering regions *south* of Imerina, is based on Betsileo and Bara oral traditions collected by Rabemanana toward the first decade of this century and apparently studied by no one.[29] A third interesting, unpublished and unexamined *Tantara* source is introduced somewhat later.

Like Betsileo or Betsimisaraka, the name Vazimba probably hides some other *tompontany*.[30] Rabozaka mentions the Rekaka and Kinitony.[31] These names are fictitious but are used to describe the local society as it was in the earliest times recalled by human memory. At the time, according to Rabozaka, there were no tombs. Instead, the deceased were thrown into lakes to become *lolorano* or water spirits (*rano* = water, *lolo* = spirit). The Kinitony were more advanced than the Rekaka. They wove mats and used a variety of wood to make fire with: *asia/seva* (*Buddleia*

[28] Rabozaka, *Notes d'histoire malgache: "tirées des récits de Rabozaka"* (1914), two manuscript notebooks, *AAM*.

[29] J. Rabemanana, *Le Pays des Kimoso et son histoire depuis les origines jusqu'à l'an 1820* (*ca.* 1912), manuscript, pp. 1–99 in-folio, *AAM*.

[30] *Fonoka, Gola, Lokoka,* and *Kimoso* (Kimosy, Chimoussi) are, for example, encountered in traditions as *tompontany* of southern Betsileo and northern Ibara. Taken literally, the first three are hardly group names. *Fonoka* means to reduce to nothing, and some of the Fort-Dauphin Antanosy named their graves as *fonoka. Gola* derives most likely from *fahagola* or, simply, legend, legendary. The term *lokoka* applies to a palm fruit from which intoxicating brew is made. Only the Kimosy, subject of an old and long controversy, still exist in Ibara. On the Kimosy, see: *De La Lande to l'Académie Royale des Sciences,* communication in the *Journal de Physique,* VIII/2 (November 1776), 357–363; Ch. Bénévent, "Note sur les Kimosy," *BAM,* IV (1905–1906), 100–103; M. Fontoynont, "La Légende des Kimosy," *BAM,* VII (1909), 51–59; Copalle, "Les Kimosy de Madagascar," *BAM,* VIII (1910), 65–67; de Maudave, "Sur un peuple singulier nommé les Quimos," *Mémoires* (1769), manuscript, 118–123, *BGT,* with an English-language extract available in the abridged edition of Abbé Rochon's *Voyage to Madagascar* (1821), pp. 47–53; and Commerson, "Note historique sur un peuple nain de Madagascar, Kimosse," manuscript pp. 1–6, *BGT.* Flacourt was the first to mention the Kimosy as purely legendary dwarfs and the controversy has been mainly on this aspect. The Kimosy of present-day Ibara differ in no way from other local inhabitants.

[31] *Kaka,* in dialects of the west coast means savage animal. *Re* is an enclitic particle used in requests and commands. *Tony* means calm, serene, quiet, but the meaning of the entire term *kinitony* could not be discerned. Rabozaka also gives *Marosboa* as another group but without further references. *Kaka,* however, in Mozambique means grandfather, grandparent.

214 Chapter 6

madagascarensis), *matsivana/fanoro* (*Gomphocarpus fruticosus*), and *fandramanana/voafotsy* (*Apholia theoeformis*).[32] Wild cattle roamed over wide areas. They were neither kept in pens nor used for food. Both the Rekaka and Kinitony were food gatherers, collecting roots, tubers, fruits, and honey.[33] An early name for the Vazimba was *manimba*, which Rabozaka translated as those with power to feed.[34] What this suggests in a very broad sense is the domestication of some plants, which are given as *akondro* (*Musa*), *ovy* (*Dioscorea*), *sakamalao* (*Zingiber*), *voamaho* (an oily edible seed), and *longoza* (species of cardamon plant).[35] A forest environment can be postulated here, while the presence of cattle implies the contraction of it. The dominant Malagasy cattle type is the African *Bos Sanga*. The term *akondro* is widespread in Africa as well.[36] That the practice of *tavy* (or the slash-and-burn method of planting) must go back to the Vazimba epoch can be deduced from the fact that even in the eighteenth century wood for construction of dwellings had to be imported into Imerina.[37]

---

[32] *Asia* and *matsivana* are no longer in use but *fandramanana* is—cf. A. Abinal and V. Malzac, *Dictionnaire malgache-français* (1888), p. 139. Abbé Dalmond, in his *Vocabulaire malgache-français pour les langues sakalava et betsimisara* (1844), p. 5, gives *asia* an entirely different meaning—to put water into salt, which suggests to dilute. *Trebo* is another type of wood mentioned by Rabozaka. It is difficult to believe that all these types of wood were used only for fire, but I have refrained from editing Rabozaka's account because it is an extremely rare attempt to depict the very beginning of his society. This account is presented as an over-all image of remote times, in which sense it has considerable value, not as a detailed memory of the more recent past to which the *Tantara* of Callet are an undisputable *detailed* testimony.

[33] Roots given: *antandena, kingiza, ataly*; tubers, *bemandry, ovinandrana, ovimariky*; fruits, *saombia, voandongoza*. *Ovi*, as noted in Chapter 2, is the prefix for a whole variety of Dioscirea.

[34] Abinal and Malzac, *Dictionnaire*, p. 392, as well as J. Richardson, *A New Malgasy-English Dictionary* (1885), p. 573, give *simba* as root, which is interesting. This root, activated by *man-*, however, is translated as spoilers and not those with power to feed. What Rabozaka is, in effect, stating is that *early agriculture in Imerina came with the Vazimba*. Such an event survives in memory by associating the Vazimba with those who do not depend on nature alone for food. Rabozaka does not say where these "men with power to feed" came from.

[35] Rabozaka, *Notes d'histoire*, Notebook I, p. 6.

[36] L. Joleaud, "Le Boeuf de Madagascar: son origine et son rôle dans les coutumes sakalaves," *L'Anthropologie*, XXXIV (1924), 103–107.

[37] "Hova dwellings are solidly constructed, in wood for the most part, although wood (supplies) are quite far away and wood is dear," according to Nicolas Mayeur, "Deuxième Voyage en Ancove, jouillet 1785," *BAM*, XII/2 (1913), 34. Earlier, in his first journey into Imerina (Ancove), in the journal entry for September 1777, Mayeur wrote: "trees are not to be seen here except those which are planted in trenches around villages and their number is small. The forests from which (the Hova) obtain their construction wood are on the southern borders, at some twenty

The Vazimba also made pottery and used mortars to prepare a dish called *varanga*.[38] The Vazimba "multiplied rapidly," absorbed the *tompontany*, formed villages, and were the first people of central highlands to have village chiefs. Rabozaka enumerated fourteen of them, seven of whom were more "prominent."[39] As signs of distinction, these chiefs wore a headgear made of animal skin, edges cut in tonguelike manner, and reddened their hair with *nato* (*Imbricaria madagascarensis*) and *anjafo*, a cosmetic mushroom (*tandroholatra*). The association of red color with chiefs and, later, with monarchs in many sections of Madagascar appears to be of ancient date. A private letter reports that the early Merina kings wore a red sash around the head, about 4 centimeters wide, with two silver crocodiles in *tête-bêche*, placed on the forehead. They were flanked on both sides by a bull horn encased in light wood, looping at the top and containing a large red pearl in the loop's center.[40] In 1595, the Dutch

---

leagues' distance," in "Voyage dans le sud et dans l'interieur des terres et particulerèment au pays d'Hancove, 1777," *BAM*, XII/1 (1913), 160. Benyowsky's interpreter and personal envoy to different parts of central, northern and western Madagascar, Nicolas Mayeur, originally from Mauritius, ranks with Mariano, Flacourt, and Guillain as one of the most accurate of early observers in the island.

[38] This dish consisted of meat cut into thin slices, broiled, sun-dried, crushed in mortar to get the pap, which is then mixed with the Zebu-hump lard and eaten. Webber, *Dictionnaire*, p. 749, gives it the equivalent of cold-cut or preserved meat. Sacleux, *Swahili-français*, Vol. II (1941), p. 995, finds *varanga* in Swahili as tumult, noise but notes it to be a non-Swahili word. The Malagasy, as noted by countless observers, do not have an original cuisine. The *Tantara*, Vol. I (1953), p. 129, note that all of the pottery *de terre a rebord* (of clay, hemmed-in edges) were called *nongo*. For the widespread diffusion of this item, root *ongo*, from Lamu to Mozambique, see Chapter 2, note 59, above. It would appear that the Comoro Islands were first populated by Africans from the mainland, whose memory survives as the Wamatsaha and Beja—cf. Said Ahmed Ali, *Essai sur l'histoire d'Anjouan* (1927), pp. 1–7, in *BGT*. All of these items are suggestive of journeys interconnecting eastern-southeastern Africa, its adjacent islands and islets, the Comoros, and Madagascar.

[39] They are given as: Imarotanjona of *Ambaravarambato* or Stone Door; Bibintany and Zanakarimaso of western *Vodivato* or Rock's-foot; Noro of *Andringitra* (site of) Quiet Waters; Ravohangy of *Analamanga*, (site of) Stunning Forest and place-name of pre-1600 Tananarive; Imanila of *Ambohitrambo* or Summit Village; and Imalaheloka of *Ambatomalaza* or Famed Rock. It should be noted that *Bibi, zana/Zanaka, maso* and the *I* prefix have a Bantu-Malagasy duality with identical meanings. Richardson, *Dictionary*, p. 453, connects *Noro* to Swahili for "light." These sites were *real*, not imagined. Since many are not listed on current maps and since *other* sites with identical names are noted, the older locations were as follows: *Ambaravarambato* (18° 17'/45° 37' 30"); western *Vodivato* (18° 35' 15"/45° 35' 30"); *Andringitra* (18° 41' 45"/45° 4' 30"); *Ambohitrambo* (18° 56' 25"/44° 49' 20"); and *Ambatomalaza* (19° 2' 10"/45° 6' 40").

[40] Father Paul Camboué, *Letter*, not dated, to A. Grandidier, cited in G. Grandidier, *Histoire politique*, p. 47, n. 2.

came across an east-coast chieftain who wore a mitrelike hat having, on
each side, *"une corne artificielle longue demi-aune, avec franges au
bout."*[41] The east-coast *tompontany*, later absorbed into the Betsimisaraka,
appear to have been Vazimba refugees from Imerina, who migrated in
small groups toward Fenerive. They were known collectively as Tsimam-
akivolana (those who see the moon no more) and somewhat later as
Betanimena (those of the red earth).[42] Both names reflect new environment, the dense eastern forests, and the very reddish soil around Fenerive.
The Vazimba, wrote Rabozaka's scribe, did not discard entirely the
lolorano burial custom but now only the human entrails were thrown
into lakes and marshes while the rest of the body was covered by stones.
Cattle-killing rituals came into being also. To arrest heavy rains, for
example, a pregnant cow (*ombinerano*) was slaughtered. If the downpour
kept coming, a sacrifice of bull and cow was made. Both had to be black
with white spots on the backs. This is also mentioned in the Merina manuscripts.[43]

In this early Vazimba epoch, neither rice nor manioc were known,
according to Callet.[44] It has been assumed until recently that manioc
came to Madagascar from the Mascarenes in 1790.[45] This may well be the
case for a portion of the eastern littoral facing Mauritius and Réunion,
but it most certainly does not apply to all of Madagascar. Nicolas Mayeur,
the first European to travel through Imerina, found manioc there to have
been both widespread and in abundant quantities by 1785.[46] The earliest
reference to manioc comes from the firsthand account of Balthazar Lobo
de Souza in 1556. He found the fields in northwestern Madagascar "full of
rice, mais and *mungo*, a plant unknown to us," in Goa.[47] As Grandidier
pointed out long ago, *mungo* is a Bantu term for manioc. Moreover,
Mariano confirmed the presence of manioc in the same area some six
decades later.[48] As is known from the list of plants by Flacourt, manioc

[41] They were sailors of Cornelius de Houtman, commander of the first Dutch fleet
to reach Madagascar. The account in French is from De Constantin's *Recueil des
voyages*, Vol. I (1725), in *COACM*, Vol. I (1903), pp. 202–203, in small print.

[42] See Boto, "Origine . . . des Betsimisaraka-Betanimena," *BODE*, XXV (1923),
252–253. Also, Fontoynont, *Etudes sur les Betsimisaraka*, not dated, manuscript, *AAM*.

[43] Cf. G. Grandidier, *Histoire politique*, p. 60, n. 4 and notule b, and Merina
Manuscripts, in *ibid.*, pp. 29–31. All pastoral Malagasy attach a whole set of sym-
bolisms to cattle colors and spots.

[44] Callet, *Tantara*, Vol. I (1953), p. 15.

[45] G. Cours and J. Fritz, "Le Manioc," *BM*, XI/178 (1961), 203–224. The Mascarene origin of Malagasy manioc in toto was developed by the Grandidiers, *Ethnographie de Madagascar*, Vol. IV, Tome 4 (1928), p. 54, n. 1, notule a.

[46] Mayeur, "Voyage en Ancove," 40.

[47] In *COACM*, Vol. I (1903), p. 101. Goa was de Souza's headquarters.

[48] Mariano *Relation* in *COACM*, Vol. II (1904), p. 12, cited in 1614 again under

was unknown along the east coast in the 1650s.[49] There is thus no doubt
that manioc reached Imerina from western Madagascar and the *Tantara*
place the advent of manioc there in the mixed Vazimba-Hova period.[50]

Old Imerina undoubtedly had commercial contacts with the western
coast although these may have been indirect for the most part. A limited
number of slaves from the *reino de Uva* in the "center of the Island,"
some with "fuzzy hair like the Cafres, which is surprising, and others with
smooth hair like ours," were brought to Mazelagem and "sold to Arabs
from Malindi" around 1613.[51] The intermediaries, in this case, might have
been the Sihanaka, who were associated with slave trade to the west
coast.[52] Two Spanish pisters, from the time of Philip II (1556–1598),
were found in an ancient Hova and not Andriana grave.[53] But, by 1668,
the *Houvs* had direct trade connections with the *Nouveau Massalege*
(Boina Bay).[54] According to information which had reached Parat, governor of Bourbon (earlier name of Réunion) in 1714, central Madagascar
already had onions, garlic and cauliflower, none of which are indigenous
to Madagascar.[55] In 1712, Robert Drury actually saw two traders from
Imerina at Mahabo (about 70 kilometers from the west-coast town of
Morondava). "They came to this country," wrote Drury, "to trade with
iron, chiefly of which they make a great deal." Drury was told that the
Sakalava "will not sell them any guns" and that they "trade sometimes to

---

the form of *mungo* (which Grandidier saw as early form of *manga*); and *COACM*,
Vol. III (1905), p. 660. For other sources which refer to manioc in Madagascar before
1790, see R. K. Kent, "Note sur l'introduction et la propagation du manioc à Madagascar," *Terre Malgache/Tany Malagasy* (January 1969), 177–183.

[49] Flacourt, *Histoire, COACM*, Vol. VIII (1913), pp. 165–206.

[50] Callet, *Tantara*, Vol. I (1953), p. 21. The same passage suggests that people of
the lowlands (Ontaiva/Antaiva) had manioc at the time of Andriampenitra, a
Vazimba chief in Vakinankaratra, whom G. Grandidier places in the middle of the
sixteenth century, cf. his *Histoire politique*, p. 358, notule c.

[51] This report is by Father Mariano, first European to mention the Hova (*Uva*),
term pronounced *hūv'*, in *COACM*, Vol. II (1904), p. 13.

[52] According to François Martin, *Mémoire . . . 1665–1668*, in *COACM*, Vol. IX
(1920), the Sihanaka "are more industrious than people in other parts [of the
island] . . . they make journeys to the west coast to sell slaves taken from their
neighbors" (p. 566); "they fired at us five or six musket shots" (p. 560); "they
pillage and ravage, without distinction, [all of] their neighbors, from whom they take
cattle and people, later sent to the west coast to be sold as slaves to English ships
which normally come for them, as well as to the Arabs and sometimes to the Portuguese" (p. 552).

[53] A. Grandidier, *Ethnographie*, p. 91 and n. 2, with one of the two pieces reproduced on page 140bis, along with other coin finds.

[54] *Journal Maritime* (1668), cited in A. Grandidier, *Ethnographie*, p. 91, n. 3.

[55] Parat to Mgr. Pontchartrain, *Letter*, September 19, 1714, copy in *BGT*. Garlic
was developed in Europe.

Mattatanna (Anteimoro-land) and Antenosa [Fort-Dauphin Antanosy], but not sufficient to furnish them with arms and ammunition."[56]

The advent of rice is a more difficult problem. Rice was found on widely divergent points of the vast coastal belt by the early European visitors.[57] Only the southwest, roughly from Antandroy to northern Menabé, had no rice fields in the sixteenth century. The *Tantara* hold that rice came to Imerina from the "heavens"[58] or else associate them with Rapeto and Rasoalao, legendary Vazimba giants, one of whom is credited with the introduction of cattle pens.[59] It would appear, nonetheless, from closer reading of the *Tantara*, that the first *wars over rice* were fought among the Hova clans.[60] Other clues emerge also from the *Tantara*. For example, Ralambo, the second Andriana of Imerina, incorporated into the nobility not only his own descendants (Zafindralambo), but also the "sons of Andriankotrina," who "had stolen a few grains of rice" from *Ambarinandrianahary* (site where God created rice, *bari/vari*/now *vary* =rice + *Andrianahary/Andria Zanahary* = roughly Almighty God).[61] This points to the very distinct possibility that rice was obtained outside Imerina. But, by whomever and from wherever it may have been first planted in Madagascar, its overseas home is clearly indicated by Javanese

---

[56] Robert Drury, *Madagascar or Robert Drury's Journal*, 7th ed. (1890), pp. 277–278.

[57] Da Cunha (1506) found rice in the northwest (as a highly developed export crop going to east Africa by tons) and Diogo Lopez de Sequeira (1508) reported it at the opposite end or southeastern Madagascar, to cite only two of the earliest sources. See *COACM*, Vol. I (1903), pp. 21, 50.

[58] Callet, *Tantara*, Vol. I (1953), p. 20. According to this particular version, a celestial princess brought along a rooster, hen, and rice grains. See also a superb short essay by Clara Herbert, "Rice and Rice Culture in Madagascar," *AA*, III (1888), 479–486. The article "Rice, a Malagasy Tradition," recorded by Ralph Linton, *American Anthropologist*, XXIX (1927), 654–660, and reprinted in S. and Ph. Ottenberg, *Cultures and Societies of Africa* (1960), pp. 110–115, bears some very marked resemblances to the one by Clara Herbert without reference to it. "Our ancestors came to this island . . . [but] there is no story of their bringing it with them or its having been introduced by strangers. Rice was known to the Kimo and Vazimba"— Ottenbergs, *Cultures*, p. 110.

[59] Callet, *Tantara*, Vol. I (1953), pp. 22–24, 442–443. The village of Rapeto, or *Ambohidrapeto* (18° 53' 45"/45° 6' 45"), was reported by Mayeur in 1777 and Reverend William Ellis in 1838. It is now a small town. A. Grandidier believed Rapeto to have been the last powerful (giant) Vazimba chieftain of Imamo, conquered by Ralambo, cf. his *Histoire de la géographie de Madagascar* (1892), p. 151, n. 1. An ancient cattle pen, along with pottery attributed to Rasoalao, have been reported at Ambohimiangara.

[60] Or between "highlanders" and "lowlanders," Callet, *Tantara*, Vol. I (1953), p. 21. For the Hova Antaivato (Antaiva), see note 71 below.

[61] *Ibid.*, pp. 20 and n. 21, 291–292.

pari (rice) and Imerina ceremonies that precede the planting of rice always begin with the incantation "Sambasamba! May the rice. . . ."[62] This term is related by Richardson to the Javanese *sambah* (reverence, homage).[63] The most developed centers of rice cultivation have been Imerina and Betsileo.

At an uncertain time but *before* Andriamanelo, the Vazimba were able to obtain the *antsy* (knives) and *fiadiana* (weapons) made of iron but their number was quite small and only the chiefs had them.[64] From strangers, they also obtained tools used in the working of silver and were noted later among the Hova for the manufacture of *ody* (amulets, charms). Silver ornaments like the *haba* (bracelets), *kavin'antsofina* (earrings) and *masombola* (rings) were buried with the dead, traded for ransom, or given to the Vazimba chiefs.[65] Silver and not gold, as in southern Madagascar, was the noble metal of Imerina. Rafohy and her mother Rangita are said to have been buried in coffins made to resemble silver outriggers.[66] And, some of the later Merina monarchs were buried with huge amounts of silver coins.[67]

Once tradition and geography are brought together, the direction from which the Hova came into Imerina can be discerned. All of the sites connected with the initial Hova penetration are in the southern subdivision of Imerina called *Vakinisisaony.* Apart from the easternmost villages of Fanangoavana and Andrarankasina,[68] the centers of movement and history are near the western boundary of Vakinisisaony, on the right bank of the Sisaony River. They are Alosara, Ambolondaha (later Imeriman-jaka), Ambohijanaka, Ambohitraina, Amboanjobe, Tsiafahy, and Ambo-hitromby.[69] One only has to read the family history of the Andriana of

[62] *Ibid.,* p. 115.

[63] Richardson, *Dictionary,* p. 546.

[64] Savaron, "Contribution" (1928), 64.

[65] *Ibid.,* and Callet, *Tantara,* Vol. I (1953), p. 134. *Haba* is something small in Swahili—Sacleux, *Swahili-français,* Vol. I (1939), pp. 260–261. As a one-piece bracelet in Madagascar it is also called *hosina,* with related African term *hosi* for a woman's scarf. It is curious indeed to note that many terms relating to anything cylindrical in shape (*zinga, maso, kibory*) are Bantu loans.

[66] Savaron, "Farihin-dRangita," 373–374. Since the west-coast Vazimba have been reported by many sources (old and recent) as skilled sweet-water fishermen and sailors, the connection of the outrigger with female rulers of the Vazimba epoch is significant because it points to the knowledge of outriggers among the inland Vazimba who had inhabited the central highlands long before the Hova arrived.

[67] The three monarchs who died between 1810 and 1861 were buried with the total of 340,000 silver piastres—cf. A. and G. Grandidier, *Ethnographie,* p. 43.

[68] *Fanangoavana* (19° 3′ 30″/45° 29′ 25″); *Andrarankasina* (19° 3′ 55″/45° 23′ 10″).

[69] *Alosara* (Hedgehog Thistle, 18° 57′ 25″/45° 12′ 25″); *Imerimanjaka* (Where the Merina Rule, 18° 58′ 40″/45° 11′ 15″); *Ambohijanaka* (Infant Village, 18° 59′ 50″/

Ambohijanaka, collected as a separate monograph by Pierre Pagès,[70] to find a specific confirmation of the wider movement. There were, Savaron was told, two Hova salients, advancing at the *same* time. The Hova clan of *Famelahy* went toward Andrarankasina and Fangoavana, then followed the westward course of the Varahina River, settling finally at Ambohijanaka. The Famelahy Hova were divided into seven subgroups led by the Antaivato, who took up residence at Ambolondaha.[71] The other salient, an advance party of Hova *Zanamihoatra*, reached Ambohitraina, leaving the main body behind, further south, toward Tsiafahy and Ambohitromby. South is thus the direction from which the Hova entered Imerina, their future home. They *had* to cross, at least in part, the lands of Betsileo.

Betsileo kingdoms do not antedate the seventeenth century. Unlike the Merina, Sakalava, or Bara, the Betsileo did not evolve into a single unified state, two vast kingdoms dominated by branches of the same family, or a multiplicity of kingdoms ruled by the same dynastic family.[72] Yet, Betsileo nobility in their four kingdoms or Lalangina, Arindrano, Isandra, and Manandriana have been uniformly called *hova*. The respect for Betsileo *hova* has good claims for being considered a part of what some anthropologists have called the divine kingship complex. It was both *manota fady* (religious transgression) and *masiavi drazana* (usurpation of ancestors) to violate their respect in any way. Punishment could lead even to decapitation.[73] Such violation could be committed in a number of ways: passing improperly in front of a *hova*; failing to render salute to a *hova-bé* (great lord) by sitting on the ground or prostrating oneself (*misava ranoniando*); by eating out of a *hova* plate, called *andapa* (palace object) when being in the owner's dwelling; eating ahead of a *hova*, or tasting food before the First (*mihinana alohambakoka*); con-

---

45° 12′ 5″); *Ambohitraina* (Village of Life, 19° 5″/45° 9′ 40″); *Amboanjobé* (Where the Peanut is Large, 19° 1′ 45″/45° 11′ 25″); *Tsiafahy* (Not to be Besieged, 19° 4′ 40″/45° 12′ 25″); and *Ambohitromby* (Cattle Village, 19° 14′ 20″/45° 12′ 25″).

[70] P. Pagès, *Histoire des Andriana d'Ambohijanaka-ouest de leur origine jusqu'à nos jours* (April 1920), manuscript, pp. 1–52, AM, Library, No. 533.

[71] Savaron, "Contribution" (1928), 63. The Hova subdivisions were: Taivato, Tambohitraivo, Tailoharano, Andavakasakay, Tatanjony, Zanakarivo, and the Tokanidina. Savaron found all of them still in the same general area.

[72] For the history of Betsileo kingdoms of Lalangina, Arindrano, Isandra, and Manandriana, see H.-M. Dubois, *Monographie des Betsileo* (1939), pp. 102–237, and G. Grandidier and R. Decary, *Histoire politique et coloniale*, Vol. V, Tome 3 (1958), pp. 1–19. A number of manuscripts dealing with Betsileo history remain in Malagasy language, the Kingdom of Isandra being the best represented. Two such texts can be cited as relatively important: J. Ralambo, *History of the Land of Isandra* (title translated), two manuscript notebooks in *AAM*; and Rainijoelina, *History of Isandra* (title translated) manuscript, pp. 1–100, on kind loan from *BDP*.

[73] Dubois, *Betsileo*, p. 568.

suming the *voditsena* or *vodi-hena* (rump of cattle), reserved for nobility.[74]

The Betsileo *hova* used a special class of slaves, called *olompady* and subdivided into four functional categories. Two of these were, in essence, guardians of the *hova* tombs. They kept permanent watch or collected and guarded the *kialo hazo*, special wood used in construction of coffins. The class of *ramanga* prevented the spilling of noble blood in cases of cuts by sucking it and chewed the *hova* nails when cut since the nails in Betsileo, too, appear to have had a sacral quality without being kept as relics. Finally, some of the *olompady* were used as supports of the body of a defunct *hova* while it was being bathed. This is another illustration of the quality being assigned to the Betsileo *hova*. It cannot at all be accounted for by way of any "recent borrowing" that could, for example, be attributed to large numbers of Merina migrants who began to settle in Betsileo in the concluding decades of the eighteenth century. Moreover, by that time, the Hova of Imerina were a class of freemen or commoners, a status in force since the time of Ralambo, second Andriana of Imerina.

The Betsileo equivalent of Hova in Imerina was *olompotsy* (commoners, freemen). This name was given—in the seventeenth century— to the Zafindraminia nobility among the Antanosy.[75] One thus obtains an interesting and curious case of progression from the extreme southeast to central Imerina: *olompotsy*, nobility in Antanosy, applied to commoners further north, in Betsileo; and *hova*, term for nobility and rulers in Betsileo, appeared in relation to commoners in Imerina, further north. The *Tantara* of Imerina regard, without ambiguity, the pre-Rafohy period as *mpanjaka Hova* (or period when the Hova ruled). Those of the Betsileo also recall that the Vohitsaomby (the ancient name for the inhabitants of Betsileo plateau) knew a period of *manjaka Hova*, extending further south into the land of Kimoso (present-day Ibara).[76]

While collecting oral traditions in the Ibara province of Betroka, early in this century, Rabemanana heard of some old ruins on the Ibara plateau and the Anteivondro massif. In the district of Ivohibé, he saw ground elevations near the Tsimanatsika River. At first, they "seemed like the work of nature." Rabemanana continued onward and came across the same pattern over four succeeding rivers. All of the elevations followed

---

[74] A. Dandouau, *Moeurs, coutumes et croyances Betsileo* (not dated but composed in the early 1920s), manuscript, pp. 51–56; and Dubois, *Betsileo*, p. 568.

[75] According to Carpeau de Saussay, *Voyage à Madagascar* (1722—but written in 1663), pp. 249–250, *Olompoutchi* (*olona-fotsy*, or white men) was applied to the *Blancs* of both sexes but (and this cannot be stressed strongly *enough*), "*les Blancs ne sont distinguez des Noirs, que par leur tein & leur chevelure; car pour ce qui est du reste, il n'y a point de difference; ils sont les uns & les autres grands, bien faits, marchant bien, fort alerte & tous braves.*"

[76] Rabemanana, *Kimoso*, pp. 39–49.

in the same line of direction.[77] On the left bank of the Iantara, there was an ancient dike, 20 meters wide, constructed with earth and crossing a deep marsh.[78] The valleys of the Iantara, Menarahaka, Ranomena, Sahambano, and Ihosy rivers, wrote Rabemanana, were full of "old sites, surrounded by circular ditches, earthen and stone walls."[79] As far as is known to me, earthen walls have been noted only in Imerina. Streamlets, according to Rabemanana, were dammed in such a way "as to have been once the means of communication over vast stretches of flatlands." The *Tantara* of Callet note that similar works were undertaken on a large scale by Andrianjaka at Alosara, on the Ikopa River, and by his successor, Andriatsitaka, in the great marshes of Betsimitatra.[80] Rabemanana also saw, "to the east of the Ivohibe peak, in the middle of these barrage works, two wooden cores which survived the vagaries of seasons [showing] that there was once a bridge at this point."[81] The only bridge construction in Madagascar, reported by early European sources, was seen by François Martin in the 1660s among the Sihanaka of the Lake Alaotra region, just north of Imerina.[82] The trails of this kind end in the northernmost area of the Sihanaka and the southernmost section of the Bara-Tanala Valley.

The barrage works referred to were locally known as the *tampindronin'Mbihiny*, in memory of Mbihiny, leader of the Andrantsay. The Andrantsay were described by traditions as *malemy volo* (men with supple hair). Three different informants—Bara, Betsileo, and Anteimoro —reported that the Andrantsay were in effect *Ambaniandro*, a name by which inhabitants of Imerina are widely called to this day. "According to the former governor of lower Matitana [Anteimoro], Ramahasitraka-rivo, a lucid historian, the Andrantsay took root on the western side of Imerina."[83] The "tradition states that the civil war which took place between Mbihiny, last Andrantsay chief, and his sister Reniseha, ended in a general migration toward the north. This migration was determined by a marine monster in serpent form, which came from the sea of the south and which brought fear to the land."[84] The *manjaka* Hova in Bet-

[77] *Ibid.*, p. 40.

[78] *Ibid.*, and sketch.

[79] *Ibid.*, p. 39.

[80] Callet, *Tantara*, Vol. I (1953), pp. 521–522.

[81] Rabemanana, *Kimoso*, p. 40.

[82] Martin, *Mémoire*, COACM, Vol. IX (1920), p. 568. "This is," he wrote, "probably the only bridge that existed in the Island of Madagascar."

[83] Rabemanana, *Kimoso*, p. 45. The Andrantsay were first reported in print by Mayeur in 1777 as inhabitants of southern Imerina, with a ruler who was Tananarive's vassal. Hubert Deschamps seems to think that the Andrantsay had *fled* southward, from Imerina. I know of no tradition that holds this.

[84] Rabemanana, *Kimoso*, p. 40.

sileo also ended with a rather long war and the ultimate expulsion of the *malemy volo*.[85]

As an architect who studied different types of construction in the Great Island, A. Jully made the observation that the Merina, Betsileo, and Antanosy dwellings revealed considerable similarities.[86] Because of his theory that an Arab family sired all of the dynasties in Madagascar, this observation was rejected at the turn of this century as unscientific by Arnold Van Gennep, one of the finest among the early anthropologists.[87] Indeed, architectural similarities are extremely tricky when relating them to the origins of a people. Comparative work in Madagascar of this century in many fields of endeavor that are not historical and that rest mainly on synchronic descriptions are unlikely to shed much light on the earlier centuries. What is even worse, it could be very misleading as well. The "basic hut," more or less longer, wider or narrower, higher or lower, with more or less openings, built with one or another type of wood and roofing material, is present from the Cape Sainte-Marie to Diego-Suarez. What may, therefore, be called the broad architectural concept does not amount to a good tool for comparison.[88]

Structural detail and the manner in which it is elaborated might be somewhat more promising. Here, by adding the Bezanozano and the Sihanaka,[89] one could find some grounds to hold that the dwelling complex of the five groups points to some unity. Nonetheless, it would still be most difficult to deduce any patterns of diffusion and chronologies are quite hard to come by. What Van Gennep, however, failed to take into account at least for the Merina and Antanosy dwellings are two types of related historical evidence. There are a number of notes on building arts of Imerina before any European influence could be present. At the same time, some two hundred years before the Merina soldiers invaded the Antanosy, Flacourt described with precision not only the dwellings of Zafindraminia Rohandrian, but also the use of the calendar and ceremonies associated with the inauguration of new homes.[90] European re-

---

[85] See in the Appendix "Political Change in Ibara as Told by Raonimpanany, Chief of Angaty Village" and "Aftermath of an Insurrection," extracts from *Kimoso* by Rabemanana.

[86] A. Jully, "L'Habitation à Madagascar," *NRE*, IV/2 (1898), 909–920.

[87] A. Van Gennep, *Tabou* (1904), p. 122.

[88] One could perhaps exempt here the pointed-roof constructions over the royal tombs among Maroserana-Sakalava, the Andriana of Imerina, and Zafindraminia of Antanosy; certain types of *zomba* (royal enclave) of Iboina Sakalava; and the Vazimba *conic* hut seen by Grandidier in the 1860s.

[89] Cf. Martin, *Mémoir*, *COACM*, Vol. IX (1920), p. 565; and Dumaine, "Voyage fait au pays d-Ancaye dans l'île de Madagascar en 1790," *AV*, IX (1810), 171–173. Ancaye was the older name for land of Bezanozano. François Martin visited the Sihanaka in 1667.

[90] Flacourt, *Histoire*, *COACM*, Vol. VIII (1913), pp. 110–112.

ports on Imerina before the 1820s, when the Merina were expanding southward, reveal a number of analogies that cannot be attributed to sheer accident.[91]

Such suggested links do not rest only on the debatable evidence of the building arts. One of the twelve royal *sampy* (guardian amulets) of Imerina, *Ramahavaly*, is reported by the reliable Flacourt in a list of Antanosy Andriana talismans.[92] The *Tantara* give two versions on the subject of where *Ramahavaly* came from. In one, it originated at Matitana, land of the Anteimoro, was thereafter the very first *sampy* of a Betsileo king, reached Imerina probably by late seventeenth century, and became there one of the four *reni-sampy* (mother protector).[93] In the other version, *Ramahavaly* came from *Rankandriana*, the legendary figure who introduced all of the *ody* (amulets, protective charms) into Imerina along with the art of divination or *sikidy*.[94] Two other sources state that Ramahavaly was brought to Imerina either in the late seventeenth century or else after *ca.* 1770.[95] It is the *function* of Ramahavaly in Imerina that shows, beyond reasonable doubt, why the Antanosy link and the previous passage through Betsileo are confirmed. The role of all of the *ody* and *sampy* was (and is) to protect against misfortune and this is certainly not the specific function in mind. In Imerina, Ramahavaly had two major roles. It could punish any person wishing ill to the monarch, in private or in public, and it screened any outside object introduced into the royal enclave. This role of Ramahavaly in Imerina is analogous to the one it had in Antanosy. But, in Imerina, Ramahavaly was also "ruler over

[91] Cf. Mayeur, "Deuxième Voyage," 40; James Hastie, "Le Voyage de Tananarive en 1817," *BAM*, II (1903), 242–243; and Jean Valette, "L'Imerina en 1822–1823 d'après les journaux de Bojer et d'Hilsenberg," *BM*, XV/227–228 (1965), 322–323. While exploring central and southeastern Madagascar in the late 1860s and early 1870s, Grandidier was able to observe that the "Merina, like the Arabized clans of the southeast, have rather complicated ceremonies for the construction and inauguration of dwellings," A. and G. Grandidier, *Ethnographie*, Vol. III (1917), p. 367. Cf. also Merina Manuscripts in G. Grandidier, *Histoire politique*, pp. 200–206.

[92] Flacourt, *Histoire, COACM*, Vol. VIII (1913), p. 276, under "Ramahavalle."

[93] Callet, *Tantara*, Vol. I (1953), pp. 333, and 425–426; description and uses, pp. 333–336, 384–394. It came to Imerina, say the *Tantara* (p. 384), during the rule of Andrianjaka's successor.

[94] *Ibid.*, pp. 151–159. Ranakandriana is also cited as having passed on to one named Kiboandrano the art of writing but that Kiboandrano was subsequently killed by the *Vorombesimba* (*ibid.*, p. 159 and Vol. III (1958), p. 229).

[95] Cf. William Ellis, *History of Madagascar*, Vol. I (1838), p. 405, who heard it came "about ninety or a hundred years ago" from his London Missionary Society informants who had been to Tananarive; and Merina manuscripts in G. Grandidier, *Histoire politique*, pp. 118–119, which—according to A. and G. Grandidier, *Ethnographie*, Vol. IV, p. 608—claim it was introduced in the time of Andriantsitakatrandriana (1665–1680).

serpents" and a national *sampy* that could arrest epidemics.[96] This connection between royal protector and serpent monarch points without much chance of error to an intermediary agency of the Betsileo, center-area of Madagascar for the belief that nobility and rulers become the *fanany* (serpents) after death.[97] The *fanany* cult, moreover, did not exist either among the Zafindraminia Antanosy or in Imerina of the earliest Andriana.

There are still other suggestive connections. The *mpisorona*, or guardian priests of tombs containing the four ancestors of Rafohy, known collectively as *Ampandranbé* (great ancestors from Ampandrana), have been traditionally Antanosy. Savaron interviewed the last Antanosy *mpisorona*, the grandson of the chief *sampy* guardian (*mpitana sampy*) under Merina queen Ranavalona I (1828–1861).[98] According to the *Tantara*, an entire group of Antanosy came from the south to serve Rabodo (the name of Queen Ranavalona I before her enthronement).[99] The *Tantara* do not reveal the reason or reasons why Ranavalona I entrusted the national *sampy* of Imerina to outsiders. Since her span of rule is accurately known, the connection with Antanosy hired as *mpisorona* would appear to be of recent date. Actually, the advent of Ranavalona I as monarch of Imerina is associated with a wide and powerful anti-European reaction and a desire to return to ancestral practices. This was especially important in the domain of religion and led to deliberate and often bloody elimination of all Christian inroads made by the London Missionary Society since about 1818. Thus, while the use of Antanosy *mpisorona* by Ranavalona I comes only into the 1830s, the memory of an older religious recollection had hardly been dead in Imerina of this time. The *Tantara* note that all of the *ody* and *sikidy* had come to Imerina through Ranakandriana's intermediaries "from whom the Tanosy themselves descend."[100] Although an "ethnic" confusion of Antanosy and Zafindraminia is not uncommon, even if there is no real ground for it, the statement points to the southeastern Antalaotra without

---

[96] Callet, *Tantara*, Vol. I (1953), pp. 334, 389–391; and Ellis, *History*, pp. 405–406.

[97] Callet, *Tantara*, Vol. III (1958), pp. 234–237, give a very detailed and unexcelled account of the *fanany* cult in Betsileo. It is reproduced in English translation in the Appendix below.

[98] Savaron, "Contribution" (1928), 65.

[99] Callet, *Tantara*, Vol. I (1953), p. 28.

[100] Callet, *Tantara*, Vol. I (1953), p. 157. Elsewhere (in *Tantara*, Vol. III (1958), p. 229), it is related that the Antanosy had been in Imerina much earlier and that some had been expelled at an undetermined epoch, fled south, and returned with Ranakandriana's amulets (*ody*). The carrier of the art of writing, Kiboandrano, is said to have been one of them.

question. It is true that the *Tantara* distinguish sometimes between imports from Matitana and Antanosy.[101] More often, however, there is a confusion of the two loci. This is, very probably, not an accident either.

The Merina did not practice *sikidy* by drawing it on the ground or sand (*langabaru alaraina*), originally an Anteimoro specialty, but used instead the grains of *fano* (Accacia).[102] One of the earliest tombs in Imerina, opened after the annexation of Madagascar in 1896, contained a silver amulet "to which were attached six crocodile teeth . . . with cylindrical pieces of wood . . . sometimes with a tooth."[103] Flacourt describes similar amulets that he saw in the area of Fort-Dauphin.[104] There is, also, a most important aspect of linguistic evidence that must not be overlooked. Following an initial analysis by Berthier,[105] Julien and Guenot, who had also worked a number of years on the Arabico-Malagasy manuscripts, found that:[106]

> . . . certain verbal forms, *passive* and especially *relative*, considered for a very long time as modern perfections of the Merina dialect alone, had been current several centuries ago among the groups in the south where, however, the modern Merina cannot be said to have exercised a profound influence.

Together with the archaeological observations of Rabemanana, which are yet to be verified,[107] it can no longer be doubted that Father Malzac's contention in respect to the Hova as being "*une* portion notable *de la* population primitive *immigré dans l'Ile*" rests on firm ground or that the *malemy volo* of traditions given to Rabemanana by his Bara, Betsileo, and Anteimoro informants represent the Hova segment.

The route of Hova migrations into future Imerina led from the general direction of the southeast, through the Ibara plateau and Betsileo. These were gradual migrations. The Hova moved continuously further to the

[101] Callet, *Tantara*, Vol. I (1953), pp. 330–331, 333. Rakelimalaza, first of the twelve *sampy* of Imerina, is associated with Ikalabé, the female who brought it from the southern area of Manambolo and who was considered as great priestess. The Arabico-Malagasy *Sora-bé* reveal consistently that only the Onjatsy living among the Anteimoro allowed women to be religious specialists.

[102] *Ibid.*, p. 35 and n. 46 of the translators.

[103] Charles Renel, "Les Amulettes malgaches: *ody et sampy*," *BAM*, new series, II (1915), 58–59.

[104] Flacourt, *Histoire, COACM*, Vol. VIII (1913), p. 273. The main similarities are crocodile teeth, six to eight in number, and the wooden encasements.

[105] H. Berthier, "Du 'Relatif en Malgache,'" *BAM*, XII/1 (1913), 177–179; and his "Des Participes passifs à suffixe," *BAM*, VI (1908), 37–53.

[106] G. Julien, "*Pages Arabico-Madécasses*," *AASC* (1929), p. 11.

[107] No archaeological work has been carried out in these localities and even suggestions for aerial photography have yet to be followed up. There is no reason to doubt the sketches and observations of Rabemanana, however.

north. On the whole, the reason for this continual movement was that the Hova encountered circumstances that were not conducive to permanent settlement until they arrived among the Vazimba. Here, as will be shown, the circumstances were to turn in favor of the Hova, for very special reasons. In their passage northward, which lasted a long time, the *tompontany* groups that the Hova came into contact with along the way had no powerful states. The *malemy volo* were thus able to remain in different localities without political arrangements and without much exogamy until sufficient conflict developed, led to "civil wars," and were resolved by means of yet further migration. But, at least the initial impulse for the Hova to abandon the southern plateau where they had remained long enough to develop an economic structure, can be attributed to some form of Antalaotra pressure, attested by the *fananimpitulaha,* or monster serpent, invariably associated with the Antalaotra as the early Anteimoro past has already more than suggested. This pressure appears in the area adjacent to the Bara-Tanala Valley and the Ivohibé Gap, which provide a break through the eastern escarpment and allow an easy passage into the interior. Moreover, the early inroads of Antalaotra Muslims among the Tanala offer convincing support in this case. But, what does not follow at all is that the Zafindraminia and Hova can be regarded as kin of any kind or that the Zafindraminia ancestors provided the Hova with their Andriana in Imerina or beforehand.

Prior to the arrival of Rangita and Rafohy (sometimes recalled as Rangita's daughter and sometimes as her sister) at Ambolondaha, southern Imerina had been familiar for some time with attempts at some form of *mpanjaka Hova.* Its beginnings, no more than its evolution for some time, hardly amount to a stabilizing force. The Hova Famelahy and Zanamihoatra were not only displacing the Vazimba *tompontany* from the Ambohijanaka Valley. They also fought among themselves. The Vazimba had their own chiefs and self-sufficient economy, and if, as the *Tantara* say, "with the Vazimba no agreement is possible" (*tsy mahay fanaraka*),[108] the Hova at least tried to reduce their own internal disagreement by first partitioning (*fifanarahana*) the Ambohijanaka Valley. Yet, the future Imerina of that time comprised peoples other than the Vazimba.

Sometime before Rangita and Rafohy, possibly at the turn of the sixteenth century, a group of "sages" and "astrologers" penetrated Imerina from the south. They assumed the role of intermediaries between the Hova and the Vazimba. This is attested by the names by which these sages and astrologers were known—*Andriamampitovy* (noble who established equality), *Andriantsiazoambakaina* (noble who knows ahead what

[108] Savaron, "Contribution" (1928), 64.

is on the mind), or *Andrianitovina* (noble by whom equality gets established).[109] It is further confirmed by an important meeting between local chiefs who decided that Rafohy's immediate ancestors should descend the Sisaony River while the northern and northwestern Imerina were to be left to the Vazimba.[110] The four ancestors of Rafohy thus took up residence at Ampandrana, a village *west* of Ambohitraina. Of this, too, there is no doubt, regardless of skepticism concerning oral history because their tombs not only exist but also have been traditional sites of pilgrimage as recently as the 1920s.[111]

From Ampandrana, say the *Tantara*, came all of the *fanjakana* (government). It was a place where princes ruled by *fenitra* (covenant). The idea and institution of *fanjakana ifanoavana* (sovereign and vassal) and of the *kabary* (discourse in public assembly) started there.[112] But, *kabary* proved a disaster in the beginning. By modifying the *fenitra* to give vassal chiefs a public voice, the principal chief (the sovereign over all others), was overshadowed by a vocal but minor chief named Baroa, and all authority collapsed. This period is recalled by tradition and proverb as either *fanjakana Baroa* (government by anarchy) or the "times of Baroa" (lack of government).[113] These early impulses toward more centralized authority at Ampandrana and the resumption of local Hova-Vazimba wars, served to unite the elders of Ampandrana with the Hova, and some 1000 warriors were assembled. They then attacked the Vazimba and waged a two-day battle. Defeated, the Vazimba fled toward Alosara, but they were intercepted by the Famelahy and wiped out. "At this moment," Savaron was told, the *"Merina* and the Hova were united under the authority of Ampandra, the Merina elders."[114] It is thus revealed by local traditions that the Merina, who now appear in them, far from being Hova, represent a mixture of original Vazimba and descendants of the sages and astrologers who had settled and intermarried among them. Western Vakinisisaony changed hands at this point and the Merina, whose elders, or *andriana*, had been hitherto neutral, threw their lot in with the Hova to the mutual benefit of both parties. The Vazimba were, nevertheless, still masters of northern Imerina, the southern Vakinisisaony was still full of them. By warfare and diplomacy, it would take another century to conquer, expel, and absorb the Vazimba. Andriamanelo, Ralambo, and Andrianjaka would certainly finish what the Hova had started but not

---

[109] *Tantara*, Vol. I (1953), pp. 28–29.

[110] Savaron, "Contribution" (1928), 65.

[111] *Ibid.*

[112] Callet, *Tantara*, Vol. I (1953), pp. 18, 540; Savaron, "Contribution" (1928), 65–66.

[113] Callet, *Tantara*, Vol. I (1953), p. 19.

[114] Savaron, "Contribution" (1928), 67.

necessarily, entirely or always to the advantage of the Hova themselves. And, during the time span in which they ruled,[115] there would gradually come into being the entity we call today the *Merina*. At its base would be the Hova, commoners whose somatological features and a great deal of material culture reflect Indonesia in the most pronounced Malagasy form. Yet, its *fanjakana* (government), *andriana* dynasty, and its special monarchical culture were no gifts from the Hova. To understand this, one must study the features in their context. Anything less would lead to the postulation of a past from the present, an enterprise that has already hidden so much of the Malagasy past and that must be discontinued altogether—or, else, it must be tightly controlled.

The *Tantara* tell of predetermined succession rule based on primogeniture. But, this *fanjakana arindra* (governmental equilibrium) is largely stated as an ideal feature of society. In reality, "chiefs of the land came [first] together and reached agreement over the heir, announcing at the same time both the death of a king that had passed away and the name of the successor [but] when there are two pretenders, the one not elected was killed along with his followers, prejudged guilty of high treason and revolt."[116] These were, on the whole, the real rules of succession and interregnum, and they span the entire history of Merina monarchy, from Andriamanelo, whose younger brother was "killed by the people," to Ranavalona I (1828–1861), who had ordered her officers to kill all the nobles related to Radama I (1810–1828) as potential heirs to the throne.[117] And, Ranavalona I herself was no daughter of Radama I.

---

[115] In earlier literature, four genealogical dates have been advanced for the first three Merina monarchs—or Andriamanelo, Ralambo, and Andrianjaka, in that order:

MALZAC	ABINAL	A. GRANDIDIER	JULLY
1540–1575	1567–1587	1590–1615	1605–1625
1575–1610	1587–1607	1615–1640	1625–1645
1610–1630	1607–1627	1640–1665	1645–1665

Cf. Malzac, *Royaume Hova* (1912), p. 31; A. Abinal, *Vingt ans à Madagascar* (1885), pp. 54–55; A. Grandidier, *Ethnographie*, pp. 83–85; and A. Jully, "Origine des Andriana," *NRE*, IV (1898), 890–898. With the exception of Malzac in the case of Ralambo, all four adhered to the "twenty-year" generation idea. Abinal can be left out completely. He obtained the dates by taking the lowest one advanced and the highest, added them together and then divided the sum total by the factor of two (1530 + 1605 = 3135 : 2 = 1567). Grandidier and Jully are closer to the mark. The *Tantara* unanimously attribute very old age to Ralambo. Rangita and Rafohy would thus cover a period of ±1550 to ±1590.

[116] Merina Manuscripts, cited in G. Grandidier, *Histoire politique*, p. 47, n. 2, notule a. See also V. Malzac, "Ordre de succession au trône chez les Hova," *NRE*, VI (1900), 607–618.

[117] For the fratricide, see Callet, *Tantara*, Vol. I (1953), p. 125. Radama's sister, her husband and their son Rakotobé (designated by Radama as his successor),

Sometimes, a monarch dictated his own choice. Ralambo, for example, selected his *younger* son, Andrianjaka, as successor. Radama I was also the personal choice of his father Andrianampoinimerina (d. 1810). According to an 1815 report, Radama had *two* older brothers, Raboudolahe and Mavoulahe. The first was shot to death by the father, while Mavoulahe, his wife, and his son were put to death by royal order.[118] Andrianjaka was himself born to Ralambo's first wife (*vadi-bé*) but only after his second wife (*vadi-kely*) had given birth to another son. The *vadi-bé* —and this should be stressed—was a daughter of a still powerful *Vazimba* chief from Ambohidrabiby and the marriage gave Andrianjaka a secure base while the Vazimba were being expelled from the north.[119]

Incest as well as features of divine kingship complex (which both Murdock and Deschamps attribute to Africa) mark the genesis of the Merina monarchy. Ralambo's own niece became his *vadi-kely* (second spouse) and she was the granddaughter of Andriamanelo's murdered brother.[120] If an informed European could state in the nineteenth century that "it is not the son of ruler who mounts the throne as such but the male offspring of his closest female relative and hence the king marries ordinarily the daughter of his own sister,"[121] the *Tantara* are quite specific that the "origin of marriages for which [special] purification [*afana*] was necessary" goes back to Ralambo.[122] "Not to displace authority, inter-

---

Radama's mother, and a number of first cousins were put to death. Most of these cousins were provincial governors. One of them, Ramanetaka, escaped to the Comoros from his gubernatorial post in Iboina. I am informed that Ramanetaka's personal *Journal*, written in Arabico-Malagasy, has been found and contains extremely interesting data.

[118] Baron d'Unienville, "Essai sur Madagascar," in his *Statistique de l'Ile Maurice et ses dépenedances*, Vol. III (1838), p. 287. The *Tantara*, Vol. IV (1958), pp. 860, 878–879, bear out the report of d'Unienville, written in November 1815 (the original manuscript [1–149] is in *ANSOMCM*, Carton X, Dossier II). It would appear that at least one of Radama's younger brothers, Rahovy, was put to death, *cf.* Leguével de Lacombe, *Voyage*, Vol. I (1840), p. 158, n.; and J. Valette, "L'Imerina en 1822–1823," *BM*, XV (1965), 334 and n. 3, which is Valette's own. Valette's doctoral dissertation deals with the rule and person of Radama I (1810–1828).

[119] *Ambohidrabiby* (Village of Rabiby, 18° 30′ 46″/45° 15′). According to the *Tantara*, this village had an earlier name or *Ankotrokotroka*. *Ra* is a personal article of respect (comparable to personal *I-*). It also means blood and often denotes kinship. The term *biby* has many meanings in Malagasy—"an animal, an insect; something extraordinary; in some provinces it is used in speaking of the petty king, and in others of the wives of such; it is also used of children in Imerina, *fig.* sensual, beastly," Richardson, *Dictionary* pp. 89–90. In some Swahili dialects, *biby* is used in addressing female spouses, in others (e.g., Ki-Amu and Ki-Gunya) it means grandfather (in the general sense of elder). *Rabiby* is believed to have been one of the last Vazimba chiefs in Vakinisisaony.

[120] Callet, *Tantara*, I (1953), 273.

[121] D'Unienville, "Essai," in *Statistique*, p. 286.

[122] Callet, *Tantara*, Vol. I (1953), p. 273.

dictions do not affect such a marriage [as for] the sovereign no interdiction exists because power cannot be inherited by others [but] among the people, if maternal cousins marry, the king and the people say 'kill them, for they are sorcerers.' "[123] It is not very difficult to perceive that (royal) *incest* in Imerina was a feature borrowed from the pre-existing society and that once it became a monarchical property, the Andriana did everything to make a monopoly of it.

Not only in the afterlife, but also while living, the new monarchs came to be eventually the *Andriamanitra hita maso* (divinity visible to the eye), deriving from *Zanahary* (God) both extranatural powers and the *hasina* (sacral personal quality) which "entitles them to unusual honors and privileges."[124] Their divine quality:[125]

> . . . *devait dès lors désigner les rois comme les intermédiaires rêvés entre le peuple et la divinité; aussi sont-ils souvent dénommé* mpisolon-Andriamanitra *(ceux qui remplacent Dieu). Là se trouve l'origine du culte particulier rendu aux anciens souverains et surtout à ceux d'entre eux qui surent d'une manière plus particulière s'implanter dans la mémoire du peuple. La personne du roi étant d'essence divine, ce qui lui a appartenu, ce qui a été en contact avec sa personne, revêt un caractère divin; le roi disparu subsiste dans ces objets, d'où la puissance attribuée notamment à la terre où son corps fut déposé. Une parcelle quelconque de ce qui a été en contact avec lui peut constituer un solo (représentant) qui jouira des mêmes pouvoirs que la personne elle-même.*

Three times during the year of mourning, subjects of the defunct monarch had to shave their heads, could not bathe in streamlets, wash their hands or feet, or do the laundry.[126] But, while the divinization of dead andriana appears with Ralambo as a manifestation of the cult of ancestors, it is not transferred to the *living* andriana until Andrianjaka, the *third* king of the new dynasty in Imerina.

The advent of ironworking in Imerina cannot be seen as originating with the Hova since two distinct traditions attribute it to Rafohy's husband, Ramanihimanjaka, who exploited the "mines" or deposits of iron at some 40 kilometers from present-day Tananarive.[127] The anonymous *Tantara*, discovered in the papers of the late André Dandouau, even

[123] *Ibid.*, p. 294.

[124] *Ibid.*, pp. 13 and n. 7 by Callet, 655–665; also Merina Manuscripts in G. Grandidier; *Histoire politique*, pp. 129–131 on rank of nobility and their privileges (*Ny fahandrianany Andriana*).

[125] M. Fontoynont, "Solo Célèbres en Imerina," *BAM*, XII/1 (1913), 115–116.

[126] Callet, *Tantara*, Vol. I (1953), p. 488; and Merina Manuscript in G. Grandidier, *Histoire politique*, pp. 262–263, following Andrianjaka's death.

[127] Savaron, "Contribution" (1928), 69 (Andrianmanelo's *uncle* according to Savaron); an independent confirmation of this is given by Lt. Lefebvre, "Les Mandiavatos," *NRE*, IV/2 (1898), 865. In this tradition, he is Ralambo's "grandfather."

mention the names of the first two smiths.[128] Thus, until Rafohy, no known tradition gives iron to the Hova. What is even more convincing, the numerous battles between the Vazimba and Hova were inconclusive to the extent that there can be no doubt that neither of the two groups knew iron *weapons* until Andriamanelo's time. Andriamanelo was the first of the andriana to adapt iron to warfare and equip his Hova levies with the iron spears against which the Vazimba clay heads were no match.[129] Without this adaptation, local history might have gone in another direction. Hence, iron, as much as the need for political centralization, explains why the Hova accepted the Merina elders as their own *andriana.* Andriamanelo and his brother were the first to construct fortifi-

---

[128] *Développement du Royaume Hova,* manuscript, p. 1. They were *Andriandranando* and *Rabesaliva. Saly vy* is an iron grill (*vy =* iron + *saly =* spit.) *Rabe* is a common male name in Imerina. *Andriandranando* is the designation of the fifth of the seven noble classes in Imerina. It was established as *third* by Ralambo himself in the hierarchy of noble clans or classes but fell to the sixth rank by the time of Andriamasinavalona (1696–1740). By that time, however, the knowledge of iron working was widespread.

[129] Callet, *Tantara,* Vol. I (1953), pp. 27, 126.

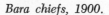

Bara chiefs, 1900.

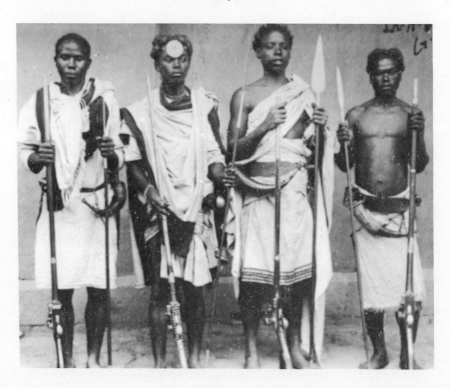

cations at Alosara. That they did not introduce fortifications into Imerina can be seen from the fact that these are nowhere described by the *Tantara* beyond a round ditch.[130] As for circumcision, Malzac's interpretation is correct because Andriamanelo—by circumcising his two sons in public—applied a *local* and apparently very old custom to the *royal family* for the first time.[131] It is clear that apart from divinized live kingship and features associated with it, a great deal more has been taken from the pre-Hova society.

When various sources discuss and describe aspects of divine kingship in Imerina, which marks the new andriana dynasty, they do so in a collective sense and manner. Thus, the weakness of oral traditions in terms of an accurate chronology is compounded by synchronism of written materials. The impression one gains under such conditions simply perpetuates the pernicious Myth of the White Chief, pernicious because it does not really emanate from the Malagasy antecedents but from Europeans obsessed with the pigmental inferiority of the darker races and because it still constitutes a powerful legacy in Madagascar of today, submerged though it is in the psyche. And its survival is by no means minimized by the tenet that political and cultural changes are inseparable and that hence outsiders, lighter in pigment and superior in culture, appear in Imerina of yore, create a state, and become divine kings from the outset. The fundamental error of Malzac was to identify the Hova *with* the Merina and argue that the same "composite" people inhabited Imerina for some quarter of a millennium (1300–1550). Suddenly, around 1550, two quite distinct groups of people, Hova and Vazimba (and all traditions agree on this point) face one another in hostility amid radical changes. It was this clear contradiction that led Alfred Grandidier to "find" his would-be Javanese-Malays, who appear at the proper moment in time and impose a superior culture on the Vazimba. For this, he needed to eliminate the Hova as "medieval" migrants and argue secondly—and not without linguistic justification—that the term *hova* was a name given to *tompontany* chiefs.[132] There is hardly a doubt that *hova* had never been a meaningful ethnic name.

Not just one or two items from the past, but a whole series of them show that the Merina from Ampandrana must have once been a cross between Vazimba women and Antalaotra migrants who had brought with them knowledge of ironworking and had introduced both the Arabic calendar and *sikidy*. By the advent of the new *andriana* dynasty, these

---

[130] *Ibid.*, p. 125.

[131] *Ibid.*, pp. 135–136.

[132] A. Grandidier, *Ethnographie*, p. 80. Although no dictionary references are cited, *hoa* would seem to mean to plan, initiate, or undertake in "classical" Polynesian, while *houa* was a title of chiefs in the Tonga Islands.

generic Merina must have been physically pure Vazimba and can never be confused with the Hova. *Rangita's* own name, which means noble with woolly hair, suggests this. But, Alfred Grandidier himself stated in one single sentence of a large volume that the *"Andriana as well as the Hova of Imerina are all in accord that, indeed, the five chiefs of Ampandrana were pure Vazimba."*[133] Only the theoretical framework of Grandidier prevented him from perceiving the true nature of this commonly held tradition—namely, that the andriana dynasty was closer to Vazimba roots than any other. And, it would be absolutely impossible to understand the internal history of the Merina state in the eighteenth and nineteenth centuries by confusing the Merina-Andriana and the Hova.[134] The Merina monarchy was not created by any sudden wave of outsiders. It evolved out of a real local necessity to cope with two contemporary and simultaneous types of conflict, among the Hova themselves and between the Hova and Vazimba. Because of the intermediary position of the Ampandrana, the Ampandrana under either of the two circumstances could have earned themselves an elite position. Together, they were hard to resist since major conflicts in any society tend to force even the most neutral of men into the taking of sides. With more advanced ideas about *fanjakana,* with their old role of astrologers and sages, and with the knowledge of

---

[133] *Ibid.,* p. 78.

[134] Modern writers have generally avoided this "delicate" topic (the Hova and Andriana provide most of the educated Malagasy, many of whom are members of the Académie Malgache, considered a high honor in Tananarive, or else writers, publicists, amateur historians. They are touchy about the past as many wish to perceive it, hence the reluctance of delving into this topic). Nonetheless, two recent works can be cited, one a bad piece of neo-Marxist "history," Pierre Boiteau, *Madagascar: contribution à l'histoire de la nation malgache* (1958), pp. 68–169; and the far more serious and scholarly one by Georges-Sully Chapus and Gustave Mondain, *Rainilaiarivony: Un homme d'etat malgache* (1953), *passim.* The middle of the nineteenth century marks the coming to power of the Hova (commoner) family and lineage of Andafy-Avaratra (now the name of the presidential palace in Tananarive), beginning with the chief minister of Ranavalona I, Rainiharo, and extending to Rainilaiarivony, chief minister under three successive queens of Imerina and the husband of Ranavalona II and Ranavalona III. The Hova, who had risen in Imerina during the first two Andriana, began to lose out with Andrianjaka in the seventeenth century. They regained much of the lost ground in government after about the 1720s and then suffered their worst downgrading under Andrianampoinimerina in the 1780s. Many of his public *Kabary* attack the Hova explicitly. Some sections of the *305 Articles' Code* of the Merina state in the nineteenth century reflect struggle between Merina-Andriana and the Hova. Cf. "Le Code des 305 articles," *NRE,* VI (1900), 93–186, particularly articles 59–63 and 113; Malzac, *Royaume Hova* (which is a misnomer title), pp. 65–238, 322–502; Callet, *Tantara,* Vol. III (1953), pp. 3–36; 45–48, and Vol. IV (1958), pp. 348–826, 873–910. Some of Andrianampoinimerina's new power rested on the *tsiarondahy,* or royal slaves, taken from the *mainty* (blacks), inhabitants of Imerina ranking below the Hova but above the slave class, or *andevo.* Sometimes the term *mpanjaka Hova* is used specifically for the period of Rainilaiarivony, or roughly the last four decades of the nineteenth century.

ironworking, a response to the need for central authority promised even greater rewards.[135]

The secular bases for the Merina state were established by Ralambo. "In the Andriana," Ralambo saw the "source from which the Merina took the princes who served them."[136] He instituted four noble castes. Three were known collectively as the *Andrianteloray* (nobility of three distinct fathers), and the fourth as *Zafindralambo* (descendants of Ralambo), to whom exogamy was forbidden.[137] In Ralambo's own time, the Andrianteloray did not have any special privileges. They served the ruler and were rewarded by him. Subsequent rulers of Imerina added three more noble castes.[138] Under Ralambo, a capitation tax, the *vadin-aina* (or price of secure life) was imposed for the first time and appears to have been used largely to support a small standing army of the *lakato* (true outriggers), who fought small expansion battles against the Vazimba.[139] The first firearm in Imerina is also traced back to Ralambo's time and was used to repel a combined Sihanaka-Bezanozano force.[140] Cattle, which until Ralambo had served mainly for work in the rice fields and for ritual sacrifices, began to be slaughtered for consumption and became a new source of meat diet. Ralambo is said to have reserved the hump (as highest peak) and the rump (as end piece) for himself and hence for royalty. But, the custom of *mandoa vody hena any andriana* (pay the king with rump) existed as a form of tribute in much of old Madagascar.

The claims of Grandidier and Malzac that *no* linguistic change took place in Imerina with the advent of the Andriana-Merina dynasty is by no means sustained by the *Tantara*, on which both European students relied. The term *Imerina* is said to have been coined by Ralambo.[141] The *Tantara* say also that a number of sites were *renamed* by him but recall

---

[135] Had the Hova *not* arrived, it is very probable that the Ampandrana elders would never have been the *andriana* of Imerina.

[136] Callet, *Tantara*, Vol. I (1953), p. 294. For the derivation of the name *Merina*, in reality a case of dialectical borrowing, see text below and note 161.

[137] *Ibid.*, pp. 287–290. Ralambo also created smith groups, with their own heads, and subdivided them into silversmiths (*Zanakaandrian-komahitsy*) and ironsmiths or *Zanakandrianfatsy*. Much later, the ironsmiths were incorporated into the Merina army.

[138] The noble castes of Imerina were, more or less, finalized through last additions by *Andriamasinavalona* (1696–1740). There are altogether seven castes recognized as constituting all of Imerina's nobility: *Zanakandriana, Zazamarolahy, Andriamasinavalona, Andriantompokoindrindra, Andrianamboninolona, Andriandranando,* and *Zandralambo.*

[139] Anonymous, *Développement du Royaume Hova*, manuscript, pp. 15–16. It seems that Andrianjaka was placed by Ralambo as head of the *lakato*, a practice duplicated later by some of the monarchs either for a chosen heir (to toughen him in battle) or rejected sons (to blame them for military defeats and thus make them "unworthy" of the throne).

[140] Callet, *Tantara*, Vol. I (1953), p. 275.

[141] *Ibid.*, pp. 284–285.

only two—Mamiomby and Langana.[142] The names of cattle, or *jamoka*, and sheep, or *besavily*, were changed respectively to *omby* and *ondry*.[143] These changes, it is worth stressing, constitute only what is remembered in the *Tantara*. *Omby* and *ondry* are, of course, Bantu terms for cattle and sheep, but the etymons of *jamoka* and *besavily* have not been resolved.[144] It is not possible to determine if the use of *i-* as a place-prefix

[142] *Ibid.*, p. 282.

[143] *Ibid.*, pp. 280–282, 284.

[144] See J.-C. Hébert, "Les Noms d'animaux en Malgache," *CM*, I/1 (1964), 311–312, 314, 379, 382.

Hazomanga in 1900.

allows for no antecedents prior to Ralambo's time since no maps of Imerina this early are available.[145] *Langana* may or may not be Malagasy.[146] The term *mamiomby* could have been applied to the site where cattle was first consumed.[147] At any rate, much more intensive research will have to be carried out in respect to dialectical and other types of borrowing for the Imerina after about 1600.

Neither Callet's *Tantara* nor other recorded traditions state or convey directly or by inference that Ralambo was a divine king. On the contrary, the *Tantara* depict Ralambo as a ruler who had sought to be popular by being a kind of "peasant monarch" to coin a term.[148] Moreover, *Rakelimalaza, Rafanataka,* and *Manjakatsiroa,* the earliest three of the twelve *sampy* of Imerina, and all three adopted by Ralambo "from the south," were not the exclusive protectors of its monarchy. Rakelimalaza was both a military *sampy,* in battles with the Vazimba, and an agent with which to control weather in connection with the planting of rice.[149] Rafanataka shielded against the Vazimba spears, and Manjakatsiroa protected both the king and his subjects against electrocutions by lightning, a not infrequent danger.[150]

The most important innovation associated with Ralambo was the *fandroana,* often called *taona tsara indrindra* or the best moment of the year. The literal translation of *fandroana* is bath. Reduced to its main ritual and simplest explanation of its meaning, the *fandroana* consisted of the sprinkling of water that symbolized the purification of the king and the people at the end of each year and the ushering in of the new one. This is why it is sometimes qualified as the "ceremony of the New Year." The *fandroana* lasted from the time of Ralambo until the fall of the Merina monarchy, shortly before the turn of this century. As it evolved in time, *fandroana,* however, is an extremely complex institution to describe. It was connected at the same time to the ancestral cult, agriculture, renovation of royal *hasina* (sacral quality), numerous *fady* (interdictions), attempts to arrest infanticide, and, at various times, to mundane manipulation.[151] Almost certainly, the *fandroana* acted as an annual

---

[145] The first *important* map of Imerina was made by Alfred Grandidier in the 1870s.

[146] *Langa* is Malagasy lofty. See also note 80 and text in Chapter V, above.

[147] *Mamy* is sweet in Malagasy, conveying delicious in taste, Richardson, *Dictionary,* p. 413. Callet's *Tantara,* I (1953), p. 282, state "At Mamiomby Ralambo tasted the meat of cattle."

[148] Callet, *Tantara,* Vol. I (1953), pp. 272–306. Under Ralambo the conflict between the Hova and the Vazimba seems to have lessened as well but this would be reversed by Andrianjaka.

[149] *Ibid.,* p. 330.

[150] *Ibid.,* p. 333.

[151] The most perceptive attempt to deal with the *fandroana* as a total cultural feature remains the sixty-page pamphlet, written in Strasbourg but published in

solvent of social stress. It also constitutes tangible proof of an early Islamic import into Imerina. The New Year in Imerina began after the month of Alohotsy (or Arabic Ramadan) at the advent of the new moon, on the first day of Alahamady (the Arab Shawual). The Merina fasted during the entire month of Alohotsy.[152] This practice was abandoned by the middle of the nineteenth century. In 1870, Alfred Grandidier was an eyewitness to an exact equivalent of the *fandroana* ritual among the Antambahoaka of Mananjary.[153] In Grandidier's time, the Ankara of the Anteimoro followed it as well. Even Etienne de Flacourt observed, on August 23, 1653, the Roandriana Antanosy in the bath ceremony.[154] In effect, among the southeastern Antalaotra as a whole, the ninth month of the year (Ramadan) was the time of *mifehivava* (closed mouth, or period of fasting). It was also customary among the Zafindraminia of Antanosy and in Imerina to decapitate fowl on New Year's Day and sprinkle blood on dwellings, but this did not occur among the Anteimoro.

All of these important features were adopted and adapted by the Andriana-Merina monarchy before the Vazimba had been displaced by the Hova as the core population group in Imerina, the point at which the old society began to recede deeper and deeper into the background. The oral tradition reveals this in connection with the once firmly entrenched institution of *ziva*, or joking relationship, well described by Hébert for west-coast groups, including the Vazimba who did survive there.[155] According to the texts of Callet, the old Vazimba of Imerina were "great jokers," but this brand of humor appeared as "insulting" to the Andriana and was not "understood" by the Hova.[156] Even if Ralambo's

---

Tananarive, by G. Razafimino, *La Signification religieuse du fandroana ou de la Fête du nouvel an en Imerina* (1924). Louis Molet's *Le Bain royal à Madagascar* (1955), solid in some aspects, is somewhat too broad, and at least one of its major conclusions may well be ill-founded altogether. See also Callet, *Tantara*, Vol. I (1953), pp. 301–329, for the *fandroana* as depicted by oral tradition.

[152] Known also by its other name Volampadina, or month of the fast. The *Tantara*, Vol. I (1953), p. 59, also say that both the sovereign and the people could do no work in the month of Alohotsy.

[153] A. and G. Grandidier, *Ethnographie*, Vol. III (1917), pp. 411–412. See also C. Colins, "The Fandroana or Annual Festival of the Taimoro," *AA*, VI (1898), 149–151.

[154] E. de Flacourt, *Relation de la grande isle Madagascar* (1661), in *COACM*, Vol. IX (1920), p. 157, and his *Histoire*, *COACM*, Vol. VIII (1913), pp. 104–109 for the Antanosy Zafindraminia Ramadan.

[155] J.-C. Hébert, "Parente a plaisanterie à Madagascar," *BM*, VIII/142–143 (1958), 182–216, 268–335.

[156] Callet, *Tantara*, Vol. I (1953), p. 13. The old *ziva* had been lost in Imerina by the nineteenth century. It is clear that the Hova had no familiarity with it and that the Andriana could not well accept it while trying to build an elevated concept of monarchy. The *fandroana*, on the other hand, partly filled the role of *ziva*, which was to reduce social tensions through "palship."

own death was mourned for a whole year, his burial had to take place at night, and the first of seven royal mausoleums, or *trano masina* (sacred homes), was erected over the royal tomb—all features pointing to increasing distance between the monarch and commoners—the really sharp differentiation between the people and the andriana developed a generation or two later. Andriana circumcision ceremonies were now conducted with greater pomp; silver chains were introduced along with dances and chants.[157] Justice became much harsher. The poison trial by ordeal through *tanghin* (T. *venenifera*), administered until then to the roosters, was applied to people by Andrianjaka's officers. The number of deaths increased apparently to such a degree that mass administration of *tanghin* was abandoned altogether for some time to come.[158] With Andrianjaka, the elevation of a deceased monarch to divinity was transferred to the living one. The *Tantara*, which nowhere in the island "speak ill" of the kings gone by, hint in numerous and round-about ways that while Ralambo was "loved," Andrianjaka was feared.

With this combination of all the sources with which to reconstruct Imerina's past before about 1700, it is no longer necessary to advocate any great mysteries or advance so many optional "explanations" that everything remains possible and nothing much more becomes known. To do so would be to transfer the cult of ancestors to history itself and transform a discipline that can only renovate itself through progress into a religion which aims at stability. The Hova were, without question, an important segment of early Malagasy, encapsulated somewhere in the southern plateaus. There is a very high degree of probability that the Hova represent the only *pure* Indonesian element in Madagascar, that they were once far more widespread, particularly in the southern half of the island, and that, as in the case of *most* Malagasy,[159] their "tribal" name, which attached itself only where the Hova could maintain a numerical concentration,[160] had nothing to do with an ethnic origin

[157] A. and G. Grandidier, *Ethnographie*, Vol. III (1917), p. 602, n. 2, 603.

[158] Some traditions attribute the introduction of both the poison ordeal and the *tsobo*, ordeal by boiling water, to the turn of the eighteenth century. On the subject of poison ordeal, see: G.-S. Chapus, "Le Tanguin," *BAM*, new series, XVII (1946), 157–188; Callet, *Tantara*, Vol. IV (1958), p. 904; and J. Valette, "Note sur l'utilisation du tanguin en Imerina en 1830," *BM*, XV/225 (1965), 173–175.

[159] The exceptions, both likely and highly probable, are few and involve associations with nearby Africa, not the earlier Indonesian antecedents: Anteimoro/Temoro/Temuru/*Temur*; Manancarunga/Mokaranga/*Karanga*; Sakalava/*Saka-lava*; Bara/*Mbara*, *Iambara*, *Barue*, *Barwe*; Vinda/*Venda*; Sakoambé/*Sacumbe*; Ajungones, Quisaju, and Kimosi (now extinct as original peoples).

[160] Groups named *Hova* and *Hovalahi ny Antara* are found even today in Ibara, but they do not resemble the Hova of Imerina. It is, nonetheless, significant that the only groups so named outside Imerina are found approximately in the same area where Rabemanana's informants placed the *malemy volo*.

outside Madagascar. No more than other contemporaries much darker in pigment, with "fuzzy" or "woolly" hair and non-Mongoloid physical features, the Hova were no state builders of the old Island society. Like most of the other Malagasy ethnicities, the Hova tried to preserve their group distinction, and like many other Malagasy they found that it was often necessary to migrate elsewhere for this very reason. This natural tendency toward group cohesion was probably facilitated not by any radical distinction from other local cultures, but by less common somatological and pigmental features of the *Malemy volo*. But, untold numbers of the Hova must have been absorbed by other Malagasy in the course of time. Equally, the genesis of the name *Merina* may well be traced back in time. It is reflected in the term *Marinh* applied, as Flacourt has told us, to the chiefs and nobility of the Antanosy society in which the Zafindraminia duplicated the same hierarchy.[161] Thus, it is very probable that the sages and astrologers who came to Imerina from the south applied *Marinh* to the existing Vazimba chiefs and nobility with whom they intermarried to become eventually the elders of Ampandrana.

Looking at Imerina of the nineteenth and twentieth centuries, its European students tended to transpose it back into time and iron out all the incongruous wrinkles that disassociated the past from the present. As can be easily calculated, the Merina state under Andrianjaka did not exceed 60 square kilometers. Even in the first half of the 1700s it was not much more than double this size. It was weakened through a partition. Reunited under Andrianampoinimerina (1787–1810), it began to extend its own borders to the size of present-day Imerina and spilled out considerably beyond under Radama I (1810–1828). By the 1870s, it could claim, at least in theory, a dominion over almost two-thirds of the Great Island, roughly the size of France herself. This spectacular success, attained to a very large extent through the Anglo-Merina alliance, is in very marked contrast to the importance of Imerina in Madagascar prior to more recent times. It is virtually impossible to discern this simple fact of relatively *recent* past either from the reading of Merina oral traditions or from the histories of Merina written by Europeans, for the printed monuments to the Merina are a reflection of the importance that the Merina attained since about 1800.

The monumental *Tantara* of Callet allot a mere thirty-three pages directly to the Vazimba and their "epoch" out of the total 1,732 pages printed so far. Yet, a careful reading of the first *Tantara* volume, along with all of the available sources beyond them, lead to the inevitable

---

[161] Flacourt, *Histoire, COACM*, Vol. VIII (1913), pp. 25–27, 78–81; also text and note 90 in Chapter 3. The term *Marinh* means The Just and derives from *arina* (balance, equity). One should recall that the names of early sages and astrologers have this very concept in them. *Merinh* is pronounced *mêrn'*.

conclusion that much of the specifically *royal* culture derives from the early Vazimba epoch, including the already present Antalaotra and more specifically both Zafindraminia *and* early Anteimoro influences. This monarchical adaptation to major aspects of pre-existing society is not an exception unique to Imerina. It obtained as well for the Maroserana rulers in Ibara, Mahafaly, and Sakalava lands. It applied to the Zafindraminia among the Antambahoaka of Mananjary and Antanosy of Fort-Dauphin. It affected considerably the Anteimoro Antalaotra as well, although as their own history and society show, part of the structure imported into Matitana continued to be superimposed over the *tompontany*.

The itinerant and semi-Islamized *ombiasa*, either trained by the Anteimoro or Anteimoro themselves, exercised influence in Imerina as they did in other Malagasy societies. The Arabico-Malagasy writing was adopted in Imerina shortly before the turn of the nineteenth century.[162] Much earlier attempts at the introduction of this writing into Imerina are suggested by the oral texts.[163] It is also impossible to overlook the impact of the Sakalava empire and Maroserana monarchy on the Andriana of Imerina, particularly with Andrianjaka when the Merina monarchy begins to differentiate itself. The use of silver chains, funerary dances and chants (mentioned earlier) suggest Sakalava inroads. The same may be said of human funerary sacrifices, of the poison ordeal applied to humans rather than animals, of the idea to "divinize" living rulers, of marking the ears of cattle. One thing is certain. Contacts between the Sakalava and Imerina, beyond warfare and slave raiding, did exist. There is a text that notes that rifles and powder were brought to Imerina by Sakalava traders, Boanahidy and Sabaly, both of whom were placed under Andrianjaka's personal protection.[164] The *Tantara* of Callet note that Andrianjaka had fifty flintlocks and three kegs of powder, but no mention is made of how or from whom these were obtained.[165] With firearm references, for example, it has been possible to up-date slightly even the most advanced

---

[162] Cf. H. Berthier, *De l'Usage de l'Arabico-Malgache en Imerina au debout de XIXe siécle* (1933), Vol. XVI of the *MAM*.

[163] See notes 94 and 100 above. On the basis of his field work among the Merina in 1965 and without reading the *Tantara*, the anthropologist Maurice Bloch, "Astrology and Writing in Madagascar," in J. Goody (ed.), *Literacy in Traditional Societies* (1968), pp. 278–297, has correctly suspected and inferred as much.

[164] Anonymous, *Développement du Royaume Hova*, manuscript, pp. 28–29. *Boana-* is an obvious reference to Iboina (Boina). *Saba-* is Swahili *saba* for copper, brass.

[165] Callet, *Tantara*, Vol. I (1953), p. 461. The Merina Manuscript cited in G. Grandidier, *Histoire politique*, p. 61 and n. 3, state that Andriamasinavalona purchased "many rifles" from the Sakalava. The *Tantara* cite the Sakalava many times—Vol. I (1953), pp. 135, 274, 278, 443, 467–469, 536, 576. Some references are clear anachronisms; others are not.

ruling spans given for Ralambo and Andrianjaka.[166] More than that, with firearms, the western Vakinisisaony were "freed" of the Vazimba and, at long last, the Merina and the Hova had a state empty of the perturbing *tompontany*. For a long time, the Merina paid annual tribute to the Sakalava coastal empire. Yet, the firearms would pave the way for the removal of this vassal status. These aspects, too, should be taken into account as antecedents of more spectacular success.

[166] M. Cheffaud, "Note sur la chronologie des rois d'Imerina," *BAM*, new series, XIX (1936), 37–47. Cheffaud believes that Ralambo mounted the throne in 1610 and Andrianjaka in 1650 (pp. 46–47).

chapter 7 AFRICA AND MADAGASCAR:
The Weight of Evidence

> At first glance these old institutions appear singular, abnormal, and above all, violent and tyrannical since they lie outside our customs . . . [but] it seemed to me that these institutions originated in a slow, gradual, and regular manner and were not at all the product of a fortuitous accident or of a sudden act of force . . . they were in harmony with the customs, the civil laws, the material interests, the forms of thought, and the frame of mind of the generations which they governed. . . . That is undoubtedly the reason why it takes many generations to establish a political regime and many other generations to tear it down.
>
> Fustel de Coulanges, *History of the Political Institutions of Ancient France* (1875)

One very simple but fundamental fact emerges from the data already presented. The Maroserana-derived *Volamena* of Menabé and of Mahafaly, the *Andrevola* of lower Fiherenana, the *Renilemi* of Mahafaly, the *Zafimanely* of Ibara, the *Zafimanara* of Antandroy, and the *Zarabehavana* of Antaisaka cannot be perceived as anything other than *Malagasy* dynastic families. The same is true of the *Anteony* of Matitana and *Andriana* of Imerina. There is no doubt that the political impulse to create kingdoms in Madagascar goes back to the oversea migrants who arrived toward the turn of the sixteenth century, migrants whom it has been necessary to call for the sake of distinction "proto-Maroserana" and "ancestral" Temoro. The idea of "kingdom" came with them, along with some associated features, from their own antecedent societies. The "experience of life teaches," wrote Marc Bloch in his *Apologie pour l'Histoire*, *ou Métier d'Historien,* "and that of history confirms, that any offense against truth is like a net and that almost inevitably every lie drags in its train many others, summoned to lend it a semblance of mutual support." In Madagascar there were no sudden enthronements of kings with superior culture, no white monarchs sliding from the cracked bellies of Indonesian and Indian ships, wrecked by convenient chance on the coast facing Asia, to bring glorious destinies to the passive *tompontany*—dark, primitive, and eager to be civilized. The very same documents abused to gratify these "fantasies" reveal their true nature. The very first notice of the Zafikazimambo-Anteony rulers at Matitana and the earliest descriptions of Volamena kings in Menabé and Iboina, seen by Europeans still relatively free of the spirit that cannot disengage pigment from culture, bear out Bloch's comment.

Whether aristocratic skins were once white or black or of some other shade, whether these shades mutated more than once is a subject of paramount importance only when restricted to the intellectual debate of those who studied and wrote about the Malagasy past. An objective value can also be given to pigment of the Malagasy, subjects and rulers alike, in a purely ethnographic sense because of the duality of "races" in the Great Island. But, what makes the proto-Maroserana and the ancestral Temoro interesting in terms of descriptive and substantive history is not their skin color, which can never be known anyway, but the fact that they were *agents* of important change in Madagascar of the 1500s and beyond. Indirectly, the earliest of their state-building activities, which were by no means successful, caused the final migration of the Hova into Vazimba-occupied central highlands. Without this event there would have been no *Andriana* dynasty, and the history of Imerina would have been very different. Again, without the Sakalava warriors the historical Maroserana would never have gained an empire or retained their prominent position in the collective memory of west-coast peoples.

The role of the Temoro in the direct building of an early kingdom at Matitana is far less impressive than the diffusion of certain features from their own society into other parts of Madagascar or the ability of itinerant Temoro and Temoro-trained *ombiasa* to manipulate the cultural and religious symbols and institutions of other Malagasy societies. The concept of *arivo*, reflected in their *Sora-bé*,[1] became the pillar of Maroserana

---

[1] None of the early Temoro ancestors were given the *arivo* ending, but this ending along with *zato*, or hundred (in *Andriamarozato*, or lord of many hundreds), begins to appear in some seventeenth-century Temoro names (cf. G. Mondain, *Histoire . . . de l'Imoro . . .* (1910), manuscript, *passim.*). In his *Histoire de la Grande Ile Madagascar* (1661), in *COACM*, Vol. VIII (1913), p. 77, Etienne de Flacourt reports that the Tanosy ruler Tsiambany (contemporary of Mariano) had a son named AndriandRamaka who was posthumously renamed *Andriamaroarivo* and "honored like a god." This event, too, is in the middle of the 1600s. However, one notes an *arivo* in

expansion and the basic political ideology of this dynastic family. The concept is simple: a real king must have at least a thousand subjects. Robert Drury in his *Journal* illustrates very explicitly the concern of adding subjects to ensure, and also to extend, the king's rule. While describing Menabé's King Tsimanongarivo as a "terrible figure" and most "cruel" of rulers, Drury reported at the same time that:[2]

> He was also very generous amongst his own subjects, making many of them who had suffered losses in serving him presents of cattle and slaves, but more especially took all the politic ways he could to entice people to come from other countries to live in Saccalavour, presenting them with slaves and cattle. . . . Civilly he treated the Feraingher [Fiherenana] people, whose families were at any time taken in war, restoring all the captives and cattle if their masters and relations would come and live in his dominions. By this means they are grown vastly populous and rich, the people living in plenty and safety. . . .

The *arivo* in association with a living Volamena king manifests itself first with Andriandahifotsy's sons, when it was not yet fully established in the *fitahina* or posthumous praise name. Both the ability of Maroserana to attract vassals and subjects *and* the branching out of royal sons who left the court to carve out new kingdoms and earn the *arivo* in death and in life are continuous and interconnected themes of local tradition. Indeed, surrounded by stretches of the savanna, living amid cattle herds and pastoralists on the move, the Maroserana also responded to this environment by shifting from low to high population-density areas.

Such terms as *misara, sikidy, kabary, tariki,* no less than the system of divination and the Arabic calendar are telltale signs of wide Temoro influence outside of Matitana. But, it is also clear that these influences were most susceptible of politicoreligious success wherever other *métis* of the *tompontany* and Antalaotra had attained various degrees of ascendancy, namely in the cases of Zafindraminia among the Antanosy and Andriana among the Vazimba and Hova and among the southwestern Maroserana. What the *ombiasa* thus promoted was the on-going dynastic change, state building, and the advent of early kingdoms. Chiefly amulets were transformed into the group *ody* and *sampy*; major religious symbols of the *tompontany* were transferred to royalty, first, to cement relationships and, later, to be manipulated as features of monarchical

---

Zafindraminia genealogy (Racoube's fifteenth descendant), which would fall into the late 1500s, certainly long after the arrival of Temoro. Thus, it is impossible to determine whether they imported the concept of *arivo* or whether the Temoro found it, like many other features, "floating about" in old Madagascar and developed it first for the Zafindraminia kinglets in Tanosy and still later for the historical Maroserana. See also note 21 below for the presence of this concept in Africa.

[2] Robert Drury, *Madagascar or Robert Drury's Journal. . . ,* 7th ed. (1890), pp. 274–275.

cultures. The *sikidy*, likewise, was employed in decisions of state. If the results were adverse, priests shielded the rulers, while in reverse instances the monarchs would take credit for success and reward their *ombiasa* by granting the rank of nobility, which passed to the descendants, by village "fiefs," and even by incorporating the *ombiasa* into the pantheon of royal relics. The shaving of heads, once applied only to the dead, was required of the living as a sign of submission to the monarchy. All of these vectors amounted to a vast enlargement of "monarchical principle" observed by Mariano from Fort-Dauphin in the southeast to Çada in the northwest. Like all of the *Antay-laut*, the Temoro underwent initial conflicts with the *tompontany* as well as among themselves, subsequent intermarriage, and monarchical differentiation. But, unlike the other *Antay-laut*, they came to the Great Island as a cohesive unit with their own religious and political institutions. This cohesiveness, moreover, was re-enforced at least once by late-arriving kinsmen. They adopted common Malagasy as their own language. They took the term *kibory* from pre-existing Antambahoaka and adopted the Zafindraminia aristocratic right of *sombili* because monopoly over the slaughter of domesticated animals gave them a clear political advantage. Yet, the rigid way in which the *sombili* was applied at Matitana, the customs which surrounded the *kibory* burials, the use of Islam as a determinant of legitimacy to rule, the preservation of scribal tradition and paper making, their age groups, and their "tribal" and not only noble-caste endogamy— all of these made the Temoro unique in Madagascar.

There is more than sufficient evidence to exclude Arabia as well as India and substitute Africa as *the* home from which both the proto-Maroserana and ancestral Temoro came to Madagascar. This alone easily eliminates the various hypotheses of the *Malgachisants*. If some were willing to perceive the presence of one or several African features in Malagasy societies and their material culture, if a few even believed in the African origin of a given Malagasy "tribe," however, *none* could adjust his entire intellect to the point where it would accord primacy in the advent of early kingdoms to *Africa* not to Asia. Yet, even this reversal, if it occurred, would constitute no more than the perception of an iceberg's top. Once more, we would be faced with the impression of culturally superior modern arrivals, "Asian" at least in part despite residence *in* Africa and capable of imposing their ideas and structures on the *tompontany*. "Life teaches and history confirms," to recall Bloch's words, that problems of this nature get lifted sooner or later out of context. Significant detail recedes into the background and the extent to which new monarchical cultures were dependent on borrowing from pre-existing society is forgotten. In the end, the older framework of thought and habit will simply reassert itself by finding "nothing revolutionary" in sight. After all, in the great variety of hypotheses about the Malagasy origins, someone had perceived somewhere connections between Africa and Madagascar either by placing the Bantu as the first arrivals to the Great Island and introducing the Indonesians later, by allowing them to "filter" through the mainland before coming to Madagascar, or by making the Malagasy jump into their outriggers to go back to Africa and raid for slaves.

All of this is, of course, possible in declining order of probabilities, from Indonesian passage on the mainland and subsequent contacts between the Malagasy and Africans to the much less likely African (pre-Bantu or Bantu) population substratum in old Madagascar. If nothing *else*, the outrigger in Africa and the Indonesian-derived language in Madagascar, attest both to the possibility and the probability of Indonesian colonies along the eastern littoral of Africa, while the Sakalava-Betsimisaraka outrigger slave raids into the western Indian Ocean area and far from Madagascar argue for pre-eighteenth-century antecedents and show distinct proof of the *capability* for maritime contact of long standing. Nonetheless, the sum total of linguistic, ethnographic, and historical data *within* Madagascar argue with far greater thrust and power for something that should have been not only discovered, but also worked out long ago. To put it in the simplest form of statement, there *must* have been in the first millenium of our era an *Afro-Malagasy race* inhabiting both sides of the Mozambique Channel, which was *then* not a barrier but a duct for movement of peoples. The use of the imprecise term race is necessary because the peoples it encompassed did not belong to any homogenous group. And, this *race* had its African and Indonesian extremes with all sorts and kinds of admixture in-between. The extremes did not survive in Africa because of the huge human migration, generally called the Bantu expansion, migrations which absorbed nearly everything in their paths. They did survive, however, in Madagascar partly because it was shielded by the sea and partly because nothing of the magnitude of these migrations occurred within it. The African extreme of this Afro-Malagasy race survived, until the 1700s, on the Bambala coast of western Madagascar, while its Indonesian counterpart won out linguistically because it had the power of numbers. Its very concentration in Madagascar rather than in Africa suggests deliberate linguistic and cultural self-preservation. Both of the extremes were assisted in this survival, despite linguistic and cultural differences, by the nearly exclusive possession of outrigger technology, retained in Africa only in pockets but flourishing along much of the Malagasy coast to this day.

Although research embodied in the previous chapters provides only a beginning of detailed investigation, evidence in the Great Island is solid enough to sustain these deductions until superior materials are presented to reveal their shortcomings as being too many and too great. Simple rejections will no longer do. To start with some of the simplest and most obvious items, to what can one attribute, for example, the clear Malagasy-Bantu parallels for a word like child (children, the young, the tender, the feeble) or *ana, anaka, zanaka, zanak* in *common* Malagasy and mu-*ana* (Tonga, Bisa, Rotse, Guha, Rue), mw-*ana* (Lunda, Teke, Gogo, Sagara, Shambala, Bondei, Taita, Nyanyembe, Sukuma, Kamba, Pokomo, Nyika, Senna, Ganda, Yao, Mozambique, Lower Congo, and the Swahili coast, where it also appears as *anana*), ny*ana* ("Kafir" of J. Torrend), uny*ana* (Zulu), ngw*ana* (Tswana, Sotho), and onw*ana* (Mpongwe)?[3] Or yet, for a word like eye, singular *maso* in *common* Malagasy and plural *meso, miso, mise* in almost as many Bantu idioms? It is moreover found as *maso* in Pokomo and *macho* in Swahili, as well as *meto/mato* in Mozambique and *mathlo* in Tswana, the last three being closest to the Malayo-Polynesian *mata* (eye), while Pokomo and Swahili are closest to the common Malagasy *maso* (eye).[4]

Malagasy and Bantu languages belong to completely different families. The parallels for two very basic vocabulary items could, in theory, be assigned to "linguistic chance" (which G. P. Murdock sees as high as 6 percent for unrelated languages). But, we are not dealing with onomatopoeia, which would account for much of this percentage (assuming its accuracy), with words children are apt to utter for father and mother; in short, we are not dealing with linguistic chance. There are other basic and important words in *common* Malagasy with clear African parallels even if these happen to be less widespread on the mainland. Here, one can cite such common Malagasy terms as chief and government, or *mpanjaka* and *fanjakana*, spear, or *lefona*, words for collectivities and numbers of people enveloped in family, class, clan, or *foko* and *fokonolona*, priest, or *ombiasa*, and custom, law, or *fomba*. All of them are found in Bantu idioms with identical or similar but broader generic meanings. The Bantu *anza/anda* appears in the generic sense of "undertake, start, initiate, begin, lead" in Swahili. It is also associated without a chance of error with places, items, and persons of government: *mapanzo*, chiefly cloth in central Africa; *mbanza*, chiefly village in the old Kongo kingdom; *mukanza*, name or title of a Lunda king, followed by *mukonzo*, or the skirt of Lunda kings; *nhampanza*, the title of a Tete chief prior to the conquest of Tete by Mwene Mutapa; *mboanjikana*, the name and form of address for the founding Lozi princess.[5] This association is far

[3] J. Torrend, A *Comparative Grammar of the South-African Bantu Languages* (1891), p. 67, item 322.

[4] *Ibid.*, p. 88, item 411.

[5] Cf. E. Axelson, *Portuguese in South-East Africa, 1600–1700* (1964), p. 5; J. M. Vansina, *Kingdoms of the Savanna* (1966), p. 334; I. G. Cunnison (ed.), *Historical Texts*, Vol. II (1962), p. 27; J. C. Chiwale, *Central Bantu Historical Texts*, Vol. III

more widespread in Africa because the examples themselves are based on preliminary research only. They are, nonetheless, sufficiently telling. The common Malagasy term for spear has already been noted in at least twelve Bantu idioms.[6] Not a few researchers in Africa have interpreted the widely diffused chiefly title *fumo* to mean invested with the spear. The Swahili *foko* and *fukua*, along with Bisa *i-fuko* cover the entire range of common Malagasy *foko/fokonolona*.[7] The common Malagasy *ombiasa* (phonetically *umbiaš*) does not correspond—as Father Birkeli believed—to the Bisa *mulosi* but to *umupashi*, the inherited familial spirit in central African societies.[8] The common Malagasy *fomba* (phonetics, *fūmb'*) is analogous to Swahili *fumba* and Congolese *fu*.[9]

One could readily explain the Bantu loans in Malagasy, common *and* dialectical, for domesticated fowl, cattle, sheep, and goat by indirect or direct borrowing in which both loans and objects were taken together because Madagascar did not have the latter. But, exactly the same case cannot be made for wild fowl, dog, lemur, snake, and crocodile. That the proto-Malagasy were familiar with these is attested by duality of synonyms, Bantu (B) and non-Bantu (non-B) derived: wild fowl, *akanga* (B) and *haka* (non-B); dog, *amboa* (B) and *alika* (non-B); lemur, *gidro* (B) and *varika, hira* (non-B); snake, *koma/akoma/ankoma, bibilava, pily/mpily/pilo, fanano/fanane/fanany/fananina/fanghane* (ancient), (all B) and *do/doa/dona, olatra/olapata* (non-B).[10] The Bantu loans for millet and even more so for manioc suggested the presence of African agricultural colonies in western Madagascar, and documentary

---

(1962), p. 5 and plate II with explanatory notes 8–9; and E. Stokes and R. Brown (eds.), *The Zambezian Past* (1966), pp. 253–254. The Luunda-*anza* association suggests, because of the Malagasy *anza*, a Lunda expansion into central Africa considerably *before* the fifteenth century. It should be understood that the present work deals mainly with *early kingdoms in Madagascar* and cannot as yet develop the myriad hints about African history itself without really going into another volume. This seminal subject should involve teamwork and several years of labor on both sides of the channel.

[6] See note 35, Chapter 2.

[7] Ch. Sacleux, *Dictionnaire swahile-français*, Vol. I (1939), pp. 224, 228; the Bisa *i-fuko* was noted by E. Birkeli in 1936.

[8] J. T. Munday, *Kankomba, Central Bantu Historical Texts*, Vol. I, Tome 1 (1961), p. xx; and A. Richards, "Bemba," in E. Colson and M. Gluckman (eds.), *Seven Tribes of British Central Africa* (1961 reprint), pp. 169, 174 *inter alia*.

[9] Sacleux, *Swahili-français*, Vol. I (1939), p. 230; and W. H. Bentley, *Dictionary and Grammar of the Kongo Language* (1887), pp. 51, 278, "*fu*, custom, manner, habit . . , practice, rule, nature . . , conduct, behaviour, usage, fashion, way." Once more, it can be noted that Malagasy *folaka* and Congolese *volaka* (bent, finished, turned over) have the same meaning, but I am uncertain whether in the Congo it was applied, as in Madagascar, to the indirect way of stating that a king was dead.

[10] J.-C. Hébert, "Noms d'animaux en Malgache," *CM*, I/1 (1964), 299–366 *passim* 378–389 for caption explanations.

materials, indeed, have confirmed these. But, the 1575 tale of Thevet about the repopulation of this section of Madagascar with men and women from Africa cannot be used as a historical "document" with which to explain how these Bambala-coast colonies formed in the first place. Rather, the extremely high probability of their genesis is revealed by the simple fact that Kapitapa's Sadians not only possessed the outriggers, but that the vessels were more than seaworthy. They went all the way to Boina Bay in the north loaded with food supplies to save the area from famine and returned home. What is, however, to be made of *akondro* (banana), a term widespread in Africa but confined in Madagascar mainly to Imerina,[11] which is not only landlocked but also regarded as a local "culture area" reflecting the most Indonesian antecedents of the Malagasy?

The spread of millet and manioc terminology *with* cultivation techniques, the roughly analogous diffusion of the palship institution (*ziwa*), tattooing (*tumbuka*), and hair-setting styles common to a number of Malagasy and African societies suggested human transmigrations within the southern half of Madagascar, not any indirect cultural borrowings from the Bambala Coast. To this must also be added the spread of the so-called *Hazomanga religion*. It is found among the Sakalava, Bara, Mahafaly, Antandroy, Vazimba of Menabé, and southwestern Betsileo of Isandra. Less intense areas of this cult are found also among some Sihanaka, Bezanozano, Tanala, Antanosy, and Betsimisaraka. It is absent in all of northern Madagascar roughly above the Sixteenth Parallel, in Imerina, in most of the Betsileo highlands outside old Isandra and in Temoro land. This *hazomanga*, or *jiro*, cult centers around wooden stakes or staffs, usually two to three meters in height, topped by wood carvings of males and females (see photograph on page 236), and normally placed in the center of villages. It is at the *hazomanga*, or *jiro*, staff that sacrifices—mainly of cattle—are made to thank or appease the departed ancestors.[12] In discussing the more or less coincidental spread of these five major features that cross-cut economy, aesthetics, group identification, and religion, one is not dealing with "monarchical" cultures but with "popular" ones that do distinguish broadly two social segments in the Great Island.

In advancing connections between Madagascar and Rhodesia, both for Ibara and the Maroserana, the items cited were, apart from gold itself, such terms as *Baramazimba, Umghabé, Zafikazimambo*, the "tribal" name of *Manankarunga*, and *-tsimibaby*. This list is far too short of what is available even for a preliminary work. It is of consequence to note that

[11] See note 63, Chapter 2.

[12] For reference, A. and G. Grandidier, *Ethnographie de Madagascar*, Vol. III (1917), pp. 339–342 and notes.

Sakoambé tombs, Moron-
dava-Menabé. The photo-
graph above was taken in
1898, at the right in 1965.

in addition to *Manankarunga/Makaranga*, three other tribal names offer African analogies that point to no coincidence: *Vinda/Venda, Bara-bé/Barwe*, and *Sakoambé/Sacumbe*. The Karanga and Barwe belong to the Shona cluster, while the Venda are often bracketed with the Shona as a Bantu tribe associated with the culture of Zimbabwe. The African *Sacumbe*, now extinct as a kingdom, occupied the area of Tete on the northeastern Karanga borderlands. Yet, one can go beyond these tribal names, and then coincidences rapidly decline. The tombs of Malagasy Sakoambé, near Morondava, *alone* have in Madagascar *bird effigies* posted on rectangular tomb enclaves. Except for being carved in wood, the bird species are similar to the soapstone ones of Zimbabwe (compare the photographs on page 251 with Zimbabwe). Bird effigies, if not of the same species, are also found among the Sotho and the Venda and in parts of Transvaal and Basuto.

According to Murdock, the Venda-Zimbabwe link is usually postulated from the Venda-incorporated Lemba who possess "markedly Semitic" physical features as well as cultural ones "that distinguish them sharply from their neighbors." Among these are "circumcision, absence of totemism, tribal endogamy . . . predilection for fish, burial in extended rather than crouched position, a distinctive new-moon ceremony, and a taboo on eating the flesh of animals unless their throats have been cut before death."[13] In this, one can recognize best the Antanosy society in Madagascar, excluding only the tribal endogamy. The throat cutting or *sombili* (itself a Bantu loan in Malagasy from *šambulia*, to jerk the head forward, in Swahili) and the new-moon ceremony offer particularly strong links.[14] Because of the classic neglect of Madagascar, it is not surprising that such major features, along with "Semitic" physical ones, have not yielded much by way of explanation, as Murdock's own guessing indicates. Therefore it should not be a complete surprise to discover that the praise names of Tswana rulers contain very pointed *Malagasy* parallels that cannot be disregarded either. For example, words in Secwana that start with the letter *f* are delineated as being of "foreign origin."[15] The Secwana vocabulary does not contain the term *soa* either. Yet, *soa* is found in the Tswana praise name *Radisoa*, while another one, *Radi-*

[13] G. P. Murdock, *Africa* (1959), p. 387; for Karanga-Shona, see J. G. Frazer and R. A. Downie, *The Native Races of Africa and Madagascar* (1938), pp. 14–16 (translated from Portuguese chronicles)—"Their greatest holy day is the first day of the moon of May; they call it *Chuavo*" (p. 14). Cf. E. de Flacourt, *Histoire, COACM*, Vol. VIII (1913), pp. 104–109. However, the Tanosy rulers did not go into an eight-day seclusion and the custom of Mwene Mutapa to put a noble to death at the end of seclusion appears in Tanosy in a different context.

[14] Sacleux, *Swahili-français*, Vol. II (1941), pp. 829–830 (under *sambua*).

[15] J. T. Brown, *Secwana-English Dictionary* (1931), p. 70.

phofu, contains the word *fu*.[16] Since we are concerned with *praise* names, it is relevant to note that *soa* in Malagasy stands for good, excellent, beautiful, and the Malagasy *fo* (phonetics, *ffóu*) means heart in both the physical and moral sense. The Secwana *Rra-* which prefixes most of the praise names, is a personal article given to mean father.[17] The Malagasy *Ra-* (phonetics, *rrâ*) is a personal prefix with which to form proper names and convey address of respect roughly between the more elevated *andriana* and the lower *I-*, or lord and mister, sir. *Ra-* is also Malagasy for blood, but it also implies kinship. Such Tswana praise names as *Ramelomana* and *Ramaubana* resemble suspiciously Malagasy names (namely, *Mamelomana, Raombana*), but one must approach this subject with caution and only after careful research. The same should be said of *diana* in the Tswana praise name *Ramodiana*. For while *diana* does resemble *andriana* in Malagasy, and even more its form found in old European accounts, or *diana-/dian-*, the Secwana *dia* happens to be third-person plural of nouns in the *di* class.[18] But, *soa* and *fu/fo* do not present the same problem while the close relationship between Malagasy *Ra-* and Secwana *Rra-* does not seem to be widely duplicated in Africa. The Rotse also have the Secwana *Ra-* (father). *Ra-* appears also as a prefix in Sierra Leone, but there it is one for creeping plants only.

To focus on the greater strength of old Madagascar-Rhodesia links does involve a danger. It is most certainly not one of inventing a false historical "reality," but rather in creating the impression that the Zimbabwe complex accounts for much that is African in Madagascar. If the matter were that simple, the reliable Father Mariano would never have perceived what *all* of the subsequent students failed to discover—namely, that the Bambala *Cafres* and the *Buki* in the rest of the Great Island possessed "much the same customs" *despite* the difference of language. Nor could he and d'Azevedo have reported two branches of Bantu in the Bambala idiom even richer in vocabulary.[19] Below Bambala, in southwestern Madagascar, where many cattle markers could recall no migrations to Birkeli and were hence were this area's *tompontany*, a south African from near the Table Bay could communicate in a meaningful way with a mere boy in 1607. No less significant, the Menabé Vazimba, whose own bilingualism was attested by Drury early in the eighteenth century, saw

[16] I. Schapera, *Praise-Poems of Tswana Chiefs* (1965), pp. 226–228 and notes.

[17] Brown, *Secwana*, p. 264; Schapera, *Praise-Poems*, p. 24. Schapera also notes that Secwana *Rra-* defines in certain cases a possessor of some special quality.

[18] Brown, *Secwana*, p. 48.

[19] Such terms as *maganga* and *cacis* (kasis) for priest and the difficult term *afo* bear out the two Bantu branches. A search is now being conducted for d'Azevedo's missing Bambala vocabulary.

themselves as either entirely or only half Makua (mainland Africans), either from overseas, from further north, or from the interior highlands from which they had fled. Although it was evident from the *Tantara* that some linguistic change did take place through royal fiat in old Imerina and that some domesticated animals thus received Vazimba names not the Hova ones, there is no evidence that the Vazimba were an African-speaking population. The pottery terms like *finga, nongo, zinga,* and Bantu loans for cattle and sheep indicate that the Vazimba already had them. Nor do the high-quality Bantu politicoreligious loans like *tromba, bilo* (possessing spirit), *lolo* (spirit, ghost), *kibory* (tomb), and *angama* (leprosy), to mention only some, suggest merely Rhodesia. *Tromba* is central African; both *bilo* and *lolo* are central African suffixes for chiefs, many of whom were priest chiefs. *Kibory* is Swahili, while leprosy figures rather prominently in royal lore among the Nyamwezi[20] and the Malagasy *angama* finds its closest equivalent in Swahili. Also, the place-name Śaka does not point to the Ila-associated Mashukulombwe, as Ferrand believed, but to the capital of the old Ozi kingdom of eastern Africa.

If the Zimbabwe of Mwene Mutapa had been paramount in Madagascar one would *not* have expected the early Europeans to find in the Great Island the small and segmented chieftainship as the uniform type of local government and real kingdoms would have preceded both the Maro-serana and Anteony. In effect, the form of government noted in old Madagascar is very similar to the one found south of the interlacustrine area of central Africa, more specifically in western Tanzania. This region is where Roland Oliver has pinpointed the concept of *arivo* as well for "almost everywhere" in this region—"and even if he only ruled a *thousand subjects,* the chief could be described as 'divine king.' "[21] Moreover, the dry-stone building techniques of Zimbabwe and the resulting structures are *absent* from Madagascar. The Shonalike combed pottery, discovered in southeastern Madagascar along with iron implements belonging to Vezo-type outrigger culture and dated by Carbon-14 to A.D. ±1100 may well be the indication of a terminal human migration of a people or peoples familiar with some features of the Zimbabwe

[20] I am indebted for this information to Miss L. White, graduate student in history, University of California, Berkeley. As regards the *bilo* and *lolo,* one can mention the *bakabilo* (councilors) and *filolo* (nobles). Cf. Chiwale, *Central Bantu Historical Texts,* Vol. III, p. 1. *Bilo* is also found in the concept of sorcery *ovu-vila* and in the term *ombila* (sorcerer), for example, in Kavirondo. Cf. G. Wagner, *The Bantu of North Kavirondo,* Vol. I (1949), pp. 141–142; Vol. II (1956), p. 103; and his "Abaluyia," in D. Forde (ed.) *African Worlds* (1965), p. 47.

[21] R. Oliver, "Discernible Developments in the Interior *ca.* 1500–1840," in R. Oliver and G. Mathews (eds.), *History of East Africa,* Vol. I (1963), pp. 191–192. The italics are added, for it is doubtful that "thousand subjects" is a simple turn of the phrase. I stand to be corrected, however, on this point.

culture. Much *later*, no doubt, links between old Rhodesia and Madagascar proved to be both familiar and useful to the gold-bearing proto-Maroserana. But, it is the *detailed* study of *how* the early kingdoms of Madagascar came into being that has revealed not only the White-King myth, but also the completely misleading notion that dynastic change itself was an imposition of superior culture simply because the kingdoms were absent in the pre-Maroserana and pre-Anteony island.

This can be dramatically illustrated through the Betsileo. They have been the *tompontany* of the central highlands at least as long as the Vazimba of Imerina, residing nowhere near the coast. The Betsileo were never ruled by a single dynasty, and their kingdoms follow those of Temoro, Bara, Mahafaly, Merina, and Menabé Sakalava.[22] Yet, the Betsileo have had the most pronounced veneration of nobility in Madagascar along with the most developed *fangane* cult (see the Appendix for a description), the longest reported interregna, as well as consistent burial of royal wives with departed kings (a feature that characterizes only the beginning of historical Maroserana rule in Menabé). Moreover, the Betsileo as a group have been the classic protectors of snakes, particularly the small Malagasy boa. This attitude toward the snake is part of popular cultures in much of east-central Africa. As in Madagascar, the *fangane* cult is connected with royalty on the mainland, from Rhodesia to Rwanda and Ganda. What the Betsileo *fangane* suggests is the transfer of common belief to royalty in both Africa and Madagascar. Indeed, the *fangane* cult may have well been a cultural link for disparate peoples of the Afro-Malagasy race. The Betsileo features cannot be explained by any simple theory of parallel evolution, by an African passage involving the proto-Malagasy, by mere dynastic change within Madagascar, or by waves of Bantu-speakers repeatedly migrating the Great Island.

Indeed, the *linguistic* victory of Indonesia in Madagascar is the root cause for *cultural* disassociation of Africa and Madagascar, underscored by the bad comparative anthropology, which Alfred Grandidier had started and which is still continued by a number of people. Blood covenant, twin infanticide, spirit possession, and trials by ordeal in Madagascar have thus been assigned to Indonesia. All are widespread in Africa to such a degree that any one of them can be labeled as cross-ethnic features.[23] The tabooing of royal names after death in Madagascar is also

[22] According to Father H.-M. Dubois, *Monographie Betsileo* (1939), p. 234 and his ruler list. The earliest king of the first Betsileo kingdom, or Lalangina, *Rahasamanarivo*, ruled from *ca.* 1650–1680. One should note again the *arivo*.

[23] Cf. groups in J. G. Frazer and R. A. Downie, *The Native Races of Africa and Madagascar* (1938), based on firsthand descriptive accounts, most of them recorded in the nineteenth century as follows: *twin infanticide*, pp. 4, 58, 88–90, 155, 208, 291, 346, 355, 360, 369; *blood brotherhood, blood covenant*, pp. 93, 127, 145, 180,

constantly attributed to Indonesia. In reality, both name and word taboos for the living and the dead (subjects and kings) in Madagascar and in Africa are *common* expressions of religious fear.[24] The dual vocabularies for royalty and commoners in Madagascar and on the mainland derive in part from this base, the duality being aided by the need to differentiate rulers from subjects and by the fact that many dynastic founders came from somewhere else.

In fact, the deeper one probes into the precolonial Malagasy societies, the more striking become the parallels with those of Africa except for the language and a very few major cultural items. Among the latter may be cited the general absence in Madagascar of eternal fire for departed rulers and rainmaking, which, itself, might be due to environmental differences. It is significant that African loan-words in Malagasy *other* than Bantu do not manifest themselves.[25] And, one only has to add up some of the pure and modified loans encountered in the course of this work in their proper place and time contexts to show that even Indonesia's linguistic victory in Madagascar cannot hide what Luis Mariano perceived early in the seventeenth century. Leaving *aside* the loans for animals and plants (cited by the *Malgachisants* either as the sole or most important loans) along with those for pottery and musical instruments, one *still* obtains an impressive list for government (including some weapons), religion, and society:[26]

224–225, 228, 258, 271, 294, 300, 321, 326 335; *trials by ordeal,* pp. 30, 49–50, 81, 137, 149, 170, 174–175, 178, 184, 204, 212, 222, 230, 242, 294, 305, 323, 330, 356, 378, 484. For *spirit possession* as an individual or private variant, called *pepo* in easternmost, or coastal Africa and *mahamba* at the opposite end, or Angola, see H. Baumann and D. Westermann, *Les Peuples et les Civilisations de l'Afrique* (1962), pp. 57, 144, 158–160, 168, 187, 214, 229, 232, 237, 304; and J. S. Trimingham, *Islam in East Africa* (1964), pp. 69, 71, 80, 113 n., 114, 117–120, 122–123. An entire trend in medical pathology was started in late nineteenth-century Brazil by Nina Rodrigues who saw spirit possession as a feature common to all Afro-Brazilians.

[24] Frazer and Downie, *Races,* pp. 45, 216, 194, 234, 287 *inter alia.* "Not only the names of certain persons related to one may not be pronounced, but common words which resemble these names are also tabooed, and other words or phrases have to be substituted for them"—E. S. Smith and A. Dale, *The Ila-Speaking Peoples of Northern Rhodesia,* Vol. I (1920), p. 369. "The people are unwilling to mention the true names of children and adults to strangers, lest through the knowledge of the names the strangers should obtain magical power over the bearer of a name and misuse it to his hurt"—Hans Meyer, *Die Barundi* (1916), p. 112.

[25] Father Birkeli believed that he detected some Bushman words in Vazimba of Menabé, but he did not conclude his study. The Arabic loans, either via Swahili or Temoro, remain Arabic as etymons despite being funneled into Malagasy from the mainland.

[26] *Ampinga* (shield, now extinct), *angama* (leprosy), *baba* (both as father and king, as in Adrian Baba, Sakalava ruler); *bahary* (from Arabico-Swahili the sea, name given to class of Sakalava funerary attendants who were sacrificed in the old

Government (24)		Religion (21)		Society (23)	
Andria- (see text below)		*andra* (-hufiki)	(DE)	*baba*	(D)
		angama	(D)	*biby*	(CM)
ampinga	(DE)	*bilo*	(D)	*foko*	(CM)
bahary	(DE)	*fanane*	(D)	*fomba*	(CM)
behava	(D)	*helo*	(D)	*haba*	(D)
-bobaka	(DE)	*-hufiki*	(DE)	*kianja*	(D)
futi	(D)	*jiro*	(D)	*kibana*	(D)
jangoa	(DE)	*kalakani*	(DE)	*kitamby*	(D)
jama	(DE)	*kasis*	(DE)	*kitomboka*	(D)
jumbe	(DE)	*kibory*	(D)	*longo*	(D)
kabeso	(DE)	*leka*	(D)	*masikoro*	(D)
kazi	(DE)	*lolo*	(D)	*ngabé*	(D)
kobo	(D)	*maganga*	(DE)	*nunu* (-na)	(D)
lefona	(CM)	*mahombé*	(DE)	*ringa*	(D)
mambo	(DE)	*misara*	(D)	*sasalia*	(D)
manda	(D)	*mososa*	(DE)	*toranga*	(D)
Monongabé	(DE)	*mpamoha*	(DE)	*tumbuka*	(D)
mpanjaka	(CM)	*ombiasa*	(CM)	*vezo*	(D)
Osa	(DE)	*moasy*	(D)	*zafi-*	(D)
samb (-arivo)	(DE)	*ody*	(CM)	*zara-*	(D)
sombili	(DE)	*sampy*	(D)	*zaza*	(D)
wazira	(DE)			*ziwa*	(D)
zomba	(D)			*zoma*	(D)
rota	(DE)				
andapa	(D)				

CM = Common Malagasy; *D* = Dialects; *DE* = Dialect Extinct

While this list by no means approaches the totality of pure and modified Bantu loans in Malagasy, it does allow a number of conclusions.

First, it contains a number of loans hitherto unperceived either as loans or as significant ones. Foremost among these belong to Common Malagasy, that is to say all the Malagasy would find them intelligible, from an Antankarana in the north to an Antandroy in the south: *lefona* (spear),

days), *bilo* (spirit possession), *biby* (by itself, royal concubine, male or female; as prefix, name for animals and insects, at times ogres; as suffix to *Ra-* also a chiefly name as in *Rabiby*, similar to *Rubibi* in Rwanda royal genealogy), *behava* (inner court), *fanane* (snake but, more precisely, a term for the worm emerging out of royal humors to become a snake with the royalty's soul and personality), *foko* (compound, community, family, clan, tribe), *bobaka* (from *Ante-i-bobaka*, pre-Zafindraminia Antanosy chiefs whose graves are still around, compound of *bu* [Swahili-Arabic, father] and *-baki* [Swahili-Arabic, to remain, survive]), *helo* (ghost, spirit), *fomba* (law, custom), *futi* (see text below), *Andra-hufiki* (see text below), *haba* (bracelet) *jangoa* (funerary attendants of Sakalava kings whose main role was to be sacrificed at burial), *jiro* (religious staff), *jama* (name given to Manambia king's subjects, the *mpanjaka* (ruler, chief), *fomba* (custom, law), and *foko* (community of any size), which only Birkeli had noted as a Bantu loan. All four are also of the highest quality, involving war, government, and society. Such loans cannot be accounted for without culturally powerful and intimate contact of the widest possible scope. Indeed, they make a convincing case for a *pre-ethnic* Malagasy in Africa who somehow merged the spear, the chief, the law, and the family into ethnic units as a result of intimate contact with Bantu speakers. As one would expect, this process was also connected with religion but in a more restricted way. Apart from *ombiasa/ umbiăš'/umupashi* and *ody/ūď/udalali* (from Swahili but ultimately from Arabic *dalal/dalîl*)[27] found with divergences in all Malagasy dialects (*ombiasse, oly, aoly*, etc.), the rest of the religious terminology is dialectical. The same is true of all other loans in government and society, excluding *biby*, which appears alone in dialects but can be found almost everywhere in commonly coined compounds (namely, *bibilava*). As for the dialectical loans in all three categories, nearly all have occurred or still occur in southern Madagascar, but the Sakalava and the Bara account for a vast majority. In government and religion, twenty-three out of forty-one dialectical loans have been lost as against none lost out of twenty such loans in society. The dialectical loan loss is highest in government (fifteen out of twenty-two), but almost half (eight out of nineteen) of the religious loans have become extinct, as well. Although no rules

submerged in Bantu), *jumbe* (old title on pre-Sakalava northwest coast for chiefs, from Swahili, *jumbe, yumbe*), *kabeso* (see text below), *kazi* and *mambo* (title of Manankarunga, chiefly daughter who married an Anteimoro and was co-founder of their *Zafikazimambo* royal clan), *kobo* and *manda* (fortification with rifle openings in old Ibara), *Monongabé* (given as the capital of Ibara in 1844), *sambarivo* (Sakalava funerary attendants, from Swahili, *šambiza*, or "attend to last rites of the dead, with *-iza* dropped and replaced by Malagasy *arivo*, thousand or many in this case), *sombili* (right to cut throats of domesticated animals, important aristocratic privilege among the Temoro and Tanosy), *wazira* (old term for southeastern chiefs, the forbidden ones in Bantu from *-zira*, abstain from forbidden), *zomba* (royal enclave, capital), *kalakani* (vital force, mentioned by Mariano on Bambala coast in 1616, along with *maganga* and *cacic/kasis* for priest) *leka* and *lolo* (spirits, malevolent or beneficial), *mahombé* (royal slaves in Ibara), *moasy* (from Malagasy, *mosavy* or sorcery, and ultimately from Swahili *mchawi*, also sorcery), *misara* (Swahili-Arabic loan for diviner from *išara*, also title of southwestern chiefs in Madagascar), *mososa* (powerful sorcerers in old Sakalava land), *zoma* (lit. Friday, but applied to big market day in Imerina), *zaza* (children), *sasalia* and *kitomboka* (see text below), *ki* (prefixed words [*kianja, kibana, kitamby*], examples of Bantu prefix and Bantu terminals, of which the *kibana* [hut] has religious meaning as a platform erected on which *tromba*-possessed persons are placed), *ngabé* (elder in general), *tumbuka* (general term for tattooing), *ziwa* (general term for joking relationship), *vezo* (general term for coastal fishermen in western Madagascar). The index at the end of this volume will lead the reader back to contexts in which the terms were found.

27 Sacleux, *Swahili-français*, Vol. I (1939), p. 162; and Vol. II (1941), p. 931.

can be postulated from a list that is itself very incomplete and also induc-
tive in nature, the greatest African impact can be said to have been in
government, followed by society and religion. The high rate of loan
survival in society and the almost corresponding loan loss in the two
other domains are easily explained by the colonial period and its impact.
This dialectical story, along with the Bara traditional system of government[28] and the composition of the Bambala Coast up to about 1700, also
suggest *postethnic* Afro-Malagasy connections in both Africa and Madagascar and give an added interest to name analogies with the Karanga,
Barwe, Venda, Sacumbe, and Šaka, leaving the *Temur* out altogether.

Special note should be made also of dialectical loans that have puzzled
local students or that have not even been suspected as Bantu loans in
Malagasy. The former problem involves, for example, the Betsileo
Kabeso (royal vocabulary address for king, ruler). It comes from the
Bantu *-eza*, or divinity, but as royal title it finds a precise analogy in
Rwanda.[29] As for the second problem, much more endemic, a cursory look
at any Swahili dictionary would have revealed long ago that the rulers
of the Betsileo Isandra and of the Antaisaka, the Zara *Behava*, were stating *in* Bantu "we are the inner-court men" of Menabé. Likewise, the Zafy
Manely rulers of Ibara were asserting their Maroserana origins through
the *futi nunu* from Bantu *futi nununa*. *Nununa* is brother, and *futi* is a
term either for kneecap or occipital bone, both of which figure prominently in Maroserana *dady*. The *-na* suffix in *nununa* is swallowed in
southern dialects. This happens as a rule in comparison with Imerina
(see the Bara-Merina vocabulary in note 34, Chapter IV). Moreover, the
terminal Malagasy *y* is barely audible. Thus, the difference is that *futi
nunu* is not the equivalent of Malagasy *fotsy nono* (white breast in
standard orthography) but a Bantu expression. If Jacques Faublée had
not recorded this term phonetically and had used instead the standard
orthography, it would have been not only impossible to uncover the
meaning but also misleading, given the legacy of pigmental myths with
which dynastic families in Madagascar have been surrounded. These
are the more dramatic examples of how extremely delicate the whole
subject is.

It is now necessary to return to one of the most abused terms in
Madagascar, the famous *andriana*. Although it figures as an important
linguistic proof for the Asian origins of kings in Madagascar, *andria*'s
etymon has never been really explained. It was supposed to have come

---

[28] See text and notes 120–132, in Chapter 4.

[29] Jan M. Vansina, *L'Evolution du Royaume Rwanda des origines à 1900* (1962),
p. 10; Alexis Kagame, *Les Milices du Rwanda précolonial* (1963), p. 17, item 5.
Around Lake Tanganyika, the spirits have been called *muzimu* but their head spirit
was *Kabezia* (The Powerful), *Annales de la Propagation de la Foi*, LX (1888), 250.

from Malay *satriyan*, from Malagasy *andry* (post, pillar), from Javanese *Andaya*, or even from the Celebes' *Dain/Dien*.[30] And, it was universally assumed that such an elevated term could not be found in the Dark Continent across the channel. One can start with the Bara *Andra-hufiki*, former funerary attendants of Bara kings with political and judicial functions. They came to be initiators in halting warfare and in the rendering of justice since the Zafy Manely kinglets created most of the tensions in Ibara. If one turns to Africa, it will be found that the *oracles* of Lugbara in Uganda have had the collective name of *andri* and that all five of the Lugbara *andri* were, in effect, initiators of action.[31] In Swahili, *anḍa* (*anḍia*, directive-imperative and *andiana* reflective) is to start, initiate, begin.[32] The Malagasy *dr* and Swahili *d* are identical labials. Since *anda* and *anza* are interchanged in Africa and both are roots associated with government (places, persons, items), there is not only a lack of mystery about Malagasy *andria* but also a crying need to acknowledge at long last that both *andria* and *mpanjaka* are simply derived from the two Bantu variants of the same *root*. As such, they may even point to earlier Malagasy transfers from the mainland, who took *anda* with them, and later ones who brought along *anza* instead. An oversight of this kind is even more dramatic for a related term, *andapa*, which designated in old Betsileo palace object or objects. This term has been given the etymon *lapa* (Malagasy, palace) by eliminating the root *anḍa*!

Still other loans illustrate some very real problems for future research. The term -*hufiki* finds its nearest orthographic relative in Malagasy *hofika* but its meaning corresponds to Swahili -*hukumu*. The Malagasy *hofika* is a plant. The Swahili -*hukumu* means "to pronounce sentence, to judge, to govern, to exercise power,"[33] and depicts exactly the role of *Andrahufiki* in Ibara. The Bara legal term *kitomboka* (false testimony) includes at the same time the Malagasy *boka* (false) and the Swahili *tambo* (insoluble enigma) as well as *tambika* (ceremonial ancestor-appeasement). The terrible admixture of *boka*, *tambo*, and *tambika* along with the orthographic distance between -*hufiki* and -*hukumu*, terms with identical and very precise meaning, suggest the high degree to which verbal and conceptual transmutations have been carried within the compound-forming Malagasy, the often deep and hidden nature of this prob-

[30] Cf. J. Richardson, *A New Malagasy-English Dictionary* (1885), p. 43 (*satriyan*); H. F. Standing, "The Tribal Divisions of the Hova," *AA* (1887), 355 (*andry*); and A. Grandidier, *Ethnographie de Madagascar*, Vol. I, Tome 1 (1908), pp. 2, n. 1, 3 (*Andaya, Dain, Dien*).

[31] John Middleton, *The Lugbara of Uganda* (1965), pp. 77–78; and his *Lugbara Religion* (1960), pp. 80, 275 (index for further references to oracles).

[32] Sacleux, *Swahili-français*, Vol. I (1939), p. 62.

[33] *Ibid.*, pp. 288–289.

lem, and the need for endless patience in investigating every word on its own merit. The next problem is one of convergence. For example, the term *Andrahufiki* led to the Lugbara of Uganda. But, the Bara judges do not occur in legal isolation. The Bara *sasalia* (immediate settlement with damages) and *tsarampilongoa* (amicable solution) reveal the Swahili *sasa* and *sasa hii* (immediately, this very instant) and *lunga* (root *unga*), to unite, bring together, along with Malagasy *tsara* (good, excellent, suitable), which is separated from Swahili *lunga* by *mpi*, or the prefix forming the habitual noun of the agent. Thus, one does not only come again to the problem of transmutation (*sasa hii/sasalia*) or dual compounds (*tsara-mpi-lunga*), but also the possible analogy between Malagasy Bara and Uganda's *Lug-bara*. Would this mean that the *Barabé/Barwe* name analogy should be seen as a simple case of "chasing" or "wishful thinking"? Again, the significant point here is *not* that such associations are advanced with "firm conviction" but that we are dealing with two branches of Bantu idioms perceived by Mariano and that the possibilities are worth stating as *signposts* for subsequent research. One cannot escape the conclusion that further discoveries of dialectical loans, more precise measurements and delineations of accurate time-and-place contexts will constitute perhaps the *most* promising area of investigation into both the Malagasy and African past.

After reviewing all of the various hypotheses about the Malagasy origins, Hubert Deschamps placed the following conclusion in italics: "*As a people, the Malagasy are a product of juxtapositions and syntheses of Indonesian and African elements.*"[34] In this very broad conclusion, one can find nothing with which to disagree. Yet, when one turns to the elements, juxtapositions, syntheses, and the manner in which the Malagasy are supposed to have formed as a *single* people, the wrinkles, incongruities, problems, and difficulties reappear in all of their magnificent splendor. While one can readily perceive that certain cultural features are shared by most Malagasy (for example, cult of ancestors, general belief in *vintana*, or fate beyond control of man), such features are not expressed in the same way everywhere and can be said to represent features diffused throughout the world. The continuously reiterated belief in the "profound unity" of Malagasy "culture and language" may be regarded as a very useful political and social myth in the present circumstances. It also happens to be a matter of convenience with which to by-pass the incongruous *detail* and substitute an ill-defined synchronic present for history itself. No one could deny that the colonial period has done much to accelerate a loss of cultural and dialectical divergences in the Great Island, a process that began in the 1820s, through the extension

[34] H. Deschamps, *Histoire de Madagascar,* 2nd ed. (1961), p. 24.

of Merina political domain and missionary work even if this change has created new divisions within Madagascar.[35] At the same time, the study of Sakalava, Bara, Anteimoro, and Merina formation and, more marginally, the note made of the Betsileo, Antanosy, Mahafaly, and Tanala-Manambia do *not* sustain the belief in the unity of traditional cultures or even of vocabulary, a fact attested by the need even in very recent times to use local-dialect interpreters. In short, an older and much different reality did exist and cannot be disregarded. An entire and well-defined political system could disappear from Ibara in a scant fifty years. All of the Bambala colonies could vanish in an equal period of time (1650–1700) almost without a trace. Within a single generation, the Tanala-Manambia could migrate several times to re-form their state with an unrelated group of Tanosy migrants. An older Temoro society could undergo considerable change from 1850 to 1900 as a result of Merina conquests, *Ampanabaka* revolts, and the advent of colonial administration. In reality, therefore, Madagascar of 1960 is not the island of two or three centuries ago, and these examples can be multiplied to prove this. The broad impact of change within Madagascar over the past 150 years has been to reduce the influence of Africa precisely where it has been most prominent as is shown by the loss of Bantu loan words.

Even the hypothesis most favorable to Africa in connection with the subject of Malagasy origins, namely an Indonesian passage on the mainland prior to the arrival of proto-Malagasy into the Great Island fails to come to grips with data available *in* Madagascar. For what these suggest strongly is that the Great Island was settled by human colonies of *any* real importance only *after* they had been on the mainland as *such*. There is already a substantial body of opinion that the ancient Azanians (old inhabitants of southern Somalia, Kenya, and Tanzania) were at least part-Indonesians. The items of evidence usually cited are: (1) the statement of Edrisi that traders from Indonesia (isles of Zabaj) and the Zenj (inhabitants of the eastern African littoral) understood each other's language; (2) the ancient presence of such vessels there as the *mtepe* and the *dau*; (3) the old technique of turtle catching; and (4) Malaysian food crops.[36] The Wak-Wak of older sources are sometimes identified with Indonesians in southeastern Africa.[37] Even this, however, is inade-

[35] As in Africa, between urban and rural, educated and illiterate, Protestants and Catholics, Muslims and "pagans," new class of Afro-Europeans (or Malagasy who live like Europeans) and "bush people." Fortunately, however, in Madagascar these divisions have not had some of the consequences apparent in Africa.

[36] Cf. Murdock, *Africa*, pp. 209–210; G. W. B. Huntingford, "Azania," *Anthropos*, 35–36 (1940–1941), 209–220; M. Posnansky (ed.), *Prelude to East African History* (1966), pp. 5, 64, 85–86, 89, 93–94, 104, 110.

[37] See E. E. Burke, "Some Aspects of Arab Contact with South-East Africa," in *Historians in Tropical Africa,* Proceedings of the Leverhulme Inter-Collegiate History

quate. We are not dealing with a single wave of proto-Malagasy, with some coastal east African colonies of Indonesians, with trans-Zambezian Wak-Wak, or even with already formed Malagasy who raid back into Africa. Rather, there must have been a vast and fairly gradual human movement from the general direction of Indonesia in the early centuries of the first millenium of our era, a movement one could call by an old Malagasy term *lakato* (or true outrigger people) because they did not belong to a single ethnicity. Moreover, these *lakato* must have spread considerably into the interior of east-central and southeast-central Africa, along the waterways and lakes, *before* the Bantu-speakers left their core area in present-day Congo-Kinshasa. Long before the Bantu reached coastal east Africa, Rhodesia, and Mozambique, they met the *lakato* in the interior. There should have been some fusion, some conflict, some flights, and some refusion, in short, an Afro-Malagasy race should have resulted from these contacts.

At the rim of most intimate contact, in the interior, the *lakato* were absorbed by the Bantu and possessed no *vy* or iron. On coastal Africa and at some points in the hinterlands there were as yet no direct contacts with the Bantu. In-between, there should have been all types of linguistic and cultural admixtures and conjugations. It was the increasing Bantu pressure into the Indonesian, semi-Indonesian, and semi-Bantu enclaves that impelled the *lakato* into another gradual but mass migration, this time to Madagascar, where a few had gone earlier as the primary but numerically minor salient.

From this second and crucial movement that can be called *lakato* II, came the *tompontany* of Madagascar—the Kimosy, Karimbola, Sihanaka, central-highlands Vazimba, some of the west-coast Vazimba, the Masikoro, Hova-Andrantsay, pre-Zafindraminia Tanosy, Vezo, Arindrano (literally, "those who balance on water, later the historical Betsileo of central highlands), the Tanala (literally, forest people), the Mahafaly, and some of the groups enumerated by Flacourt but now extinct, namely the Vohitsangombe (men of cattle) and Alfissach. These *lakato* II gave the island its Indonesian linguistic matrix, which would never be dislocated. They also introduced agriculture (including the cultivation of rice), the megaliths, terracing, stone-walled villages, cattle and pens, ancestral cults including the *fanane* variant, village chiefdoms, water and stone burials, ritual slaughter of cattle, the idea that red is the color of chiefs, and the root *anda*. The loans for domesticated animals and plants and for pottery came with the semi-Bantu component of the *lakato* II as well.

Conference, Salisbury (1962), p. 98. The African Wak-Wak were mentioned principally by Maçudi, in his *Golden Meadows*, and by Buzurg Ibn Shahriyar in *Livre des merveilles de l'Inde*.

Among the *lakato* II, the Vazimba and Arindrano appear to have been culturally the most influential. The *ovi* (yams), the power to feed, the stone villages, and *andria* are associated with the Vazimba as attested by tradition. The earliest village toponymy was based on the *vato* or stone (Ambato, Varambato, etc.) and chiefly names were formed with *andria* long before the Hova arrived in Imerina. On the other hand, rice cultivation and agricultural terracing have been most developed among the Betsileo while both megaliths and stone villages overlap in old Imerina and old Betsileo areas.

The basic formation of the *tompontany* in Madagascar should have occurred by the tenth century. Their African antecedents extend very likely from the lake regions of central Africa to Rhodesia where they could be connected with the Inyanga and Ziwa complex, spanning—by the available Carbon-14 dates—the period A.D. ±300 and the end of the first millenium, and revealing such items as combed pottery, "stone-faced agricultural terracing with which are associated many hundreds of stone-walled enclosures, stock pits, and a certain number of strongholds, the remains covering about 3000 square miles."[38] In contrasting Inyanga from Zimbabwe, Roger Summers saw the difference in terms of two human segments, the culture of ordinary people at Inyanga and that of nobility at Zimbabwe. It is also interesting to note that the Iron Age scarcely touched Inyanga, while the use of copper was minimal.

Early in the second millenium of our era, the *lakato* left behind on the mainland were considerably reduced and confined to much more limited areas of the eastern coast and southern Africa, where the proto-Shona, Venda, and Sotho were just arriving.[39] The Swahili commercial empire in eastern Africa and the Bantu expansion into southern Africa produced the *lakato* III movement to Madagascar, the last important migration of peoples to which the "Legend of Raminia" applies. The arrival of Raminia in the Great Island has been viewed as an isolated event, a single migration. In effect, as Ferrand has shown long ago, *Ramini* is not a personal name. It designated one of the Indonesian islands, and *Raminia* may well stand for Indonesians who had been on the mainland and disappeared from it by the twelfth century, as can be deduced from Ibn al-Mujāwir. Hence, the Raminia legend is an account of the *lakato* III movement from Africa to the Great Island. This time, however, new elements were present as well. The *lakato* III possessed iron both in eastern and southern Africa.[40] They included groups wholly Bantu in language as well as semi-

---

[38] R. Summers, "The Southern Rhodesian Iron Age," *JAH*, II (1961), 10.

[39] A. J. E. Jaffey, "A Reappraisal of the History of the Rhodesian Iron Age Up to the Fifteenth Century," *JAH*, VII (1966), 189–190.

[40] It is well-known that iron was present in southern Rhodesia before the arrival of Bantu-speakers. If the Indonesians are to be seen as iron carriers into southern

Islamized elements that had been in contact for some time *in* Africa with the Persian and Arab colonizers and traders.[41] The *lakato* III gave Madagascar, on the one hand, the Antambahoaka and Zafindraminia and, on the other hand, such groups as the Bambala, Manankarunga, Bara, Sakoambé, Antaifasy, and Antamby (or people of iron, *antam-by/vy*) reported in the traditions of southern Madagascar. The migrations of *lakato* III should have ended with the southern African arrivals by the turn of the 1300s at the latest. During the same period, there also formed in northwestern Madagascar and at Vohemar in the northeast the Antalaotra-Swahili cultures and trading outposts, which were, however, oriented entirely toward external commerce. The *lakato* II and III paved the way for the Maroserana, the Temur, and their Anteony, both from the mainland as well. In short, the traditional past of Madagascar makes absolutely no sense without Africa.

Africa, then they could only be the *lakato* III peoples who moved from the eastern coast of Africa (where they got the iron through trade with Zabaj and from where iron was exported to India) into southern Rhodesia. The earliest Carbon-14 date for iron in Madagascar is A.D. ± 1100. It is doubtful that this date will be rolled back more than two centuries by archaeological work yet to be done on the island. Apart from a trickle of *lakato* I into Madagascar possibly by A.D. ± 400, median date by "convention," I do not envisage the *lakato* II movement to have taken place much before *ca.* 600–700 precisely because they first colonized the mainland.

[41] Gabriel Ferrand and Alfred Grandidier, and more recently Jacques Faublée, found that the *Sora-bé* contain certain Persian and even Syrian antecedents. The two earlier *Malgachisants* even had a running quarrel over whether these antecedents were imported by the Anteimoro or whether the Anteimoro reproduced them from pre-existing Zafindraminia texts. Actually, this problem has nothing to do with the "origins" of the Zafindraminia or Anteimoro but with their residence *in* Africa.

BIBLIOGRAPHY

MADAGASCAR

Unpublished

Abdallah. "Généalogie des Maroserana." Not dated. *BP*. Document 629. Manuscript. Short but interesting for the problem of Maroserana formation.

Anonymous. *Bara Oral Texts* (without title). 1924. *BP*. Document 664. Typescript. Partially reproduced in the Appendix below, these texts have been collected by a Bara among his own people.

Anonymous. *Développement du Royaume Hova*. Not dated. *BDP*. Typescript. Forty-five in-quarto pages of Merina oral texts, collected and edited probably in the 1890s. Fairly important supplement to Callet's *Tantara*. Extract in Appendix below.

Anonymous. "Mémoire sur l'estat présent de l'Isle Dauphine." February 10, 1668. *ANSOMCM*. Carton I, Picce 15. Manuscript. A kind of incomplete periplus for the Malagasy coast.

Anonymous. *Niandohan'ny Fivavahan'ny Sakalava*. *AM*. No. 2238/2. Manuscript notebook. An important source for the origin of monarchical Sakalava *dady* cult as well as for its description.

Anonymous. "Relation des remarques qui ont estes faites sur les principalles bayes, ances & havres de l'Isle Dauphine & Isles Adiaçantes." February 22, 1670. *ANSOMCM*. Carton I, Piece 26. Manuscript. Up-dated and expanded version of the February 10, 1668 "Mémoire" attributed to the captains, pilots, and merchants of the vessel *Petit St. Jan*.

Anonymous. "Renseignements sur les Bara." 1912. *BGT*. Manuscript. An ethnographic list of Bara subgroups at Ivohibé.

Anonymous. *Tantaran'ny Andrian' Sakalava*. *AM*. No. 2238/1. Manuscript notebook. A history of Sakalava kings. Valuable especially for the nineteenth century.

Bernard. "Notice sur le *Vy Lava*." Not dated. *BP*. Document 623. Manuscript. Short but good description of the *vy lava* (long knife), symbol of Sakalava royal authority.

Bernier, Ch. *Rapport sur une mission sur la côte nord-est de Madagascar.* December 27, 1834. *ANSOMCM.* Carton XVII, Dossier 8. Manuscript. A 136-page document, mostly on the Antankarana, written in 1834 but based on a visit in 1831. For an edited and published version of this manuscript, see Fleury, below.

Betoto, Ch. "Histoire de la royauté sakalava." Paris, 1950. Typescript, in author's own possession. A 32-page paper prepared at the Ecole Nationale de la France d'Outre-Mer.

Birkeli, E. "Rapport relatif à la découverte de la langue vazimba." July 3, 1917. *AAM.* Typescript letter of three pages.

Commerson. "Note historique sur un peuple nain de Madagascar, Kimosse." Not dated. *BGT.* Manuscript. Referred to by de la Lande (see entry below), this 6-page report has been at the center of a long controversy about the Kimosy as "dwarfs" of Madagascar.

Cossigny, Ch. de *Mémoires.* 1773. *ANSOMCM.* Carton III, Dossier 10. Manuscript. Basically, a document discussing the possibilities of a French colony in eastern Madagascar.

Dandouau, A. "Funerailles des rois sakalava." 1901. *BDP.* Manuscript. An interesting ethnohistorical account with a genealogical list of Maroserana kings.

———. *Moeurs, coutumes et croyances betsileo.* Early 1920s. *BDP.* Manuscript notebook. A very useful 191-page addendum to Father Dubois' (see entry below) massive work on the Betsileo.

Dargèlas, A. *Notes.* December 26, 1837. *BGT.* Manuscript. Fairly important recollections of a former sea captain and long-time resident of southeastern Madagascar.

De la Motte Saint-Pierre, R. *Nossi-bé, 13° latitude sud.* 1949. *AAM.* Typescript. A 238-page attempt to deal with Sakalava history. Uneven.

Dreyer. *Letter.* December 9, 1915. *BP.* Manuscript. Appended to Document 620. See under Tovonkery below.

Duhamel, Comte de Précourt. *Mémoire.* April 1784. *ANSOMCM.* Carton VIII, Dossiers a-c. Manuscript. An argument for a French colony in Madagascar.

Grandidier, A. *Notes et souvenirs.* 1917. *ARM.* Manuscript. 413 pages. Alfred Grandidier's autobiography, completed shortly before his death.

Grandidier, A. *Notes manuscrites* (Sakalava). The original manuscript has not been located. *Extensive* references to these have, however, been made both by Alfred and Guillaume Grandidier in print as well as in G. Grandidier's unpublished "Essai," cited below.

Grandidier, G. "Essai d'histoire des Malgaches de la région occidentale: les Sakalava." Paris, not dated. Manuscript. In private library of Hubert Deschamps. An unfinished and useful work of 78 pages with extensive notes, based mainly on the *Notes Manuscrites* of his father, period 1868–1870.

Hoffmann, B. H. *Vocabulaire français-hova-sakalava-tsimihety.* Compiled 1940–1948. *BP.* Manuscript. 218 pages and a 116-page index. An important supplement to other vocabularies and dictionaries.

La Serre, Sieur de. *Journal du voyage fait à Madagascar.* 1776–1777.

ANSOMCM. Carton VII, Dossier 8. Manuscript. Some 60 pages with addenda, dealing mainly with the east coast of Madagascar. Copy in *BGT*.

Louis, Dr. M. *Mémoire sur les moeurs et coutumes des peuplades de Madagascar.* 1950. *AAM.* Manuscript. Interesting ethnographic paper of 48 pages.

Mamelomana, E. *Les Mahafaly.* Not dated. *BP.* Typescript. A 78-page, heavily edited essay based on oral texts. Extract in the Appendix below.

Mamory-bé. *Sakalava Oral Traditions.* 1965. Tape 1 (*OTT/1*). Mirinarivo, Majunga. My own recording of oral texts given, in part, by this aged guardian of Sakalava royal relics. See also *OTT* below.

Maudave, Comte de. *Journal.* 1768. *ANSOMCM.* Carton II, Dossier 1. Manuscript. Copy in *BGT.* See also Pouget de St. André, below.

Mayeur, N. *Histoire de Ratsimilahoe.* Not dated. Original manuscript in the Farquhar Collection, Department of Manuscripts, the British Museum. Typescript copy in *ARM.*

Mellis, J. *Autour du Tombeau du prince qui fait peur.* Not dated. IRSM Library. Document 0752. Typescript. 123 pages. Edited oral texts and speculations on Sakalava past and psychology.

Merina Manuscripts. See G. Grandidier (1942) below.

Nintsy. *Sakalava Oral Traditions.* 1965. *OTT/1.* Texts given to author by the *mpanjaka* of Mirinarivo, Majunga.

OTT (Oral Traditions Taped). Collection of tape recordings of Sakalava oral texts made by the author at Majunga and Morondava mainly between June and September 1965. Most of these texts will be reproduced in English translation in a forthcoming "Sakalava History, 1650–1896." For extracts, see Appendix, below.

Pagès, P. *Histoire des Andriana d'Ambohijanaka-ouest de leur origine jusqu'à nos jours.* April 1920. *AM* Library. No. 533. Manuscript notebook. An important family monograph of 52 pages. Throws light on broader history of Imerina.

Parat. *Mémoire.* September 19, 1714. Manuscript. Copy in *BGT.* Actually a 10-page letter addressed to Pontchartrain. Mentions the presence of onion and garlic in central highlands.

Rabemanana, J. *Le Pays des Kimoso et son histoire depuis les origines jusqu'à l'an 1820.* Not dated—probably *ca.* 1912. *AAM.* Manuscript. 99 in-folio pages. Although it borders occasionally on fantasy, this is a most important work based on oral texts and area descriptions.

Rabozaka. *Notes d'histoire malgache.* Set on paper in 1914 by an anonymous French administrator at Anjozorobé. *AAM.* Two manuscript notebooks. Unusual for its recollection of the "legendary times" for northern Imerina.

Rainijoelina. *Histoire d'Isandra. BDP.* No date. In Malagasy. Manuscript notebook of 100 pages. A contribution to Betsileo history.

Ralambo, J. *Histoire de pays d'Isandra. AAM.* In Malagasy. Two manuscript notebooks. Overlaps with Rainijoelina above.

Ramaherison. "Anteimorona de Vohipeno." 1915. *AAM.* Manuscript. For the most part, an enumeration of Anteimoro subgroups at Vohipeno.

Raphael, F. "Ny Famohazan'ny Sikily." Not dated. *AAM.* Manuscript. 5 pages. Account of the "awakening of sikidy."

Rombaka, J.-P. *Tantaran' drazan'ny Anteimoro Anteony.* 1933. Manuscript. A French translation, listed as being in the IRSM Library, could not be found. A summary outline in French in *AAM* indicates that it is based on old *Sora-bé.* Has the earmarks of novel contribution to the history of Anteony.

Said Ahmed Ali. *Essai sur l'histoire d'Anjouan.* December 29, 1927, IRSM Library No. 0751. Typescript. 45 pages. Important but unevenly written paper.

Tombo, Tsimanohitra. *Sakalava Oral Traditions.* 1965. *OTT/1.* Texts given to author by this well-informed and relatively young guardian of royal Sakalava relics at Mirinarivo, Majunga.

Tovonkery. *Lovantsofina Milaza ny Tantara Nihavian'ny Mpanjaka Sakalava Samy Hofa Eto Amin'ny Faritany Maromandia.* 1915. *BP.* Document 620. Manuscript. An often important history of Sakalava kings dictated by *mpanjaka* Tovonkery to the district head of Maromandia.

Tsarovana, V. *Notes sur les Sakalava.* 1912–1913. Collection of the Human Sciences Department, University of Madagascar. Notebook No. 173. Manuscript. Relatively interesting social and ethnographic materials by a schoolteacher in northwestern Madagascar.

Published

Abinal, A. *Vingt ans à Madagascar: colonisation, traditions historiques, moeurs et croyances.* Paris, 1885.

———, and Malzac, V. *Dictionnaire malgache-français.* Tananarive, 1888.

Ardant du Picq, Col. "L'Influence islamique sur une population malayo-polynésienne de Madagascar: Tanala," *RTC,* XXVI (1932), 191–208, 266–279, 370–401.

Aujas, L. *Les Rites du sacrifice à Madagascar.* Tananarive, 1927.

Aymard, Capt. "Le Pays sakalava," *BSGT,* XXVI (1907), 90–124.

Baron, R. "The Bara," *AA,* II (1881), 82–84.

Bastard, E.-J. "Mémoires d'un roi bara," *RM,* VI (1904), 385–508; VII (1905), 232–246, 321–354.

Batchelor, R. T. "Notes on the Antankarana and Their Country," *AA,* I (1877), 27–31.

Battistini, R., and Verin, P. "Vohitrandriana haut-lieu d'une ancienne culture du Lac Alaotra," *CM,* I/1 (1964), 53–90.

Bénévent, Ch. "Etude sur le Bouéni," *NRE,* I (1897), 355–379; II (1897), 49–77.

———. "Note sur les Kimosy," *BAM,* IV (1905–1906), 100–103.

Bensch, E. "De Tuléar à Fianarantsoa," *NRE,* V (1899), 529–538.

———. "La Faune dans le sud de Madagascar," *RM,* IV (1902), 133–153.

Benyowsky, M. A. de. *Memoirs and Travels.* Vol. II. London, 1790.

Bernard-Thierry, S. "A Propos des Emprunts sanskrits en Malgache," *JA,* (1959), 311–348.

Berthier, H. *De l'Usage de l'Arabico-Malgache en Imerina au debut de XIXe siécle.* Tananarive, 1933. Vol. XVI of *MAM.*

———. "Des Participes passifs à suffixe," *BAM,* VI (1908), 37–53.

———. "Du 'Relatifs en Malgache,'" *BAM,* XII/1 (1913), 177–179.

————. "Fragment du folklore bara," *RM*, VIII (1906), 1062–1066.

————. *Notes et impressions sur les moeurs et coutumes du peuple malgache.* Tananarive, 1933.

————. "Rapport ethnographique sur les races de Madagascar," *NRE*, IV (1898), 1111–1142.

Birkeli, E. *Marques de boeufs et traditions de race: document sur l'ethnographie de la côte occidentale de Madagascar.* Oslo, 1926. *Bulletin* No. 2 of the Oslo Etnografiske Museum.

————. *Les Vazimba de la côte ouest de Madagascar: notes d'ethnologie.* Tananarive, 1936. Vol. XXII of *MAM.*

Boothby, R. *A Briefe Discovery or Description of the Most Famous Island of Madagascar, in Asia, near the East Indies.* London, 1640.

Boto, J. "Tradition relative à l'origine des Betsimisaraka-Betanimena," *BODE*, XXV (1923), 252–253.

Boudou, A. *Les Jésuites à Madagascar au XIXe siécle.* Paris, 1942. In two volumes.

Cadet, A. "Pages oubliées," *BAM*, I (1902), 125–127.

Callet, F. *Tantaran'ny Andriana.* Tananarive, 1873–1902. Five volumes in two editions. Translated into French by G. S. Chapus and E. Ratsimba as *Histoire des rois.* Tananarive, 1953–1958. In four volumes. See entry below.

Carpeau du Saussay. *Voyage à Madagascar.* Paris, 1722. Written in 1663. An English translation in serial form appeared at Mauritius.

Catat, L. *Voyage à Madagascar.* Paris, 1895.

Chamla, M.-C. *Recherches anthropologiques sur l'origine des Malgaches.* Paris, 1958. *Mémoires.* Vol. XIX, No. 1, Series A. Museum National d'Histoire Naturelle.

Champion, P. "La Tache pigmentale congenitale à Madagascar," *JSA*, VII/1 (1937), 79–92.

Chapus, G.-S. "Le Tanguin," *BAM*, new series, XVII (1946), 157–188.

————, and Ratsimba, E. (trans. and eds.) *Histoire des rois (Tantaran'ny Andriana).* Vols. I–IV. Tananarive, 1953–1958.

Cheffaud, M. "Note sur la chronologie des rois d'Imerina," *BAM*, new series, XIX (1936), 37–47.

COACM. Collection des ouvrages anciens concernant Madagascar. Paris, 1903–1920. In nine volumes. Alfred and Guillaume Grandidier are listed as general editors.

Colançon, M.-M. "Note sur la fabrication du papier dit Anteimoro," *BEM*, (1921), 267–269.

————. "Premier Chapitre du *Tantaran'ny Andriana*," *BAM*, XII/1 (1913), 21–114.

Collins, C. "The Fandroana or Annual Festival of the Taimoro," *AA*, VI (1898), 149–151.

Copland, S. *A History of the Island of Madagascar.* London, 1822.

Coppalle, A. "Les Kimosy de Madagascar," *BAM*, VIII (1910), 65–67.

————. "Sikidy and Vintana: Half-Hours with Malagasy Diviners," *AA*, III

Cours, G., and Fritz, J. "Le Manioc," *BM*, XI/178 (1961), 203–224.

Cowan, D. W. *The Bara Land: A Description of the Country and People.* Tananarive, 1881. Pamphlet. 72 pages.

————. "Geographical Excursions in the Betsileo, Tanala and Bara Countries," *Proceedings*, Royal Geographical Society, London (June 1882), 521–537.

Cultru, P. *Un Empereur de Madagascar au XVIIIᵉ siécle: Benyowszky*. Paris, 1906.

Dahl, O. Chr. *Malgache et Maanjan*. Oslo, 1951.

————. "Le Substrat bantou en Malgache," *NTS*, XVII (1953), 325–362.

Dahle, L. "The Influence of the Arabs on the Malagasy Language, as a Test of Their Contribution to Malagasy Civilization and Superstition," *AA*, I (1876), 75–91.

————. "The Race Elements of the Malagasy and Guesses: A Truth with Regard to Their Origin," *AA*, II (1883), 216–228.

————. "Sikidy and Vintana: Half-Hours with Malagasy Diviners," *AA*, III (1886), 218–234; III (1887), 315–327; III (1888), 457–467.

————. "The Swaheli Element in the New Malagasy-English Dictionary," *AA*, III (1885), 99–115. See also entry under Richardson.

Dalmond, Abbé. *Vocabulaire malgache-français pour les langues sakalave et betsimisara*. Paris, 1844.

Dandouau, A. *Contes populaires des Sakalava et des Tsimihety de la région d'Analalava*. Algiers, 1922.

————. "Coutumes funéraires dans le nord-ouest de Madagascar." *BAM*, IX (1911), 157–172.

————, and Chapus, G.-S. *Histoire des populations de Madagascar*. Paris, 1952.

Dandouau, B., and Fontoynont, M. "Ody et Fanafody," *BAM*, XI (1913), 151–218.

David, R. "Notes d'ethnographie malgache," *BAM*, new series, XXII (1939), 65–72.

————. "Le Problème anthropobiologique malgache," "Observations anthropométriques et sérologiques chez les Mahafaly du sud-ouest de Madagascar," *BAM*, new series, XXIII (1940), 1–11, 12–32.

Decary, R. *L'Androy*. Paris, 1930–1933. In two volumes.

————. "La Chasse et le piégeage chez les indigènes de Madagascar," *JSA*, IX/1 (1939), 3–41.

————. *Coutumes guerrières et organisation militaire chez les anciens malgaches*. Vol. I. Paris, 1966.

————. *L'Habitat à Madagascar*. Paris, 1958.

————. *Moeurs et coutumes des Malgaches*. Paris, 1951.

————. *La Mort et les coutumes funéraires à Madagascar*. Paris, 1962.

————. *Les Ordailles et sacrifices rituels chez les anciens malgaches*. Paris, 1959.

————. "Les Tatouages antandroy," *RM*, new series (October 1933), 37–54.

————. "Les Tatouages chez les indigènes de Madagascar," *JSA*, V/1 (1935), 1–39.

Defoort, E. "L'Androy," *BEM*, XIII/2 (1913), 127–246.

D'Escamps, H. *Histoire et géographie de Madagascar*. Paris, 1884. Published originally in 1844 under the pseudonym of Macé-Descartes.

Deschamps, H. *Les Antaisaka*. Tananarive, 1936.

———. *Le Dialecte antaisaka.* Tananarive, 1936.

———. *Histoire de Madagascar.* 2nd ed. Paris, 1961.

———. *Les Migrations intérieures passées et présentes à Madagascar.* Paris, 1959.

———, and Vianès, S. *Les Malgaches du sud-est.* Paris, 1959.

Drury, R. *Madagascar or Robert Drury's Journal during Fifteen Years Captivity on That Island.* 7th ed. Edited by Capt. Pasfield Oliver. London, 1890. Original ed. 1729. The French edition, consulted less frequently, was published in 1906 as Volume IV of the *COACM* (see entry above).

Du Bois. *Les Voyages faits par le Sieur D. B. aux Illes Dauphine ou Madagascar, & Bourbon, ou Mascarene, és années 1669–1672.* Paris, 1674.

Dubois, H.-M. *Monographie des Betsileo.* Paris, 1939.

———. "Les Origines des Malgaches," *Anthropos,* XXI (1926), 72–126; XXII (1927), 80–124; XXIV (1929), 218–311; XXIX (1934), 757–774.

Du Bois de la Villerabel. "Etude sur le secteur des Bara Imamono," *NRE,* V (1899), 523–528.

———. "La Tradition chez les Bara," *NRE,* VI (1900), 263–273.

Dumaine. "Voyage fait au pays d'Ancaye dans l'île de Madagascar en 1790," *AV,* XI (1810), 146–218.

D'Unienville, Baron. "Essai sur Madagascar," in his *Statistique de l'Ile Maurice et ses dépendences.* Vol. III. Paris, 1838. Pp. 223–344.

Elle, B. "Note sur les tribus de la province de Farafangana," *BAM,* VI (1905–1906), 97–103.

Ellis, Wm. *History of Madagascar.* London, 1838. In two volumes.

———. *Three Visits to Madagascar.* . . . London, 1859.

Englevin, A. *Les Vézos ou "enfants de la mer": Monographie d'une soustribu Sakalava.* Bellevue (Seine-et-Oise), 1936.

Estragon, M. "La Fabrication du papier anteimoro," *RM,* new series (October 1933), 59–62.

Fagering, E. "Etude sur les immigrations anciennes à Madagascar et sur l'origine des principalles dynasties du sud et de l'ouest de l'ile," *BAM,* new series, XXV (1942–1943), 165–174.

———. "Histoire des Maroserana du Menabé," *BAM,* new series, XXVIII (1947–1948), 115–135.

Faublée, J. "L'Alimentation dès Bara," *JSA,* XII (1942), 157–201.

———. *La Cohésion des sociétés bara.* Paris, 1954.

———. *Les Esprits de la vie à Madagascar.* Paris, 1954.

——— (ed.). *Ethnographie de Madagascar.* Paris, 1946.

———. *Récits bara.* Paris, 1947.

———. "Techniques divinatoires et magiques chez les Bara de Madagascar," *JSA,* XXI/2 (1951), 127–138.

———, and M. "Pirogues et navigation chez les Vezo du sud-ouest de Madagascar," *Anthropologie,* LIV (1954), 432–454.

———, and Léandri, J. "Noms indigènes de végétaux du Menabé septentrional," *Bulletin,* Museum National d'Histoire Naturelle, XVII (1945), 435–442, 514–516.

Faustin, L. "Moeurs et coutumes de l'Androy," *BM,* VIII/144 (1958), 359–394.

Fenies, J. "Migrations tandroy," *BM*, VII/138 (1957), 923–940.

Ferrand, G. "L'Elément arabe et souahili en Malgache ancien et moderne," *JA*, 10th series, II/3 (1903), 451–485.

———. "La Légende de Raminia," *JA*, 9th series, XIX/2 (1902), 185–230.

———. "Les Migrations musulmanes et juives à Madagascar," *AMGRHR*, LII (1905), 381–417.

———. *Les Musulmans à Madagascar et aux Iles Comores*. Paris, 1891–1902. In three volumes.

———. "Note sur l'alphabet arabico-malgache," *Anthropos*, IV/1 (1909), 190–206.

———. "Note sur le calendrier malgache et le fandrauna," *REES*, (April–May 1908). Extract of 33 pages.

———. "L'Origine africaine des Malgaches," *JA*, 10th series, XI/3 (1908), 353–500.

———. "Le Pays de Mangalor et de Mangatsini," *T'oung-pao* (Leiden), 2nd series, X/1 (1909). Extract of 16 pages.

———. "Un Texte arabico-malgache du XVIᵉ siécle," *NEMBN*, XXXVIII/2 (1906), 450–576.

———. "Les Voyages des Javanais à Madagascar," *JA*, 10th series, XV/2 (1910), 281–330.

Firinga, Sgt. "La Dynastie des Maroserana," *RM*, III (1901), 658–672.

Flacourt, E. de. *Histoire de la Grande Ile Madagascar*. 2nd ed. Paris, 1661. Expanded edition of 1658 original. Reprinted in 1913 as Vol. VIII of *COACM* (see entry above).

———. *Relation de ce qui s'est passé en Ile de Madagascar depuis l'année 1642 jusqu'en 1660*. Paris, 1661. Reprinted in 1920 as first section of Vol. IX of *COACM*.

Fleury, Th. "Quelques Notes sur le nord de Madagascar," *SGCBB*, (1886), 194–209, 226–245, 257–282, 290–312. See unpublished entry above on Bernier.

Fontoynont, M. "La Légende des Kimosy," *BAM*, VII (1909), 51–59.

———. "Solo Célèbres en Imerina," *BAM*, XII/1 (1913), 115–137.

———, and Raomandahy, E. "Les Antaifasy: origines et guerres avec les tribus voisines," *BAM*, new series, XXII (1939), 1–28.

Froberville, E. de. "Aperçu sur la langue malgache et recherches sur la race qui habitait l'ile de Madagascar avant l'arrivé des Malais," *BSG*, XI (1839), 29–46, 257–274.

———. "Historique des invasions madécasses aux Iles Comores et à la côte orientale d'Afrique," *AVG*, II (1845), 194–208.

Gallieni, Gen. J.-J. *La Pacification de Madagascar: opérations d'octobre 1896 à mars 1899*. Paris, 1900.

Gaudebout, P., and Vernier, E. "Notes sur une campagne de fouilles à Vohémar," *BAM*, new series, XXIV (1941), 91–114.

Gautier, E.-F. "Les Hovas sont-ils des Malais" *JA*, 9th series, XV (1900), 278–296.

———. *Madagascar: essai de géographie physique*. Paris, 1902.

Grandidier, A. *Ethnographie de Madagascar*. Vol. I. Paris, 1908. In two parts.

————. "Les Canaux et les lagunes de la côte orientale de Madagascar," *BSGP*, (1886), 132–140.

————. *Histoire de la géographie de Madagascar.* Rev. ed. Paris, 1892.

————. "Les Hova," *BCM* (June 1895), 113–125.

————. "Note sur les Vazimba de Madagascar," *MSP*, commemorative issue, (1888), 155–161. English translation by J. Sibree, *AA*, V (1894), 129–135.

————. *Notice sur les travaux scientifiques.* Paris, 1884. Pamphlet of 54 pages, with 2 maps.

————. *L'Origine des Malgaches.* Paris, 1901. Shorter version of *Ethnographie de Madagascar.*

————. "Un Voyage de découvertes sur les côtes occidentale et méridionale de l'isle de Madagascar en 1613–1614 par le P. Luiz Mariano," *BCM* (1899). Extract of 28 pages.

————. "Un Voyage scientifique à Madagascar," *RS*, 2nd series, I (1872), 1077–1088.

———— and G. (eds.). *COACM.* See entry above on *COACM.*

———— and G. *Ethnographie de Madagascar.* Vol. III. Paris, 1917.

Grandidier, G. *Bibliographie de Madagascar.* Paris and Tananarive, 1905–1957. Three volumes in four tomes.

————. "Histoire de la fondation du royaume des Betsimisaraka," *BCM* (June 1898), 275–286.

————. *Histoire politique et coloniale.* Vol. V, Tome 1. Paris, 1942. Vol. V, Tome 2. Tananarive, 1956.

————. "A Madagascar—anciennes croyances et coutumes," *JSA*, II/2 (1932), 153–207.

————, and Decary, R. *Histoire politique et coloniale.* Vol. V, Tome 3, Fascicule 1. Tananarive, 1958.

Gravier, G. *La Cartographie de Madagascar.* Rouen-Paris, 1896.

————. *Madagascar.* Paris, 1904.

Guillain, Ch. *Documents sur l'histoire, la géographie et le commerce de la partie occidentale de Madagascar.* Paris, 1845.

Haile, J. H. "Some Betsileo Ideas," *AA*, VI (1900), 385–400.

Hamond, W. *Madagascar, the Richest and Most Fruitful Island in the World.* London, 1643.

————. *A Paradox Proving That the Inhabitants of Madagascar Are the Happiest People in the World.* London, 1640.

Hastie, J. "Le Voyage à Tananarive en 1817," *BAM*, II (1903), 91–114, 173–192, 241–269. Edited by J. Sibree and A. Jully.

Hébert, J.-C. "La Cosmographie malgache," *AUM*, special issue (1965), 83–149.

————. "Noms d'animaux en Malgache," *CM*, I/1 (1964), 295–389.

————. "La Parente a plaisanterie à Madagascar," *BM*, VIII/142–143 (1958), 182–216, 268–335.

Hildebrandt, J. M. "Ausflug zum Ambergebirge in Nord-Madagaskar," *ZGE*, XV (1880), 268–287.

Hornell, J. "Outrigger Boats of Madagascar," *Asia* (New York), XXX (1930), 168–170.

Huet, G. "Histoire de l'occupation du territoire des Anteimorona par les Hova (1842–1896)," *RM*, II (1901), 761–767.

Jacquet, E. "Mélanges malays, javanais et polynésiens," *JA*, 1st series, XII/3 (1833), 97–159.

Jakobsen, D. "Notes sur Andriamaro, idole célèbre chez les Mahafaly," *BAM*, I (1902), 50–52.

Jensenius, O. "Dictionnaire bara-hova," *BAM*, VII (1909), 165–194.

Joleaud, L. "Le Boeuf de Madagascar: son origine et son rôle dans les coutumes sakalava," *Anthropologie*, XXXIV (1924), 103–107.

Jorgensen, S. E. "Notes on the Tribes of Madagascar," *AA*, III (1885), 51–59.

Julien, G. "Le Culte de boeuf à Madagascar," *Revue d'Ethnographie et des Traditions Populaires* (1924), 246–268.

———. "Le Fananimpitulaha ou monstre heptacéphale de Madagascar," *Comptes Rendu, ASC*, VIII (1926–1927), 205–212.

———. *Institutions politiques et sociales de Madagascar*. Paris, 1908–1909. In two volumes.

———. "Notes d'Histoire Malgache," *BAM*, new series, IX (1926), 2–13.

———. "Notes et observations sur les peuplades sud-occidentales de Madagascar," *RETP* (1925), 113–123, 237–247; (1926), 1–20, 212–226; (1927), 4–23; (1928), 1–15, 153–175; (1929), 2–34.

———. "Pages arabico-madécasses," *AASC* (1929), 1–123; (1933), 57–83. Two separate extracts.

Jully, A. "Ethnographie de Madagascar," *RM*, VIII (1906), 1025–1054.

———. "L'Habitation à Madagascar," *NRE*, IV (1898), 909–920.

———. "Origine des 'Andriana' ou nobles," *NRE*, IV (1898), 890–898.

———. "L'Origine des Malgaches," *BAM*, I (1902), 11–22. Review of A. Grandidier's *L'Origine des Malgaches*.

Kent, R. K. "Alfred Grandidier et le 'mythe des fondateurs d'états Malgaches d'origine asiatiques,'" *BM*, No. 277–278 (June–July 1969), 603–620.

———. *From Madagascar to the Malagasy Republic*. New York, 1962.

———. "How France Acquired Madagascar, 1642–1896," *Tarikh*, II/4 (1969), 1–20.

———. "Madagascar and Africa: The Anteimoro, a Theocracy in Southeastern Madagascar," *JAH*, X/1 (1969), 45–65.

———. "Madagascar and Africa: The Problem of the Bara," *JAH*, IX/3 (1968), 387–408.

———. "Madagascar and Africa: The Sakalava, Maroserana, Dady and Tromba Before 1700," *JAH*, IX/4 (1968), 517–546.

———. "Note sur l'introduction et propagation du manioc à Madagascar," *Terre Malgache–Tany Malagasy*, V (1969), 177–183.

———. "The Sakalava: Origins of the First Malagasy Empire," *RFHOM*, LV/199 (1968), 145–189.

Lacaille, L. *Connaissance de Madagascar*. Paris, 1863.

La Lande, de. "Communication," *Journal de Physique*, VIII/2 (1776), 357–363.

Lapeyre, P. *Dialectes hova et sakalava: essai d'etude comparée*. Tananarive, 1891. Pamphlet of 8 pages.

Laverdant, D. *Colonisation de Madagascar*. Paris, 1844.

Le Barbier, C. "Notes sur le pays des Bara-Imamono, région d'Ankazoabo," *BAM*, new series, III (1916–1917), 63–162.

Leclerc, M. "Les Peuplades de Madagascar," *RE*, V (1886), 397–432; VI (1887), 1–32, 463–469 ("Notes sur Madagascar").

Lefort, Capt. "Une Mission dans le sud," *NRE*, III (1898), 196–225, 267–293.

Leguével de Lacombe, B.-F. *Voyage à Madagascar et aux Iles Comores*. Paris, 1840. In two volumes.

Linton, R. "Culture Areas in Madagascar," *American Anthropologist*, XXX/3 (1928), 363–390.

———. "Culture Sequences in Madagascar," *Papers*, Peabody Museum, No. 22 (1943), 72–78.

———. *The Tanala: A Hill Tribe of Madagascar*. Chicago, 1933.

Little, H. W. *Madagascar, Its History and People*. London, 1884.

Lyautey, Marshal. *Lettres du sud de Madagascar, 1900–1902*. Paris, 1935.

McMahon, E. O. "First Visit of a European to the Betsiriry Tribe," *AA*, IV (1891), 273–280.

Magnes, B. "Essai sur les . . . Tsimihety," *BM*, No. 89 (1953), 1–95.

Malotet, A. *Etienne de Flacourt ou les origines de la colonisation française à Madagascar, 1648–1661*. Paris, 1898.

Malzac, V. *Histoire du Royaume Hova depuis ses origines jusqu'à sa fin*. Tananarive, 1912. Reprint, 1930.

———. "Les Hova, premiers habitants de l'Imerina," *NRE*, V (1899), 341–349.

———. "Ordre de succession au trône chez les Hova," *NRE*, VI (1900), 607–618.

Marchand. "Les Habitants de la province de Farafangana," *RM*, III (1901), 481–491, 569–580.

Marcuse, W. D. *Through Western Madagascar in Quest of the Golden Bean*. London, 1914.

Mariano, L. *Letters*. Six letters dated July 1616; September 17, 1616; October 22, 1616; August 20, 1617; August 24, 1619; and September 9, 1630. One of these appears to have been authored by his companion, Father d'Azevedo. A seventh letter is a kind of periplus, cited as "Relation . . . 1613–1614." See *COACM*. Vol. II. Paris, 1904.

Martin, F. *Mémoire concernant l'ile de Madagascar, 1665–1668*. In *COACM*. Vol. IX. Paris, 1920.

Mattei, L. "Les Tsimihety," *BAM*, new series, XXI (1938), 131–196.

Mayeur, N. "Deuxième voyage en Ancove" (July 1785), *BAM*, XII/2 (1913), 14–49.

———. "Voyage dans le sud et dans l'interieur des terres et particulièrment au pays d'Hancove, 1777," *BAM*, XII/1 (1913), 139–173.

Mazurier, Capt. "Aperçu géographique sur la contrée entre le Manambao et la Tsarabisay," *NRE*, V (1899), 259–289.

Mellis, J. *Volamena et Volafotsy*. Tananarive, 1938.

Michel, L. *Moeurs et coutumes des Bara*. Tananarive, 1957. Vol. XL of *MAM*.

Millot, J. "Considérations sur le commerce dans l'Océan Indien au moyen age et au pré-moyen age, à propos des perles de Zanaga," *Mémoires,* Institut de la Recherche Scientifique de Madagascar, Série C, I/2 (1952), 159–165.

————, and Pascal, A. "Notes sur la sorcellerie chez les Vezo de la région de Morombé," *Mémoires,* IRSM, Série C, I/1 (1952), 13–28.

Molet, L. *Le Bain royal à Madagascar.* Tananarive, 1955.

Mondain, G. *L'Histoire des tribus de l'Imoro au XVIIᵉ siécle d'après un manuscrit arabico-malgache.* Paris, 1910.

Mouren and Rouaix. "Industrie ancienne des objets en pierre de Vohémar," *BAM,* XII/2 (1913), 3–13.

Mullens, J. *Twelve Years in Madagascar.* London, 1875.

Nielsen-Lund, J. "Travels and Perils Among the Wild Tribes in the South of Madagascar," *AA,* III (1888), 440–457.

Nöel, Captain. "Le Pays bezonozano," *NRE,* II (1897), 1–27.

Nöel, V. "Recherches sur les Sakkalava," *BSG,* 2nd series, XIX (1843), 275–295; 2nd series, XX (1843), 40–64, 285–306; 3rd series, I (1844), 385–416.

Oliver, R. "The Great African Island," *JAH,* I/2 (1960), 319–321. Review of H. Deschamps, *Histoire de Madagascar.*

Pfeiffer, I. *Voyage à Madagascar.* Paris, 1881.

Poirier, Ch. *Ethnographie malgache.* Tananarive, 1950. Vol. XXXVIII of *MAM.*

————. "Généalogie des rois maroserana du sud de l'Onilahy," *BAM,* new series, XXXI (1953), 29–34.

————. *Notes d'ethnographie et d'histoire malgaches.* Tananarive, 1939. Vol. XXVIII of *MAM.*

————. "Réflexions sur les ruines de Mailaka . . . et sur les tombes anciennes de Vohémar," *BAM,* new series, XXVIII (1947–1948), 97–101.

————. "Terre d'Islam en Mer Malgache," *BAM,* special issue (1954), 71–116.

Poirier, J., and Dez, J. "Les Groupes ethniques de Madagascar: rapport préliminaire sur un inventaire des tribus." Tananarive, University of Madagascar, 1963. Mimeograph.

Poisson, H. *Etude des manuscrits de L.A. Chapelier, voyageur-naturaliste.* Tananarive, 1940.

Pouget de St. André, H. *La Colonisation de Madagascar sous Louis XV, d'après la correspondance inédite du Comte de Maudave.* Paris, 1886.

Prud'homme, Lt. Col. "Considerations sur les Sakalava," *NRE,* VI (1900), 1–43. Translated into English, *AA,* VI (1900), 408–437.

Quesnot, F. "Moeurs et coutumes des Mahafaly," *BM,* No. 93 (1954), 99–123.

Ratsimamanga, A. R. "Tache pigmentaire héréditaire et origine des Malgaches," *RA* (1940), 5–130.

Razafimino, G. *La Signification religieuse du Fandroana ou de la fête du nouvel an en Imerina.* Tananarive, 1924.

Renel, Ch. "Les Amulettes malgaches: *ody* et *sampy,*" *BAM,* new series, Vol. II (1915), 35–255.

Richardson, J. *A New Malagasy-English Dictionary.* Tananarive, 1885.

Rochon, Abbé. *Voyage à Madagascar.* Vol. I. Paris, 1787.

Rusillon, H. *Un Culte dynastique avec evocation des morts chez les Sakalaves de Madagascar: le "Tromba."* Paris, 1912.

————. "Notes d'histoire sakalava: notes explicatives à propos de la généalogie maroserana zafimbolamena," *BAM,* new series, VI (1922–1923), 169–184.

————. *Un Petit Continent: Madagascar*. Paris, 1933.

————. "Le *Sikidy* malgache," *BAM*, VI (1908), 115–162.

Sachs, C. *Les Instruments de musique de Madagascar*. Paris, 1938.

Savaron, C. "Contribution à l'histoire de l'Imerina," *BAM*, new series, XI (1928), 61–81; XIV (1931), 57–73.

————. "Notes sur le Farihin-dRangita," *BAM*, X (1912), 373–377.

Sibree, J. "An Ancient Royal Tomb at Ambohidrabiby," *AA* (1896), 498–499.

————. "Curiosities of Words Connected with Royalty and Chieftainship Among the Hova and Other Malagasy Tribes," *AA* (1887), 301–310.

————. *The Great African Island*. London, 1880.

————. "Ifangoavana," *AA* (1877), 34–35.

————. *Madagascar and Its People*. London, 1870.

————. *Madagascar Before the Conquest*. London, 1896.

————. "The Malagasy Custom of Brotherhood by Blood," *AA* (1897), 1–6.

————. "Malagasy Place-Names," *AA* (1896), 401–413; (1898), 152–166.

————. "Remarkable Ceremonial at the Decease and Burial of a Betsileo Prince," *AA* (1898), 195–208. Translation of a Malagasy manuscript.

————. "The Sihanaka and Their Country," *AA* (1877), 51–69.

————. "The Western Bara and Their Customs," *AA* (1876), 45–50.

Solheim, W. G. "Indonesian Culture and Malagasy Origin," *AUM*, special issue (1965), 33–42.

Soury-Lavergne, P. "Un Chapitre du *Tantara*," *BAM*, new series, IV (1918–1919), 76–130.

Thomas, R. P. "L'Origine des noms de mois à Madagascar: notes de philologie comparée," *BAM*, VI (1908), 17–36.

Thomassin, Lt. "Notes sur le Royaume de Mahabo," *NRE*, VI (1900), 395–413.

Toquenne and de Thuy, Capts. "Etude historique, géographique et ethnographique sur la province de Tuléar," *NRE*, V (1899), 101–116.

Urbain-Faublée, M. *L'Art malgache*. Paris, 1963.

Vacher, Capt. "Etudes ethnographiques," *RM*, V (1903), 323–339, 385–423, 498–519; VI (1904), 3–25, 106–130, 136–150, 324–336.

Valette, J. "De l'Origine des Malgaches," *AUM*, special issue (1965), 15–32.

————. "L'Imerina en 1822–1823 d'après les journaux de Bojer et d'Hilsenberg," *BM*, XV (1965), 297–341.

————. "Madagascar vers 1750 d'après un manuscrit anonyme," *BM*, XIV/214 (1964), 211–258.

————. "Le Naturaliste sonnerat à Madagascar," *BM*, XV/226 (1965), 195–243.

————. "Note sur l'utilisation de tanguin en Imerina en 1830," *BM*, XV/225 (1965), 173–175.

————, and Raharijaona, S. "Les Grandes Fêtes rituelles des Sakalava du Menabé ou 'Fitampoha,'" *BM*, IX/155 (1959), 281–314.

Vallier. "Etude ethnologique sur les Bezanozano," *NRE*, III (1898), 65–84.

Van Gennep, A. *Tabou et totémisme à Madagascar*. Paris, 1904.

Verneau, R. "Note sur les caractères céphaliques des Baras," *Anthropologie*, XXXIII (1923), 475–507.

Webber, J. *Dictionnaire français-malgache*. Ile Bourbon, 1855.

————. *Dictionnaire malgache-français*. Ile Bourbon, 1853.

AFRICA

Abraham, D. P. "The Early Political History of the Kingdom of Mwene Mutapa (850–1589)," in *Historians in Tropical Africa*. Salisbury, 1962. Mimeo. Edition. Pp. 61–90.

Alexander, C. S. "Fish Poisoning Along the North Eastern Coast of Tanganyika," *TNR*, No. 62 (1964), 57–60.

Ashton, E. H. "Political Organization of the Southern Sotho," *BS*, XII (1938), 287–320.

Axelson, E. *Portuguese in South-East Africa, 1600–1700*. Johannesburg, 1964.

Bascom, Wm., and Herskovits, M. J. (eds.). *Continuity and Change in African Cultures*. Chicago, 1959.

Baumann, H., and Westermann, D. *Les Peuples et les civilisations de l'Afrique*. Paris, 1962.

Béguin, E. *Les Ma-Rotsé*. Lausanne, 1904.

Bent, J. T. *The Ruined Cities of Mashonaland*. London, 1893.

Bentley, W. H. *Dictionary and Grammar of the Kongo Language as Spoken at San Salvador. . . .* London, 1887.

Bernardi, B. "The Age-System of the Nilo-Hamitic Peoples: A Critical Evaluation," *Africa*, XXII/4 (1952), 316–332.

Bertrand, A. *The Kingdom of Barotsi*. London, 1899.

Blakney, Ch. P. *On "Banana" and "Iron," Linguistic Footprints in African History*. M.A. Thesis. Hartford Seminary Foundation, Hartford, Conn., 1963. Typescript.

Bleek, W. H. I. *Languages of Mozambique*. London, 1856.

Bösch, F. *Les Banyamwezi*. Münster, 1930.

Brelsford, W. V. "Shimuwalule: A Study of Bemba Chief and Priest," *ASBS*, I/3 (1942), 207–223.

———. *Aspects of Bemba Chieftainship*. Lusaka, 1944. *RLC*, No. 2.

———. "Bird-lore of the Babemba," *NADA*, No. 20 (1945), 28–35.

Broomfield, G. W. "Development of the Swahili Language," *Africa*, III/4 (1930), 516–522.

———. "Re-Bantuization of the Swahili Language," *Africa*, IV/1 (1931), 77–85.

Brothwell, D. R. "Evidence of Early Population Change in Central and Southern Africa: Doubts and Problems," *Man*, LXIII/132 (1963), 101–104.

Brown, J. T. *Secwana-English Dictionary*. Tigerkloof, 1931.

Bullock, Ch. *The Mashona*. Cape Town, 1928.

Carvalho, H. D. *Ethnographia e História dos Povos da Lunda*. Lisbon, 1890.

Caton-Thompson, G. *The Zimbabwe Culture*. Oxford, 1931.

Cerulli, E. *Somalia, scritti vari editi ed inediti*. Rome, 1957–1964. In three volumes.

Chiwale, J. Ch. (trans. and ed.) *Royal and Praise Names of the Lunda Kazembe. . . , Central Bantu Historical Texts*. Vol. III. Lusaka, 1962. *RLC*, No. 25.

Colson, E. "The Role of Cattle Among the Plateau Tonga," *RLJ*, 11 (1951), 10–46.

————, and Gluckman, M. (eds.) *Seven Tribes of British Central Africa.* New York, 1961, reprint.

Cory, H. "The Buyeye: A Secret Society of Snake Charmers in Sukumaland," *Africa*, XVI/3 (1946), 160–178.

Coupland, R. *East Africa and Its Invaders.* London, 1965, reprint.

Crawford, J. R. *Witchcraft and Sorcery in Rhodesia.* Oxford, 1967.

Culwick, A. T. and G. M. "Indonesian Echoes in Central Tanganyika," *TNR*, No. 2 (1936), 60–66.

Cunnison, I. G. *The Luapula Peoples of Northern Rhodesia: Custom and History in Tribal Politics.* Manchester, 1967, reprint.

————. "Perpetual Kinship," *RLJ*, 20 (1956), 28–48.

———— (trans. and ed.) *Historical Traditions of the Eastern Lunda, Central Bantu Historical Texts.* Vol. II. Lusaka, 1962. *RLC*, No. 23.

————, ———— *King Kazembe.* . . . Lisbon, 1960. In two volumes. See entry under Gamitto below.

Darroch, R. G., and Samson, M. "Some Notes on the Early History of the Tribes Living in the Lower Tana," *JEAUNHS*, 47 (1943), 244–254.

Devic, L.-M. *Le Pays des Zendj ou la côte orientale d'Afrique au moyen-age.* Paris, 1883.

Dobbs, C. M. "Fishing in the Kavirondo Gulf, Lake Victoria," *JEAUNHS*, 30 (1927), 97–109.

Doke, C. M. *A Comparative Study in Shona Phonetics.* Johannesburg, 1931.

————. *The Lambas of Northern Rhodesia.* London, 1931.

Duyvendak, J. J. L. *China's Discovery of Africa.* London, 1949.

Earthy, D. E. "Note on the Decorations of Carved Wooden Bowls from Southern Chopiland," *Annals*, Transvaal Museum, 11 (1925), 118–124.

————. *The Valenge Women.* London, 1933.

Ehret, Chr. "Cattle-Keeping and Milking in Eastern and Southern African History: The Linguistic Evidence," *JAH*, VIII/1 (1967), 1–17.

————. "Sheep and Central Sudanic Peoples in Southern Africa," *JAH*, IX/2 (1968), 213–221.

Fagan, B. *Southern Africa During the Iron Age.* New York, 1965.

Fage, J. D. "Anthropology, Botany and the History of Africa," *JAH*, II/2 (1961), 299–309. Review of G. P. Murdock's *Africa.* See entry for Murdock below.

————. "Xylophones and Colonists," *JAH*, VI/3 (1965), 413–415. Review of A. M. Jones' *Africa and Indonesia.* See entry for Jones below.

Ferrand, G. *Les Çomalis.* Paris, 1903.

Forde, D. (ed.) *African Worlds.* London, 1965. Paperback reprint.

Fortes, M., and Evans-Pritchard, E. E. *African Political Systems.* London, 1966. Paperback reprint.

Frazer, J. G., and Downie, R. A. *The Native Races of Africa and Madagascar.* London, 1938.

Freeman-Grenville, G. S. P. (ed.) *The East African Coast—Select Documents.* . . . London, 1962.

————. *The Medieval History of the Coast of Tanganyika.* London, 1962.

Gamitto, A. C. P. *O Muata Cazembe.* . . . Lisbon, 1845. Translated into English by Ian G. Cunnison.

Gelfand, M. *Medicine and Magic of the Mashona.* Cape Town, 1956.

————. "The Mhondoro-Chaminuka," *NADA*, No. 36 (1959), 6–10.

————, and Swart, Y. "The *Nyora*," *NADA*, No. 30 (1953), 5–11.

Gillman, C. "An Annotated List of Ancient and Modern Indigenous Stone Structures in Eastern Africa," *TNR*, 17 (1944), 44–55.

Giorgetti, F. *Musica africana.* Bologna, 1957.

Gluckman, M. *Order and Rebellion in Tribal Africa.* New York, 1963.

Grant, C. H. B. "Some African Royal Burials and Coronations in Western Tanganyika," *African Studies*, X/4 (1951), 185–193.

Gray, R. F. "Positional Succession Among the Wambugwe," *Africa*, XXIII/3 (1953), 233–243.

Greenway, P. J. *A Swahili-Botanical-English Dictionary of Plant Names.* Dar-es-Salaam, 1937.

Grottanelli, V. L. "Asiatic Influences on Somali Culture," *Ethnos* (Stockholm), IV (1947), 153–181.

————. *Pescatori dell'Oceano Indiano.* Rome, 1955.

Gulliver, Ph. H. "The Age-Set Organization of the Jie," *JRAI*, LXXXIII/2 (1955), 147–168.

Hambly, W. D. *Serpent Worship in Africa.* Chicago, 1931.

Hannan, M. *Standard Shona Dictionary.* London, 1959.

Harding, J. R. "Conus Shell Disc Ornaments in Africa," *JRAI*, XCI/1 (1961).

Harris, G. "Possession 'Hysteria' in a Kenya Tribe," *American Anthropologist*, LIX/6 (1957), 1046–1066.

Hatchell, G. W. "The 'Ngalawa' and the 'Mtepe,'" *TNR*, 57 (1961), 211–215.

Hébert, J.-C. "Analyse structuralle des géomancies comoriennes, malgaches et africaines," *JSA* (1961), 115–208. Offprint.

Hiernaux, J. "Bantu Expansion . . . ," *JAH*, IX/4 (1968), 505–515.

Hincle, C. J. *Spirit Possession in Negro Africa, with Particular Reference to the Guinea Coast and East African Cattle Area.* M. A. Thesis. Philadelphia, University of Pennsylvania, 1950. Typescript.

Hirth, F., and Rockhill, W. W. (trans. and eds.) *Chau Ju-Kua: His Work on the Chinese and Arab Trade in the Twelfth and Thirteenth Centuries Entitled "Chu-fan-chi."* St. Petersburg, 1911.

Historians in Tropical Africa. Proceedings of the Leverhulme Inter-Collegiate History Conference, September 1960. Salisbury, 1962. Mimeo. edition.

Hoch, E. *Bemba Pocket Dictionary.* Tabora, 1966, reprint.

Holleman, J. F. *Accommodating the Spirit among some North-Eastern Shona Tribes.* London, 1953. *RLOP*, No. 22.

Hollis, A. C. "Notes on the History of the Vumba, East Africa," *JAI*, XXX (1900), 275–297.

Hornell, J. "The Baganda Canoe: The Problem of Its Origin," *MM* (October 1933), 439–445.

————. "Boat Oculi-Survivals: Additional Records," *JRAI*, LXVIII (1938), 339–348.

————. "The Common Origin of the Outrigger Canoes of Madagascar and East Africa," *Man*, XX/67 (1920), 134–139.

————. "Indonesian Influence on East African Culture," *JRAI*, LXIV (1934), 305–333.

————. "The Outrigger Canoes of Madagascar, East Africa and the Comoro Islands," *MM* (January 1944), 3–18; (October 1944), 170–185.

————. "Les Pirogues a balancier de Madagascar et de l'Afrique orientale," *La Géographie*, XXXIV/1 (1920), 1–23.

————. "The Sea-going *Mtepe* and *Dau* of the Lamu Archipelago," *TNR*, 14 (1942), 27–37.

————. "The Sewn Canoes of Victoria-Nyanza," *TNR*, 15 (1943), 7–24.

Huntingford, G. W. B. "The Azanian Civilization of Kenya," *Antiquity*, VII (1933), 153–165.

Hutton, J. H. "West Africa and Indonesia: A Problem of Distribution," *JRAI*, LXXVI/1 (1946), 5–12.

Irstam, T. *The King of Ganda*. Stockholm, 1944.

Jaffey, J. E. "A Reappraisal of the History of the Rhodesian Iron Age . . . ," *JAH*, VII/2 (1966), 189–195.

Jaspan, M. A. *The Ila-Tonga Peoples*. London, 1953.

Jaubert, A. (trans. and ed.) *Géographie d'Edrîsî*. Paris, 1836–1840. In two volumes.

Jensen, A. E. "Elementi della cultura spirituale dei conso nell'Etiopia meridionale," *Rassegna di Studi Etiopici*, II/3 (1942), 217–259.

Jones, A. M. *Africa and Indonesia: The Evidence of the Xylophone and Other Musical and Cultural Factors*. Leiden, 1964.

Junod, H. P. "Les cas de possession et exorcisme chez les Vandau," *Africa*, VII/3 (1934), 270–299.

————. *The Life of a South African Tribe*. New York, 1962, reprint. In two volumes.

Kagame, A. *L'Histoire des Armées-Bovines dans l'ancien Rwanda*. Brussels, 1961.

————. *Les Milices du Rwanda précolonial*. Brussels, 1963.

Kirkman, J. *Men and Monuments on the East African Coast*. London, 1964.

Lewis, H. S. "Origins of the Galla and Somali," *JAH*, VII/1 (1966), 27–46.

Lima, M. *Tatuagens da Lunda*. Angola, 1956.

Lindblom, K. G. *Spears and Staffs with Two or More Points in Africa*. Stockholm, 1940. Publication No. 14 of the Stockholm Ethnographic Museum.

Livingstone, D. and Ch. *Narrative of an Expedition to the Zambezi and Its Tributaries . . . 1858–1864*. New York, 1866.

Lofgren, L. "Stone Structures of the South Nyanza, Kenya," *AZ*, II (1967), 1–14.

Lystad, R. A. (ed.) *The African World*. New York, 1965.

Mackenzie, D. R. *The Spirit-ridden Konde*. London, 1925.

Maclaren, P. I. R. *The Fishing Devices of Central and Southern Africa*. Livingstonia, 1958. *RLOP*, No. 12.

McCullock, M. *The Southern Lunda and Related Peoples*. London, 1951.

McMaster, D. N. "Speculations on the Coming of the Banana to Uganda," *UJ*, XXVII/2 (1963), 163–176.

Macquarie, C. "Water Gypsies of the Malagarasi (River)," *TNR*, 9 (1940), 61–67.

Maupoil, B. *La Géomancie à l'ancienne côte des esclaves*, Paris, 1943.

Mayer, Ph. "The Joking of 'Pals' in Gusii Age-Sets," *African Studies*, X/1 (1951), 27–41.

Middleton, J. *The Lugbara of Uganda*. New York, 1965.

——. *Lugbara Religion*. London, 1960.

——, and Winter, E. H. (eds.) *Witchcraft and Sorcery in East Africa*. London, 1963.

Mitchell, J. C. "Chidzere Tree: A Note on a Shona Land Shrine and Its Significance," *NADA*, No. 38 (1961), 28–35.

Molitor, H. "La Musique chez les nègres du Tanganyika," *Anthropos*, VIII (1913), 714–735.

Monneret de Villard, U. "Note sulle influenze asiatiche nell'Africa orientale," *Rivista degli Studi Orientali* (University of Rome), XVII/4 (1938), 303–349.

Montez, C. "Os Indígenas de Moçambique," *Moçambique*, XX (1939), 5–31.

Moreau, R. E. "The Joking Relationship in Tanganyika," *TNR*, 12 (1941), 1–10.

Mugane, B. *The Pre-Colonial Lango-Omiru: An Ethnic History*. Berkeley, 1968. Typescript. Pp. 1–175.

Munday, J. T. *Kankomba, Central Bantu Historical Texts*. Vol. I, No. 1. 1961. *RLC*, No. 22.

Murdock, G. P. *Africa: Its Peoples and Their Culture History*. New York, 1959.

Ntahokaja, J. B. "La Musique des Barundi," *Grands Lacs*, LXIV/4–6 (1948–1949), 45–59.

Nyirenda, S. "History of the Tumbuka-Henga People," *BS*, V/1 (1931), 1–75. Translated by T. C. Young.

Oliver, R. "Ancient Capital Sites of Ankole," *UJ*, XXIII/1 (1959), 51–63.

——. "The Problem of Bantu Expansion," *JAH*, VII/3 (1966), 361–376.

——. "The Royal Tombs of Buganda," *UJ*, XXIII/2 (1959), 129–133.

——, and Mathew, G. (eds.) *History of East Africa*. Vol. I. London, 1963.

Ottenberg, S. and Ph. (eds.) *Cultures and Societies of Africa*. New York, 1960.

Pauwels, M. "La Divination au Rwanda," *Kongo Overzee*, XX/4–5 (1954), 293–368.

Peristiany, J. C. "The Age–Set System of the Pastoral Pokot," *Africa*, XXI (1951), 188–206, 279–302.

Perraudin, J. "Mort et funérailles chez les anciens Barundi," *Missions*, III (1952), 46–47.

Philipott, R. "Makumba: The Baushi Tribal God," *JRAI*, LXVI (1936), 189–208.

Pigott, D. W. I. "History of Mafia," *TNR*, 11 (1941), 35–40.

Posnansky, M. "Bantu Genesis—Archaeological Reflexions," *JAH*, IX/1 (1968), 1–11.

————. "Kingship, Archaeology and Historical Myth," *UJ*, XXX/1 (1966), 1–12.

———— (ed.). *Prelude to East African History*. London, 1966.

Posselt, F. W. T. *Fact and Fiction*. Bulawayo, 1935.

Prins, A. H. J. *The Coastal Tribes of the North-Eastern Bantu*. London, 1952.

————. *East African Age-Class Systems*. . . . Groningen, 1953.

————. *The Swahili-Speaking Peoples of Zanzibar and the East African Coast*. London, 1967.

————. "Uncertainties in Coastal Cultural History: The 'Ngalawa' and the 'Mtepe,'" *TNR*, 53 (1959), 205–213.

Randles, W. G. L. "South East Africa and the Empire of Monomotapa as Shown on Selected Printed Maps of the 16th Century," *Studia* (Lisbon), No. 2 (1958), 103–163.

Rayner, Wm. *The Tribe and its Successors*. New York, 1962.

Reusch, R. "How the Swahili People and Language Came into Existence," *TNR*, 34 (1953), 20–27.

Reynolds, B. *Magic, Divination and Witchcraft among the Barotse of Northern Rhodesia*. Berkeley, 1963.

Reynolds, V. "Joking Relationship in Africa," *Man*, LVIII/21 (1958), 29–30.

Richards, A. I. *East African Chiefs*. London, 1959.

Rita-Ferreira, A. *Agrupamento e Caracterização étnica dos Indigénas de Moçambique*. Lisbon, 1958.

Roberts, J. G. "Totemism, Zimbabwe and the Barozwi," *NADA*, 24 (1947), 48–51 and 65–70 (Totem).

Roscoe, J. *The Baganda*. . . . London, 1911.

————. "Python Worship in Uganda," *Man*, IX/57 (1909), 88–90.

————. "Worship of the Dead as Practiced by Some African Tribes," *Harvard African Studies*, I (1917), 33–47.

Sacleux, Ch. *Dictionnaire swahili-français*. Paris, 1939–1941. In two volumes.

Sangree, W. H. "The Bantu Tiriki of Western Kenya," in J. L. Gibbs (ed.) *Peoples of Africa*. New York, 1965. Pp. 41–79.

Schapera, I. (trans. and ed.). *Praise-Poems of Tswana Chiefs*. London, 1965.

Scrivenor, T. V. "Some Notes on *Utani*," *TNR*, 4 (1937), 72–74.

Sicard, H. von. "The Ancient Barwe Accession to Chieftainship," *NADA*, 31 (1954), 54–56.

————. "Occam's Razor," *NADA*, 30 (1953), 53–56.

————. "The Origin of Some of the Tribes in the Belingwe Reserve," *NADA*, 25 (1948), 93–104; 27 (1950), 7–19; 28 (1951), 5–25; 29 (1952), 43–64; 30 (1953), 64–71.

Smets, G. "Funérailles et sépultres . . . de l'Urundi," *Bulletin*, Sessions of the Belgian Royal Colonial Institute, XII/2 (1941), 210–234.

Smith, E. W. *A Handbook of the Ila Language* (*Seshukulombwe*). London, 1907.

———— and A. M. Dale. *The Ila-Speaking Peoples of Northern Rhodesia*. London, 1920. In two volumes.

Speares, J. "The Burial and Succession Rites of a Mashona Chief," *NADA*, 6 (1928), 89–91.

Stayt, H. A. *The Bavenda.* London, 1931.

Stefaniszyn, B. "Clan Jest of the Ambo," *NADA*, 28 (1951), 94–107.

———. "Funeral Friendship in Central Africa," *Africa*, XX (1950), 290–305.

Stierling, Dr. "The Hehe Royal Graves," *TNR*, 46 (1957), 25–28. Translated.

Stokes, E., and Brown, R. (eds.) *The Zambezian Past.* Manchester, 1966.

Strandes, J. *The Portuguese Period in East Africa.* Nairobi, 1961. Translated from German by J. F. Wallwork, with topographical notes by James S. Kirkman.

Stubbings, B. J. J. "Notes on the Native Methods of Fishing in the Mafia Islands," *TNR*, 19 (1945), 49–53.

Summers, R. "The Southern Rhodesian Iron Age," *JAH*, II/1 (1961), 1–13.

Tanghe, J. "Le Swahili. . . ," *Bulletin*, Sessions of the Belgian Royal Colonial Institute, XV/2 (1944), 1–24.

Thomas, F. M. *Historical Notes on the Bisa Tribe.* Lusaka, 1958. *RLC*, No. 8.

Torrend, J. *A Comparative Grammar of the South-African Bantu Languages.* London, 1891.

———. *An English Vernacular Dictionary of the Bantu-Botatwe Dialects of Northern Rhodesia.* Mariannhill (Natal), 1967, reprint.

———. "The Sabeans on the Zambezi," *Proceedings*, Rhodesia Scientific Association, V/2 (1905), 1–14.

Tracey, H. *Chopi Musicians, Their Music, Poetry and Instruments.* London, 1948.

Trautmann, R. *La Divination à la côte des esclaves et à Madagascar. Le Vôdôu Fa-Le Sikidy.* Dakar, 1939. *Mém. Institut Français de l'Afrique Noire*, I/1.

Trimingham, J. S. *Islam in East Africa.* London, 1964.

———. *Islam in Ethiopia.* London, 1952.

Vansina, J. M. *L'Evolution du Royaume Rwanda des origines à 1900.* Brussels, 1962.

———. *Introduction à l'ethnographie du Congo.* Kinshasa, 1966.

———. *Kingdoms of the Savanna.* Madison, Wis., 1966.

———. "Long-Distance Trade Routes in Central Africa," *JAH*, III/3 (1962), 375–390.

———. *Le Royaume Kuba.* Tervuren, 1964.

———, Mauny, R., and Thomas, L. (eds.). *The Historian in Tropical Africa.* London, 1964. Pp. 104–411.

Wagner, G. *The Bantu of North Kavirondo.* London, 1949–1956. In two volumes. Volume II was published posthumously, edited by L. P. Mair.

Werner, A. "A Pokomo Funeral," *Man*, XIII/38 (1913), 66–68.

———. "Some Notes on the Wapokomo of the Tana Valley," *Journal*, Royal African Society, XII (1913), 359–384.

———. "A Swahili History of Pate," *Journal*, Royal African Society, XIV (1915), 148–161, 278–296, 392–413.

———. "Tribes of the Tana Valley," *JEAUNHS*, IV/7 (1913), 37–46.

White, C. M. N. "A Note on Luvale Joking Relationship," *African Studies*, XVII/1 (1958), 28–33.

Whiteley, W. H. *A Selection of African Prose.* Vol. I. London, 1963.

Williams, F. L. "Blood Brotherhood in Ankole," *UJ*, II/1 (1934), 33–41.

Wieschhoff, H. A. *The Zimbabwe-Monomotapa Culture, General Series in Anthropology.* Vol. 8. Menasha, Wis., 1941. Pp. 1–115.

Young, C. T. *Notes on the Customs and Folklore of the Tumbuka-Kamanga Peoples.* Livingstonia, 1931.

GENERAL

Barnes, H. E. *The New History and the Social Sciences.* New York, 1925.

Barnett, H. G. *Innovation: The Basis of Culture Change.* New York, 1953.

Beier, H. U. "The Historical and Psychological Significance of Yoruba Myths," *Odu,* 1 (1955), 17–25.

Biobaku, S. O. "Myths and Oral History," *Odu,* 1 (1955), 12–17.

Bloch, M. *The Historian's Craft.* New York, 1962. Translated from French by P. Putnam.

Bloomfield, L. *Language.* New York, 1966, reprint.

Boas, F. *Race, Language and Culture.* New York, 1966. Paperback.

Bogišić, V. *Narodne Pjesme iz starijih, najviše Primorskih Zapisa.* Belgrade, 1878.

Clark, G. K. *The Critical Historian.* London, 1967.

Dauzat, A. *Les Noms de personnes: origine et evolution.* Paris, 1950.

Dyen, I. "Language Distribution and Migration Theory," *Language,* XXXII (1956), 611–626.

————. (Review of Dahl's *Malgache et Maanjan*) *Language,* XXIX (1953), 577–590.

Evans-Pritchard, E. E. *Social Anthropology and Other Essays.* New York, 1964.

Gabel, C., and Bennett, N. (eds.). *Reconstructing African Culture History.* Boston, 1967.

Greenberg, J. *Essays in Linguistics.* Chicago, 1963.

————. "Historical Linguistics and Unwritten Languages," in A. L. Kroeber (ed.), *Anthropology Today.* Chicago, 1953. Pp. 265–286.

————. "Linguistic Evidence for the Influence of the Kanuri on the Hausa," *JAH,* I/2 (1960), 205–212.

————. "Linguistics and Ethnology," *Southwestern Journal of Anthropology,* XL (1948), 140–148.

Guiraud, P. *L'Etymologie.* Paris, 1964.

Hymes, D. (ed.). *Language in Culture and Society.* New York, 1964.

Jongmans, D. G., and Gutkind, P. C. W. (eds.). *Anthropologists in the Field.* Assen, 1967.

Karadžić, V. S. *Prvi i Drugi Srpski Ustanak.* Belgrade, 1947.

————. *Skupljeni Istoriski i Etnografski Spisi.* Belgrade, 1898.

Kent, R. K. "The Real Magnitude of a Small Historical Problem," in L. P. Curtis, Jr. (ed.), *Historian's Workshop.* New York, 1970.

Kroeber, A. L. *An Anthropologist Looks at History.* Berkeley, 1963.

Lehmann, W. P. *Historical Linguistics: An Introduction.* New York, 1962.

Lewis, I. M. *History and Social Anthropology*. London, 1967.

Lord, A. B. *The Singer of Tales*. New York, 1965.

Lowie, R. H. *The History of Ethnological Theory*. New York, 1937.

McCall, D. F. *Africa in Time-Perspective: A Discussion of Historical Reconstruction from Unwritten Sources*. Boston, 1964.

Malinowski, B. *The Dynamics of Culture Change*. New Haven, 1961.

Mandelbaum, D. G. (ed.). *Selected Writings of Edward Sapir in Language, Culture, and Personality*. Berkeley, 1949.

Panić-Surep, M. *Filip Višnjić, Pesnik Bune*. Belgrade, 1956.

Rostaing, Ch. *Les Noms de lieux*. Paris, 1945.

Samarin, Wm. *Field Linguistics*. New York, 1967.

Sapir, E. *Language: An Introduction to the Study of Speech*. New York, 1949.

Schmidt, W. *The Culture Historical Method of Ethnology*. New York, 1939. Translated from German by S. A. Sieber.

Stimson, J., and Marshall, D. S. *A Dictionary of Some Tuamotuan Dialects of the Polynesian Language*. The Hague, 1964.

Sturtevant, E. H. *Linguistic Change*. Chicago, 1965.

Toussaint, A. *Histoire de l'Océan Indien*. Paris, 1961.

Van Gennep, A. *La Formation des légendes*. Paris, 1910.

Vansina, J. M. "Anthropologists and the Third Dimension," *Africa*, XXXIX/1 (1969), 62–68.

———. "A Comparison of African Kingdoms," *Africa*, XXXII/4 (1962), 324–335.

———. *De la Tradition orale. Essai de méthode historique*. Tervuren, 1961.

———. "Ethnohistory in Africa," *Ethnohistory*, IX/2 (1962), 126–136.

———. "The Use of Ethnographic Data as Sources for History." Madison, Wis., 1963. Typescript. Pp. 1–32.

———, Mauny, R., and Thomas, L. (eds.). *The Historian in Tropical Africa*. London, 1964. Pp. 1–103.

Vlekke, B. H. *Nusantara: A History of the East Indian Archipelago*. Cambridge, Mass., 1943.

Whiteley, W. H. "Social Anthropology, Meaning and Linguistics," *Man*, new series, I/2 (1966), 139–157.

Winner, Th. G. *The Oral Art and Literature of the Khazaks of Russian Central Asia*. Durham, N.C., 1958.

APPENDIX

PRINCIPAL ARISTOCRATIC FAMILIES, LINEAGES, CLASSES, AND CLANS

MAROSERANA

(Dynastic family of Mahafaly, Sakalava, Bara, Antaisaka, Antandroy, Fiherenana, and Masikoro)

Volamena (Mahafaly and Sakalava)
Zafy Manely (Bara)
Zara Behava (Antaisaka)
Zafy Manara (Antandroy)
Andrevola (Fiherenana and Masikoro)

ANTEONY

(Aristocratic clans from which Anteimoro obtained their kings, or Andrianoni)

Anteoni (founders of Anteimoro colony, *ca.* 1500)
Zafikazimambo (most powerful between *ca.* 1550–1660)
Ankara (most powerful in the 18th and 19th centuries)

ANDRIANA-MERINA

(Nobility from which Merina kings were chosen)

Ampandrana
(now extinct ancestral line of Andriana-Merina)
Zafindralambo ⎫
Andriandranando ⎪
Andriamasinavalona ⎪
Andriantompokoindrindra ⎬ Seven Noble Classes of Imerina
Andrianamboninolona ⎪
Zanakandriana ⎪
Zazamarolahy ⎭

DYNASTIC FOUNDERS
AND EARLY RULERS

MAROSERANA

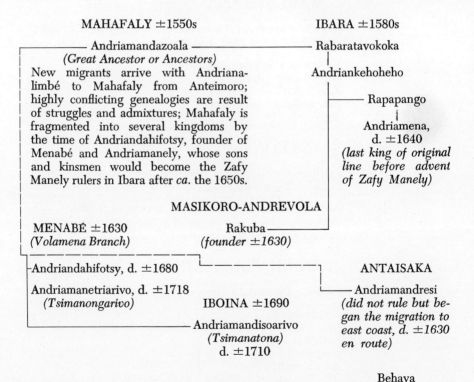

MAHAFALY ±1550s

Andriamandazoala
(Great Ancestor or Ancestors)
New migrants arrive with Andrianalimbé to Mahafaly from Anteimoro;
highly conflicting genealogies are result
of struggles and admixtures; Mahafaly is
fragmented into several kingdoms by
the time of Andriandahifotsy, founder of
Menabé and Andriamanely, whose sons
and kinsmen would become the Zafy
Manely rulers in Ibara after *ca.* the 1650s.

IBARA ±1580s

Rabaratavokoka

Andriankehoheho

Rapapango

Andriamena,
d. ±1640
*(last king of original
line before advent
of Zafy Manely)*

MASIKORO-ANDREVOLA

MENABÉ ±1630
(Volamena Branch)

Rakuba
(founder ±1630)

Andriandahifotsy, d. ±1680

Andriamanetriarivo, d. ±1718
(Tsimanongarivo)

IBOINA ±1690

Andriamandisoarivo
(Tsimanatona)
d. ±1710

ANTAISAKA

Andriamandresi
*(did not rule but be-
gan the migration to
east coast, d. ±1630
en route)*

Behava
*(founder of the Zara-
behava)*

ANDRIANA-MERINA

(Ampandrana)
Rangita and Rafohy
*(transitional Vazimba-Merina-Hova
period queens, ca. 1550s–1590s)*

Andriamanelo, d. ±1625
(founder of Andriana dynasty)

Ralambo, d. ±1645

Andrianjaka, d. ±1665

ANTEONY-ANTEIMORO

(rulers)

Ramakararubé
(Great Ancestor)

In the first few decades of the 1500s, the Anteimoro state
did not fully form despite the "ruler list"

Ali
±1510–1535

Ramasomari
±1535–1540

Ramarohala
±1540–1565

Andriakazimambobé*
±1565–1580

Rabésirana
±1580–1615

Andriamarofotana
±1615–1630

Andriamarofotana and Andriapanolaha
(alternating)
±1630–1660

* Very probably the advent of a fully developed Anteimoro
kingdom can be attributed to this leader of the last oversea
migrants to arrive at Matitana. Religion and state merge under
the Zafikazimambo.

SOURCE READINGS

THE CULT OF FANANE IN CENTRAL HIGHLANDS OF MADAGASCAR

This abridged account from the *Tantara* collected by Father Callet gives a detailed description of the *fanane* cult among the Betsileo as reported by informants in Imerina. It comes from the original Malagasy text as transcribed by Callet, pp. 635–637. A French translation by G.-S. Chapus and E. Ratsimba will be found in the *Tantara*, Vol. III (1958), pp. 234–237.

The following customs are observed upon the death of a Betsileo Prince. All of his kin are brought together. Following this reunion, an outrigger is constructed. When the outrigger is finished, his dwelling is arranged and the deceased is prepared for envelopment in the *lamba*. Once enveloped in the *lamba*, the remains are placed upon an elevated post . . . and the finished outrigger is set at its foot. Then, singers are called upon, and the assembled kin are made to enter the dwelling. Cattle are slaughtered, rice is boiled, and much intoxicating beverage is purchased for the invited kin and all others who gather around the remains. . . . The deceased is stretched across the central post over against the outrigger so as to collect humors which are to flow from the remains. When ooze from the corpse becomes ample and the resulting humors become abundant, they are left intact. When . . . the entire stomach has decayed and all of the issuing humors are deposited within the outrigger, and the putrid odor becomes very strong . . . everyone in the vicinity is supposed to be intoxicated enough not to notice it. . . . This condition lasted a week or two, even longer . . . to allow the humors to become infested with worms. When the presence of worms inside the outrigger is ascertained and when one of them has attained the size of a thumb, the remains are buried. . . . Following the funeral . . . the out-rigger itself is taken to a pond and deposited there, for the Betsileo have ponds where their ancestors are left. . . . [Later] children of the deceased watch the fattest among the worms in the outrigger . . . he feeds on the smaller ones until all alone inside the outrigger . . . [to grow ever larger] . . . first like a *mandotra* [species of snake], later like [large] eel . . . and when . . . really long and fat, the children then know that it is indeed their father . . . in the outrigger. They provide servants to guard the beast and call it *fananompitulaha* . . . and the reason why it is guarded by the servants is the fear that someone might do him harm. But, no one among the Betsileo would even dare touch the *fananompitulaha* since he is considered to be an *Andriana*. It was thus that the sovereigns of Betsileo believed that the *fanano* are their ancestors . . . that the remains of defunct princes transformed into worms, the worms into *mandotra*, and the *mandotra* into the *fanano*. It is said in respect to these *fanano* that if they die no one ever sees them for they go underwater. Others state that if they die, their guardians inform members of the family who then envelop them into another *lamba* again. It is only then that the defunct becomes an *angatra* [spirit] departing on the way to Ambon-drombé.

When the [common] people of Betsileo die, some say that the soul refuses to become a beast and departs for Ambondrombé. Others say, on the contrary, that when such and such Betsileo dies, the entire stomach is taken out and thrown into the water. This produces a *tona* [large eel]. . . . Thus, the Betsileo commoners transformed [upon death] into eels. It is [also] believed that should [the *tona*] appear, new deaths will come to the family of those who had thrown . . . the stomach [into the water]. [And] if some [should] eat the *tona*, they will die . . . because these are ancestors of the Betsileo.

HISTORICAL ACCOUNT OF
MALAGASY INVASIONS OF
THE COMORO ISLANDS AND
THE EAST AFRICAN COAST

Some hundred and twenty-five years ago, Eugene de Froberville, then one of the most active students of Madagascar, published this account in *Annuaire des Voyages et de la Géographie*, Vol. II (1845), pp. 194–208. The author was completely mistaken in attributing the origin of these invasions to an accident of travel involving Count de Benyowsky in 1785. Apart from this aspect, however, there is no better essay on the subject itself. What follows is an abridged and at times paraphrased rendition of de Froberville's essay in English.

This is how the expeditions were organized. When the idea of invasions became widely accepted in eastern Madagascar, the influential chiefs would determine how many men each would contribute. They then canvassed each district slated to participate with men and outriggers. The total number of warriors was known through a system of notch markings in strips of leather, and the levies were both legally binding and scrupulously provided. The time of departure varied, but the expeditions took place between August and October. The main point of rally was established on the northwestern coast facing the Comoros. Outriggers from around the Tamatave area, with thirty to forty men, left first, sailing along the coast and recruiting more along the way. At Vohémar, secondary point of rally, more outriggers would be waiting in concentration. This force would then continue, circling past the Cap d'Ambre and arriving at the principal point of rally either at the islet of Nossi-bé or one of the nearby large bays. Here, it would be met by a smaller number of outriggers dispatched from the western coast. The combined force would consist at times of 400 to 500 outriggers carrying 15,000 to 18,000 men. This would take place every five years. Fleets assembled, however, in the intermediary years would be much smaller, hardly more than fifty outriggers because the Comoro Islands could not renovate their wealth sufficiently fast to accommodate annual invasions from Madagascar.

If the winds were not favorable for the journey toward the Comoros, the outriggers would let the currents carry them across the Mozambique Channel to the coast of Africa where the Malagasy would then land. This happened not a few times. For example, the township of Ibo on one of the Querimba islets, defended moreover by a Portuguese fort, was attacked three times by the Malagasy between 1808 and 1816. In the first two invasions, they ravaged the whole archipelago, burning the dwellings and plantations, killing and taking prisoners. They even set fire to a French vessel docked at Ibo and, after massacring the crew, looted its cargo. On another occasion, they attacked and captured a Portuguese sloop of war with sixteen cannons and a crew of eighty. But, despite the success they had in the first of two expeditions, these Malagasy pirates lost more than half of their outriggers and men during the second as much by lack of provisions and smallpox as by relative ignorance of high-sea navigation. And, still, they were not discouraged and sailed again toward Ibo for a third time in 1816. This was a fatal expedition. Surprised by a storm, only 68 of the 250 outriggers that had left Madagascar arrived at the Querimba islets. These were, in turn, completely destroyed by the Portuguese so that of the 6,250 Malagasy who had started out not even one managed to return to Madagascar. These Malagasy even had the audacity to attack Kilwa and push on to the Mofia Island, where they took about 3000 slaves. But, once again at sea, some twenty dhows armed with cannon and sent in pursuit by the Sultan of Zanzibar encountered the Malagasy at the Bay of Mzimbaty, north of the Ruvuma, and massacred every last one of them.

The Malagasy expeditions were, however, really directed against the Comoros and particularly Anjouan. When the Malagasy were sighted, everyone at Anjouan would seek refuge in towns that were supplied with provisions to withstand sieges. But, although arms were distributed for defense, a general feeling of worry and terror was prevalent. A part of the invaders would disembark and construct huts around the Anjouanese towns they wanted to take while another part would comb the countryside and bring the provisions. Sometimes these sieges lasted until the change of monsoons since the Malagasy would not navigate without the winds behind them. In cases of these long sieges, famine inside the walls plagued the Anjouanese, particularly women and children. In 1808, Matsamoudo, capital of Anjouan, sustained such a long siege and so many repeated attacks, that two hundred women [with children] who had taken refuge in a powder-housing structure . . . eventually perished under the ruins by setting the powder on fire. The memory of this terrible event is still present among the Anjouanese who relate it to foreigners. . . .

When the time for their departure would come, the Malagasy would stop their activities and embark on their outriggers with what they could loot as well as with prisoners. These were normally turned into slaves because the Malagasy did not kill the inhabitants of the Comoros except when it was unavoidable. The Comoreans, on the contrary, would kill immediately any of the Malagasy that could be surprised, not because of any thirst for cruelty but because the very name of the Malagasy inspired them with an unwelcome terror. One should note that at times some of the European captains present at the Comoros during these calamities, instead of defending the local inhabitants, aided with everything they had the Malagasy to take prisoners since these brigands promised them slaves as compensation. More than that, some captains even helped direct the Malagasy expeditions toward Anjouan. . . . The Anjouanese, on many occasions, pleaded for help from English and French colonies in the Indian Ocean. In 1812, the Sultan of Anjouan sent an ambassador to the Cape of Good Hope. The contemporary governor of this colony, Sir J. F. Cradock (now Lord Howden) . . . sent the frigate *Nisus*, commanded by Captain Beaver, with orders to visit the main ports of Madagascar and arrest these barbaric expeditions either through threats or by negotiation. . . . [As these and other measures failed, and following the efforts of Sir Robert Farquhar, the governor of Mauritius], a diplomatic agent signed with commissioners of Radama I a treaty on October 23, 1817, on behalf of England to abolish these slave raids and slave trade in general. This treaty, which was to insure the security of the unfortunate Comoreans, was not however executed until three years later because the governor who [temporarily] succeeded Sir Robert Farquhar refused to pay Radama I the indemnity of 2000 pounds sterling that the British government contracted to furnish him every three years. The treaty was signed again in 1820 putting an effective end to the Malagasy invasions; and the Comoreans could breathe again after thirty years of terror. . . .

THE BARA ACCORDING
TO THEMSELVES

Extracts from a collection of Bara oral texts, now Document 664 of the Department of Human Sciences, University of Madagascar. The texts were collected in 1924 and are anonymous. The language used indicates that they were set on paper by a Bara who had gone to school and had learned the official language. The Malagasy texts below are immediately followed by translations.

Talohalohan'ny nahatongaran'ny Frantsay teto Madagasikara ny Bara dia niady nifanafika samy nanana basy lefon-droana lefon-tokana, ireo fiadana ireo; ny ampingaratra, ny pondry dia tody tao Tulear naondran'ny Inglisy, fa ny lefona dia ny Bara hiany no nanefy azy, omby 4 kahat-ramin'ny 7 ny vidin'ny basy iray loy ny basiany, vato manja, tombo-hilanivy, ary vy tefen'ny mpanefy Bara, nanana tsifam-pondry izy ireo, hiditr' omby ny fitondram-balany, sy ny fehikibony na anjaka. Raha mikasa handeha antafika izy, ny zavatra voalohany tsy maintsy ataony, dia misikisy, faminaniana, hahalany ny loza hanjo, ka raha efa tsara ny sikidy sy ny andro tiana, ka hahazakoana moramora my sy handresy, dia manampankevitra izy ireao ny andeha, dia mamory ny vahoakany ny mpanjaka, na manao fotana hiany-hoeananona dia mpanjaka iray no lohan-ny tafika io, ny fanalohahy, ny ombiasa, ny ranitrampanjaka, ary ny safo, rehefa mandeha izany dia samy misadika fanafody maromaro mohara, Tohiresy hazo; berano mandriko, amin-izany ny ombiasa amin'anjarany dia tsy minjanona ny manondraka ny tafika ny fanafody Berano io mba tsy ho latrain'ny balan'ny fahavalo, fa ny fanafody man-driko kosa hampandavo ny fahavalo izay naratran'ny balany, rehefa tonga eo amin'ny tanin'ny fahavalo dia maniraka ny safo 4 na 5 hijery ny tany firakandrovany, raha sendra ao ny ombiny, ka raha miverina hilaza, amin'ny mpanjaka dia mitoran-ravik'azo ho faman-tarana fao ao ny omby, raha fahamatazana ny marika ny tafika izany, dia mihetsiket-sika hamonjy. Raha favantany tonga eo amin'ny omby dia mandraoka azy mindray lomay, dia lasa lomay hazolava any antanana ny mpiandry omby hampandre ny olona, rehefa tonga ny hazolava, dia rofotra ny ady, mifapitifotra, mifandefana, ny maty, ny maratra, raha tsy latsaka ny omby, ka efa lavitra ny niadiana, dia jarainy ny omby, indraindray aza raha tanana no veleziny dia misy babo ny zaza amambehivavy. Alohan'ny hanaovana ny fizarana dia fidina ny omby tsara, olona babo, ho an'ny mpanjaka, faha 2 ny anjaran'ny ranatra-mpanjaka, faha 3 alavan'ny anjarany ombiasa, fahefa 4, ny anjaran'ny iraka, ny sisa dia anjaran'ny tafika. Amin'ny andro andehanan'ny lehilahy antafika iny, dia miatomboka miatsa mirary ny apela, antsa fisaorana, mba handresy ny lehilahinay hahazo omby moramora. Amin'ny maraina anenoman'ny akoho iny no amotorany miatsa dia samy mitondra tehikely atao hoe: matsotsoraka, vindana, ravisevana, misadika folivelona izy rehetra, mandrampiverin'ny lehilahy ny vehivavy manambady tsy mahasahy mandry amin'olona fa tena fady, ka ny vehivavy azo manao izany dia heverina ho mpamosavy. Ka rehefa tonga iny lehilahy dia mitantara ny vaovao izay nitranga, nadritra ny nandehanany maimaika ery'ny vehivavy amin'izany hanan-dron'ny fotsimbarim-balavo nasisa.

Translation   Just before the arrival of the French in Madagascar, the Bara warred among themselves, group against group. Each man had a rifle and one or two spears; these weapons, rifle and powder, came from Tulear, being sent ashore by the English, while the spears were made by us Bara. One rifle cost from four to seven head of cattle; its bullets were of lead, pebbles (*manja*), jug stems, or iron forged by the Bara smiths; they had powder horns, leather cartridge-pouches or leather belts. When the Bara were to go to war, the first thing they had to do was to ask the *sikidy* and learn the dangers, and if the *sikidy* and the selected favorable day were good for a victory and an easy take of cattle, they would decide to have a go at it, the king gathering his men or telling them to meet him at a chosen site. The group was [usually] composed of the king, warriors, ombiasa, subchiefs, and emissaries (*safo*). At departure, each has on him the *fanafody* (protective amulets) in horns and pieces of wood: either *Berano* or *Mandriko*, while the ombiasa, in turn, arouses the men through the *fanafody Berano*, which is a protector against enemy bullets, while *fanafody Mandriko* is to make those among the enemies who are wounded by their bullets go mad. Upon arriving at the enemy's border, the emissaries, some four or five of them, go to examine the grazing area to see if the cattle are there and report back to the *mpanjaka*. If they are there, they signal by placing on their heads the *bozaka*, or tree leaves. When the men get their tip-off, they advance, and once near the herd they steal them on the run as guardians run to the village to warn the inhabitants. And, when the latter arrive, there is a fierce fight on, rifles go off, spears are thrown, there are wounded and dead. If the cattle (herd) is not abandoned far from the battle site, it is divided up and sometimes, when the village is attacked, even children and women become captives. Before the spoils are divided, the choice of the best cattle and best-looking captives goes to the *mpanjaka*, (after that) two (head of cattle) go to each subchief, three to the ombiasa, four to all the emissaries, and only then the men divide the rest. On the day when men leave for war, women sing chants of hope, pray for the victory and good fortune and an easy capture of cattle. (This takes place) especially at cock's crow and each (woman) wears (carries) a wand called *matsot-soroka*, the *vindana*, leaves of *seva,* and wear on their bodies a piece of cotton called *folivalo*. In the absence of their husbands, the women are extremely *fady* for copulation with other men and any woman who does such an act is taken to be a sorceress. When the men, upon return, start telling of their exploits during the journey, at that moment the women start boiling the *fotsimbarim-balavo*.

FATI-DRAN'NY SAMY MPANJAKA

Raha hifanao fati-dra ny mpanjaka dia maniraka alona iray ilay mila mba hampandre ny anankiray, na hanaiky izy, na tsia, ka raha manaiky izy, dia mila ilay iraka fa manaiky tsara izany, rehefa reny iny fa manaiky dia mampandre ny vahoakany izy mba ho tonga rehefa amin'ny andro tononiny. Ka raha efa tonga ny andro nofidiny, dia mandeha ny mpanjaka miaraka amin'ny vahoakany sady mitondra omby iray hanao-vana ny fati-dra. Rehefa tonga akaiky ny tanana handrehanany dia maniraka olona roalahy mba hampandre ilay anakiray hoe: tonga ny sakaiza nao, hanao ny fihavananareo, ka dia mamaly izy, asaovy tonga izy, fa izaho dia efa miandry azy, miverina ireo iraka milaza io teny io, dia mandroso moramora, manao laharana lavabe ny zazalahy sy ny olona andevo dia mitondra hazo kitay, rehefa tonga eo amin'ny tokon-tan'ny mpanjaka izy rehetra dia mimpetraka daholy, dia izao no lahateny ataon'ny ranitrampaka: Tsy avao ahay eto miandry anareo fa mifanao tsatok'andro itsika, ka raha tonga hianareo dia soa, hivitan'ny bivitan'ny fiahavan-tsika, dia mamaly ilay ranitrin'ny mpivahiny, eny marina fa tsy maintsy anay tokoa hiana-reo satria efa mampandre anareo mialoha izahay mba handehandehananareo ka dia mamaly ireo mpanjaka roalahy hoe: Tsy misy fiovana ny efa voalaza teo, fa arakiny my ohabolana hoe: lalana amorokeaky ka tsy misy fiovana intsony. Amin'izay ny vehivavy eto an-tanana efa akaiky rahateo mitondra vary fotsy, mangahazo, voamanga, ary omby iray, hafaha ny vahiny, dia tetoanan-trano hisy azy, mandrampandehany, amin'io andro hiany na ampitson'io dia mivory ambody hazo, na amin'ny hazomanga, dia vahorana eo akiakin'ny hazo-manga na hazo ny omby, mitandoha miatsinana ny lohany, mitodika mianatsimo ny hatrefany dia samy maka ny lefony avy izy roalahy samy mpanjaka izay samy atsattony eo amin'ny kibon'ilay omby, tanan'ny tanany havanana avy dia efa eo koa lahy antitra anankiray hanompa azy, ary hanao ny kabary momba ny famarana ny fatridra. Nefa io omby io hiany dia mbola tsy ampy fa ampiana ranombolamena, atao antain'ny vilia madio, dia sotro koa iray, hisotroana ny ra dia tsihy madio indray ao ambany, mitsanga aorian'ilay treo mpanjaka roalahy, amin'izay ila antidahy hanompa azy mificka ny vantan'io omby io, amin'ny kibay na lefona sady atsipiny ambony indray maka ny fanombolamena, miantsoa anao Ndriananahary tsielaela fa ity raha kely na dia handeha ho avy avaratra, hiantsinana, na hiahandrena, na hianatsimo hianao dia mijanona aloha, fa io.

BLOOD COVENANT AMONG KINGS

When the kings are to become blood brothers, the one who asks for this sends someone to find out if the other (king) will refuse or not. When the one asked responds favorably, the emissary will repeat the message of acceptance. While waiting for it, the one who demands will inform his subjects to come on a designated day to attend the ceremony. When that day comes, the king departs with his men and must take along an ox for sacrifice in this blood covenant. Upon arriving near the village to which they are to go, two men are sent to let the other party know that his friend is coming to gain friendship. He answers: "Let him come, I am waiting," and the envoys return and repeat what was said. Advancing slowly and forming a long line, the young and the slaves carry wood for burning. Once at the royal court, they all sit down while the subchiefs tell them the greeting words: "We are here awaiting you on the appointed day, and it is good you come, we will accept your brother." And the arriving subchiefs answer: "Yes, it is indeed a truth that you are awaiting us, for we have asked you in advance not to be absent." Then, two notables answer that the recitals just made change nothing and say this proverb: "A road crossed near an abyss cannot be traversed backward." At that moment, the village women are in sight, carrying white rice, amioc, potatoes, or an ox to be offered to the travelers; then the huts for their use during the stay are pointed out. On the same day or the next, they all reunite at a foot of a tree or at the *hazomanga* [altar] where, at its foot, the ox is attached, its head toward the east but facing the south. The two *mpanjaka*, each with a spear in his hand, place them into the belly of the ox, with their right hands holding it, while an old man insults and cites maledictions that can affect the blood brothers [if the covenant is violated]. But the ox is not enough. Water and gold have to be added into the spoon from which blood is drunk. With a clean mat below the plate, the two kings behind the animal, the old man taps the body with a large knife or a spear while throwing the gold water into the air. "I call upon God for a moment for here is something which goes north, east, south, and west, hear, stay first, for here is . . . [name of one king and then the other].

FIALANA NY VOLY VOKATRA

Tsy mahasahy mihimina ny rahalahy sy ny sanaka raha voalohamboly raha tsy efa manomezana ny ray, satria fady dia fady . . .

THE CROP HARVEST

The brothers and the sons can never eat until the first crop harvested is given to the father for this is absolutely forbidden . . . .

NY AO ANANTIN'NY TRANO

Ny fiavakavahan'ny toerana: milapy ny rindrina andrefana ny farafara, mitandoha mianatismo, mianavaratra ny tongotra, ny rindry atsinana dia voatokana ho an' ny olon-dehibe ny akaiky ny varavana andrefana dia an' ny apela, sy ny andevo, milapy ao atsinan'ny kibany dia ny fatanafo, dia kihotrano eo akaikiny varava aniloha, dia an'ny tompotrano, ny rindry atismo an'ny vahiny, ka ny tena afovoan'ny trano indrindra eo toerana tsy sahin'olona itoerana.

PLACE DISTINCTIONS IN THE HOUSE

Against the western wall, the bed: head facing south and the feet north. The eastern section is reserved for important persons (while) near the western door are women and slaves. At the eastern side of the bed is the hearth. In the northeastern corner, at the side of the window, is the proprietor; the southern wall section is for travelers and the exact center of the house is not for anyone to stay.

NY FOMBAN'NYZ AFIMANELY

Ka raha tena mpanjaka ny Zafimanely dia manambady hatraminy 1 ka hatramin'ny 20 ka dia ny vehivavy no manatona azy ao antranondahiny tsiraray, nefa izay tiany indrindra no asainy manantona matetika. Rehefa maty izy dia lovan'ny zanany ireo vadiny.

THE ZAFIMANELY CUSTOM

A Zafimanely king can marry one to twenty wives and it is the wife who comes to sleep in his own house who is called *tranondahy*, in turn with others.[1] But, the one he likes a lot comes most often and when he dies his wives are inherited by his sons.

NY FIANA APELA BARA

Raha mila apela Bara ny voalohany ialan azy io saika tsy ahazoana azy, fa manao fialana tsiny manao magnelo izy aloha hoe: isika olona mifakahita eto avao isan' andro androany hianao vao mila anaky, dia manome fotoana roa na telo andro izay vao mazoto, io faneloa ataony io fiala tsiny io, izany hoe miambolany heviny mba tsy hahazoana mandeha tsy anajy, ka voatery manaraky ny andro ampadinasiny. Reha te-hanao hifamary amin'ny atoandro dia mifanoro toerana hoe; ao ananona dia mifakahita isika nefa matetika tsy hita ny iaviany-ho solon'izy tsy minday tsihy dia andriana ny lambany misy zavitrazo no atao lafika, rehefa miala tao dia fafafana ny loha mba tsy ho fantatr'olo, indrindra moa raha manambady, mba tsy ho vambe. Fa ny apela aleony nifampandry amin'ny atoandro nohon'ny miafana harivasao rohon'ny lehilahy amin'ny hoe: iny apela lavahana, sady lavahana ny apela manao izany ka menatra, aleony koa Betsileo, na ambaniandro fa raha bara menatra izy ny hifanakariva.

HOW BARA WOMEN ARE TAKEN

When Bara women are sought, they are not won with the very first words. She usually excuses herself, pleading to be ill, and [complains about] being sought [only] today although the demanding male sees her every day. [But] she promises herself within two or three days [so as] to pretend to be well again in order to avoid gossip. Then the waiting takes place, and, if the desire is mutual, a day is selected for a meeting at [a given place]. Very often it can be seen where the women have been, when they return, by the dislocation of their matting, since the sleeping takes place on their *lambas*, or else by the tree leaves that remain after they get up and clear their hair of the bits of *bozaka*, particularly if they happen to be married. The Bara women prefer to copulate in broad daylight rather than in the evenings, being ashamed of talk among men that "here goes that rake of a woman." But, if she does it now and then in the evenings, she prefers to be with either a Betsileo or a Merina, for their gossip will not reach too many of the young Bara.

[1] Lehimanjaka, King of Imamono, had a harem of eighty wives.

POLITICAL CHANGE IN IBARA AS TOLD BY RAONIMPANANY, CHIEF OF ANGATY VILLAGE, CA. 1910

Extracts from Rabemanana's unpublished manuscript *Le Pays des Kimoso et Son Histoire*: *a*, pp. 84–85; *b*, p. 87; *c*, p. 87; *d*, pp. 59–60; and *e*, pp. 46–49. Items *a*, *b*, and *c* are based on the oral account of Raonimpanany. Items *d* and *e* are from unidentified Betsileo sources.

After the departure of the Andrantsay, the Kimoso returned bit by bit to the Valley of Manarahaka and to the Valley of Ranomena. In the Horombé [plateau], the Tambahy held the forested escarpments. . . . To the east of Ivohibé peak, a small kingdom began to form. It was composed of some villages having the Vohitovo as chiefs. Then, at the source of Manarahaka, came to dwell the Mananatra who originated from Arindrano. But the chiefs did not get along and the Mananatra split into two clans. The first remained in the high valley of Manarahaka and took the name of Maroentana. The second grouping joined the Vohitovo at the edge of the Iantara, to the east of the peak, in order to form the Antaivohibe clan. [Then] Ralahiroso, father of Rakalandria of the village of Manampy [Ambalavao], son of Ramatahimanana, went to the source of Manarahaka, among the Manantara or, better, the Maroentana . . . [during a feast] as the [Maroentana] got drunk . . . Ralahiroso deemed the moment had come to establish a kingdom, took the axe, and cut the heads of all those stone drunk. He spared the women and the children and had himself proclaimed king of the high Manarahaka [valley]. His subjects were called the Taimanarahaka or simply Manarahaka. [Then] Rataboaka, Ramaitsomanana, and Ravangalahy, men of Zafimatahimanana origin according to some or of Zafimbetsiry [Zafimbetsiriry?] origin according to others, hardened by the adventures of Ralahiroso, had themselves recognized by the Kimoso of the Manarahaka Valley and of the lower valleys of the Tomampy [Itomampy] and the Onaivo [Ionaivo]. But, there was one insurrection among the Kimoso. The insurgents delegated Trosa and Rabahary to appeal for help to any king of the south. . . . [a]

The *Andrahofika* are descendants of Rabehala [ombiasa from Antai-saka]. They can marry the Zafimanely women without being punished. They alone can wash the Zafimanely bodies and enter them. . . . [b]

Rabiby may have ruled between 1745 and 1769. Toward the end of his rule, he made incursions among the Zafirambo [Tanala] of Manan-driana and died of a disease on the banks of the Sahateno River, in the high valley of Manarahaka. His son, Andriamanely II, succeeded him. [c]

Andriamanalina I of Betsileo and Andriamanely II, King of the Bara: at five days' journey south of Mahazoarivo, between the Rivers Tomampy and Onaivo, lived a celebrated king who was called Andriamanely. [One day] the King of Sandra [Isandra, Betsileo Kingdom] went to see him with an army of considerable size, intent on being recognized as King of the Bara in the same way his father, Ralambovitaony, set himself up among the Sandra. His army captured Ambinaninony when Andria-manely sent envoys to ask him what he was up to. Andriamanalina answered: "I want Andriamanely to come and tell me that he is my son." Surprised by such arrogance, Andriamanely shouted: "On the contrary, it is he, Andriamanalina, who is my son since he is coming to visit me. If not, let him prepare for war, for I have as many men as he (has)." This time, Andriamanalina employed a jest. He sent a huge jug to Andria-manely with the following word: "Let Andriamanely make each of his men carry a pinch of rice to be placed in the jug. If they [can] fill it up, I am his son. If not, he is mine." Andriamanely accepted the game. He carried out his task, but the jug was not filled up. Then Andriamanely returned the jug saying: "Let Andriamanalina, in his turn, have each of his men spit into the same jug like cats. If they fill it up, I am his son. If not, he is mine." Andriamanalina had this done in front of judges composed of Bara and Betsileo. It was filled up and there were still some of his men who had not spat into the jug. Andriamanely had lost twice in this game which appeared to have been a mere jest but which was, in reality, quite serious. He accepted to be the son . . . of Andriamanalina. The latter then told him: "As you are my son, after my death you will prepare a memorial stone at the spot where I had come to see you." At the death of Andriamanalina, a stone in his memory was erected at the confluence of three rivers, the Tomampy, Onaivo, and Manarahaka. [d]

AFTERMATH OF AN INSURRECTION

The Vohitsaomby did not know how to profit from the expulsion of the Malemy Volo. They devoured one another. Families got together to form new clans, the clans subdivided into component families, villages disappeared to make way for other villages, a continuous state of war was on. And in its wake came the famine and the diseases and claimed many victims. Those who fled to the rocky mountain tops believed to be seeing the sea mount toward them and started to "swim" in the fog, killing themselves by the fall. There was a small clan of Beminena, from the west of Manandriana, now settlers near Fianarantsoa. After having, in succession, constructed and abandoned their villages, these newcomers moved from Avonomby to Vohitsavolona and Vohitsarivo. Barely settled, they attacked the Kianjasoa-Manolafaka, who put them to flight and who killed their principal chiefs. The endless war made it impossible for the Vohitsaomby to cultivate their rice fields. A bit of potatoes or manioc, they say, was worth a large bull. The epidemic, that twin of famine, lost no time in appearing and claimed so many victims that there were not enough men to bury the victims, who had to be dragged and rolled down into the crevices nearest to the villages. All of these calamities saddened the land of the Vohitsaomby. The Beminena survivors who had escaped the epidemics left their infected villages and sought refuge on the Vohibola Mountain where, weak of body and of spirit, they started one morning to "swim" in the fog which surrounded their village, thinking that the sea had come up, and fell crushed to death at the bottom. Those who refused to kill themselves in this manner, some of the richest men, made their cattle charge the mountain they so vainly sought to displace. This mountain took the name of Ankarambohibola. The mothers forgot their little children in the fields and spent the night home without the slightest worry. They did not remember their children until the following morning. Finally, the general deterioration had reached such a point that people did not know any longer if an egg placed in boiling water could really harden by being boiled. The old men attributed this general moment of brutality of the Vohibola inhabitants to the influence of the source from which they obtained potable water. This source was later filled with earth and named Andranomahagaigy or "water which gives madness." But, the real cause of the [collective] folly was the misery of vast proportions that the *manjaka Hova* brought about not only to the Vohibola inhabitants but also to the entire Fianarantsoa province, equally afflicted by this general madness. The Vohitsaomby were never in greater misfortune than during the time of *manjaka Hova*. Suffering from endless misfortune, these peoples of the central interior asked for nothing better than to have chiefs and kings who alone could provide security. [e]

THE EARLY ANDRIANA-MERINA
AMONG THE VAZIMBA

These two extracts are from an anonymous collection of unpublished *Tantara* of Imerina recorded around 1890. The first reveals that pure and simple conflict did not constitute the sole relationship between the Andriana and the Vazimba. Its main event is the political marriage between the Merina ruler Andriamanelo and the daughter of Rabiby, a powerful Vazimba chief, each of the two parties having, however, a different purpose in mind. The second extract points to the advent of royal fratricide as method of succession which marked and distinguished the Andriana.

Andriamanelo could not expel the Vazimba of Analamanga as well as the Vazimba inhabiting the western region. Only the Vazimba residing in the smallest of villages were attacked. Then, Andriamanelo reached Ambohidrabiby. With his advisers, he decided that it would be an advantage to take as spouse the only daughter of Rabiby, chief of Ambohidrabiby, and of his wife Raolomasina. The king and his advisers knew that if this marriage could be concluded, the king's estates would extend greatly. . . . And, so, Andriamanelo and his advisers decided to ask for the hand of Ramaitsoanala, the daughter of Rabiby and Raolomasina. Andriamanelo did not go to Ambohidrabiby himself. He sent Andriamitondra, who gave Andriamanelo's message: "tell Rabiby and Raolomasina that I have come to be their son for we are of the same family of Analamaitso, that I have come to knock on their door to ask for Ramaitsoanala. Here are the cattle. . . . They are not a gift but a sign of my presence. *Aoka mba hahazo manantena aho* (let them not dim my hope)." Since then, the site named Ambohimanantena became Ambohitrantenaina instead. "Yes," said Rabiby and his wife, "it is to our liking that . . . this lord of many subjects comes to ask with respect the hand of our daughter but we are only parents of her body and not of her will . . . and must thus ask her first. . . ."

Ramaitsoanala consented . . . and Andriamanelo sent gifts. One of these became known later as *vodiondry* (rump of sheep, gift made by groom to bride's parents). From this comes the saying *Mahasaikatsai-katra hoatry ny mitari-bady tsy lasam-bodiondry* (it is embarrassing to walk with a wife for whom no sheep's rump was given). Thus, the *vodiondry* became a sacred covenant. The marriage was concluded. Pisalahy and Manjenitany were called upon to assist Rabiby in the blessing since—at that time—it was the Vazimba custom to have this done by three men. Here is how this was done: Seven mats made of *hisatra* (bark of the *zozoro* or sedge) are placed at the site of benediction and then two drums are put in the middle of the seven mats. On the drums will sit the two spouses. Some dried-up *hisatra* are added along with the *herana* (an aquatic plant) and some dry *tsotsoraka* (arbusta). Following the Vazimba custom, here is their significance. *Hisatra* is meant to multiply those who will till the fields. *Tsotsoraka* and *herana* are there to fulfill any wish, and the *zozoro*, taken while still green, is meant to give happiness to the village dwellers. As for the drums, if the spouses make a son, the earth and the sky will know it, and if it is a daughter, she will have much posterity to fill up the fields with. Pisalahy, after placing these objects on the spouses' heads, spoke the following words: "O my ancestors . . . creators of life, of feet and of hands, Andriamanelo and Ralapavola (another name of Ramaitsoanala) are being joined. May this day be to their favor, may their destinies not cross, may they be rich, grow old, have many subjects. . . ." Rabiby and Manjenitany then blessed the spouses in the same way. This Vazimba manner of blessing was adopted by all the descendants and subjects of Andriamanelo and Ralapavola and also by all the princes that followed. . . ."

✿   ✿   ✿

The sovereignty of Andriamanelo at Alosara expanded much with the help given by the people of Loharano and Ambohidrabiby as well as the support of powerful and celebrated individuals long since with him: diviner Andriambenamelavahoaka, Andriamanaraianandobé, Beroka, Andriantsilavimbahoaka, Andriankimboro, Andriamamilazabé, Rabesaboa and others. At that time, Andriamanelo—angry at an act committed by his younger brother—violated the recommendation of his father . . . and put him to death to leave also the kingdom to Ralambo instead. It used to be said then *Miova tokoa lahy ity fa he ireto andriana iray tam-po mifamono* (everything has changed, the princes kill one another) and it is still customary to say *Aza manao fihavanan'andriana* (do not be two-faced like the *andriana*).

TRADITIONS OF THE SAKALAVA

The first of two oral texts given below was recorded by the
author at Morondava in 1965 (Informant: Mahonjobé) and
the second, also in the same year, at Mirinarivo-Majunga
(Informant: Tsimanohitra Tombo). One deals with a custom
concerning a dead Sakalava king. The other is an account
of "Who Were the Sakalava."

When a Sakalava monarch dies, the entire custom of his ancestors must
be invoked. The moment he expires, his last breath out, pieces of bone
from the forehead, arm, and foot are taken off. Ten castrated bulls are
sacrificed. Their right horns are removed, and the points are shunted.
The horns are then given a fire burn. Afterward, they are washed with
water from an area over which no bird was observed in flight [for a
while] and brought early in the morning, at cock's crow. Then, with
greatest care, the horns are enveloped in a red *lamba* [cloth for dead
royalty] and the ends are sewn together. With this done, the *lamba* is
ornamented with different types of beads: white, red, black-spotted.
Afterward, the councilors and the royal ministers get together and pronounce the following words: *"Matsereoke, Matsereoke raekko"* ["May
our father be a saint"]. They then take three pieces of gold or three of
them take three pieces of gold and carry them above their heads while
repeating *"Matsereoke raiko,"* as was done earlier. Then they put the
three pieces of gold into a horn and step back a pace or two to let others
closer so that they can bring a fistful of earth from the eight regions over
which the dead monarch had ruled. These last then cede the place to
others who bring the strong drink distilled from the alembic and pour
it over the earth previously inserted into the horns. Then they, in turn,
step back while others bring along razors from which the handles were
taken and only the blades are then introduced into the horns because
this means that the king, while alive, ruled the land indeed. Then they
step back, and others come up to introduce the scissors, which is to say
that the king, while alive, did indeed govern the people. When all of these
acts are accomplished, the royal councilors and ministers who had been
in the residence of the dead monarch blow seven times on their marine
shell and the people assemble at once around it. With this done, the royal
wives are made to come out of a certain place, all bedecked, hair down,
and crying. They carry incense in a small and beautiful earthen plate.

They enter the royal residence and place some charcoal into the incense plate. Soon, there is a fine aroma within the residence, and the royal councilors and ministers start calling on Andriananahary and on the ancestors. After that, the royal wives leave the residence. Then start the piercing screams, sounds, and chants of all kinds. A castrated red bull is then killed. He is skinned, and the skin is hung over a fire. Pieces of meat are placed in baskets and taken into the royal residence for the councilors and ministers to eat. Although the decomposing body has a very strong and unpleasant odor, it is forbidden to spit, and the one who spits while eating is killed instantly with axes or beaten to death with wooden canes. He then becomes the "rug" on which the royal body is to be placed in the tomb. The open tomb would be guarded so that no one comes near the victim's body before interment. Then, the cured skin of the killed bull is taken from above the fire and the king's body is enveloped in it. Several head of cattle are then killed. They are fat and serve as food for those who had come to attend the royal funeral. But, these attendants bring their own cattle and gold. The dead [king] emits a repelling odor for a month and is taken early in the morning to a far-away forest. When the tallest tree is located, the body is suspended from it. Underneath the body, a great earthen jug is placed in order to collect the humors that flow from it. And when the humors stop after a month and the body is dry, the bones enveloped in the skin are taken down and placed on a mat. The humors are taken to the *zomba*, along with royal relics in horns. When all of this is done, the dead king is taken to the tomb of his ancestors, or more precisely, his bones on the mat are taken there. Then trees are felled so that the royal bones can be placed on them, this without counting the head of cattle (constantly) killed since the monarch's death. With this done, more wood for matting is introduced into the mortuary pit [*Sasa-Poana*], arranged in an even manner over the body of the one killed for spitting near the decomposing body of the king because of repellent odor. Pieces of wood are placed on four sides of the dead. This burial lasts six months so that no one could possibly count all the head of cattle killed for this occasion and, everywhere, the fires burn. The people are not only given the meat, but also manioc from all of the regions, without forgetting the alcoholic beverage consumed. When all of this is done, everyone starts to cry and every single person cuts his own hair to mark the mourning of the dead monarch.

WHO WERE THE SAKALAVA

When we speak of the Sakalava, these are the Anjaramay, the Tampala, the Jongoho, and the Mpilokoly who scattered into the forests, led by Andriandahifotsy. The Tiamanongo . . . have all emigrated; the Bezano who went to Anjamba, the Maromainty who went to Ambaniala, to Miarimandroso in the land of the Sihanaka, to Ambanialabe and Ambanialakely. The Andreba went into the forest. The Antandrona who are Tsimihety and who were called before *Omamay*. These Antandrona were brought along by the Zafinifotsy, under Andrianianinarivo, a great conqueror. Among the Betsileo, he had left children who remain forever Andriandahifotsy. He left some at Avarirano and at Maranibato. He was the chief of all these peoples. And he left children in the north, like a vagabond. They all descend from Andriandahifotsy. He literally filled up the whole region. Here, however, in the north, he was hated and could not stay. But the land was not in peace, and he called upon his sons and grandsons [particularly] Andriamandisoarivo. It was in Morondava that the ancestors of Zafimanely formed, and it was there that Andriamisara appeared, Andriamisara whose descendants came all the way to here [at Majunga]. Thus came the Sakalava to beat the Manandabo who ruled here as masters of the land [*tompontany*]. The Manandabo were won over but without a drop of blood, or a rifle shot. . . . When the Islamos came from Mahore, they were called Antalaotra but still became (like everyone else) Sakalava . . . they hardly fought to the point of bloodshed . . . they rather engaged in commerce and erected strong houses. In effect, they have aided us a great deal, us Sakalava. The Islamos were one of the earliest tribes here. They made arrangements with Andriamisara, Andriamandisoarivo, and all the Sakalava of the region. They married Sakalava women. Their children became Sakalava. . . . The real Sakalava came out of the Mahajamba region and went both south and north of Maevatanana. These are the real Sakalava. They crossed a valley and found themselves in the heart of Menabé. These are the real Sakalava. . . . There was once here, long, long, ago, the rich Kingdom of Borifotra, but it had no king as all of the Borifotra ruled and the king came later, much later. . . . That was the government of the Borifotra, before the Manandabo. . . . After the Borifotra it was Andriamandisoarivo who ruled, and this was the reason why the Tsimihety and the Sihanaka left. . . .

ON BARA DANCERS,
HAIR DRESSING,
THEIR ODY AND SAMPY

Reverend George A. Shaw of the London Missionary Society paid a visit to northern Ibara when it was still *terra incognita* for the outsider. While sharing the tendency common to many of the Tananarive-based missionaries to look down on "provincial" Malagasy, Shaw made some interesting notes, published in the *Antananarivo Annual* (1876), 227–237, as "Rough Sketches of a Journey to Ibara." The following extracts are from page 232.

The girls of the village [of Bèsikaona] assembled and sang us some of their native songs. It was the first Ibara singing we had heard, and a more barbarous noise coming from human throats it is scarcely possible to imagine the word "singing" attached to. A couple of those not engaged in the vocal exercise [for *exercise* it certainly was, and would have made me hoarse in five minutes] stood up and danced. Besides the usual ugly style of hair dressing, they had horns branching like those of oxen, made of the split rush used in making their mats. The dance did not materially differ from that of the Hova and Betsileo, except that each carried a staff made of polished iron, about five feet long and ornamented with some half-a-dozen links of a chain at the top, which rattled with every motion.

The style of hair dressing differs considerably from that of any other tribe I have seen. Once a month, and in some cases once in six weeks, the hair is washed and then rolled up into a great number of knots, varying in size from that of a marble to that of an orange, and always round. After being carefully rolled up and tied or sewn . . . it is then thickly coated with beeswax melted with fat, so that when cold each knob is firmly cemented to those adjacent to it, and all appearance of hair gone. When freshly done it looks like lumps of grey clay stuck on their heads, each of which when struck gives back a sound like striking a piece of hard wood. . . .

At noon next day we stayed at a village called Ivíly for tiffin, and while our men were discussing their rice, I had a chat with the chief and some of his principal men about their *òdy* (charms) and *sàmpy* (gods). He had one of the former round his neck, consisting of a piece of wood shaped like a flowerpot, about an inch long, with a piece of iron stuck horizontally near the bottom. The inside was filled with tinder. For this he had given an ox, and he said, and seemed firmly to believe, that it would protect him from the power of bullets fired at him. Outside the gate of this village is a pair of *sàmpy*. Pieces of wood about two feet long are roughly shaped like busts, male and female, with a bent spearhead stuck in the ground between them. They are surrounded by a double fence like the *rova* of a town. They are the presiding protectors of the town, and are believed to have the power of warning the inhabitants of approaching danger.

THE HAZOMANGA AND BILO IN MAHAFALY

Two descriptive extracts from Mahafaly traditions collected by Mamelomana (see the Bibliography), not dated but probably recent.

The *hazomanga* is made of hard wood, the *katrafay*. The crossbar is called *folakara*, while the poles are 1.50 to 2 meters high. The crossbar itself is about 20 centimeters from the top and is about 20 centimeters wide and 50 to 60 centimeters long. The subjects of the Maroserana kings did not have, at one time, the *hazomanga* since it was strictly a royal prerogative to preside over the sacrifices and offerings, but (the subjects) were eventually permitted to have the *hazomanga*. When the moment arrives to make the sacrifice, the one who does it must turn his head toward the east. North of the *hazomanga*, at some two to three meters' distance, are planted other poles of wood to which the heads of sacrificed cattle are later attached. These are called the *fatora*. It is at the foot of the *hazomanga* that prayers are said along with demands for blessings or cures. Each *hazomanga* has its own sacrificer, called *mpisoro*, and upon his death the *hazomanga* is called *hazomanga maty* (*maty* = dead) and a new ceremony must be made for a successor who will have his own *hazomanga*. He can implant it anywhere, as long as it is to the east of the village or dwelling within it. No one can touch the *hazomanga*, which is sacred.

❖   ❖   ❖

Among the Mahafaly, the *bilo* is a person haunted by mean spirit. First come the chants by professionals, if the person or family is rich, then comes the dancing with the *bilo*. The next day, the *bilo* selects from a passing herd an ox that is later speared to death through its armpit. The ox is called *tiambilo* [*bilo*'s favorite]. But, before it is killed, its forehead is washed with water, and the same water is given to the *bilo* to drink. Then, in the afternoon, comes the *mampino-bilo*, the drinking of blood. When the ox is killed, the *bilo* puts his mouth to the bleeding spot while the people tap the abdomen of the dead ox and say *kamino, ka minon-dra* [do not drink blood or the very opposite of what is being done just to incite the *bilo* to drink more]. After this blood drinking, the *bilo* is taken to a water source and plunged [dunked?] into the water by assistants who "test" his body by tickling the *bilo* out of it through laughter. And the *bilo* laughs, and the ill one is cured at once! *Sandratse* is a feast organized after the recovery. It is one of chants, like the *beko*, and of dances, which last two or three days, as the kin and the *fatidra* [blood brothers] bring one head of cattle each. *Jiny* is the person possessed by the dead spirits. . . .

ON MALAGASY ORIGINS

In 1883 (*Antananarivo Annual*, II/7, 216–228), the Norwegian missionary and linguist Lars Dahle published an essay on the subject of Malagasy origins. It was then far ahead of its time and is still superior to the more recent brief discussions of this great problem, partly because many of Dahle's seminal points were never heeded. The cross-disciplinary approach outlined by Dahle is only now beginning to be followed. Although at times Dahle is misguided and even departs from his own rules, overstressing one aspect or minimizing another, the essay is still replete with insights of the first order and is hence reproduced with as little abridgement as possible, stating what has been left out. Its full title is "The Race Elements of the Malagasy and Guesses at Truth with Regard to Their Origin."

The question before us is by no means an easy one; in fact, the present writer is so far from thinking himself able to solve the problem, that he thinks it is impossible to do so in a satisfactory manner at present. Before this can be done, the different tribes constituting the Malagasy nation must be better known than they are now; their different dialects must be compared and subjected to a close examination and a scientific analysis, reducing all words to their root elements, and pointing out what is common to the language of the people as a whole, and what is peculiar to each dialect. The East African peoples and languages, too, must be more extensively studied, as there can be no doubt that we must look in that direction for new light on many questions concerning Malagasy philology and—what is to me almost the same thing—ethnography. Until this work is done, we can scarcely hope to produce anything better than "guesses at truth," suggestions for further investigations, hypotheses to be proved or disproved in the future.

I am sorry to say that my residence here has not enabled me to make any extensive researches with regard to what may have been written on this question in books and periodicals in other countries. Many contributions toward solving the difficulty may have been given without my being at all aware of it; but considering that I have, in common with many others in my position, for thirteen years been excluded from access to any other books than those on my own shelves, I hope the reader will kindly excuse any deficiencies, and that if these lines should fall into the hands of any who have written on this question, and who may be disappointed in not finding their views noticed and criticized, they will kindly keep in mind that this is simply owing to my ignorance of what they have written. . . . It is certainly my opinion that a man who is going to write on such a question as this ought, if possible, to know, and pay a fair attention to, everything written by his predecessors, avail himself of their labors, and write nothing at all if he does not feel satisfied that he is able to throw some light on the question, or at least advance new proofs in support of old views, if he has not himself any new theory to set forth. . . . [Omitted here are the next five paragraphs, pp. 216–218, in which Dahle questions not so much the conclusions of some writers advancing such origins and influences as Jewish, Siamese, Bechuana, but rather the premises on which these conclusions or usually simple assertions rested.]

Before setting my own views on the subject, I shall take the liberty of making a few remarks with regard to the means available for an investigation into the origin of a people, and the relationship between different nations. These are, in my opinion, the following: (1) *The geographical position of the countries occupied by the peoples in question.* We are not justified in deriving one people from another if there is not, geographically viewed, a possibility, or even some probability, of communication between the countries they inhabit. Nobody, for instance, would look to Greenland for the origin of the Malagasy. This does not, however, depend merely on the distance between the countries, but quite as much on the means of communication, the mountains, deserts, intervening seas, currents, winds, etc.; (2) *Similarity of manners and customs among the dif-ferent peoples*, including also their domesticated animals and cultivated plants. This is, however, in my opinion, the least important of all the criteria in question, because (*a*) these manners and customs are often very much the same amongst even widely different nations and races, provided the moral, intellectual, and social standpoint of such races is nearly the same. (*b*) They are, on the other hand, frequently strangely different amongst different tribes of the same people, where the common language and physiognomy prove the unity of the race beyond contro-versy. The different tribes in Madagascar afford a very good instance of this. (*c*) They vary widely at different times, according to the progress and the development of the nation, and its more or less frequent contact with other nations and races. The Malagasy, for instance, have changed their customs considerably in the course of the last half-century, but they are still the same race and have substantially the same language as before. (3) *The physiognomy of the different peoples*: their stature, color, hair, eyes, the form of their head, their facial features, etc. This is, no doubt, of considerable weight, especially if extensive measurements of the craniums can be made in a scientific manner. There seems, however, yet to be much difference of opinion with regard to the reliability of the con-clusions to be drawn from this test. (4) *Their language*. This is, no doubt, next to history, the best criterion of relationship. It must, however, be borne in mind that similarity in the grammatical structure of the lan-guages . . . proves more than does similarity of vocabulary; and that in their vocabulary the *quality* . . . is often more telling than the *quantity* of similar words. . . . (5) *Their traditions and history*. These are, of course, quite conclusive, as far as they go; for if a nation can be proved historically to have originated from another, their relationship is settled beyond dispute. Unhappily, this argument is not very often accessible, as few nations can be traced historically to their origin. Generally, we have only very vague traditions to guide us; but even these may be of importance as an additional help—a corroboration of the results we have arrived at by means of other sources of information.

In the following remarks I shall confine myself chiefly to the fourth and fifth of these points, but especially to the fourth. [Omitted here are two paragraphs on p. 219 in which Dahle essentially offers an apology both for not working with other points because of lack of means and sources and for advancing at this time more "guesses" and "hypotheses."]

Taking this view of the question, I feel it my duty first to state the facts to be explained, and then adduce the hypothesis by which to account for them. By these facts I mean the actual condition of the Malagasy tribes, viewed ethnologically. The hypothesis then is only a suggestion with regard to the question how their ethnological position originated and can be accounted for. The facts in question are, in my opinion, the following: (1) *That the inhabitants of Madagascar, broadly speaking, are one people.* This seems clear from the fact of the language spoken over the whole island is substantially the same, although differing very much as to the dialects of the different tribes. This unity of language must now be considered as a tolerably well-established fact. . . . I freely admit that I have had great difficulty in understanding some of [the dialects] or making myself understood [in] them; but this is not more than any Londoner would experience amongst country people in Yorkshire or Northumberland, who would nevertheless still maintain that the language spoken in these counties is English. [Omitted are 26 lines on p. 220 in which Dahle rejects any great linguistic influence of the Hova upon other Malagasy to account for the basically same linguistic matrix.] That the different dialects have many words peculiar to them is a matter of course, as such is the case in dialects everywhere. Some of the dialects in the most distant parts of the country may in these respects differ so much from the dialect of Imerina [the dialect generally used in books] as to justify saying that they are slightly verging on the boundary line of a new language. . . . [Omitted are 21 lines on pp. 220–221 where Dahle gives further detail to show that the Hova domination of Madagascar in the past century is not synonymous with their linguistic influence.] (2) *This language is closely related to the Malayo-Polynesian, partly also to the Melanesian, which clearly indicates that there must have been an emigration to Madagascar from the island world in the East. But at the same time there are certainly many elements in the Malagasy language not to be traced to this source.* [Omitted are 8 lines on p. 221 where Dahle notes that the general premise has been established while more precise and more specific affinities need to be looked into.] But the matter is quite different with respect to the non-Malayo-Polynesian element, as absolutely nothing has as yet been done to explain it and point out its relationship. I have been collecting materials for an essay on it, but I am not yet in a position to publish it. At present I must confine myself to the bare statement that I believe much of it can be traced to east African sources. (3) *An examination of the physiognomies of the Malagasy people leads to the same result, viz., that they represent a mixture of Malayo-Polynesian and African elements.* [Omitted are the next 70 lines on pp. 221–223. Here, Dahle states that the Hova are the most "Malayan type" and that the true Hova are also "fairest" in color while "all other tribes, even those on the east coast, are decidedly less Malayan, and more African in their physiognomy." To the two major elements should be added the Arabs "or their descendants, pure or hybrid, from the Comoro Islands or east Africa" but "seldom direct from Arabia" and still later-day Europo-Malagasy intermixtures.]

Of course, it is impossible to give a decided answer . . . but when I suppose the emigration from Africa to have been the first, it is for the following reasons [paraphrased]: (*a*) proximity of Africa; (*b*) native tradition points the same way, particularly for the Vazimba, earliest inhabitants of central highlands; (*c*) "If the more clever and warlike Malayo-Polynesian race had been the first to take possession of the country, the Africans would scarcely have been able to gain ground here at all; whilst it is quite natural that the former should be able to get a footing in a country previously occupied by the latter;" (*d*) that since the Malayo-Polynesian element won in language and "social influence" it must have been the conquering one and the other the conquered, "a state of things . . . most in keeping with the general lot everywhere of the sons of Ham, who were to be 'servants of servants to their brethren'." Only on the supposition "that the whole African element here is owing simply to the import of slaves from Africa could I suppose that element to be of a more recent introduction than the Malayo-Polynesian; but I have too firm an impression of its strength to be able to accept this solution of the problem." [The rest of the text, pp. 223–225, and two long notes, pp. 225–228, are mainly devoted to an argument for African origin of the Vazimba.]

THE ONJATSY

The Onjatsy (phonetics, *Undzatse*), who appear in many parts of Madagascar but mainly in the northeast (Vohémar) and southeast (Vohipeno and Matitana) are extremely interesting from the ethnographic point of view. In this *Sora-bé*, reproduced from Gabriel Ferrand's *Les Musulmans à Madagascar et aux Iles Comores*, Vol. II (1893), pp. 41–49, (both Malagasy and French texts), the Onjatsy are connected with magicoreligious powers, often in comparison with the Anteimoro clans of Tsimeto (spelled here Tsimaito) and Ankara. Ferrand's explanatory notes are left out in this English translation.

The tribe of Onjatsy lives in the southeast of Madagascar. They are found in greatest numbers at Vohipeno and at Matitana. Their ancestors came from over the seas with Raminia, founder of the tribe of Antambahoaka [after he had left Mecca]. There were the Antaivandrika, the Onjatsy, the Tsimaito, the Ankara, the Antaimasay, etc. These are the first to have arrived on the southeastern littoral of Madagascar. Their ancestors knew the science of amulets and passed it on to them. The Onjatsy and the Tsimaito possess the science over things that are on the earth itself, that is to say over everything living. They have known also, it is said, to divine if the future will be good or bad. [For example] if a wild boar enters a village from the west and moves toward the east, they announce that a misfortune is on the way. But, before it comes about, they make an amulet that is to turn [the misfortune] back. They then say that this ill was conjured when it was [traveling] on its way. In the old days, the Onjatsy and the Tsimaito bore the title of counselors of the earth and of the peoples.

When the wild boar comes from the south and goes north, they say that a misfortune will arrive from the south; and they then engage in practices that are to force it back. There is also another belief that when wild fowl crosses a village it is [in effect] heralding the arrival of a stranger at this village [his point of expected entry being determined by the direction from which the bird came]. The people believe all this; and they dress up, slaughter cattle and fowl or chickens, all in honor of strangers whose arrival is announced by the sorcerers.

They also knew how to transform the wind into a storm. They could destroy many things and force, it is said, the wrecking of ships over the reefs. Here is what they do to throw ships against the reefs: they take an earthen pot having an external hem and put into it water from a river coming from an unknown source. Then, they take a firebrand and throw it into the pot along with other things. The pot is then taken to the edge of the sea. At this point, it is said, the storm manifests itself immediately, and the ship cracks up. [But] they also have protective charms that stop the storm at that very moment. They also knew how to descend a lightning in broad daylight [even when the weather is clear]. They start out by forming clouds in the sky; the flashes burst out, the thunder that announces the rain is heard, and the lightning strikes, it is said, the one for whom it is intended.

The Onjatsy and the Tsimaito are especially renowned for having knowledge of amulets that protect from bullets and spear thrusts. If a bullet is fired at them, they catch it, as is said, in their hand or in their *lamba*. They are never wounded. They can also transform the powder found in a flintlock into water. And, thanks to their knowledge of this magic, no firearm can harm them. They are real sorcerers. When an army begins to march, they would already know. If they wanted to avoid war, all they had to do was to make a peace amulet and the warring factions engaged in combat would become friends and form an alliance instead. Whatever war might be taking place, the army they accompanied would never be defeated. On the contrary, oftentimes the tribes that came to their ministrations ended by becoming friends. On the other hand, they could cause a war if they so desired. . . . It is said . . . that they can pre-tell the future by following the books left them by their ancestors.

The Ankara [spelled Anakara in the original text], they have knowledge of the skies, that is to say of the sun and the moon. They knew when a misfortune would befall on the earth. If the sun is red, if a circle sur-rounds it, or if the sun is hiding, this is a sign that there will be a terrible disaster, an epidemic, or much bloodshed. . . . But, one of the most extraordinary of powers possessed by the Onjatsy is the power to make birds in flight fall down. . . . When a bird is observed in flight and they wish to bring it down, they look at the shadow made by the bird's body on the ground, and the bird, by its own will, would dive down into their interlocked hands. The Onjatsy, it is said, also knew the stars, their posi-tions and their phases. . . .

HOW THE ANTALAOTRA COLONIES WERE ESTABLISHED ON THE NORTHWESTERN COAST OF MADAGASCAR

The ensuing tradition was collected by Captain Charles Guillain from local informants and published in his *Documents* . . . (1845), pp. 357–360. It should be compared with the Swahili chronicles and with Neville Chittick's article "The 'Shirazi' Colonization of East Africa," *JAH*, VI/3 (1965), 275–294.

The township or the district of Boukdadi, located near Bassora, was once under the authority of a sheik named Hassani who lived there with his family. One day, a son of his—having been reprimanded by the father in a public assembly—was so overcome with anger that it impelled him as far as to strike his father's face. The attendants, outraged at this hideous act, were about to put to death at once the transgressing son; but Hassani stopped them, being satisfied with his incarceration. None-theless, his own sense of dignity, profoundly wounded by this outrage he had no will to purify in the blood of his [own] son, forced him to consider as impossible a prolonged stay in the country and [thus] he conceived a plan to expatriate himself. He then made all of the preparations for departure; embarking with all those who were to follow him, with his slaves, and with his wealth, he sailed away forever from the lands that bore witness to his affront. The fleet carrying the emigrants consisted of seven dhows. It came out of the Persian Gulf and went toward the eastern coast of Africa. The landings took place in a small bay just to the south of Monbaze. [In a note, Guillain states that this event probably occurred toward the end of the 1500s.]

Hassani [then] . . . established himself on the left bank of a river that emptied into this bay, founding a village he named *Pangani*. . . . At his death, Hassani left behind two sons. The elder son, named Amadi, inherited the authority of his father while the other, named Kambamba, transferred with his followers to the other bank of the river where he built the village of *Bouéni*.

The wars that took place some years later in the neighboring areas frightened the colonists and made them decide to leave the coast of Africa and search for a land where they could live more peacefully. The two brothers then boarded the ships they had with all of their people going toward the land of *Kom'ri*, the name by which Madagascar was being designated by the Arab navigators. The fleet docked near the northernmost tip of the island . . . where the emigrants landed to set up a colony. They already had made some constructions and built a wall around the site chosen for their village when it was discovered that the nearby lands were not suited for cultivation. They left and went south, first to the islet of Nossi-Comba, which was also abandoned, and later to the Matzamba Bay. There, they founded a new village, which was called Pangani, from the name of their first colony in Africa. The name of Langani, by which this village was subsequently called, is simply a corruption of Pangani. The settlers had always been subdivided into two groups, each more directly under the authority of one of the brothers. While the larger of the two groups, under Amadi, remained established at Langani, the other, under Kambamba, pushed further south and stopped at the islet of Makambi. Kambamba had two children, a son and a daughter. At the father's death, the son—named Amadi like his uncle— took the group under him to a bay of the mainland [of Madagascar] facing Makambi. First, they lived on a small islet in the bay but moved again to the end of the bay itself, where the village they erected was called Bouéni, parallelling the name of the village Kambamba had founded on Africa's coast.

The Amadi of Langani had many children, of whom the oldest [son] Mikdadi succeeded him [to be in turn succeeded by his son also named Amadi]. It was [this] Amadi that ruled at Langani when Andriamandiso-arivo [Sakalava-Maroserana] came to his land. . . . Upon their arrival, the Arab settlers were given by the local inhabitants the name of *Anti-Alaoutsi* (men from over the seas) of which the term Antalaots' is a simple contraction. Since then, this name has served to designate them and their descendants as well as to distinguish the Arabs who used to come to live there temporarily in order to do commerce. These settlers, active and industrious, engaged mainly in commerce. They expanded and regulated the system of exchanges that had already existed on the western side of the island . . . [and] at the period when the Sakalava took hold in the north, there were four colonies of Antalaots on the western coast of Madagascar. . . .

WORD CHANGES IN BETSILEO

From James Sibree's article "Curious Words and Customs Connected with Chieftainship and Royalty Among the Malagasy," *JAI*, XXI (1891), 223–224. James Sibree was the long-time editor of the *Antananarivo Annual*, the best London Missionary Society diplomat in Tananarive, and a fine reporter about the Malagasy.

	PEOPLE	CHIEFS, ELDERS, NOBILITY
Children	Kilonga	Anakova
To Eat	Mihinana	Misoa, Mifanjotra
Plate	Vilia	Fisoavana, Fifanjorana
Farewell	Veloma	Mahazoa nono Masina
Dead	Maty	Folaka
Corpse	Faty	Volafolaka
Old	Antitra	Masina
Head	Loha	Kabeso
Eye	Maso	Fanilo
Ear	Sofina	Fihainoana
Hand	Tanana	Fandray
Foot	Tongotra	Fandia
Tooth	Nify	Faneva
Belly	Troka	Fisafoana
To sit	Mipetraka	Miarina
To go	Mandeha	Mamindra
To sleep	Mandry	Mirotra
Wife	Vavy	Fitana
House	Trano	Lapa
Ill	Marary	Manelo
To sing	Miandravana	Manpiotraka
To bury	Mandevina	Maniritra

THE TROMBA—
THE RAZANA OR ANGABÉ

This concluding item was written by the late André J. Dandouau, one of the best informed students of north-western Madagascar. It is left as written. I am grateful to his widow, Mme Berthe Dandouau, and his daughter, Mme Gabriel Pain of Tananarive for the permission to reproduce it.

1. LE TRUMBA

Les Sakalava et les Tsimihety croient qu'après la mort les esprits ne montent pas au ciel rejoindre les Zangahari. Ils restent sur la terre, vont et viennent, rôdent dans l'air, se déplacent avec une rapidité prodigieuse d'un point à un autre, voient tout ce que font les hommes, soit de nuit, soit de jour, peuvent rendre malade ou guérir, rendre faible et languissant ou plein de force et de santé, indiquer les remèdes de toute espèce, faire retrouver les boeufs égarés dans la brousse et les objets perdus.

On les désigne sous le nom générique de "Razana" (ancêtres) ou "Angabe" (fantômes puissants). Ce sont eux que l'on invoque au cours des différentes cérémonies familiales que nous venons de décrire afin qu'ils soient toujours favorables à leurs descendants.

L'esprit des rois est soumis à cette règle commune, mais il est beaucoup plus puissant, beaucoup plus saint que l'angabe vulgaire. Il peut résider s'il le veut, dans le corps de certaines personnes étrangères à sa famille. On l'appelle alors "trumba" et les personnes qu'il possède (littéralement: sur lesquelles il aime à se poser) prennent le nom de "saha." Ce sont tantôt des hommes tantôt des femmes, quelquefois même des enfants; mais les femmes sont les possédées de prédilection.

Lorsque le trumba vient agiter le saha, l'esprit de celui-ci quitte son corps pour lui céder la place. Le trumba seul le gouverne et le fait agir. Quand il se retire, l'esprit revient, mais le saha ne se souvient ni de ce qu'il a fait, ni de ce qu'il a dit pendant la possession; il a oublié qu'il a bu, chanté, dansé, prescrit des "udi," des "fadi," etc. . . .

Il y a des "trumba" mâles et des "trumba" femelles. Lorsqu'un "trumba" mâle possède une femme, la voix de celle-ci change et présente des intonations masculines. Elle fuit le "sambuadi" (met son lamba en bandoulière suivant la coutume des hommes, des guerriers) elle se saisit d'un bâton ou d'une sagaie, elle se caresse les lèvres et le menton comme quelqu'un qui lisse ses moustaches ou joue avec sa barbe. Lorqu'un trumba femelle possède un homme, celui-ci se féminise dans sa voix et dans son attitude.

Les "trumba" sont bons ou mauvais. Les "trumba ratsi" (trumba mauvais) sont ceux qui rendent malades, font perdre la fortune, attirent les malheurs, rendent les femmes stériles, égarent les boeufs dans la forêt. Ce sont des ennemis dangereux qu'il faut expulser dès qu'ils exercent leur action nuisible.

Les "trumba tsara" (trumba bons) indiquent les remèdes efficaces pour guérir tous les maux, font retrouver tout ce qui est perdu, ordonnent des prescriptions pour combattre l'influence des trumba ratsi, président l'avenir et, si celui-ci paraît trop sombre, indiquent les moyens infaillibles de le rendre plus souriant. Ce sont des bienfaiteurs qu'il faut choyer pour qu'ils continuent à être favorables. Ils affectionnent certaines personnes qu'ils ont choisies eux-mêmes, des femmes généralement, et à l'appel desquelles ils accourent pour répondre aux questions qu'on désire leur poser. Ces personnes sont très considérées et on vient les consulter parfois d'assez loin. La reconnaissance des malheureux consolés et des malades guéris se traduit par d'abondants cadeaux en boeufs, volailles, riz, piastres etc. Les trumba tsara sont, en général, les esprits d'Andriamisara, d'Andriamaudisuariou, d'Andriamandazuala, anciens rois sakalava et celui de Ramarufali, le plus puissant de tous, devant lequel tous les autres s'inclinent.[1] Mais ils deviennent "trumba ratsi" très facilement si on les offense en n'exécutant pas leurs prescriptions, ou en violant les fadi qu'ils ont imposés.

La même personne peut avoir à sa disposition deux ou trois "trumba tsara" qui l'agitent différemment. Le même "trumba ratsi" peut tourmenter dix ou douze personnes soit l'une après l'autre, soit simultanément.

L'appel du "trumba tsara" se fait d'une façon très simple.

Appel du Trumba Tsara Lorsque quelqu'un est malade et que toutes les prescriptions du "mpisikidi" n'ont pu le guérir, il se rend auprès d'une personne, généralement une femme, renommée pour être possédée par un bon "trumba" connaissant bien les "udi." Arrivé près d'elle, il lui remet, suivant la gravité de son cas, une somme variant entre un franc et une piastre. Le mari de la femme prend l'offrande et la dépose dans une assiette en faïence qu'il remplit d'eau et dans laquelle il délaie un peu de terre blanche. Il pose contenant et contenu sur une natte neuve

[1] Les Hovas établis depuis longtemps dans la région sakalava ont adopté une partie des coutumes du pays et croient au "trumba". Les esprits qui les agitent sont ceux de leurs anciens rois: Andrianampoinimerina et Radama I.

étendue dans la case. Il met auprès un "fanimbuhana" garni de quelques charbons allumés sur lesquels on fait brûler un peu de "embuka" ou résine de copalier.

Quand la fumée de l' "embuka" s'élève, le mari appelle le trumba à voix haute, sa femme l'appelle ensuite et, après elle, le consultant. Le trumba ne se fait pas longtemps attendre, il vient tout de suite. La femme s'agite marquant ainsi que son esprit est parti et que le trumba le remplace. Le mari interroge ce dernier pour s'assurer de son identité.

"Oui, répond celui-ci, je suis Andriamisara et je suis venu parce que vous m'avez appelé."

"Kuezi, ô notre maître! Voilà pourquoi nous vous appelons. C'est que "Ranuna" votre esclave, ici présent, et malade et voici qu'elle est sa maladie. Il a mal au ventre et dans son estomac il y a comme une grosse boule qui monte et qui descend. Il ne peut pas manger, il ne peut pas travailler, il ne peut pas dormir. On l'a soigné mais il n'a pas guéri. Nous venons vous demander ce qui le rend malade et quels 'fanafudi' il faut lui donner pour lui rendre la santé. Répondez à vos esclaves et nous saurons nous montrer reconnaissants!"

Tout d'abord le trumba fait des réponses évasives,[2] il ignore la cause de la maladie, il ne connait point d'udi qui puisse guérir un cas aussi difficile, aussi spécial. Mais le consultant insiste, il prie, fait des promesses. Il fait boire du toka au saha afin quele trumba se délecte d'abord, n'ait pas honte de parler ensuite.[3] Lorsque le saha est ivre, le trumba satisfait, se décide à parler. Il indique la cause de la maladie, les feuilles, bois et racines qui doivent entrer dans la composition du remède, la façon de préparer celui-ci, et enfin, prescription de la plus haute importance, les fadi que le consultant devra observer désormais.

Alors le malade satisfait, renouvelle ses promesses, mais sous forme conditionnelle.

"Si je guéris, dit-il, je vous donnerai ceci ou cela, une ou deux piastres, un boeuf, des poules, etc. . . .

Le trumba prend acte de ces promesses, se retire satisfait et le saha cure son ivresse en attendant que son esprit soit revenu.

Lorsque, par hasard, le malade guérit, le saha vient lui rappeler ses engagements.

"Voilà que vous êtes guéri, maintenant, dit-il, et je suis tourmenté par le trumba parce que vous ne lui avez pas encore donné ce que vous lui avez promis. Je vous prie de me le remettre afin qu'il me laisse dorénavant en repos!"

[2] Il est bien dans le caractère sakalava de ne jamais répondre franchement lorsqu'on l'interroge pour la première fois.

[3] Un vieux Sakalava, ivrogne invétéré appelait un jour devant nous le "toka famaki baràka" qui enlève la honte et la vergogne.

Il s'exécute sur l'heure de crainte que le trumba ne s'indispose contre lui et ne le rende malade à nouveau.

Si un dénouement fatal se produit, la renommée du saha n'est pas le moins du monde diminuée. Il a soin d'entourer ses prescriptions d'un tel luxe de recommandations minutieuses que le malade risque fort d'en oublier quelqu'une. Cet oubli fait s'évanouir complètement les vertus des udi absorbés et excite la colère du trumba qui se venge.

Expulsion du Trumba Ratsi Les trumba ratsi ne quittent pas ceux qu'ils possèdent avec la même facilité. Ils s'obstinent à peser sur eux, les tourmentent de mille façons, les rendent malades. Il faut les expulser en les forçant à dire leur nom[4] ce qui souvent est très long et très difficile, et exige un cérémonial assez compliqué: c'est le "rumbu."

On commence d'abord par préparer du toka: tokamainti, tokasatrana, tokadrazana, on achète du tokamena, de l'absinthe, de l'eau-de-vie anisée. Le nombre de bouteilles doit être un multiple de six ou de huit, avec un minimum de douze. On en prend deux, trois fois six, deux, trois fois huit, etc. . . .

Au jour fixé pour la cérémonie, on invite toutes les personnes que l'on connait et qui croient au trumba, condition essentielle, la présence d'incrédules empêchant souvent le trumba de dire son nom. On dresse dans la cour de la case une grande tente à l'aide de voiles de boutre. On y apporte à l'Est une grande table orientée Nord-Sud. Au Sud de la table on dispose un lit orienté Est-Ouest que l'on recouvre d'une natte neuve. Entre le lit et la table, il y a un espace suffisant pour que deux personnes puissent s'y promener de front. Sur le sol on étend des nattes neuves car toute l'assistance revêt ses plus beaux habits. Quelquefois, cependant, le mpisikidi, toujours consulté au préalable, prescrit une tenue particulière. Toute l'assistance doit se draper dans un simple lamba, laissant les épaules et les bras nus, et s'abstenir de vêtements confectionnés, la moindre couture étant fadi et très désagréable au trumba qu'il s'agit d'expulser.

Avant l'arrivée des invités on dispose sur la table le "fumban' ni fauyatahana", ce que l'on a coutume de réunir pour les demander.

1. les bouteilles pleines de toka au nombre de douze ou dix-huit, seize ou vingt-quatre. Elles seront remplacées au fur et à mesure qu'on les videra. On marque chacune d'elles de quatre lignes verticales tracées avec de la terre blanche délayée dans l'eau;

2. un "fanimbuhana" garni de charbons allumés;

3. une assiette contenant de la terre blanche délayée dans l'eau;

[4] Lorsqu'un trumba a dit son nom, il est considéré comme n'étant plus dangereux. On peut l'invoquer personnellement, lui faire les offrandes et les sacrifices que l'on sait, par tradition, lui être agréables.

4. une piastre "tsangan'ubu" et des bijoux en argent;

5. un ou plusieurs bâtons pourvus d'un petit pommeau en argent.

C'est dans l'après-midi, après le repas que la cérémonie a lieu. Les invités arrivent par groupes et s'accroupissent sur la natte. Puis le malade possédé par le trumba (généralement une femme) vient, à son tour, s'asseoir au premier rang.

On met alors de l' "embuka" dans le "fanimbuhana." La fumée s'élève et se répand sous toute la tente. Le mari de la malade invoque le trumba et le prie de dire son nom. On commence à chanter en battant des mains, le toka est bu à pleins verres. La possédée surtout, boit à longs traits. Lorsque l'ivresse la gagne, elle grogne et s'agite, ou plutôt, comme le croient les Sakalana, le trumba lui-même grogne et s'agite; il parle en mots sans suite, s'empare d'un bâton, fait le "sambuadi," trempe ses doigts dans la terre blanche que contient l'assiette et en fait des points sur sa figure et sur celle des assistants. Les personnes ainsi marquées s'inclinent et saluent d'un "kuezi" respectueux qui s'adresse au trumba.

Les chants redoublent d'intensité, les paroles sont simples, un seul couplet par chanson, mais se répétant indifiniment:

> Montons au Mahabu
> Duani de notre maître
> qui peut regarder des millions (de sujets)
> Célèbre est celui à qui nous appartenons.

ou encore:

> Pour bénir avec cette eau
> Apportez des feuilles d'arbres
> Voici venir ceux qui ne sont pas vos ancêtres.

ou bien:

> De même que nous sommes prosternés,
> De même aujourd'hui, vous à qui nous appartenons,
> Nous vous implorons, ô notre maître.

et surtout:

> Nous portons notre maître
> Qui a beaucoup d'esclaves

Pour accompagner ces chants de poésie plus qu'indigente, les battements de main se font plus vifs; l'assistance à grands cris prie le trumba de dire son nom; la malade danse et chante jusqu'à ce que, fatiguée, épuisée, elle se couche sur le lit, souvent en poussant de grands cris. Cela indique que le trumba l'a quittée, mais sourd aux prières, aux supplications, insensible au toka dont on l'a abreuvé il refuse de dire son nom.

Tout à coup, du milieu de l'assistance une femme commence à s'agiter.

D'abord elle balance doucement sa tête, puis le buste oscille dans tous les sens, des soupirs saccadés s'échappent de sa poitrine, de plus en plus profonds, tournant au râle et faisant bientôt place à des grognements et à des cris inarticulés. Ses mouvements deviennent plus violents, plus brusques, l'agitation gagne tous ses membres; enfin elle se lève et s'avance vers la table en dansant et en gesticulant. Le trumba est entré en elle et refuse d'en sortir. Une deuxième imite son exemple, puis une troisième: d'autres s'agitent tout en demeurant à leur place. L'assistance chante alors de plus en plus fort, comme gagnée par une sorte de délire frénétique, les rasades de toka se succèdent fréquentes et copieuses: c'est avec des hurlements que l'on adjure le trumba de sortir et de dire son nom.

Souvent il résiste pendant plusieurs heures; quelquefois il ne se décide que le matin au chant du coq, au moment où l'assistance va se séparer. Parfois même des trumba particulièrement entêtés ou indisposés contre leurs victimes ne se sont décidés qu'après deux ou trois séances et après avoir montré de grandes exigences, allant jusqu'à envoyer de temps en temps à leur place des trumba de qualité inférieure, trumba de "maruvavi," par exemple, dire leur nom particulier et ajouter:

"Nous venons ici à la place du 'Puissant Trumba' notre maître. Il ne vient pas lui-même parce que vous avez oublié telle et telle prescription, vous n'avez pas apporté telle et telle chose. . . ."

Ces oublis sont réparés au fur et à mesure qu'ils sont signalés, et la consommation de toka devient réellement effrayante.

Enfin le trumba se décide à sortir. Au milieu des cris et souvent des hoquets convulsifs, une des femmes possédées tremble de tous ses membres. L'assistance se tait, et, dans le silence relatif qui s'établit, on entend un nom sortir de ses lèvres. Alors le calme renaît peu à peu, des chants d'allégresse succèdent aux invocations, tout le monde se retire sauf ceux que l'alcool a terrassés et qui cuvent leur ivresse sur les nattes. Il ne reste plus qu'à consulter le mpisikidi pour savoir ce qui a si fort fâché le trumba et ce qu'il faut faire pour ne plus encourir sa colère. Le mpisikidi ordonne des remèdes divers et surtout prescrit des fadi qui seront religieusement observés.

2. LES RAZANA OU ANGABE

La croyance aux Razana ou Angabe est plus spéciale aux Tsimihety.

"Personne, disent les Sakalava, ne peut se poser sur la tête de quelqu'un s'il n'a été autrefois un muasi fameux ou un roi ayant réellement régné" . . . Les Tsimiheti reconnaissent aux esprits de tous leurs ancêtres le pouvoir de se poser sur eux et de les tourmenter. Ce sont ces esprits que l'on appelle plus spécialement Razana ou Angabe.

L'Angabe manifeste sa présence d'une façon un peu différente de celle du trumba et il se chasse par d'autres procédés. Il rend surtout malade et la maladie résiste à toutes les médicamentations. Devant l'insuccès répété de ses udi, l'attention du mpisikidi ou muasi est éveillée. Il consulte ses graines pour être exactement fixé. Le sikidi lui apprend infailliblement si c'est un Razana qui est cause de la maladie et lui indique très souvent ce que réclame ce dernier pour se tenir coi dans son séjour: boeufs, toka, volailles etc. . . .

La famille s'exécute et fait les offrandes demandées. La cérémonie s'appelle "Rasahariana" ou partage des biens, les Ancêtres demandant à recevoir leur part des richesses possédées par leurs descendants. Elle se fait suivant un certain cérémonial.

Si les Ancêtres demandent un boeuf, on le choisit "vazaha tànana" aux quatre membres blancs. On le conduit au milieu du village. On l'étend par terre pour le tuer et près de sa tête on met deux assiettes blanches contenant chacune un bracelet en argent ou "vanguvangu," une piastre "tsangan'ulu," et un peu de terre blanche. On ne fait jamais brûler d'"embuka" comme on le fait pour le trumba. On invoque ensuite les Razana. On les prie de trouver agréable le sacrifice que l'on fait en leur honneur et on les convie à en prendre leur part. On boit, on chante, on danse et le malade ne tarde pas à recouvrer la santé.

Mais quelquefois le Razana se montrent entêtés et refusent de prendre leur part des richesses qu'on leur offre. Il faut pour s'en débarrasser employer des moyens beaucoup plus énergiques.

La cérémonie se déroule pendant la nuit dans la case du malade. On dispose celle-ci d'une façon spéciale. Au pignon Sud et à la paroi Est, on fixe des morceaux de toile blanche, voiles de pirogue ou de boutre, formant ainsi au Sud-Est, au coin sacré, le coin des dieux et des ancêtres, une sorte de tente triangulaire: c'est la "tranu-lay." On conduit la personne malade auprès de cette tente, jamais dans l'intérieur. Près d'elle se tient le "mpika baru," manière d'orateur servant d'intermédiaire entreles Razana et elle. Tout le monde ne peut pas jouer ce rôle. Il faut d'abord avoir été soi-même tourmenté par les Razana; de plus il faut parfaitement connaitre la généalogie du malade afin de pouvoir faire les appels et les invocations sans oublier un seul ancêtre, le Razana oublié (délaissé) pouvant se fâcher et faire expier cruellement cet oubli. Mais les personnes réunissant cette double condition se rencontrent assez facilement, les Tsimiheti vivant groupés par familles, dans leurs villages, et ne tolèrant pas le voisinage d'étrangers.

Le mpikabaru se tient debout auprès du malade et invoque tous les Razana en commençant par le plus ancien. Quand il suppose que tous sont là, il leur adresse directement la parole:

"Si par hasard, dit-il, vous voulez demeurer chez vos descendants, et si vous ne voulez pas les faire mourir, sortez, venez dans cette maison.

Voilà la 'tranu lay' que nous avons faite pour que vous y entriez, pour que vous y demeuriez. Dites-nous votre nom, dites à vos descendants toutes les choses qu'ils ont faites et qui vous ont déplu, car le malade souffre trop. On l'a soigné et il n'a pu guérir, on lui a donné des remèdes et ils sont restés inefficaces. C'est vous que le rendez malade et qui les faites souffrir. Pourquoi vous acharnez-vous après vos enfants et vos petits-enfants, après vos descendants? Aussi nous vous demandons de venir. Notre argent est entièrement dépensé, nous l'avons tout donné aux 'muasi' et aux mpisikidi, et cependant le malade n'est pas guéri. Si vous ne voulez pas qu'il meure, si vous voulez qu'il vive, venez dans cette maison causer avec nous vos petits-fils!"

L'invocation terminée on chante, on danse et on boit jusqu'à ce que les Ancêtres se décident à pénétrer sous la tente. Lorsqu'ils sont là la toile s'agite un peu, ils grognent, ils font du bruit en froissant les feuilles du toît sur lesquelles ils se posent avant d'entrer.*

Alors le mpikabaru les interroge sur les causes de la maladie. L'un d'eux prend la parole au nom de tous les autres et, par l'intermédiaire du mpikabaru s'adresse au malade:

"Vous Ranuna, moi un tel, un tel et un tel (et il énumère les noms de tous les parents morts qui sont là rassemblés) voici ce que nous avons à vous dire:

Vous avez mangé de l'anguille et vous saviez que cela nous déplaît;

Vous avez tué un 'Tuluhu' (espèce de coucou: Centropus tolou Gm) et vous saviez que cet oiseau doit être sacré pour tous les membres de notre famille;

Vous ne nous avez pas offert les prémices de votre dernière récolte de riz;

Et vous faites cuire vos poissons dans une marmite en fer!

Voilà pourquoi nous vous avons rendu malade! Mais puisque vous vous repentez et que vous demandez notre aide pour guérir, voici ce que nous vous prescrivons:

Vous allumerez ce soir du feu dans votre case. Dans une marmite neuve, pleine d'eau vous mettrez un hameçon et des panicules de "manevika"[5] (Imperata amndinacéa Cyr. Graminis). Vous ferez bouillir le tout et vous vous laverez avec cette eau. Votre maladie sera enlevée et ne reviendra plus."

Alors on continue à danser, à chanter et à boire. On dépose dans la

---

* [A note about hut construction is omitted.]

[5] L'hameçon, dans cet udi servira à enlever le mauvais sort comme il enlève les poissons hors de l'eau.

Quant au manevtka il a la vie extrêmement dure et ses panicules sont ornées de barbes blanchâtres: le malade, grâce à son influence guérira et vivra assez longtemps pour que ses cheveux blanchissent.

trano-lay une assiette pleine de rhum destinée aux Ancêtres. Les Tsimiheti croient que ceux-ci viennent le boire.

Quelquefois la chose est plus sérieuse. La maladie est particulièrement grave, un des ancêtres s'acharne et ne veut pas céder. Les autres Razana qui voudraient soulager leurs descendants intercèdent auprès de lui, mais rien n'y fait, il ne pardonne pas. Alors tous s'assemblent à l'appel du "mpikabaru" en sorte de réunion plenière et là ils disent:

"C'est l'ombre de Ramuna qui vous fait ainsi souffrir. Nous avons essayé de la calmer, mais nous n'avons pas pu. Si elle ne meurt pas, aucun udi ne pourra vous guérir, donnez-nous la permission de la tuer!"

La permission est accordée. Alors les Razana ajoutent:

"Ayez confiance en nous, nos petits-fils, nous allons chercher ce 'maditra' (entêté) pour l'amener ici et le tuer!"

Tous se dispersent pour se mettre en quête de l'ombre si méchante. Quand ils l'ont rencontrée, ils usent de ruse pour la décider à les suivre. Ils lui disent:

"Venez, nous allons assister à un 'fidzuruana' tous ensemble, car il y a une grande réunion que les hommes font là-bas. Il y a beaucoup de monde, on y boit beaucoup de toka, il y a de grands jeux, de belles danses et de beaux chants. Allons ensemble voir et entendre tout cela!"

L'ombre n'a aucune méfiance et les suit. On la conduit dans la case sous la "tranu lay." La troupe des Razana, en entrant, fait du bruit. Alors la famille du malade assemblée insulte et maudit l'"angabe masiaka" (l'ombre méchante) qui n'a pas voulu se laisser fléchir, et les autres Razana le tuent sans autre forme de procès, mais avec force désordre et vacarme, dans l'intérieur du "trano lay."

Dès qu'il est mort, le malade se sent soulagé. Le mpisikidi lui prescrit les "udi" qui parachèveront la guérison, à moins que l'un des Razana ne lui indique lui-même le traitement à suivre.

INDEX